Postcolonial Theory and Organizational Analysis: A Critical Engagement

Postcolonial Theory and Organizational Analysis: A Critical Engagement

Edited by

Anshuman Prasad

POSTCOLONIAL THEORY AND ORGANIZATIONAL ANALYSIS: A CRITICAL ENGAGEMENT

First published 2003 by
Palgrave Macmillan™
175 Fifth Avenue, New York, N.Y. 10010 and
Houndmills, Basingstoke, Hampshire, England RG21 6XS.
Companies and representatives throughout the world.

Palgrave Macmillan is the global academic imprint of the Palgrave Macmillan division of St. Martin's Press, LLC and of Palgrave Macmillan Ltd. Macmillan® is a registered trademark in the United States, United Kingdom and other countries. Palgrave is a registered trademark in the European Union and other countries.

ISBN 978-0-312-29405-2   ISBN 0–312–29405–0 hardback

Library of Congress Cataloging-in-Publication Data
Postcolonial theory and organizational analysis: a critical engagement/edited by Anshuman Prasad.
      p. cm.
   Includes bibliographical references.
   ISBN 0–312–29405–0
   1. Postcolonialism. 2. Organization. 3. Organizational sociology.
I. Prasad, Anshuman.

JV51.P653 2003
325'.3—dc21   2002033305

A catalogue record for this book is available from the British Library.

Design by Newgen Imaging Systems (P) Ltd., Chennai, India.

First edition: March, 2003
10 9 8 7 6 5 4 3 2 1

Transferred to Digital Printing in 2012

This book is for Bhabhi and Bhauji ... with affection

Contents

Part IV   Conclusion

Acknowledgments

The idea for this book emerged, in part, during the course of organizing the postcolonialism stream of the inaugural Critical Management Studies (CMS) Conference, University of Manchester, UK. I am grateful to Hugh Willmott, the prime mover behind the first CMS Conference, for enthusiastically responding to my suggestion to include a postcolonialism stream in the conference.

Early versions of some of the chapters in this book were initially presented at the first two CMS Conferences, and have benefited from the criticism of participants at those meetings. Sincere thanks to all those who provided suggestions and criticisms on the conference papers. My grateful thanks to all the contributing authors for making the book possible. Warm thanks to my many friends and colleagues—in particular, Mats Alvesson and Yvonne Due Billing, David Barry, David Boje and Grace Ann Rosile, Paul Carlile, Paula Caproni, Mike and Pat Cavanaugh, Barbara Czarniawska, Wayne Eastman, Mike Elmes, Dafna Eylon, Brad Jackson, Ulla Johansson, Ashwin Joshi and Kiran Mirchandani, Mike Rouse, Maureen Scully, Ralph Stablein, Dvora Yanow, Larry Zacharias and Cathy Schoen, and all the others—for their friendship and intellectual support. I would also like to remember Richard Sotto, who so unexpectedly passed away recently. He would have enjoyed arguing with this book over a bottle of fine scotch. A special word of thanks for my good friend Alison Konrad who, in inviting me several years ago to share some of my postcolonial theoretic ideas at an Academy of Management annual meeting, paved the way for what, in all likelihood, was the very first conference presentation on postcolonialist themes at the Academy.

Warm thanks to Toby Wahl, Editor at Palgrave, for his support, and to Toby, Ian Steinberg, Jennifer Yoon, Paige Casey, and others there for piloting the book through the publication process and beyond. Sincere thanks also to V. S. Mukesh and his colleagues at Newgen Imaging Systems (P) Ltd., Chennai, India, for their wonderful production work.

Last but definitely not the least, Pushi has been closely involved with this book project in more ways than one. A mere "thank you" is hardly enough to convey my appreciation of all that she has done. Of course, without the love and affection of my family in India, nothing would have been possible. Finally, I would not be guilty of forgetting Derri(da), our kitty-cat, who has been a constant and joyous reminder that there are indeed many ways in which one can "play" with the text.

Grateful acknowledgment is made for permission to reprint in Chapter 11, material previously published under the title, "Whose Land Is It Anyway?" by Subhabrata Bobby Banerjee, *Organization & Environment* (Volume 13, Issue 1) pp. 11–29 (copyright © 2000 by Sage Publications, Inc.; reprinted by permission of Sage Publications, Inc.).

Figures 7.1, 7.2, and 7.3 are reproductions of artworks that originally appeared in different Surveys of India published by the *Economist*. We are grateful to Katie Hird, Rights and Syndication Executive of the *Economist*, London, and to the following copyright holders: (a) Ardea London Ltd., 35 Brodrick Road, London, for permission to reprint artwork published in the *Economist*, Survey of India dated January 21, 1995 and (b) Matilda Harrison, c/o Arena, 108 Leonard Street, London, for permission to reprint artwork published in the *Economist*, Survey of India dated February 22, 1997. Artworks reprinted by permission of the said copyright holders.

Every effort has been made to identify and contact copyright holders with a view to obtaining their permission to reprint in this book materials that originally appeared elsewhere. We would be grateful to hear from any copyright holder who could not be acknowledged here as a result of circumstances beyond our control, and will gladly rectify in future editions of the book any errors or omissions that might have occurred in the present edition.

Notes on the Contributors

Subhabrata Bobby Banerjee (Ph.D., University of Massachusetts at Amherst) is Professor of Strategic Management at the International Graduate School of Management, University of South Australia, Adelaide, Australia. Previously he taught at RMIT University where he was the Director of the Doctor of Business Administration Program, and at the University of Wollongong where he headed the doctoral program. His current research interests include cultural, political, and economic aspects of indigenous-settler relations in Australia, corporate environmentalism, sustainable development, and critical management studies. He has published scholarly articles in many journals including *Journal of Management Studies; Journal of Marketing; Organization Studies; Organization; Management Learning; Journal of Advertising; Media, Culture and Society;* and *Advances in Consumer Research.*

Bill Cooke is Senior Lecturer in Organizational Analysis at the University of Manchester Institute of Science and Technology (UMIST), U.K. He researches the history of management ideas, and the contemporary use of management ideas by international development organizations like the World Bank, the United Nations, and NGOs. He is particularly interested in change management. Previously he taught at the Institute for Development Policy and Management, University of Manchester, where he directed the M.Sc. in Organizational Change and Development, and at the University of Teesside. He is the co-editor, with Uma Kothari, of *Participation: The New Tyranny?* (Zed Books, 2001).

Abhijit Gopal (Ph.D., University of Georgia) is Associate Professor in the Richard Ivey School of Business Administration at the University of Western Ontario, Canada. He works in the area of information systems and has taught in China, the Czech Republic, Poland, and the United States. His work has appeared in such leading journals as the *MIS Quarterly* and

Information Systems Research. His recent research focuses on critical analyses of management information systems and new information technologies.

Yasmin Gopal (Ph.D., University of Georgia) is an aspiring potter, and an independent researcher who is currently teaching part-time in the distance program offered by the Centre for Innovative Management at Athabasca University, Alberta, Canada. Her research interests are focused on mediated communication and the reciprocal impact of humans and their technological artifacts. A self-professed dabbler, she has several years experience as an advertising copywriter in India, has tried her hand at elementary school teaching, and has had a brief stint as a freelance journalist.

Gavin Jack (Ph.D., Heriot-Watt University, Edinburgh, UK) is Lecturer in Marketing at the University of Keele, U.K., and a Visiting Lecturer in Cross-Cultural Management at the University of Linz, Austria. His research interests articulate around the relationships among production, consumption, and identity politics in areas such as organizational diversity, intercultural management communication, and tourism. He is a member of the Editorial Board of the journal, *Language and Intercultural Communication*, a member of the Executive Board of the Standing Conference on Organizational Symbolism (SCOS), and the Book Reviews Editor for *International Marketing Review*.

Dennis Kwek is pursuing a Ph.D. in Management Studies at the University of Essex, U.K. A Singaporean wrenched from his home, he has a confusing identity which attempts (sometimes unsuccessfully) to bridge the East/West cultural divide. This is often reflected in his resistance toward disciplinary boundaries. His research interests include post colonial implications of international management research, cultural identities and diaspora, cultural formations in persistent online communities, Eastern religions and comparative philosophies, computer simulations of organizations, and chaotic and complex processes at the workplace. A winner of the ORS Award by the Committee of Vice-Chancellors and Principals of the Universities of the United Kingdom, his research has been published in the *British Journal of Management*.

Anna Lorbiecki is Lecturer in the Department of Management Learning, Lancaster University, U.K. Her research interests revolve around international management, and managing diversity within intra- and international contexts. Currently, she is specifically looking at how postcolonial ideas could enhance inclusive plurality within management education and development. She has recently conducted a two-year Leverhulme-funded study of

Diversity Management and Being "British" within the British Broadcasting Corporation (BBC), British Aerospace, and British Telecomm. Previously, she was involved in a range of research and consultancy projects with the chemical industry, the European Commission, and the U.K. National Health Service. She has written an e-learning booklet on diversity for senior managers in the British Cabinet Office, and her research has been published in a number of journals, including *Management Learning*, the *British Journal of Management*, and *Health Services Management*.

Ali Mir (Ph.D., University of Massachusetts at Amherst) is Associate Professor of Management at William Paterson University, New Jersey. His research focuses on transformation of work in late capitalism. He is currently working on the new forms of international divisions of labor in information technology industries. His research has appeared in such journals as *Cultural Dynamics, Information Systems Management,* and *Management Learning*. He has written and consulted for the World Wide Web project of the *Encyclopedia Britannica*, and has appeared as an expert commentator on the international high-tech industry for the New York city radio.

Raza Mir (Ph.D., University of Massachusetts at Amherst) is Associate Professor of Management at William Paterson University, New Jersey. He grew up in India and has been witness to the expansion of international capital there, particularly over the last decade. His research interests are based on those experiences. Currently, he is studying the process of knowledge transfer in multinational corporations, especially their political and power-laden dimensions. His research has appeared in such journals as *Cultural Dynamics*, and the *Strategic Management Journal*.

Dean Neu (Ph.D., Queen's University, Canada) is the Future Fund Professor of Accounting at the University of Calgary, Canada. His recent research focuses on the ways in which accounting mediates the relations between governments and indigenous peoples. Author of more than fifty scholarly and practitioner articles in leading journals like *Accounting, Organizations and Society*, and *Critical Perspectives on Accounting*, he is a recipient of the Outstanding Researcher Award at the University of Calgary. He has served on the executive committee of the Canadian Academic Accounting Association (CICA), and has acted as expert commentator on public finance matters for the Canadian Broadcasting Corporation (CBC).

Anshuman Prasad (Ph.D., University of Massachusetts at Amherst) is Associate Professor of Management and Director, Doctoral Program, at the School of Business, University of New Haven, Connecticut. He has also taught at the University of Calgary, Canada, and in the International M.B.A. Program of the Helsinki School of Economics and Business Administration. His research mostly deals with organizational culture and ideology, workplace diversity and multiculturalism, resistance and empowerment in organizations, and the strategic search for corporate legitimacy, and has been published in several journals including *Human Relations, Journal of Applied Behavioral Science, Journal of Business Communication, Organization Science,* and *Research in the Sociology of Organizations.* He has coedited *Managing the Organizational Melting Pot: Dilemmas of Workplace Diversity* (1997), as well as a special issue on interpretivism and critique for *Organizational Research Methods* (2002), the journal of the Research Methods Division of the Academy of Management. Before joining the academe, he earned an M.B.A. degree, and served as an executive in State Bank of India for a number of years.

Pushkala Prasad (Ph.D., University of Massachusetts at Amherst) is the Arthur Zankel Chair Professor of Management and Liberal Studies at Skidmore College, New York. Prior to this, she was the Chair Professor of Public Administration at Lund University, Sweden. She has held teaching appointments at Clarkson University and the University of Calgary, Canada, besides being a Visiting Professor at the Helsinki School of Economics and Business Administration, and a Visiting Scholar at MIT's Sloan School of Management. Her research interests are in the areas of organizational culture and symbolism, the management of workplace diversity, organizational legitimacy, and post-positivist methodologies of organizational research. Her research has been published in reputed journals such as the *Academy of Management Journal, Human Relations, Journal of Management Studies,* and *Organization Science.* She has coedited *Managing the Organizational Melting Pot: Dilemmas of Workplace Diversity* (1997), as well as a special issue on interpretive research for *Organizational Research Methods* (2002).

Esther Priyadharshini (Ph.D., Lancaster University, U.K.) is Lecturer of Education at the Centre for Applied Research in Education (CARE), University of East Anglia, U.K. Her research interests are in the areas of sociology of education (especially, management education), the experience of globalization in everyday lives of educational communities, postcolonial and feminist pedagogy, and methodological issues in research. She was awarded the prestigious Commonwealth Scholarship from the Association of Commonwealth Universities for completing her doctoral dissertation, *A Critical Ethnography on the Production of the Indian MBA Discourse,* which explored the complex relationships between pedagogy, industry, and the creation of student identities within the M.B.A. discourse. In addition to the Ph.D., she holds an M.B.A. degree, and has worked for several years as a Research Executive with market research agencies in India.

Punya Upadhyaya (Ph.D., Case Western Reserve University) is an independent scholar who has taught most recently at Emporia State University, Kansas. His research interests include postcolonial theory, alternative forms of organizational learning, Indian history and religion, and cross-cultural issues in management. His articles have appeared in a number of journals including the *Journal of Management Inquiry*, and the *Journal of Organizational Change Management*.

Robert Willis (Ph.D., University of Calgary, Canada) is Assistant Professor (M.I.S.) in the College of Business Administration at Marquette University, Wisconsin. His research interests are in the areas of social impacts of technology, critical analyses of management information systems, and the use of new information technology in the small business setting.

PART I

Introduction

CHAPTER 1

The Gaze of the Other: Postcolonial Theory and Organizational Analysis

Anshuman Prasad

> ...the peoples of the periphery return to rewrite the history and
> fiction of the metropolis.
>
> Homi K. Bhabha, *Nation and Narration*
>
> Europe is literally the creation of the Third World.
>
> Frantz Fanon, *The Wretched of the Earth*

In the year 1496, the Portuguese seafarer Vasco da Gama set out on a long and arduous journey. Sailing down the western coast of Africa, he rounded the Cape of Good Hope on the southern tip of the continent, entered the Indian Ocean, and eventually landed at the port city of Calicut. According to a well-known story (cf. Sprinker, 1995: 2), when asked why da Gama and his men had come to India, they replied: "We seek Christians and spices." Four years before da Gama embarked on his perilous search for spices and Christians, a Genoese sailor, Christopher Columbus, had obtained a royal warrant from Spain—and venture capital from financiers in Genoa—and had journeyed across the Atlantic in search of Oriental gold[1] and the opulent kingdom of the great Khan of Cathay. As we know, he never made it that far.

However, although Columbus reached only as far as America—and, not surprisingly, failed to make contact with the royal court of the Grand Khan[2]—the log book of his first voyage duly records that, in these Indies, there are "great mines of gold and of other metals" (*The Journal of Christopher*

Columbus, quoted in Hulme, 1986: 42). Columbus further records in his *Journal* that the inhabitants of the Indies "refuse nothing that they possess ... [and] are content with whatever trifle ... may be given to them" in exchange, and that even those among the natives who "are regarded ... as very fierce ... are ferocious among these ... people who are cowardly to an excessive degree, but I make no more account of them than of the rest" (Hulme, 1986: 42). Already, during his first voyage, we may discern in Columbus the germs of the idea for violently subduing the native populations to grab their riches: the horrific genocide of the "Indians" is quick to follow. The voyages of Columbus and da Gama prefigure that confluence and commingling of commercial and financial interests, (religious) ideology and belief, military force and political cunning, and the deployment of unimaginable violence and cruelty, which was to become the hallmark of modern Western colonialism. The question that the present book attempts to grapple with is whether (and in what ways and forms) modern Western colonialism—and non-Western resistance to this colonialism—may have some important implications for how we choose to manage, think about, and work in contemporary formal organizations. This introductory chapter sets the stage for such an inquiry.

Postcolonial Theory and the Colonial Encounter

With the late fifteenth century as a provisional point of departure, modern Western colonialism has a history of over five hundred years. In addition to this long history, modern Western colonialism is notable for its geographical extent. By the early years of the twentieth century, Western colonial empires covered some 84.6 percent of the area of the earth (Loomba, 1998: 15). Indeed, as Young (2001: 2) notes, if we consider control rather than actual occupation of territory, by the early decades of the twentieth century a handful of Western countries directly or indirectly controlled about 90 percent of the globe.

In some respects, one might say, there is nothing new about conquest and colonization: the Aztec Empire, the Byzantine Empire, the Empire of Ghana, the Inca Empire, the Empire of Mali, the Maurya Empire, the Mongol Empire, the Mughal Empire, the Ottoman Empire, the Roman Empire, the Vijayanagara Empire, and other similar empires all attest to the fact of repeated territorial conquest in world history. Despite the existence of such earlier empires, however, scholars (e.g., Loomba, 1998; Young, 2001) argue that there is indeed something new and unique about modern Western colonialism. One important difference between modern Western colonialism and the earlier empires relates to the economic dimension. In economic terms, what was new about modern Western colonialism was that it not only extracted wealth and tribute from the peoples and territories it conquered, it also linked the West and its colonies in a complex structure of unequal exchange and industrialization that made the colonies economically dependent upon the Western colonial nations. Significantly, the economic imbalance created by modern Western colonialism served as a condition of possibility for the very emergence of European capitalism (cf. e.g., Loomba, 1998: 4). Along with the above, modern Western colonialism was new in that it attempted to subjugate its colonies in the realm of culture and ideology as well. Modern Western colonialism, thus, represents a unique constellation of complex and interrelated practices that sought to establish Western hegemony not only politically, militarily, and economically, but also culturally and ideologically. Not surprisingly, right from its early years, the battles of non-Western resistance to Western colonialism were fought along all these lines.

The long history of Western colonialism, its global reach, and the uniqueness of many of its constitutive practices and structures imply that Western colonialism and non-Western resistance to such colonialism have played a significant role in shaping the contours of the world as we know it today. Indeed, the continuing imprint of colonialism and anticolonialism is discernible in a range of contemporary practices and institutions, whether economic, political, or cultural. Postcolonial theory and criticism (or postcolonialism, in short)[3] represents an attempt to investigate the complex and deeply fraught dynamics of modern Western colonialism and anticolonial resistance, and the ongoing significance of the colonial encounter for people's lives both in the West and the non-West.

Colonialism and imperialism are highly debated concepts with multiple and shifting meanings (Loomba, 1998: 2 ff.; Young, 2001: 15 ff.).[4] Generally speaking, however, whereas colonialism involves the actual physical conquest, occupation, and administration of the territory of one country by another, imperialism is an exercise of economic and political power by one country over another that may or may not involve direct occupation. The British and French empires that reached their fullest expansion during the late nineteenth and early twentieth centuries were mostly *colonial* empires, with both Britain and France being in actual physical possession of vast territories all over the globe. By contrast, the current system of American imperialism is one that is seen as primarily non-colonial: to a considerable degree, American imperialism seeks to exercise power not through new conquests and occupation but through the control of powerful economic institutions such as the World Trade Organization (WTO), the World Bank, the International Monetary Fund (IMF), and the like (Young, 2001).

Neocolonialism is a term that came into use after the period of decolonization—a period that began during the middle of the last century and, within a few decades, led to the formal political independence of almost all of the erstwhile colonies of Europe. Such achievement of political independence marked an important victory for the various anticolonial movements waged in the non-West. However, these newly independent countries found that, despite political independence, they continued to be economically dependent on their ex-colonial masters because of the far-reaching restructuring of their economies during the colonial era. Such continued economic dependence of the ex-colonies implied that their formal independence was often of only somewhat limited political value. Neocolonialism is a term that refers to such continuation of Western colonialism by nontraditional means (cf. Young, 2001: 44 ff.). Frequently, neocolonialism is seen as having not only economic and political dimensions, but a dimension of Western cultural control as well.

Western colonialism/imperialism, thus, has a long history and an enormous geographical scope involving a range of different peoples, cultures, and territories. Not surprisingly, therefore, colonial/imperial institutions, structures, and practices are characterized by considerable heterogeneity. It is important for the critic of colonialism and imperialism to be aware of the existence of such heterogeneity. The existence of such heterogeneity, moreover, also seems to place certain limits on the kinds of generalizations we may draw about colonialism/imperialism (Loomba, 1998). However, as Young (2001: 18 ff.) rightly notes, while colonialism was indeed marked by a diverse range of practices, the overriding consequence of such practices, *as far as the colonized peoples were concerned*, was broadly the same, to wit, the attempted domination and subjugation of the colonized. From the perspective of the colonized, therefore, it makes ample sense to see a kind of overall *uniformity*, rather than heterogeneity, in colonial/imperial practices.

It follows from the above, therefore, that postcolonialism, which "identifies with the subject position of [the colonized and the] anticolonial activists" (Young, 2001: 19), may legitimately seek to draw theoretical generalizations about modern Western colonialism/imperialism as such. While so doing, nevertheless, the postcolonial critic needs to take into account the fact that, from the perspective of the Western colonizers themselves, colonial policies and practices may frequently exhibit important heterogeneities in their operational details. However, one implication following from the preceding is that the conceptual differences characterizing terms like "colonialism" and "imperialism" may not be overly significant in so far as the theoretical project of postcolonialism is concerned. Unless otherwise noted, therefore, we will employ the terms "colonialism" and "imperialism" somewhat interchangeably.

Postcolonial theory and criticism is explicitly committed to developing a radical critique of colonialism/imperialism and neocolonialism. In doing this, postcolonialism is not attempting something entirely new; quite to the contrary, the critique of colonialism offered by postcolonialism forms a part of that long and impressive history of oppositional criticisms of, and resistance to, Western colonialism, which is as old as Western colonialism itself. Postcolonialism, hence, needs to be seen as building upon the contributions of a number of earlier thinkers, freedom fighters, and anticolonial activists, including Cabral (1973), Césaire (1972), Fanon (1967a,b), Mahatma Gandhi (1927, 1928, 1938), Ho Chi Minh (1962), Kaunda (1967), Kenyatta (1938), Lenin (1947), Lumumba (1963), Mariátegui (1971), Mannoni (1964), Memmi (1965), Nkrumah (1965), Nyerere (1968), Senghor (1964), and many more.

Postcolonialism, thus, is rooted in—and, in some ways, may even be seen as a logical outcome of—the historical processes of European/Western[5] colonization and decolonization. Starting with the recognition that the neocolonial world order of our times is extremely unfair and unjust, postcolonialism is grounded in the belief that justice and human freedom are indivisible, and that achieving true freedom and justice requires a genuine global decolonization at political, economic, and cultural levels. The postcolonial perspective takes seriously the call by the Kenyan novelist Ngugi wa Thiong'O (1981) to "decolonize the mind." Such a project of the decolonization of the mind is strongly committed to contesting and subverting the unquestioned sovereignty of Western categories—epistemological, ethicomoral, economic, political, aesthetic, and the rest. In a word, postcolonial theory and criticism is committed to the project of "provincializing Europe" (Chakrabarty, 1992, 2000; Prasad, 1997a).

Postcolonialism is not a narrowly systematized and unitary theory. Rather, postcolonial theory is a set of productively syncretic theoretical and political positions that creatively employ concepts and epistemological perspectives deriving from a range of scholarly fields (such as anthropology, African American studies, cultural studies, film and media studies, women's studies, history and art history, literary theory, philosophy, political science, sociology, etc.) as well as from multiple approaches to inquiry (e.g., variants of Marxism and neo-Marxism, feminism, psychoanalysis, post-structuralism, deconstruction, queer theory, and so on). Inevitably, this has meant considerable internal debates, tensions, and heterogeneities within postcolonialism. Partly as a result of the close links—during the early years of the development of postcolonial theory—between literary theory and postcolonialism, the latter is often seen as an approach for critically analyzing the discourse (or, discourses) of colonialism and neocolonialism. It is important to keep in mind here that the term "discourse" does not merely refer to writing and/or speech, narrowly understood. Rather, discourses are better understood as "ways of constituting knowledge, together with the social practices, forms of subjectivity and power relations which inhere in such knowledges and the relations between them" (Weedon, 1997: 105). We may note here that, in Weedon's preceding definition, the term "knowledge" needs to be seen as referring to both scholarly and non-scholarly knowledge, and relating to all spheres of life including intellectual, cultural, economic, political, religious, social, ethico-moral, aesthetic, and so forth. Hence, the use of the term "discourse" in postcolonial theory and criticism serves to underscore the point that intellectual, social, cultural, political, economic, and other similar processes and structures form an intricately articulated ensemble of great complexity that seeks to (re)produce and perpetuate relations of colonialism and neocolonialism.[6] In so doing, postcolonialism draws attention toward the "intersection of ideas and institutions, knowledge and power" (Loomba, 1998: 54).

Postcolonialism's deployment of the notion of discourse, therefore, is meant to highlight—in the context of exercise of imperial power—the mutual imbrication of the material and the ideological, and to emphasize the importance of not collapsing either of these categories into the other. In practice, however, scholars often violate this injunction, and seem to privilege one of these two categories at the expense of the other. Somewhat simplifying Moore-Gilbert's (1997) detailed discussions of the dynamics attending these developments, one could say that the term "postcolonial theory" is *sometimes* used to refer *only* to the works of those scholars who (a) tend to privilege language and ideology over materiality and history and who, moreover, (b) extensively rely upon French "high theory" coming from Derrida, Foucault, Lacan, and others. On the other hand, works of those scholars who value history/materiality at the expense of language/ideology are sometimes said to belong to the domain of "postcolonial criticism." As our use of the term "postcolonial theory and criticism" suggests, we seek to go beyond such distinctions in postcolonial studies, without however trying to deny or ignore the heterogeneities that mark this field. Moreover, partly in view of the fact that a definition of postcolonial theory as analysis of colonial discourse may be considered appropriate only if the word "discourse" largely holds its more comprehensive meaning—one that points to the intersection of language and materiality—we consider the twin terms "postcolonial theory" and "postcolonial theory and criticism" as full substitutes for one another.

Following common scholarly practice, "postcolonialism" serves as a short-form for referring to either of these two terms (cf. e.g., Young, 2001: 57 ff.). Postcolonial theory has influenced a wide range of disciplines such as anthropology, cultural studies, development studies, geography, history, literary criticism, philosophy, political science, religious studies, sociology, and the like. Such developments point to the wide recognition of the usefulness of the postcolonial perspective in scholarly inquiry. One disciplinary field of knowledge, however, which, for a variety of reasons, remains largely untouched by such postcolonial ferment taking place in the social sciences and the humanities, is the field of management and organization studies. Interestingly enough, during the last few decades, organizational research has seen fit to liberally draw upon a number of different scholarly approaches, such as critical theory, feminism, Marxism and neo-Marxism, postmodernism, post-structuralism, and so forth. Partly as a result of such intellectual traffic, there now exists a fairly vigorous *critical* tradition within management and organization studies. Surprisingly, however, even critical organizational scholarship has mostly elected to ignore the insights offered by postcolonial theory and criticism. This state of affairs is intriguing, to say the least.

Be that as it may, this book contends that postcolonial theoretic insights can help management scholarship in meaningfully enhancing the current understanding of management and organizations. The concluding part of this chapter discusses in relatively greater detail the relevance of postcolonialism for management and organization studies. Before that, however, we will first offer a general overview of some of the intellectual contributions made by postcolonial theory.

Key Scholars and Their Contributions

In this section, we will primarily focus upon four influential scholars (namely, Edward Said, Ashis Nandy, Homi Bhabha, and Gayatri Chakravorty Spivak), and seek to develop an understanding of some of their more important theoretical insights. Although the overall field of postcolonial theory includes a number of other theorists, in many respects it is these four scholars who have, arguably, provided the field with some of its most productive lines of inquiry.

Edward Said and the Discourse of Orientalism

In the intellectual history of postcolonial theory, Edward Said's path-breaking book, *Orientalism* (1978), is commonly regarded as a "canonical event" (Gandhi, 1998: 66). *Orientalism* is an attempt to explore the complicity of power and knowledge and, in so doing, to produce an understanding of colonialism/imperialism at the level of representation. This book is generally seen as being in the nature of an inaugural text for the academic field of post-colonial theory and criticism, and both Said's admirers (e.g., Spivak, 1993) as well as his detractors (e.g., Ahmad, 1992) frequently attest to its lasting influence and significance.

Orientalism emerged in a scholarly context in which the field of literary and cultural analysis in the West mostly maintained a studied silence on issues of colony and empire (Young, 1990). This book's publication, hence, needs to be viewed as something akin to an intellectual rebellion on Said's part. Moreover, it may be claimed without exaggeration that it was the phenomenal success of this book that was responsible, at least in part, for reorienting sections of literary, cultural, and social-scientific scholarship in radically new directions. In some ways, *Orientalism* is also an expression of Said's frustration with the inadequacies of orthodox Marxist theory in the context of investigating the dynamics of colonialism and imperialism. Hence, for instance, Said's recourse in this book to the Foucauldian category of discourse. However, even though *Orientalism* employs a post-structuralist analytical device (namely discourse), the book itself must be seen as an extended critique of the ethnocentrism frequently exhibited by Western post-structuralist writings, which are often reluctant to seriously engage with different aspects of Western colonialism and/or to acknowledge the imprint of the empire on the West. Such tension—between postcolonialism and Marxism on the one hand, and between postcolonialism and post-structuralism, on the other—continues to be a part of the epistemological make up of postcolonial theory and criticism right up to the present.

Orientalism, for Said, has three interrelated meanings. First, Orientalism is a specialized field of Western scholarship having the Orient as its object of inquiry. Second, Orientalism is a Western "style of thought" (Said, 1978: 2) that adopts a starkly dichotomous view of "the Orient" and "the Occident" and makes essentialist statements about the former. Finally, Orientalism is a discourse—in Michel Foucault's (1972, 1977) sense of the term[7]—that serves as a "corporate institution for dealing with the Orient" (Said, 1978: 3). This third meaning subsumes the other two, and conceptualizes Orientalism as a complex ensemble of enunciatory, representational, and material and/or institutional practices that enabled the West "to manage . . . the Orient politically, sociologically, militarily, ideologically, scientifically, and imaginatively" (Said, 1978: 3).

Orientalism is a book that is remarkably ambitious in its scope. In geographical terms, for instance, while the book primarily focuses upon the West's relations with the Middle East and Islam, Said's analysis frequently breaches this boundary and, in so doing, seems to draw conclusions for the entire colonized world as a whole. Similarly, not only does Said's analysis range over a wide array of scholarly disciplines including literature, philosophy, history, theology, anthropology, archeology, and philology, it also frequently steps outside the domain of scholarly writing as such to cast a critical gaze upon other genres of writing, examining in the process such things as journalistic pieces, travel books, official reports, and other similar documents produced by colonial governments in the course of their dealings with political, military, and administrative issues. Likewise, *Orientalism* is impressive in its historical scope, which extends in some ways from ancient Greece to the era of modern European and U.S. colonialism/imperialism.

In his book, Said argues that the Orient is not so much a fact of geography as "a European invention" and "one of... [Europe's] deepest and most recurring images of the Other" (1978: 1). According to Said, the European invention of the Orient was accomplished by means of the discourse of Orientalism, a discourse that went "hand in hand with, or... [was] manufactured and produced out of, the actual control or domination" of the Orient by the West (1993a: 109). Said contends that the discourse of Orientalism is premised upon the positing of a fundamental "ontological and epistemological distinction... between 'the Orient' and 'the Occident'" (1978: 2). In other words, one of the foundational fictions of Orientalism is the belief that "the Orient" and "the Occident" are polar opposites, and that the inhabitants of these two "binomial" (1978: 227) entities do not participate in the same humanness.

Starting with the preceding fictive assumptions, Orientalism has grown into a massive "discursive formation" (Said, 1978: 23) that displays and authorizes something approximating a Western cultural consensus about the *essence* of being Oriental, and supplies the "enunciative capacity... [for making] a statement of any consequence about the Orient" (Said, 1978: 221). This cultural consensus, Said (1978) notes, includes such stereotypes, among others, as those of "Oriental despotism, splendor, cruelty, and sensuality" (p. 4), of the Oriental lack of logic, untruthfulness, intrigue, cunning, lethargy, suspicion, irrationality, depravity, and childishness (pp. 38–40), as well as of the Orient's "eccentricity, backwardness, indifference, feminine penetrability, and supine malleability" (p. 206). With the help of these and other similar devices, Orientalism depicted the Orient as characterized by "decline, degradation, and decadence" (Dirks, 1992a: 9), and successfully created the portrait of the Oriental as someone belonging (in an ontological sense) to a subject race who, therefore, had to be subjugated. In so doing, the discourse of Orientalism "justified in advance" and prepared the ground for Western colonialism (Said, 1978: 39).[8]

An Orient constructed along the preceding lines served also as a focal point for distilling the *opposites* of all those moral, ethical, and aesthetic attributes that gradually accreted to constitute the very core of the West's own self-definition. Thus, Orientalism's construction of the Orient "helped to define...the West...as [the Orient's] contrasting image, idea, personality, experience" and the like (Said, 1978: 1–2). In this way, Orientalism sought to produce the so-called essence of both the Orient (or even the entire non-West) as well as the Occident. The Occident/Orient (or West/non-West) dichotomy was based upon the elaborate fiction of a system of hierarchical binary oppositions such as active/passive, center/periphery, civilized/savage, developed/undeveloped, masculine/feminine, modern/archaic, scientific/superstitious, and so on (cf. Prasad, 1997b). These binaries were hierarchical in the sense that the first term in each of the foregoing combinations was the *privileged* term, and was considered superior to, and more desirable than, the second term.

The discourse of Orientalism linked the West with the superior pole of these binaries, and relegated the non-West to the inferior pole. This conceptual maneuver proved useful for developing a moral justification for colonialism: once the identity of the non-West had been thoroughly fleshed out with terms designating "inferiority," colonialism could be successfully portrayed as a project designed to civilize, improve, and *help* those peoples who were "lagging behind" in the March of History and Civilization. Indeed, once this conceptual maneuver had been made, colonialism almost became a *moral obligation* for the West.

The foregoing Orientalist dogma functioned as a hegemonic (Gramsci, 1971) common sense for the West. According to Said (1978), the hegemonic authority wielded by Orientalism was linked to a number of factors including a long history of Western productions of minutely detailed and closely worked over written representations of the Orient,[9] a widely accepted "system for citing works and authors" dealing with the Orient (p. 23) that had its own "pioneers, patriarchal authorities, canonical texts...exemplary figures" and the like (p. 22), as well as the growth and development over time of a highly productive and influential network of institutions (e.g., learned societies, university departments, scholarly conferences, governmental bodies such as foreign services, diplomatic corps, military establishments and colonial administrations, and so forth) that provided the material grounding for Orientalism.

The hegemonic authority enjoyed by Orientalism, however, implied that Orientalist vocabulary, images, stereotypes, and dogmas inevitably furnished the overarching framework within which any Western discussion of the

Orient and/or the non-West could be carried on. Hence, Said's (1978: 206) judgment that "every [Western] writer on the Orient...saw the Orient as a locale requiring Western attention, reconstruction, even redemption," and his pointed observation that "every European, in what he could say about the Orient, was consequently a racist, an imperialist, and almost totally ethnocentric" (p. 204).

In thus laying bare the inner dynamics of Orientalism, Said underscored the close complicity of Western systems of knowledge and representation with brute colonial control and domination. In this process, he also delivered a serious blow to the conventional Western liberal understanding of scholarship as being an autonomous pursuit of pure, objective, and disinterested knowledge. *Orientalism* is the first book of a trilogy that includes *The Question of Palestine* (1979) and *Covering Islam* (1981). These two later books further investigate the persistence of the Orientalist discourse, and bring the arguments of *Orientalism* to bear upon current Western relations with the Middle East.

Notwithstanding, however, its canonical status (or, perhaps, *because* of it[10]), *Orientalism* has drawn criticism from many sides (see, e.g., Ahmad, 1992; Bhabha, 1983; Clifford, 1988; Fox, 1992; Porter, 1983; Young, 1990). In brief, such criticisms contend that in this book Said: (a) disregards and flattens historical variations in Western representations of the Orient, and seems to argue that these representations remained virtually unchanged from classical Greece to the modern times, (b) adopts an unduly monolithic and homogenized view of Orientalism as a result of giving inadequate attention to heterogeneities across individual Orientalist authors and different national traditions of Orientalism existing within the West, (c) exhibits an uncertain theoretical vacillation between Orientalism as a discourse, on the one hand, and Orientalism as an ideological misrepresentation, on the other, (d) insufficiently grounds Orientalism in the material processes of capitalism and colonialism and, in so doing, seemingly overstates the significance of representational and ideological aspects of colonialism, and (e) that by virtue of theorizing a starkly hegemonic and pessimistic "prisonhouse of Orientalism" (Pathak, Sengupta, & Purkayastha, 1991), he ignores non-Western as well as Western resistance and opposition to Orientalism.

Undoubtedly, it is possible to see some merit in many of these criticisms. Subsequent postcolonial scholarship, however, has also sought to reconsider some of the earlier criticisms of *Orientalism*. Moore-Gilbert (1997), for instance, points out that Said does recognize, albeit somewhat unevenly, the fractured and heterogeneous nature of Orientalism, and does not depict it as a completely homogeneous discourse. Similarly, Loomba (1998) and

Moore-Gilbert (1997), among others, have noted that, contrary to some of his critics' assertions, Said's work does not foreclose the possibility of resistance to Orientalism. Said himself has responded to the criticisms of *Orientalism* partly by offering explicit commentaries on such criticisms (e.g., Said, 1985), and partly by providing, in his later writings, relatively greater emphasis on some of those themes that his critics saw as missing in *Orientalism*. In *Culture and Imperialism*, for instance, Said (1993b) presents an extended analysis of resistance to colonialism.

In any event, and notwithstanding the validity or otherwise of criticisms of this book, the importance and originality of *Orientalism* continues to be acknowledged even today (Loomba, 1998; Young, 2001). *Orientalism* is important not because it is the first (or even an early) critique of Western colonialism. As we saw earlier, critiques of Western colonialism are as old as Western colonialism itself. Rather, the importance and originality of *Orientalism* is to be found in its insistence that colonialism functioned not only as military violence and economic control and subjugation, but also as a discourse of domination. In so doing, the book convincingly argued that Orientalism (as a field of scholarship, for instance) was intimately implicated in the dynamics of colonialism, empire, and power. If, on the one hand, the historical circumstances of colonial domination served as the very conditions of possibility of Orientalism, on the other hand, the "knowledges" produced by Orientalist scholarship in diverse fields (e.g., literature, art, anthropology, philology, etc.) developed a specific representation of the Orient, which made the deployment of particular imperial technologies of power and control possible. *Orientalism*, thus, challenged the traditional liberal view of knowledge, scholarship, and "high" culture as somehow being "above" the more profane, violent, and bloody world of colonialism. Concomitantly, by introducing the concept of discourse in the study of colonialism, Said inaugurated an entirely new scholarly field of colonial discourse analysis.

The Psychology of Colonialism

If Edward Said occupies a deservedly well-respected and iconic place in the field of postcolonial theory and criticism, a full realization of the significance of Ashis Nandy's contributions to this field has just begun to dawn (Miller, 1998; Young, 2001). Nandy's work primarily focuses upon the *psychology of colonialism* (cf. e.g., Nandy, 1980a, 1983, 1987). In this process, Nandy not only recuperates some of the earlier insights on colonialism offered by such important figures as Fanon (1967a,b), Mannoni (1964), and Memmi (1965), he also creatively draws upon the cultural, ethical, and political philosophy of Mahatma Gandhi (1869–1948) who has been, somewhat surprisingly perhaps, relatively ignored by postcolonial scholars (Young, 2001). Nandy's writings are almost always intended as forceful and explicit interventions in contemporary politics, be it the politics of awareness (1987), the politics of self (1994), the politics of fashioning "a plural human future" (1995: x), or "the politics of cultural choices and . . . visions in South Asia" (2000: xi). Moreover, as Miller (1998: 302) has noted, Nandy's writings always bring with them an "acute knowledge of the politics of knowledge."

Nandy's analyses of the consequences of the fateful colonial encounter between the West and the non-West range over a number of substantive concerns including, *inter alia*, science, technology and development (1980a, 1988), nationalism (1994), religion and fundamentalism (1998, 2001), and cricket—"an Indian game accidentally discovered by the English" (2000: 1)—as a metaphor for understanding popular cultures and cultural choices. In many respects, however, his general intellectual and ethico-political approach for analyzing colonialism and its aftermath was laid out in some detail in his remarkable book, *The Intimate Enemy: Loss and Recovery of Self under Colonialism*, and Nandy's subsequent works have continued to follow, in important ways, the broad contours of the overall approach outlined in that book.

The Intimate Enemy contends that although military conquest and economic domination are indeed important aspects of colonialism, what is perhaps even more important is the colonization of mind and imagination effected under the colonial situation.[11] Usually these two moments (or phases) of colonialism are chronologically distinct, and ideological colonization may frequently lag behind the actual physical conquest and control of the colony by several years. In the case of the British in India, for instance, ideological colonialism seems to have lagged behind military conquest by some 75 years (Nandy, 1983: 2). Nandy refers to such ideological colonialism as the second colonization, and points out that the instruments of the second colonization are not greedy marauders and "bandit-kings" commonly responsible for colonial conquest, but "well-meaning, hard-working, middle-class missionaries, liberals, modernists, and believers in science, equality and progress" (1983: xi). *The Intimate Enemy* offers an analysis of the structures of this psychological and ideological domination, and of resistance to such domination.

In psychological terms, according to Nandy (1983: 2), colonialism seeks to "alter the original cultural priorities *on both sides* and bring to the center of the colonial culture subcultures previously recessive or subordinate *in the two confronting cultures*. . . . [while simultaneously] remov(ing) from the center of *each*... [those] subcultures [that may have been] previously salient in them" (italics added). An important example offered by Nandy in this regard involves the redefinition, during later years of British colonialism, of the cultural meanings attached to the category of sex.

Nandy notes that during the early years of British colonialism there seems to have been little attempt to see a strong link or correspondence between British politico-military dominance (in India, for instance) and the traditional dominance within British culture and society of men/masculinity over women/femininity. During the later years, however, a highly aggressive and violent form of masculinity—or what Nandy calls "hyper-masculinity"—came to be seen as the very foundation of British imperial dominance. Along with this, the ideology of imperialism also began to offer explanations and justifications for the empirical fact of European military domination of the world partly in terms of European masculinity and non-European femininity/effeminacy.

These moves, which contributed to the setting up of a homology between sexual dominance and political/military dominance, were accompanied by a redefinition of the very category of masculinity within British culture. The result was the development of a very narrow and restrictive notion of masculinity that came to regard any hint of femininity in men (i.e., the existence of psychological bisexuality in males) as highly dangerous and harmful. Such reordering of the cultural priorities of the colonizers was accompanied by somewhat parallel developments in the world of the colonized. For instance, in certain sections of India, the experience of colonialism led to an internalization of the aforementioned homology between sexual and political dominance and, as a result, some Indians engaged in attempts to "reform" and "rejuvenate" India by construing *Kshatriyahood* (the Indian ideology of martial races, warriorhood, violence, and virility) as true Indianness, and by proposing to fashion a new cultural identity for India, with *Kshatriyahood* occupying the very core of this new identity.[12]

Thus, the psychological forces released by colonialism seek to devalue the tender and humane aspects of culture in both societies, the society of the colonizer as well as that of the colonized. Hence, colonialism is a highly fraught enterprise even for the colonizing society itself, which must pay a heavy price in terms of its own "psychological decay" (Nandy, 1983: xvi). For instance, in the case of Britain, notes Nandy (1983), this psychological decay and degradation included such "cultural pathologies" (p. 35), among others, as "ruthless social Darwinism" (p. 35), an instrumental view of human relationships, denigration of femininity and debasement of women, deemphasizing intellectual speculation, and relative lack of cultural self-scrutiny and marginalization of internal cultural criticism.

In thus highlighting the psychological cost of colonialism for the colonizers themselves, Nandy questions the conventional wisdom that sees colonialism as "a one-way flow of benefits" in which the colonized are "the perpetual losers" and the colonizers "the beneficiaries" (1983: 30). Indeed, Nandy crucially insists that colonialism is a game without victors: both the colonizers and the colonized are merely *victims* of colonialism. For Nandy (1983: 31), a stark example of the psychic degradation and victimhood of the colonizer is provided by Fanon (1967b) who offers the case of the French police officer in Algeria whose violent torture of Algerian freedom fighters was matched only by the violence that he inflicted on his own wife and children.[13]

As regards resistance to colonialism, Nandy maintains that since "colonialism is first of all a matter of consciousness" (1983: 63) it needs to be ultimately defeated at the level of the human imagination itself. His focus, therefore, is on some of the psychological aspects of resistance to colonialism. Significantly, moreover, in keeping with the priority accorded in his thinking to the notion of second colonization, his analyses of resistance to colonialism are crucially informed by a desire to defeat that insidious neocolonialism, which survives at the level of imagination—in significant parts of the world—the formal dissolution of the Western empires, and which seeks to "generalize the concept of the modern West from a geographical and temporal entity to a psychological category" (Nandy, 1983: xi).

In his analyses of resistance to colonialism, Nandy makes an important distinction between the resistance, on the one hand, of those he calls the counterplayers—who continue to pay "homage to the victors" even in defiance (1983: xii)—and, on the other hand, of the innocent nonplayers who are unwilling to be either players or counterplayers. Noting that the modern colonizing West has produced in the colonies "not only its servile imitators and admirers but also its circus-tamed opponents and its tragic counterplayers performing their last gladiator-like acts of courage in front of appreciative Caesars" (1983: xiv), Nandy observes that both the imitative players as well as the defiant counterplayers continue to offer obeisance to the idea of the West as a universal: what distinguishes the counterplayers from the players is that, unlike the latter, the former seek to surpass and defeat the West at its own game (e.g., by fashioning a national culture that is more aggressively hypermasculine than even the dominant culture of the West). Drawing upon the example of Mahatma Gandhi's politics of national and cultural liberation, however, Nandy insists that what finally defeats colonialism is not the opposition waged by the tragic counterplayers but a resistance informed by the authentic innocence of the nonplayers—an innocence "which includes the vulnerability of a child but which has not lost the realism of its perception of evil or that of its own 'complicity' with that evil" (1983: xiii).

Nandy refuses to see the unheroic nonplayers in the colonies as passive victims of colonialism. Rather, he insists that they must be viewed as active agents making cognitive and moral choices and judgments in their battle of survival against colonialism. As Nandy famously observes, even the lowly Indian clerk—the babu—must be seen "as an interface who processes the West on behalf of his society and reduces it to a digestible bolus" (1983: xv), and in so doing "turns the West into a reasonably manageable vector within the traditional worldview still outside the span of modern ideas of universalism" (1983: xiii).[14] It is this psychological resistance—sometimes conscious, sometimes unselfconscious—on the part of the innocent nonplayers that Nandy takes seriously, and analyzes with a view to contributing to the overall postcolonial project of contesting and subverting the second colonization of the erstwhile colonies.

Nandy's focus upon psychological resistance is motivated by a desire to understand how the unheroic, innocent, nonplayers in the colonies mobilized the wisdom of their own stock of cultural traditions (e.g., traditions dealing with the issue of, among other things, fashioning an appropriate response to oppression) with a view to successfully responding to, and surviving under, conditions of unprecedented violence and bloody subjection unleashed by modern Western colonialism. The purpose of this exercise on Nandy's part is to grasp the nature of the anticolonialism of the innocent nonplayers, and to fashion our own resistance to colonialism (and, perhaps even more importantly, to the second colonization) along parallel lines.

Nandy, thus, follows in Gandhi's footsteps, and explicitly acknowledges that the anticolonialism of the nonplayers is the more effective form of resistance to colonialism and neocolonialism. There seem to be at least two reasons for this position on his part. First of all, like Gandhi, Nandy (1983) accepts the "moral and cultural superiority of the oppressed" (p. 49) and recognizes the value of the "ethically sensitive and culturally rooted" (p. xvii) response to colonialism offered by colonialism's innocent subjects. "It was that innocence," declares Nandy famously, "which finally defeated colonialism, however much the modern mind might like to give the credit to world historical forces, internal contradictions of capitalism and to the political horsesense or 'voluntary self-liquidation' of the rulers" (1983: xiii). In addition, Nandy contends also that, in the master–slave relationship, the slave "represents a higher-order cognition" (1983: xv). The slave's cognition would seem to be of a higher order, in part, because it accepts the master as a human being and, therefore, has access to a larger repertoire of cognitive categories for dealing with the world. In contrast, the master's cognition rejects the humanness of the slave and, therefore, possesses a relatively narrower repertoire of cognitive categories.

Following Gandhi, Nandy too emphasizes the continuity between the experiences of the colonized and the colonizer—both of whom are co-victims of colonialism—and sees the resistance waged by the colonized as simultaneously being a project to liberate and save the colonizers themselves. In this mutual project of resistance to (neo)colonialism, the colonized have an important ally in "the other West" (Nandy, 1983: 48), or the "west's other self" (Nandy, 1983: xiii), which represents many of the precious cultural values and priorities that have been marginalized and rejected by the colonizing West's dominant self. Nandy's subsequent works continue to follow, in different ways, the broad agenda (of contesting second colonization with a view to imagining a different universalism that would serve as an alternative to the universalism offered by the modern West's dominant self) set in *The Intimate Enemy*.

The influence of Nandy, and of *The Intimate Enemy*, in the field of postcolonial theory and criticism has been immense. Indeed, in Robert Young's view, for instance, *The Intimate Enemy* is comparable in significance to Said's *Orientalism*, and is "one of the books that contributed most to setting up the basic framework of the theoretico-political environment of postcolonial studies...across the whole field" (2001: 339–340). In part, Nandy's contribution to postcolonialism is rooted in his recognition of "the subversive radicality of...Gandhi's counter-modernity" (Young, 2001: 340), and his creative appropriation of Gandhi for this field. Following Gandhi, Nandy refuses to see a clear-cut separation between "India" and "the West," between "victors" and "victims," or between the colonizers and the colonized, and offers instead a hybrid and unstable conceptualization of these categories. Nandy, thus, greatly contributes toward making hybridity into an important intellectual and political category in the field of postcolonial theory and criticism. Similarly, Nandy's notion of psychological resistance creatively borrows from Gandhi's idea of internal resistance and, in this process, successfully establishes the psychology of resistance as a key concern for postcolonialism. Moreover, Nandy's inventive use of psychoanalysis anticipates some of the nimble creativity of Homi Bhabha's deployment of psychoanalytic categories in the latter's own works.

Ambivalence, Mimicry, Hybridity

Among postcolonial scholars it would appear to be Homi Bhabha more than any one else whose name, for a variety of reasons, seems to have become most closely identified with such important concepts as ambivalence, mimicry, and hybridity (Bhabha, 1983, 1990, 1994).[15] Following some of the leads and openings offered by Said in *Orientalism*—leads and openings that, according to Bhabha, *Orientalism* itself does not seem to have fully explored—Bhabha argues that colonial discourse is characterized not by monolithic homogeneity and hegemonic fixity, but by ambivalence, fissure, and contradictions.

For instance, as suggested in *Orientalism* itself, even though colonialism seeks to identify the non-West as inferior and undesirable, the non-West is also regarded by colonial discourse as a highly desirable and prized object of Western possession. Similarly, although colonialism defines the non-West as weak and effeminate, it simultaneously views the non-West as a grave threat capable of destroying the Western world. Or, while colonialism sees itself as being spurred by a moral drive to "improve" and recast the non-West in the West's own image, somewhat paradoxically, colonialism also evinces an intense belief in some changeless *essence of* non-Western cultures, which already dooms such cultural improvement projects to failure. In a parallel fashion, although colonial discourse claims that the moral purpose of colonialism is to civilize the dark and savage races of the world, this discourse simultaneously posits savagery to be a fixed, biological condition, incapable of being changed. Along similar lines, as Bhabha (1994: 82) notes, for colonial discourse:

> The black is both savage (cannibal) and yet the most obedient and dignified of servants (the bearer of food); he is the embodiment of rampant sexuality and yet innocent as a child; he is mystical, primitive, simple-minded and yet the most worldly and accomplished liar, and manipulator of social forces.

Hence, observes Bhabha, one of the effects of colonial discourse is the ambivalent production of "that 'otherness' which is at once an object of desire and derision" (1994: 67). Moreover, colonial discourse is ambivalent also because it simultaneously recognizes as well as disavows differences— of race, culture, history, and so on—with the result that this discourse "produces the colonized as a social reality which is at once an 'other' and yet entirely knowable and visible" (Bhabha, 1994: 70–71). That is to say, colonial discourse is ambivalent about the *boundary* that it posits as separating the West and the non-West. On the one hand, this discourse views such a boundary as being absolutely firm and non-permeable, such that the non-West and the West become radical "others" of each other. Such radical otherness implies that the non-West occupies a conceptual space fully *outside* that of the West, as a result of which Western categories/epistemologies are rendered incapable of knowing/understanding the non-West. On the other hand, however, colonial discourse regards the non-Western colonized as also being fully knowable with the help of Western categories/epistemologies and, in so doing, draws the non-West *inside* the West and thereby breaches the very boundary that this discourse itself has erected.

At this point, diverging somewhat from the Said of *Orientalism*, Bhabha insists that such ambivalence of colonial discourse as an instrument of power implies that this discourse forever fails in accomplishing the one thing that is crucial for establishing the hegemonic domination of the colonizers over the colonized, namely, fully and finally fixing the subjectivity of the colonized "as a population of degenerate types on the basis of racial origin" (Bhabha, 1994: 70), and as peoples occupying the lower rungs on the hierarchy of civilizations and races. It is this ambivalence of the colonial discourse, and the inevitable failure of this discourse to successfully fix the subject positions of the colonized, which ensures that colonialist stereotypes—as devices that are integral to the overall disposition of colonial discourse—are incessantly repeated such that "the *same old* stories of the Negro's animality, the Coolie's inscrutability or the stupidity of the Irish *must* be told (compulsively) again and afresh" (Bhabha, 1994: 77, italics in the original). As Bhabha notes, it is "as if the essential duplicity of the Asiatic or the bestial sexual license of the African that needs no proof, can never really, in discourse, be proved" (1994: 66). In contradistinction to *Orientalism*, therefore, for Bhabha, the ambivalence of colonial discourse[16] underscores the fatal instability of colonial power and opens up a space for anticolonialist struggle.

If the ambivalence of colonial discourse points toward the *necessarily* unstable nature of colonial power, Bhabha introduces the notion of colonial mimicry to highlight an even greater loss of authority and control on the part of the colonizer. Conventionally, in the colonial context, mimicry—that is, the miming and imitation of colonizers by the colonized—has been theorized as an effect of the colonizers' power and authority. In other words, the argument has been that the colonizers' power and authority—politico-economic as well as cultural and ideological—force the colonized to internalize the norms and values of the former. Traditionally, therefore, mimicry has often been viewed as one more "proof" of the colonizers' hegemony and of the dependency and subservience of the colonized (e.g., Naipaul, 1967). In a crucial departure from such earlier arguments, however, for Bhabha, mimicry is the space of resistance that destabilizes and undermines colonial authority.

"Mimicry *repeats* rather than *re-presents,*" says Bhabha (1994: 88, italics in the original), with the result, for instance, that the colonized are only partial copies of the colonizers. In other words, the imitation of the colonizers by the colonized does not produce colonial subjects who are identical in all respects to the colonizers, but, rather, merely gives rise to figures who are "*almost the same but not quite . . . almost the same but not white*" (Bhabha, 1994: 89, italics in the original). Mimicry thus becomes a process designating "an ambivalent mixture of deference and disobedience" (Gandhi, 1998: 149) through which the colonized successfully retain their difference and refuse to obey the colonizers' narcissistic demand/command to be the "same." Hence, mimicry—sometimes as camouflage, sometimes as mockery, parody, and irony—constantly menaces the colonizing project of the civilizing mission that seeks to transform the culture of the colonized by making it into a replica of the colonizers' culture. Somewhat related to mimicry, colonial hybridity may be seen as referring to a process of cultural appropriation or "translation" on the part of the colonized that, following "the logic of inappropriate appropriation" (Gandhi, 1998: 150) or "mistaken reading" (Spivak, 1999), combines/articulates the colonizers' discourse "with a range of differential knowledges and positionalities that both estrange . . . [the] 'identity' of [that discourse] and produce new forms of knowledge . . . new sites of power" (Bhabha, 1994: 120), and thus effects a "strategic reversal of the process of domination" (Bhabha, 1994: 112) and enables the rise of active anticolonial resistance.

Postcolonial Feminism and Subalternity

In addition to the writings of Said, Nandy, and Bhabha, the work of Gayatri Chakravorty Spivak—sometimes described as a "feminist Marxist deconstructivist" (MacCabe, 1987: ix)—is widely recognized as "one of the most substantial and innovative contributions to postcolonial [theory and criticism]" (Moore-Gilbert, 1997: 74). Spivak addresses a range of diverse concerns including the limits of First World feminism, the usefulness of deconstruction and Marxism within a broad postcolonialist agenda and framework, the tensions between essentialism and anti-essentialism in the context of a critical and progressive praxis, globalization and the contemporary international division of labor, and so forth. In many respects, Spivak's emergence as a key critic of (neo-) imperialism was heralded by the publication of her important essay, "French Feminism in an International Frame" (Spivak, 1981),[17] an essay acclaimed for being "exemplary in its attention to the narcissism of the [First World] liberal-feminist investigator" (Gandhi, 1998: 86).

In this essay, Spivak analyzes some of the problems that invest First World feminists' vanguardist claims regarding their own liberated status, which supposedly renders them into fully formed agents for emancipating/saving the Third World Woman. In parts of this essay, Spivak engages in a critical reading of the French feminist Julia Kristeva's, *About Chinese Women* (1977), and argues that Kristeva's text is not so much interested in understanding Chinese women as it is in Kristeva's own self-constitution and self-elaboration. "Her [Kristeva's] question, in the face of those silent [Chinese] women," notes Spivak (1987: 137), "is about her *own* identity rather than theirs" (italics in the original). Spivak, therefore, is skeptical about the value or relevance of Kristeva's kind of First World feminism in an international/Third World context.

Along with the above, Spivak is critical of many First World feminists for their "colonialist benevolence" (1987: 138) and sense of privilege that impels them to act to "save" their so-called less-privileged Third World sisters. "The academic [First World] feminist," contends Spivak (1987: 135), "must learn to learn from . . . [the Third World women], to speak to them, to suspect that their access to the political and sexual scene is not merely to be *corrected* by . . . [the First World feminist's] superior theory and enlightened compassion" (italics in the original). In short, Spivak insists, "the First World feminist must learn to stop feeling privileged *as a woman*" (1987: 136, italics in the original).[18] In another essay (cf. Spivak, 1985), Spivak's criticism of First World feminism leans toward the latter's Anglo-American, rather than French, variant. Focusing, in part, upon Anglo-American feminism's attempts in the 1970s to celebrate Jane Eyre—the heroine of the nineteenth-century British novel of the same name—as a triumphant proto-feminist, Spivak (1985) critiques such attempts not only for ignoring the novel's investment in reproducing the axioms of imperialism, but also for uncritically conflating feminist *individualism* with feminism *as such.*

Arguably, Spivak is best known within the field of postcolonial theory and criticism for her celebrated essay, "Can the Subaltern Speak?"[19] The term "subaltern" owes its origins to Gramsci (1971), who used this word in his *Prison Notebooks*—written during the 1920s and 1930s—to broadly refer to the oppressed and subordinated groups and classes of society. During more recent years, however, the term has gained considerable prominence as a result of the scholarly work done by a group of intellectuals—commonly known as the *Subaltern Studies* Collective (cf. e.g., Chaturvedi, 2000; Guha, 1997; Guha & Spivak, 1988)—which has devoted itself to studying the condition of subalternity in South Asian history, society, and culture. This group of scholars understands the word "subaltern" as referring to "the general attribute of subordination in South Asian society whether this is expressed in terms of class, caste, age, gender and office or in any other way" (Guha, 1982a: vii). Guha (1982b: 8) further elaborates this definition by adding that the terms "people" and "subaltern classes" are synonymous, and that the subaltern classes "represent *the demographic difference between the total Indian population and all those whom we have described as the 'elite'*" (italics in the original). Thus, adopting a politics of the people perspective, the early works of the *Subaltern Studies* Collective were concerned with searching for the essential structure of subaltern consciousness (Chatterjee, 1999), and with retrieving that consciousness such that the subaltern may finally be able to speak "within the jealous pages of elitist historiography" (Gandhi, 1998: 2). "Can the Subaltern Speak?" represents, among other things, a radical attempt on Spivak's part to raise some serious questions about the project of letting the subaltern speak.

Focusing for the most part on the doubly marginal figure of the female subaltern under conditions of (neo-)colonial domination—a figure subordinated by imperialism on the one hand, and by patriarchy, on the other—Spivak's essay contends, in brief, that any project of retrieving the consciousness of the female subaltern subject is doomed to fail. Spivak seems to be arguing that such a project of consciousness retrieval must fail because: (a) a "subject is only constituted as a subject through the [subject] positions that have been [discursively] permitted" (Young, 1990: 165), and (b) that there simply does not exist in discourse (nor has ever existed) a subject position, or a "position of enunciation" (Young, 1990: 164) through which the female subaltern may speak. As a result, the female subaltern is never "allowed to speak: everyone else speaks for her, so that she is rewritten continuously as the object of patriarchy or of imperialism" (Young, 1990: 164). Given the absence of an adequate discursive position for the female subaltern as a speaking subject, Spivak concludes that "(t)he subaltern as female cannot be heard or read" (1988a: 308; 1999: 308).

Earlier versions of this essay (e.g., Spivak, 1988a) follow the preceding conclusion by insisting that "(t)he subaltern cannot speak" (p. 308). Hence, it becomes the task of criticism to critique those discourses that show an investment in the idea of retrieving subaltern consciousness, and to investigate the complicity of such discourses in the production of subalternity. In her revised version of the essay, however, Spivak (1999) has taken into consideration the fact that—notwithstanding the absence of a discursively authorized enunciative position for the female subaltern—through our acts of "reading," "translation," and "distanced decipherment" (p. 309), the subaltern does seem to speak. Nevertheless, even as she subtly repositions the earlier essay, she injects a note of caution by asking us to ponder over an important question: "What is at stake when we insist that the subaltern speaks?" (1999: 309).

Notions of subalternity and subaltern consciousness, and the project of retrieving the essential structures of such consciousness may, of course, be seen as falling prey to the problem of essentialism. In brief, essentialism may be said to refer to the idea that any specific group of objects or people (e.g., a race, gender, or class) is marked, identified, and defined by pure, immutable, and transhistorical characteristics and essences that inhere in the specific group in question, and that determine the fundamental and unique nature of that group. Not surprisingly, post-structuralism—with its emphasis upon, among other things, the untenability of rigid boundaries between socially constructed categories, and the radical embeddedness of such categories in history—is critical of the idea of essentialism. Notwithstanding her (partly) post-structuralist leanings, however, Spivak (1988b: 13) considers the *Subaltern Studies* Collective's deployment of essentialism to be legitimate because it represents "a *strategic* use of positive essentialism in a scrupulously visible political interest" (italics in the original).

Following this, Spivak's idea of strategic essentialism—broadly indicating the theoretically "impure" practice of occasionally employing essentialism for purposes of practical politics—has gained considerable prominence in critical circles. Even while endorsing the practical usefulness of strategic essentialism, Spivak continued to caution that it was important "not to be theoretically committed to . . . [essentialism], and . . . to take a stand against the discourses of essentialism" (1990: 11). Spivak has noted that her subsequent work exhibits a "shift from (anti-)essentialism to agency" (Spivak, 1993: ix). In part, Spivak understands this shift as an acknowledgment of "the unavoidable usefulness of something [e.g., essentialism] that is dangerous" (1993: 5). Hence, strategic essentialism now becomes marked with the recognition that "the critique of essentialism is [to be] understood not as an exposure of error . . . but as an acknowledgement of the dangerousness of something one cannot *not* use" (Spivak, 1993: 5, italics added).

As the foregoing suggests, along with the scholarly contributions of Said, Nandy, Bhabha, and Spivak, it is the work of the *Subaltern Studies* Collective that has greatly influenced the intellectual contours of postcolonial theory and criticism. While attempting to understand the *Subaltern Studies* project—a project that has attained the "status of a global academic institution" (Chaturvedi, 2000: vii)—it is useful to draw a distinction between the early and later works of the Collective. As we noted earlier, the *Subaltern Studies* Collective's early works began as a project for retrieving the essential structures of subaltern consciousness in South Asia, and revising the elitist historiography (both colonialist and nationalist) relating to that region. Later works of the Collective, however, mark a shift away from essentialist notions of subaltern consciousness and identity, and toward more complex, relational, and discursive conceptions of identity. This shift has also been accompanied by a greater emphasis upon questions of secularism, caste, and gender (cf. Chatterjee, 1999). At the same time, the *Subaltern Studies'* approach has transcended its own initial geographical focus upon South Asia, and has entered several other locales such as Africa, China, Ireland, Japan, Latin America, and Palestine (Chaturvedi, 2000).

The overall postcolonial oeuvre is truly immense, with important contributions coming from a number of scholars. Apart from the themes discussed above, researchers have contributed to this field by way of focusing critical attention upon such issues, among others, as the language, rhetoric, and literature of empire (Brantlinger, 1988; Pratt, 1992; Sharpe, 1993; Spurr, 1993; Suleri, 1992; Teltscher, 1995), the relationship between the rise of the novel as a genre and the project of imperialism (Azim, 1993), the construction of the category of English literature as an ideological device in colonial India (Viswanathan, 1989), the role of Western women in imperialism (Chaudhuri & Strobel, 1992; Jayawardena, 1995), the universalistic pretensions of First World liberal feminism (Mohanty, Russo, & Torres, 1991), the discourse of development (Escobar, 1995; Rahnema & Bawtree, 1997; Sachs, 1992), critical genealogies of science (Nandy, 1988; Prakash, 1999), the complicitous links between colonialism and scholarly "knowledge" in several fields including anthropology (Clifford, 1988; diLeonardo, 1998; Stocking, 1985) and mathematics (Bishop, 1990), the discourse of the nation and nationalism (Bhabha, 1990; Chatterjee, 1986, 1993), cultural dimensions of globalization (Appadurai, 1996), the idea of a distinct *mestizo* Latin American identity and culture (Retamar, 1989), relationship between postcolonialism and postmodernism (Adams & Tiffin, 1990; During, 1987), reinterpretation and critique of received colonialist histories and modes of historiography (Chakrabarty, 1992, 2000; Dirks, 1992b; Mani, 1989; Prakash, 1995), and so forth.

Considerations on the Postcolonial

In addition to the issues just mentioned, a number of scholars have contributed to postcolonialism by engaging in extensive debates about the very nature of the project of postcolonial theory and criticism. To begin with, the key terms—"postcolonial," "postcoloniality," and "postcolonialism"—have themselves been at the center of an intense debate (Appiah, 1991, 1997; Ashcroft, Griffiths, & Tiffin, 1998; McClintock, 1992; Shohat, 1992).

While there is, indeed, a general agreement among scholars that the term "postcoloniality" refers to a specific historical condition, and the term "postcolonialism" refers to the theory, broadly speaking, that seeks to intellectually engage with the historical condition of postcoloniality (Gandhi, 1998; Young, 2001), other differences are quick to surface.

One such scholarly disagreement concerns the prefix "post" in terms like postcolonialism or postcoloniality. Some critics are troubled by the presence of this prefix because, according to them, the prefix "post" is a temporal marker. Hence, such critics contend that a term like "postcoloniality" suggests that colonialism belongs to the past—or that colonialism has decisively ended—and thereby downplays the significance of the continuation of colonialism under contemporary neocolonialism. Others, however, argue that the term "postcolonial" does not refer to a distinct historical epoch—one that supposedly follows the final end of colonialism—but rather points to a specific form of critical practice (i.e., postcolonial theory), which investigates the past and present of colonialism with a view to developing a better understanding of the contemporary conjuncture.

The preceding is a valid enough argument but, at the same time, yet other scholars note that there is indeed some value in the temporal connotation of the prefix "post." For these scholars, the "post" in postcolonialism is useful in drawing attention toward an important historical process—namely, decolonization and the formal end of European empires—that served as one of the very conditions of possibility for the remarkable growth of postcolonial theory. Partly in order to get around concerns such as these, several scholars use the term "post-colonial" (i.e., with a hyphen) as a temporal expression referring to decolonization and what comes after, whereas they use the term "postcolonial" (without the hyphen) to suggest a way of thinking about colonialism and its apparatuses and consequences (cf. Barker, Hulme, & Iversen, 1994; Gandhi, 1998; Mishra & Hodge, 1991; Mongia, 1996). We propose to follow this very practice with respect to spelling.

Despite the preceding, however, other unanswered questions remain. Modern Western colonialism is over five-hundred-years old. Different countries were colonized at different historical moments, and they became politically independent at different times. For instance, several African and Asian countries gained their independence during the middle of the last century. On the other hand, many Latin American countries became independent during the nineteenth century. If the postcolonial gestures toward the moment of decolonization, when precisely do we fix that moment? Moreover, what about white settler colonies such as Australia, Canada, New Zealand, and the United States, all of whom gained their independence from

Britain, but where conquered indigenous populations continue to be subjugated. Do these countries count as "postcolonial" too? Questions like these continue to divide the postcolonial field. Some scholars insist on treating the Third World alone as the site of postcoloniality. Others use the term somewhat indiscriminately to refer to the entire world, thereby raising charges of careless universalization and homogenization of the concept. Lately, however, several scholars have stressed the importance of recognizing that postcoloniality is primarily "a descriptive and not an evaluative term" (Hulme, 1995: 120). Hence, scholars like Frankenberg and Mani (1993), Hall (1996), Hulme (1995), Loomba (1998), and others argue that the entire world may indeed be conceived of as being "postcolonial" *provided* it is clearly recognized that different countries and societies are *not* postcolonial *in the same way*.

This formulation seems to have at least two advantages. First, it recognizes that colonialism, anticolonialism, decolonization, and neocolonialism are processes of enormous significance on a global scale. Second, it guards against hasty universalization. Hence, while both India and Britain may indeed be postcolonial, they are postcolonial in *different ways*. Or, while both Britain and the United States are postcolonial, they are postcolonial in *different ways*. This view, therefore, sees the postcolonial as a global phenomenon having certain shared characteristics, but emphasizes, at the same time, the necessity of investigating postcoloniality as a variegated historical situation that is embedded in specific locations. In addition, a number of scholars have debated other issues including the implications of prestigious metropolitan institutional locations of certain well-known Third World postcolonial theorists, the relative roles of Marxism and post-structuralism in postcolonial theory, tensions between hybridity and cultural nationalism, and so forth (Ahmad, 1992, 1995; Dirlik, 1994, 1997, 1999; Duara, 2001; Parry, 1987, 1994).

Postcolonialism and the Study of Management and Organizations

As noted earlier, scholars in the field of management and organization studies have mostly tended to ignore postcolonial theory and criticism. Undoubtedly, there are some exceptions to this rule, especially in more recent organizational research (e.g., Jaya, 2001; Mir, Calás, & Smircich, 1999; Prasad, 1997a,b; Prasad & Prasad, 2002a,b). Nevertheless, the generally lukewarm reception of postcolonialism in organization studies is in sharp contrast to the marked enthusiasm with which many organizational researchers have responded during the last few decades to other so-called "non-traditional" scholarly approaches, such as critical theory, postmodernism, post-structuralism and so on (cf. Alvesson & Deetz, 2000; Clegg, Hardy, & Nord, 1996; Kilduff & Mehra, 1997). As a result, even *critical management studies*—a fairly thriving subfield within the wider domain of management and organization studies—continues to remain mostly aloof from postcolonial theory. This book is motivated, in part, by a genuine concern that in thus neglecting postcolonial theory, organizational scholars might be missing a valuable opportunity for advancing knowledge within the discipline. In this section, we will discuss some of the ways in which postcolonial theoretic insights can enrich our understanding of management and organizational processes.

Organizational scholars (and, in particular, critical organizational scholars) have frequently emphasized the productive role of *defamiliarization* in developing a fresh understanding of everyday, taken-for-granted organizational phenomena (Alvesson, 1993; Alvesson & Deetz, 2000). Briefly stated, the purpose of defamiliarization is to turn the seemingly familiar and well-known into something relatively strange and unexpected. Defamiliarization invites us to literally see and observe new aspects and meanings of commonplace organizational phenomena. As a result, an organizational phenomenon that might have ceased to surprise us—that might even have become banal—becomes capable of offering new surprises once again. Defamiliarization, thus, adds a fresh layer to our current understanding of common organizational phenomena, and sometimes may even enable us to see an old organizational phenomenon in a radically new light.

By way of providing an example of defamiliarization, Alvesson and Deetz (2000: 175 ff.) cite a cultural study of female clerical work (conducted by Tepperman) that reports and comments upon racialized division of labor. Alvesson and Deetz note that a "majority of organizational culture researchers" (2000: 175) do not seem to notice racialized structuring of work in organizations. According to Alvesson and Deetz, this suggests that either those culture researchers "find the phenomenon [of racial division of labor] irrelevant to an understanding of... [organizational culture], or they are not surprised by it and consequently do not observe it" (2000: 175). Rather than ignore the phenomenon of racialized work (as an aspect of organizational culture), however, the Tepperman study takes note of, and comments upon, this phenomenon and, in so doing, defamiliarizes organizational culture, transforming the latter from being something "well known" to "something strange" (Alvesson & Deetz, 2000: 176).

Here, an important question that arises is why this difference between Tepperman and most other organizational culture researchers? In other words, why should it be the case that the Tepperman study takes notice of racial division of labor as an aspect of organizational culture, whereas many other studies do not? In brief, the answer of Alvesson and Deetz to this question is that, among other things, it is also Tepperman's specific theoretical framework—with its "implicit regulatory ideal of non-racial division of labor" (2000: 176)—that prepares Tepperman to *observe* the phenomenon of racialized work at the organizational site of his study. As Alvesson and Deetz perceptively note, without such a theoretical framework Tepperman's "observations [about racialized work] would be pointless" (2000: 176). Even in a relatively straightforward example, therefore, Alvesson and Deetz point to the important role of new theoretical frameworks in facilitating defamiliarization, and generating new understandings of old organizational phenomena. Similarly postcolonial theory can work to defamiliarize common organizational phenomena and, thereby, meaningfully enhance our current understanding of such phenomena.

While most *new* theoretical perspectives are likely to defamiliarize common organizational phenomena, needless to say, different theories would tend to defamiliarize these phenomena *differently*. Simplifying somewhat, for example, it could be claimed that critical theory helps to defamiliarize organizational processes partly by means of ideology critique (cf. Alvesson & Deetz, 2000). In a similar fashion, we could argue that, to some extent, feminist theory (cf. e.g., Alvesson & Billing, 1997) defamiliarizes by providing a critique of phallocentrism and patriarchy that continue to invest contemporary organizational processes and structures. Hence, in order to appreciate the significance of postcolonialism for organization studies, we need to understand some of the ways in which postcolonial theory might defamiliarize organizational phenomena.

In recent years, researchers in several fields have begun taking note of the significant role played by the colonial encounter in the development and growth of a number of important social, cultural, political, and economic practices, movements, and institutions in the West. In this connection, mention has already been made of colonialism as having provided a condition of possibility for the emergence of Western capitalism. Others have noted that such major cultural developments in the West as the Renaissance and the Enlightenment, if they are to be comprehensively understood, must be studied with reference to the colonial encounter between the West and the non-West (cf. Loomba, 1998: 64). Similarly, researchers have pointed out the major role played by Native American political philosophy (and Native American leaders) in the development of the Constitution of the United States and the American political system (Mander, 1991, cited in Clarkson, Morrissette, & Regallet, 1997: 43).

In a related vein, scholars like Torgovnick (1990: 85) and others have commented upon African influences on Pablo Picasso's art, while Chopra (2002) recently discusses the likely influences of the artistic traditions of India—specifically of the sculptures of the Guptas, the Chandelas, and the Paramaras, and of Kalighat and Chitpur prints—on Picasso. The colonial encounter, thus, is seen as being consequential even for the development of modernism in European art. In other fields, Grove (1995: 90), for example, notes that Linnaeus's system of plant classification—a system that emerged in the early eighteenth century, and continues to be in use today—is indebted to the Ezhava classificatory system of India, whereas Cole (2001) has pointed out that fingerprinting as a forensic practice began in Europe only after British administrators learnt the technique from old practices that had long existed in India.

The colonial experience has influenced the development of numerous other practices in the West. For example, both hydraulic engineering (cf. Shiva, 1988: 187) and reconstructive plastic surgery have greatly drawn upon indigenous expertise that the British encountered during their colonial rule in India. On a somewhat different register, Viswanathan's (1989) work has made the point that the practice of English literary study was first introduced in colonial India, and only later imported into Britain. Even the coffeehouse—that quintessential French/European cultural institution—has non-Western roots, and came to Europe from Ottoman Turkey only in the seventeenth century (Darnton, 2002). Scholars have also looked at the influence of the colonial and the postcolonial on such philosophical developments as post-structuralism and deconstruction (Bhabha, 1994; Young, 2000, 2001).[20]

None of this, of course, should come as a big surprise. Modern Western colonialism is a long and extensive encounter between the West and the non-West that, not surprisingly, served to produce and/or influence a number of important practices and institutions in both sites, Western as well as non-Western. This implies, however, that several practices, institutions, and discourses that are often seen as being "purely" Western—and as having emerged "independently" within the West—need to be reconceptualized as having been constituted in and through the colonial encounter. Viewed from this perspective, postcolonialism can help management scholars examine and understand the influences of colonialism in constituting/producing current practices and discourses of management. One result of such analysis would be that, rather than being viewed as autonomous Western productions, management practices and discourses would come to be understood as having emerged from (and/or bearing the imprint of) the colonial encounter between the West and the non-West. This aspect of postcolonialism has the potential of defamiliarizing important aspects of management scholarship and practice, and a number of chapters in this book attempt defamiliarization partly along these lines.

Postcolonial theory can serve to defamiliarize organizational practices and discourses in a number of other, somewhat overlapping, ways. For example, the postcolonial perspective is useful for analyzing the role played by different management disciplines and subdisciplines in establishing/furthering colonial or neocolonial control. This kind of investigation would help us see these (sub-)disciplines in a new light. Postcolonial analysis is also helpful in unveiling the persistent imprint of colonialist ways of thinking and behaving in fields such as cross-cultural management and international management. Such understanding can be useful in giving a new orientation to current management practices as well as research.

In a similar vein, the postcolonial perspective is useful in the context of trying to understand non-Western management practices. Traditionally, Western management has often been regarded as a universal norm, and non-Western management practices have usually been judged against this norm (Kao, Sinha, & Wilpert, 1999). As a result, if a practice (which is commonly followed in Western management) is absent within the realm of non-Western management, such an absence has frequently been treated as a sign of lack or deficiency in the latter. Conversely, if non-Western management is found to have practices that may be absent in Western management, such practices may sometimes be seen as residues of "traditional" cultural practices that impede organizational efficiency, effectiveness, and so forth. The postcolonial perspective can be helpful in addressing such ethnocentrism, and thereby, developing an alternative understanding of non-Western management. Relatedly, the postcolonial approach can be useful for offering a new understanding of the "transfer" of management knowledge and practice from the West to the non-West. In addition, postcolonialism's nuanced and in-depth analysis of colonizer–colonized dynamics can be usefully employed in management research for developing fresh insights about power, control, and resistance in organizations.

Researchers working within the broad domains of institutional theory (Powell & DiMaggio, 1991; Scott & Meyer, 1994) have noted that organizations frequently play important roles in the construction of social and cultural boundaries. For instance, DiMaggio's (1992) institutionalist analysis examines organizational processes contributing to the creation of the boundary between "high" and "low" culture in American theater, opera, and dance. Other researchers (e.g., Beisel, 1992) have investigated the role of organizations in creating boundaries between literature and obscenity. We may usefully note here that the construction of even these boundaries is not untouched by the cultural consequences of colonialism. Therefore, postcolonial theory can add to the institutionalist insights provided by scholars such as these. In addition, postcolonial theory can be useful in understanding how the legacy of colonialism inflects the work of organizations in constructing ethnic, racial, and sexual boundaries. By these and other means, postcolonial theory can play a highly productive role in the future development of institutional theoretic organizational research.

Postcolonialism is relevant for the study of management and organizations also because of a massive transformation during the last few decades of the overall context in which contemporary organizations operate. At the macro level, the global economy, for instance, has witnessed large-scale changes during these years. For one, the global concentration of economic activities is slowly but surely moving away from the West. In 1950, for example, North America, Western Europe, Australia, and New Zealand collectively accounted for over 64 percent of global economic output; by 1990, this proportion had fallen to about 49 percent, and by the early years of the second decade of the twenty-first century, this proportion may further decline to about 30 percent of global output (Huntington, 1996: 87). Similarly, at the middle of the twentieth century, the combined economic output of China, India, and Japan seems to have been just about 10 percent of the world's output; by the middle of the twenty-first century, these three economies may well account for over 50 percent of global gross economic product (Huntington, 1996: 87). According to some estimates, China, with about 25 percent of the then global output, will be the largest economy by the year 2025 (Burki, 2002).

Along with the aforementioned changes, the global scene is marked also by a number of other important developments including globalization and a new international division of labor, rapid growth of new information technologies, the rise of the service economy in Western countries, the accelerating pace of large-scale environmental degradation, an ever-widening gap between the rich and the poor, growth of demographic diversity and multiculturalism, an eroding faith in the universality (and infallibility) of the master narratives of Western modernity, and so on. Postcolonial theoretic insights can be immensely valuable in developing a fresh understanding of the significance and implications of these and similar other changes. And above everything else, perhaps, one could say that postcolonial theory is relevant for management and organization studies because it offers a uniquely radical and ethically informed critique of Western modernity and modernity's overdetermined accoutrements like capitalism, Eurocentrism, science, and the like.

Broadly guided by these and other considerations discussed earlier, the remaining chapters of the book mobilize varied insights of postcolonial theory with a view to investigating a wide range of theoretical and empirical issues. The themes taken up by the contributors to this volume include control in organizations (chapter 2), action research and group dynamics as part of Organization Development (OD) techniques for managing organizational culture (chapter 3), workplace resistance (chapter 4), cross-cultural management research (chapter 5), the colonialist legacy of ethnography in contemporary institutions (chapter 6), the rhetoric of otherness in business journalism (chapter 7), the intersection of accounting and (neo-)colonialism (chapter 8), the cross-cultural training industry (chapter 9), information technology and globalization (chapter 10), and the fraught dynamics of colonial and anticolonial discourses in the context of conflicting Aborigine and Settler-Government interests surrounding a uranium mine in Australia (chapter 11). The final chapter offers some thoughts by way of a provisional conclusion.

Notes

1. "Gold" is the most extensively employed word in Columbus's log book, and appears more than 140 times there (cf. Hulme, 1986: 271, n. 11).
2. In any event, the dynasty of the Mongol Khans was no longer ruling China in the late fifteenth century (Hulme, 1986: 36; Rossabi, 1988: 228). Columbus seems to have been misinformed on more than one count.
3. For reasons to be explained later in this chapter, we employ the three expressions—"postcolonialism," "postcolonial theory," and "postcolonial theory and criticism"—interchangeably.
4. Young (2001: 25) notes that between 1840 and 1960 there were at least twelve changes in the meaning of the word "imperialism."
5. We will mostly use the expressions "Europe" and "the West" synonymously. Any departure from this usage will normally occur in precisely defined contexts where the distinct meanings of the two expressions will be self-evident. Here it may be useful to note also that our use of seemingly monolithic terms like "Europe," "the West," etc. does not imply that postcolonial theory is unaware of the arbitrariness of these terms, or of the existence of internal differences within the geographical and cultural space designated by these categories. Despite such awareness, however, postcolonialism continues to value the use of such terms for at least two reasons. First, postcolonialism recognizes that terms such as these, while they may well be somewhat arbitrary and/or fictive, continue to be terms of great material and symbolic significance. Second, although the West may indeed contain internal differences, postcolonial theory points out that insofar as the political effect of Western colonialism on the non-West is concerned, the West has indeed

"spoken with one voice" (Radhakrishnan, 1996: 178, n. 3). See also, in this connection, Chakrabarty (1992), and Prasad (1997b: 306, n. 4), among others.

6. Niranjana (1992: 7) glosses colonial discourse as "the body of knowledge, modes of representation, strategies of power, law, discipline, and so on, that are employed in the construction and domination of 'colonial subjects.'"

7. For discussions of some differences on this score between Said and Foucault, see, e.g., Clifford (1988: 255 ff.), and Young (2001: 383 ff.).

8. In all fairness, we must note that Said does recognize the presence of ambivalence and heterogeneities in the discourse of Orientalism, and does not treat this discourse as absolutely monolithic. However, Said seems to contain the force of such ambivalence by positing a *unified* Western will to power. This issue is creatively taken up by Homi Bhabha, discussed later in this chapter.

9. Said (1978: 204) points out that between 1800 and 1950, for instance, some 60,000 books dealing with the Near Orient were published in the West.

10. Young (2001: 384) considers a critique of *Orientalism* to be a necessary "ceremony of initiation by which newcomers to the field...take up the position of a speaking subject within the discourse of postcoloniality."

11. As we discuss later, Nandy sees both the colonizer and the colonized as being the victims of such colonization of the mind and imagination. Nandy is following Mahatma Gandhi here.

12. Although important, the project of hyper-*Kshatriyahood* in colonial India was only marginally successful, and was circumvented with relative ease by Mahatma Gandhi who, rejecting the colonial ideology of hyper-masculinity, reaffirmed the earlier Indian cultural traditions that consider *Kleevatva* (androgyny) to be a more potent principle than either masculinity or femininity (cf. Nandy, 1983, 1987).

13. Interestingly, the case of the Israeli peace movement offers an example of the recognition that colonization degrades the colonizers themselves. For instance, an open letter published in January 2002 by a group of Israeli combat officers and soldiers opposed to Israel's occupation of Palestinian territories declares that "the price of occupation is the loss of... [our] human character and the corruption of the entire Israeli society" (Gordon, 2002: 24). For a discussion of colonial aspects of the Israeli occupation of Palestinian territories, see Ahmad (2002), among others.

14. These ideas have parallels in Homi Bhabha's views on mimicry and hybridity discussed later in the present chapter.

15. Bhabha's writings are famously dense. In some respects, the denseness of his writings seems to be a function of their uniquely productive and creative nature. Mostly for reasons of space, the following brief overview is forced to rely upon a somewhat sweeping, though unavoidable, simplification of Bhabha's ideas.

16. Like Nandy, Bhabha also is concerned with problematizing the traditional colonizer/colonized dichotomy. Accordingly, in Bhabha's writings, colonial discourse is seen as being involved with the colonial subject, *both as colonizer and colonized*. While reading Bhabha, therefore, it is important not to treat his use of

the term, "colonial subject," as a narrowly precise, fully functioning, and invariant substitute for the word, "colonizer," or, for that matter, "colonized." At the risk of some simplification, it could possibly be argued that, in Bhabha's hands, the term, "colonial subject," leans sometimes toward the colonizer, sometimes toward the colonized, and sometimes attempts to encompass both the colonizer and the colonized and/or the *relationship* between the two. For Bhabha, the term "colonial" frequently acts as a referent for the "interstitial" space (or "the third space") in-between colonizers and colonized. In many respects, Bhabha's work serves also as an interesting exemplar of how to write about the colonial situation without treating the colonizer as the only subject or locus of agency.

17. The essay has also been reprinted in Spivak (1987), *In Other Worlds*, pp. 134–153.
18. In some of her later works (e.g., Spivak, 1993), Spivak revisits French feminism and, instead of primarily focusing upon the "inbuilt colonialism of First World feminism toward the Third" (Spivak, 1987: 153), sees the possibility of a fruitful "exchange between metropolitan and colonized feminisms" (Spivak, 1993: 144). The important question for Spivak then becomes: "How does the postcolonial feminist negotiate with the metropolitan feminist?" (1993: 145).
19. Several versions of this essay exist. The essay first appeared in 1985—under the title, "Can the Subaltern Speak? Speculations on Widow Sacrifice"—in *Wedge*, 7/8 (pp. 120–130). A revised version of the *Wedge* piece was subsequently published as Spivak (1988a), the latter, in turn, being carried in such edited collections as Williams and Chrisman (1994b), and Ashcroft, Griffiths, and Tiffin (1995). The editors of *The Spivak Reader* (1996), however, were unsuccessful in adding this essay to their collection because of Spivak's desire to extensively revise the 1988 version of the essay (cf. Landry & MacLean, 1996: 8). The result of these revisions appears in Spivak (1999: 248 ff.).
20. Radhakrishnan (1996: 163) refers to Mahatma Gandhi, for instance, as an "early deconstructive thinker." Somewhat similar sentiments on Gandhi have been expressed by Young (2001) as well.

References

Adams, I., & Tiffin, H. (Eds.). 1990. *Past the last post: Theorizing postcolonialism and postmodernism.* Calgary, Canada: University of Calgary Press.

Ahmad, A. 1992. *In theory: Classes, nations, literatures.* London: Verso.

Ahmad, A. 1995. The politics of literary postcoloniality. *Race and Class, 36,* 1–20.

Ahmad, A. 2002. Israel's colonial war. *Frontline, 19* (4), February 16–March 1 (www.flonnet.com).

Alvesson, M. 1993. *Cultural perspectives on organizations.* Cambridge: Cambridge University Press.

Alvesson, M., & Billing, Y. D. 1997. *Understanding gender and organizations.* London: Sage.

Alvesson, M., & Deetz, S. 2000. *Doing critical management research.* London: Sage.

Appadurai, A. 1996. *Modernity at large: Cultural dimensions of globalization.* Minneapolis: University of Minnesota Press.

Appiah, K. A. 1991. Is the "post-" in "postmodernism" the "post-" in "postcolonial"? *Critical Inquiry, 17* (Winter), 336–357.

Appiah, K. A. 1997. Is the "post-" in "postcolonial" the "post-" in "postmodernism"? In A. McClintock, A. Mufti, & E. Shohat (Eds.), *Dangerous liaisons: Gender, nation, and postcolonial perspectives* (pp. 420–444). Minneapolis: University of Minnesota Press.

Ashcroft, B., Griffiths, G., & Tiffin, H. (Eds.). 1995. *The post-colonial studies reader.* London: Routledge.

Ashcroft, B., Griffiths, G., & Tiffin, H. 1998. *Key concepts in post-colonial studies.* London: Routledge.

Azim, F. 1993. *The colonial rise of the novel.* London: Routledge.

Barker, F., Hulme, P., & Iversen, M. 1994. Introduction. In F. Barker, P. Hulme & M. Iversen (Eds.), *Colonial discourse/postcolonial theory* (pp. 1–23). Manchester, UK: Manchester University Press.

Beisel, N. 1992. Constructing a shifting moral boundary: Literature and obscenity in nineteenth century America. In M. Lamont & M. Fournier (Eds.), *Cultivating difference: Symbolic boundaries and the making of inequality* (pp. 104–128). Chicago: University of Chicago Press.

Bhabha, H. K. 1983. Difference, discrimination, and the discourse of colonialism. In F. Barker, P. Hulme, M. Iversen, & D. Loxley (Eds.), *The politics of theory* (pp. 194–211). Colchester, UK: University of Essex Press.

Bhabha, H. K. (Ed.). 1990. *Nation and narration.* London: Routledge.

Bhabha, H. K. 1994. *The location of culture.* London: Routledge.

Bishop, A. 1990. Western mathematics: The secret weapon of cultural imperialism. *Race and Class, 32,* 51–65.

Brantlinger, P. 1988. *Rule of darkness: British literature and imperialism, 1830–1914.* Ithaca: Cornell University Press.

Burki, S. J. 2002. Pakistan and West Asia. *Dawn* (Internet ed.), February 5 (www.dawn.com).

Cabral, A. 1973. *Return to the source: Selected speeches by Amilcar Cabral.* New York: Monthly Review Press.

Césaire, A. 1972. *Discourse on colonialism.* New York: Monthly Review Press [originally published in 1955].

Chakrabarty, D. 1992. Postcoloniality and the artifice of history: Who speaks for "Indian" pasts? *Representations, 37* (Winter), 1–26.

Chakrabarty, D. 2000. *Provincializing Europe: Postcolonial thought and historical difference.* Princeton: Princeton University Press.

Chatterjee, P. 1986. *Nationalist thought and the colonial world: A derivative discourse.* London: Zed Books.

Chatterjee, P. 1993. *The nation and its fragments: Colonial and postcolonial histories.* Princeton: Princeton University Press.

Chatterjee, P. 1999. Interview: Partha Chatterjee in conversation with Anuradha Dingwaney Needham. *Interventions, 1* (3), 413–425.

Chaturvedi, V. (Ed.). 2000. *Mapping subaltern studies and the postcolonial.* London: Verso.

Chaudhuri, N., & Strobel, M. (Eds.). 1992. *Western women and imperialism.* Bloomington: Indiana University Press.

Chopra, S. 2002. Broad canvas, narrow presentation. *Frontline, 19* (2), January 19–February 1. (www.frontlineonnet.com).

Clarkson, L., Morrissette, V., & Regallet, G. 1997. Our responsibility to the seventh generation. In M. Rahnema & V. Bawtree (Eds.). *The post-development reader* (pp. 40–50). London: Zed Books.

Clegg, S., Hardy, C., & Nord, W. (Eds.). 1996. *Handbook of organization studies.* London: Sage Publications.

Clifford, J. 1988. *The predicament of culture: Twentieth century ethnography, literature, and art.* Cambridge, MA: Harvard University Press.

Cole, S. 2001. *Suspect identities: A history of fingerprinting and criminal identification.* Cambridge: Harvard University Press.

Darnton, R. 2002. A Euro state of mind. *The New York Review of Books, XLIX* (3), February 28, 30–32.

diLeonardo, M. 1998. *Exotics at home: Anthropology, others, American modernity.* Chicago: University of Chicago Press.

Dirks, N. 1992a. Introduction: Colonialism and culture. In N. Dirks (Ed.), *Colonialism and culture* (pp. 1–25). Ann Arbor: The University of Michigan Press.

Dirks, N. (Ed.). 1992b. *Colonialism and culture.* Ann Arbor: The University of Michigan Press.

Dirlik, A. 1994. The postcolonial aura: Third world criticism in the age of global capitalism. *Critical Inquiry, 20* (Winter), 328–356.

Dirlik, A. 1997. *The postcolonial aura: Third world criticism in the age of global capitalism.* Boulder: Westview Press.

Dirlik, A. 1999. How the grinch hijacked radicalism: Further thoughts on the postcolonial. *Postcolonial Studies, 2,* 149–163.

DiMaggio, P. 1992. Cultural boundaries and structural change: The extension of the high culture model to theater, opera, and dance, 1900–1940. In M. Lamont & M. Fournier (Eds.), *Cultivating difference: Symbolic boundaries and the making of inequality* (pp. 21–57). Chicago: University of Chicago Press.

Duara, P. 2001. Leftist criticism and the political impasse: Response to Arif Dirlik's "How the grinch hijacked radicalism: Further thoughts on the postcolonial." *Postcolonial Studies, 4,* 81–88.

During, S. 1987. Postmodernism or postcolonialism today. *Textual Practice, 1,* 32–47.

Escobar, A. 1995. *Encountering development: The making and unmaking of the Third World.* Princeton, NJ: Princeton University Press.

Fanon, F. 1967a. *Black skin white masks.* (C. Markmann, Trans.). New York: Grove Press.

Fanon, F. 1967b. *The wretched of the earth.* (C. Farrington, Trans.). Harmondsworth, UK: Penguin.

Foucault, M. 1972. *The archeology of knowledge.* New York: Pantheon.

Foucault, M. 1977. *Discipline and punish.* New York: Pantheon.

Fox, R. 1992. East of Said. In M. Sprinkler (Ed.), *Edward Said: A critical reader* (pp. 144–156). Oxford, UK: Blackwell Publishers.

Frankenberg, R., & Mani, L. 1993. Crosscurrents, crosstalks: Race, "postcoloniality" and the politics of location. *Cultural Studies, 7* (May), 292–310.

Gandhi, L. 1998. *Postcolonial theory: A critical introduction.* New York: Columbia University Press.

Gandhi, M. K. 1927. *An autobiography: Or the story of my experiments with Truth.* Ahmedabad: Navajivan Publishing House.

Gandhi, M. K. 1928. *Satyagraha in South Africa.* Ahmedabad: Navajivan Publishing House.

Gandhi, M. K. 1938. *Hind swaraj: Or Indian home rule.* Ahmedabad: Navajivan Publishing House.

Gordon, N. 2002. An antiwar movement grows in Israel. *The Nation* (February 25), 24.

Gramsci, A. 1971. *Selections from the Prison Notebooks.* (Q. Hoare & G. Nowell-Smith, Trans.). London: Lawrence and Wishart.

Grove, R. H. 1995. *Green imperialism.* Cambridge: Cambridge University Press.

Guha, R. 1982a. Preface. In R. Guha (Ed.), *Subaltern studies I: Writings on South Asian history and society* (pp. vii–viii). Delhi: Oxford University Press.

Guha, R. 1982b. On some aspects of historiography of colonial India. In R. Guha (Ed.), *Subaltern studies I: Writings on South Asian history and society* (pp. 1–8). Delhi: Oxford University Press.

Guha, R., & Spivak, G. C. (Eds.). 1988. *Selected subaltern studies.* New York: Oxford University Press.

Guha, R. (Ed.). 1997. *A subaltern studies reader.* Minneapolis: University of Minnesota Press.

Hall, S. 1996. When was the "post-colonial"? Thinking at the limit. In I. Chambers & L. Curti (Eds.), *The post-colonial question: Common skies, divided horizons* (pp. 242–260). London: Routledge.

Ho Chi Minh. 1962. *Prison diary.* Hanoi: Foreign Language Publishing House.

Hulme, P. 1986. *Colonial encounters: Europe and the native Caribbean, 1492–1797.* London: Routledge.

Hulme, P. 1995. Including America. *Ariel, 26,* 117–123.

Huntington, S. P. 1996. *The clash of civilizations and the remaking of world order.* New York: Simon & Schuster.

Jaya, P. S. 2001. Do we really "know" and "profess"? Decolonizing management knowledge. *Organization, 8,* 227–233.

Jayawardena, K. 1995. *The white woman's other burden.* New York: Routledge.

Kao, H., Sinha, D., & Wilpert, B. (Eds.). 1999. *Management and cultural values: The indigenization of organizations in Asia.* New Delhi: Sage.

Kaunda, K. 1967. *Humanism in Zambia and a guide to its implementation*. Lusaka: Zambia Information Services.

Kenyatta, J. 1938. *Facing Mount Kenya*. London: Secker and Warburg.

Kilduff, M., & Mehra, A. 1997. Postmodernism and organizational research. *Academy of Management Review, 22*, 453–481.

Landry, D., & MacLean, G. 1996. Introduction: Reading Spivak. In G. C. Spivak, *The Spivak reader* (pp. 1–13). New York: Routledge.

Lenin, V. I. 1947. *Imperialism: The highest stage of capitalism*. Moscow: Foreign Language Publishing House [originally published in 1916].

Loomba, A. 1998. *Colonialism/postcolonialism*. London: Routledge.

Lumumba, P. 1963. *Lumumba speaks*. Boston: Little Brown.

MacCabe, C. 1987. Foreword. In G. C. Spivak, *In other worlds: Essays in cultural politics* (pp. ix-xix). New York: Methuen.

Mander, J. 1991. *In the absence of the sacred*. San Francisco: Sierra Club Books.

Mani, L. 1989. Contentious traditions: The debate on Sati in colonial India. In K. Sangari & S. Vaid (Eds.), *Recasting women* (pp. 88–126). New Delhi: Kali for Women.

Mariátegui, J. C. 1971. *Seven interpretive essays on Peruvian reality*. Austin: University of Texas Press [originally published in 1927].

Mannoni, O. 1964. *Prospero and Caliban: The psychology of colonization*. (P. Townsend, Trans.). New York: Praeger.

McClintock, A. 1992. The angel of progress: Pitfalls of the term "post-colonialism." In P. Williams & L. Chrisman (Eds.), *Colonial discourse and postcolonial theory* (pp. 291–304). New York: Columbia University Press.

Memmi, A. 1965. *The colonizer and the colonized*. (H. Greenfield, Trans.). New York: The Orion Press.

Miller, D. 1998. Nandy: Intimate enemy number one. *Postcolonial Studies, 1* (3), 299–303.

Mir, R., Calás, M., & Smircich, L. 1999. Global technoscapes and silent voices: Challenges to theorizing global cooperation. In D. Cooperrider & J. Dutton (Eds.), *Organizational dimensions of global change* (pp. 270–290). London: Sage Publications.

Mishra, V., & Hodge, B. 1991. What is post(-)colonialism? *Textual Practice, 5*, 399–414.

Mohanty, C. T., Russo, A., & Torres, L. (Eds.). 1991. *Third World women and the politics of feminism*. Bloomington: Indiana University Press.

Mongia, P. 1996. Introduction. In P. Mongia (Ed.), *Contemporary postcolonial theory: A reader* (pp. 1–18). London: Arnold.

Moore-Gilbert, B. 1997. *Postcolonial theory: Contexts, practices, politics*. London: Verso.

Naipaul, V. S. 1967. *The mimic men*. London: Penguin.

Nandy, A. 1980a. *At the edge of psychology: Essays in politics and culture*. Delhi: Oxford University Press.

Nandy, A. 1980b. *Alternative sciences: Creativity and authenticity in two Indian scientists.* New Delhi: Allied Publishers.

Nandy, A. 1983. *The intimate enemy: Loss and recovery of self under colonialism.* Delhi: Oxford University Press.

Nandy, A. 1987. *Traditions, tyranny and utopias: Essays in the politics of awareness.* Delhi: Oxford University Press.

Nandy, A. (Ed.). 1988. *Science, hegemony and violence: A requiem for modernity.* Delhi: Oxford University Press.

Nandy, A. 1994. *The illegitimacy of nationalism: Rabindranath Tagore and the politics of self.* Delhi: Oxford University Press.

Nandy, A. 1995. *The savage Freud and other essays on possible and retrievable selves.* Princeton, NJ: Princeton University Press.

Nandy, A. 1998. The twilight of certitude: Secularism, Hindu nationalism and other masks of deculturation. *Postcolonial Studies, 1* (3), 283–298.

Nandy, A. 2000. *The Tao of cricket: On games of destiny and the destiny of games.* Delhi: Oxford University Press.

Nandy, A. 2001. A report on the present state of health of the gods and goddesses in South Asia. *Postcolonial Studies, 4* (2), 125–141.

Niranjana, T. 1992. *Siting translation: History, post-structuralism, and the colonial context.* Berkeley: University of California Press.

Ngugi wa Thiong'O. 1981. *Decolonizing the mind: The politics of language in African literature.* London: James Currey.

Nkrumah, K. 1965. *Neo-colonialism.* London: Heinemann.

Nyerere, J. 1968. *Ujamaa: Essays on socialism.* Dar es Salaam: Oxford University Press.

Parry, B. 1987. Problems in current theories of colonial discourse. *Oxford Literary Review, 9,* 27–58.

Parry, B. 1994. Resistance theory/theorizing resistance: Or two cheers for nativism. In F. Barker, P. Hulme, & M. Iversen (Eds.), *Colonial discourse/postcolonial theory* (pp. 172–196). Manchester, UK: Manchester University Press.

Pathak, Z., Sengupta, S., Purkayastha, S. 1991. The prisonhouse of Orientalism. *Textual Practice, 5,* 195–218.

Pollock, S., Bhabha, H., Breckenridge, C., & Chakrabarty, D. 2000. Cosmopolitanism. *Public Culture, 12* (3), 577–589.

Porter, D. 1983. *Orientalism* and its problems. In F. Barker, P. Hulme, M. Iversen, & D. Loxley (Eds.), *The politics of theory* (pp. 179–193). Colchester, UK: University of Essex Press.

Powell, W., & DiMaggio, P. (Eds.). 1991. *The new institutionalism in organizational analysis.* Chicago: University of Chicago Press.

Prakash, G. (Ed.). 1995. *After colonialism: Imperial histories and postcolonial displacements.* Princeton: Princeton University Press.

Prakash, G. 1999. *Another reason: Science and the imagination of modern India.* Princeton, NJ: Princeton University Press.

Prasad, A. 1997a. Provincializing Europe: Towards a postcolonial reconstruction. *Studies in Cultures, Organizations and Societies, 3,* 91–117.

Prasad, A. 1997b. The colonizing consciousness and representations of the other. In P. Prasad, A. Mills, M. Elmes, & A. Prasad (Eds.), *Managing the organizational melting pot: Dilemmas of workplace diversity* (pp. 285–311). Thousand Oaks, CA: Sage Publications.

Prasad, A., & Prasad, P. 2002a. Otherness at large: Identity and difference in the new globalized organizational landscape. In I. Aaltio & A. Mills (Eds.), *Gender, Identity and the Culture of Organizations* (pp. 57–71). London: Routledge.

Prasad, P., & Prasad, A. 2002b. Casting the native subject: The ethnographic imagination and the (re)production of difference. In B. Czarniawska & H. Hopfl (Eds.), *Casting the other: The production and maintenance of inequality in organizations* (pp. 185–204). London: Routledge.

Pratt, M. L. 1992. *Imperial eyes: Travel writing and transculturation.* New York: Routledge.

Radhakrishnan, R. 1996. *Diasporic mediations.* Minneapolis: University of Minnesota Press.

Rahnema, M., & Bawtree, V. (Eds.). 1997. *The post-development reader.* London: Zed Books.

Retamar, R. F. 1989. *Caliban and other essays.* Minneapolis: University of Minnesota Press.

Rossabi, M. 1988. *Khubilai Khan: His life and times.* Berkeley: University of California Press.

Sachs, W. (Ed.). 1992. *The development dictionary.* London: Zed Books.

Said, E. 1978. *Orientalism.* New York: Vintage Books.

Said, E. 1979. *The question of Palestine.* New York: Times Books.

Said, E. 1981. *Covering Islam.* London: Routledge.

Said, E. 1985. Orientalism reconsidered. In F. Barker, P. Hulme, M. Iversen, & D. Loxley (Eds.), *Europe and its others* (Vol. 1, pp. 14–27). Colchester, UK: University of Essex Press.

Said, E. 1993a. Expanding humanism: An interview by Mark Edmundson with Edward Said. In M. Edmundson (Ed.), *Wild orchids and Trotsky* (pp. 99–123). New York: Penguin.

Said, E. 1993b. *Culture and imperialism.* New York: Alfred A. Knopf.

Said, E. 2000. *The Edward Said reader.* (M. Bayoumi & A. Rubin, Eds.). New York: Vintage Books.

Scott, W. R., & Meyer, J. (Eds.). 1994. *Institutional environments and organizations.* Thousand Oaks, CA: Sage Publications.

Senghor, L. S. 1964. *On African socialism.* London: Pall Mall.

Sharpe, J. 1993. *Allegories of empire: The figure of woman in the colonial text.* Minneapolis: University of Minnesota Press.

Shiva, V. 1988. *Staying alive.* New Delhi: Kali for Women.

Shohat, E. 1992. Notes on the "post-colonial." *Social Text, 31/32,* 99–113.

Spivak, G. C. 1981. French feminism in an international frame. *Yale French Studies, 62,* 154–184.

Spivak, G. C. 1985. Three women's texts and a critique of imperialism. *Critical Inquiry, 12,* 242–261.

Spivak, G. C. 1987. *In other worlds: Essays in cultural politics.* New York: Methuen.

Spivak, G. C. 1988a. Can the subaltern speak? In C. Nelson & L. Grossberg (Eds.), *Marxism and the interpretation of culture* (pp. 271–313). Urbana: University of Illinois Press.

Spivak, G. C. 1988b. Subaltern studies: Deconstructing historiography. In R. Guha, R. & G. C. Spivak (Eds.), *Selected subaltern studies* (pp. 3–32). New York: Oxford University Press.

Spivak, G. C. 1990. *The postcolonial critic: Interviews, strategies, dialogues.* New York: Routledge.

Spivak, G. C. 1993. *Outside in the teaching machine.* New York: Routledge.

Spivak, G. C. 1996. *The Spivak reader.* (D. Landry & G. MacLean, Eds.). New York: Routledge.

Spivak, G. C. 1999. *A critique of postcolonial reason: Toward a history of the vanishing present.* Cambridge, MA: Harvard University Press.

Sprinker, M. 1995. Introduction. In R. de la Campa, E. A. Kaplan, & M. Sprinker (Eds.), *Late imperial culture* (pp. 1–10). London: Verso.

Spurr, D. 1993. *The rhetoric of empire: Colonial discourse in journalism, travel writing, and imperial administration.* Durham, NC: Duke University Press.

Stocking, G. (Ed.). 1985. *Objects and others: Essays on museums and material culture.* Madison: University of Wisconsin Press.

Suleri, S. 1992. *The rhetoric of English India.* Chicago: University of Chicago Press.

Teltscher, K. 1995. *India inscribed: European and British writings on India, 1600–1800.* Delhi: Oxford University Press.

Torgovnick, M. 1990. *Gone primitive: Savage intellects, modern lives.* Chicago: University of Chicago Press.

Viswanathan, G. 1989. *Masks of conquest: Literary study and British rule in India.* New York: Columbia University Press.

Williams, P., & Chrisman, L. 1994a. Colonial discourse and postcolonial theory: An introduction. In P. Williams & L. Chrisman (Eds.), *Colonial discourse and post-colonial theory* (pp. 1–20). New York: Columbia University Press.

Williams, P., & Chrisman, L. (Eds.). 1994b. *Colonial discourse and postcolonial theory.* New York: Columbia University Press.

Weedon, C. 1997. *Feminist practice and poststructuralist theory* (2nd ed.). Oxford, UK: Blackwell.

Young, R. 1990. *White mythologies: Writing history and the West.* London: Routledge.

Young, R. 2000. Deconstruction and the postcolonial. In N. Royle (Ed.), *Deconstructions: A user's guide* (pp. 187–210). New York: Palgrave.

Young, R. 2001. *Postcolonialism: An historical introduction.* Oxford, UK: Blackwell Publishers.

PART II

Postcolonial Engagements with Management and Organization Theory

CHAPTER 2

Toward a Postcolonial Reading of Organizational Control

Raza A. Mir, Ali Mir, and Punya Upadhyaya

The notion of organizational control has been a constant theme in the construction and representations of euromodern[1] organizations. The discourse of control has been justified in organizational theory on a variety of counts, such as the need to eliminate stubborn "soldiering" by recalcitrant employees (Taylor, 1911), the inducement of collaborative enterprise (Barnard, 1938), the curtailment of opportunist practices in organizational transactions (Williamson, 1985), the management of bounded rationality (Simon, 1957), the development of adaptive mechanisms (Hannan & Freeman, 1977), the facilitation of diverse organizational conversations (Srivastava & Cooperrider, 1990), the management of organizational knowledge (Davenport & Prusak, 1998), or even the need to create a paradigmatic consensus in organizational research (Pfeffer, 1993). On the other hand, mainstream theories of organizational control have been critiqued as being coercive (Braverman, 1974), insensitive to noncontractual trust-based control systems (Perrow, 1979), or unmindful of the fundamental causal determinants of conflict (Jermier, Knights, & Nord, 1994). Scholars have pointed to the enacted nature of organizational reality (Weick, 1979), the constructed nature of academic practices (Canella & Paetzold, 1994), and the anthropocentric biases that have dominated management research (Shrivastava, 1996), thereby seeking to destabilize the platform of positivism on which much of the mainstream discourse of organizational control stands.

This chapter seeks to add to the "paradigmatic confusion" that these critiques of mainstream theories of organizational control have induced. Our argument however, is derived from different premises; we believe that the construction of the modern organization, and the control systems it has fostered, is inextricably linked to the construction of the discourse of modernity, a discourse that owes its primacy to the processes of colonialism. Colonialism, which was experienced by a significant section of the currently impoverished regions of the world over the past 500 years, not only facilitated the process of wealth appropriation by the colonial powers, but also served to impose a certain homogenizing discourse on the colonies, a discourse that denied legitimacy to a variety of perspectives and epistemes. In this chapter, we seek to explore the material and discursive aspects of euromodern control, and offer alternative perspectives of organizing and control, which we term "postcolonial." The postcolonial perspective is developed first by contextualizing euromodern theories of organizing in the power imbalances that were fostered by colonialism, and then by offering alternative theories of organizing (Castle, 2001; Chaturvedi, 2000).

The spirit of our argument is important. We offer it neither as a plea for the inclusion of particular epistemologies into the discourse of managerial control nor as an act of representation of excluded subjectivities. Nor is our intention to valorize all that is non-modern as implicitly emancipatory. We do, however, believe that the unilinear nature of modernist discourse simplifies and reduces the multiplicity of perspectives that are available to the realm of organizational inquiry. This chapter represents our attempt to articulate our own understanding of these multiple perspectives that may be available to open-minded and non-parochial scholarship, and to share it with those who are willing to undertake this journey with us.

The chapter is organized in four parts. First, we explore the reciprocal relationship between colonialism—as a dominating but non-hegemonic practice—and various structures and processes of the euromodern organization. This section may be visualized as a historical or contextualizing process, whereby the "natural" in organizational theory is shown to be a "construction" of colonial practices. In the second section, we adumbrate the theoretical underpinnings of postcolonial epistemology as a tool to engage in the examination of various organizational systems and practices. In the third section, we use the postcolonial perspective to subject various conceptualizations of organizational control to scrutiny. This is done by identifying and classifying the different ways in which control has been theorized, renaming them, and examining their underlying assumptions. Finally, we attempt to explore some aspects of a postcolonial notion of control—which we call "control as liberation"—through a vignette from a nontraditional organization.

Colonialism and the Euromodern Organization

The modernist concept of the industrial organization has been predicated on the hope that the technologized society would create better worlds for all the peoples of the world. Studies of industrialized organizations, from Weber onwards, have treated the formal, task-centered, bureaucratized organization more as a fact of nature than as a construction. For instance, Chandler (1962, 1977), documenting the historical development of organizations in the United States in the post–World War I era, points to technology as a marker of organizational progress. This understanding has been fostered by the belief that the advent of modern corporations was linked to the rise of powerful technology that opened up newer possibilities of organizing. This, in turn, is seen as having facilitated newer organizational structures like the M-Form organization, and newer instruments of control such as contractual systems, newer avenues of growth such as internationalization, and newer micro-practices of control from scientific management and the human relations school down to the latest theories of TQM and reengineering.

However, such a perspective presents an extremely limiting view of organizations, for it does not pay attention to the political and coercive forces that accompanied, and indeed facilitated, not only the processes of organizing, but the very aspects of technological development that rendered them possible. In doing so, it implicitly legitimizes the manner in which the global diversity of progress, technological advancement, and wealth creation has been subordinated to the history of a small group of nations and peoples (Nandy, 1993). Despite the failed promise of euromodernity—as manifested in increasing wealth disparities across and within nations, ecological crises, and the growth of weapons of mass destruction—this view continues to be perpetrated; one may only conclude that eurolimited[2] scholars have consciously chosen to ignore the possibilities that may be articulated by alternative epistemologies.

The relationship between the discourse of colonialism and the discourse of euromodern organizing systems needs little historical uncovering, it lies before us in resplendent transparency.[3] In brief, there are five major areas where these two discourses intersect, namely: (a) the linkages between colonialism and industrialization, (b) the creation of the colonial subject as a ground for the creation of the docile worker, (c) the relationship between colonial practices and organizing practices, (d) the convergence between colonial and organizational ideologies, and (e) the similarity between colonial regimes and modern international regimes as control systems.

Colonialism as the Financier of Industrialization

The nurturance of industrialization by colonialism has been well documented using various points of departure, such as the financing of James Watt's steam engines by West Indian slave owners (Rodney, 1974), the subsidization of textile labor in industrial England by slavery-based plantations (Mintz, 1985), and the creation of a market for Lancashire cloth through the systematic destruction of the cotton industry of India accomplished by the imposition of tariffs and the brutal maiming of Indian weavers in order to prevent them for spinning cloth for their own markets (Dutt, 1970). Indeed, colonial rulers themselves admitted that the industrial revolution was predicated not on inventions but on the suddenly available massive capital outlays from colonialism (Cunningham in Dutt, 1970: 111). Thus, the first transnational forays of capital were not the products of industrialization, but more the products of imperialism, serving to further the spatial displacement of industrialization toward the west (Polanyi, 1957).

The spatial displacement of capital that was unleashed during colonialism is conspicuous even today. The patterns of wealth availability indicate that 500 corporations, which employ only 0.005 percent of the global population, control over 25 percent of the global output (Korten, 1995). The growth in wealth concentration has not really "trickled down" to the periphery, for instance, even today, the world's largest six grain merchants control over 90 percent of the global grain trade, even as several million people die of famine each year (Escobar, 1994). Nor have global organizations been model citizens in their operations; on the contrary, they have to answer to the growing criticisms of their role in specific geographical exploitation (Kozul-Wright, 1995), the feminization of poverty (Pearson, 1986), the violation of human rights (Chodos & Murphy, 1974), the extinction of many animal species, and the depletion of several natural resources around the world (MacKerron & Cogan, 1993).

Colonial Subjects, Organizational Subjects

As far as the creation of the colonial subject was concerned, the colonial rulers did not even find it necessary to couch their arguments in rhetoric. Speaking in his capacity as the Legal Member of the Council of Indian Education in 1785, Lord Thomas Macaulay (Macaulay, 1972: 249) stressed,

> We must at present do our best to form a class who may be interpreters between us and the millions we govern; a class of persons, Indian in blood and colour, but English in taste, in opinions, in morals, and in

intellect. To that class, we may leave it to refine the vernacular dialects of the country, to enrich those dialects with terms of science borrowed from the western nomenclature, and to render them by degrees fit vehicles for conveying knowledge to the great mass of population.

Macaulay's statements did not represent an isolated individual utterance; his words along with the actions of his adherents decisively tilted the future of education policy in British India to a colonialist mode, whereby the learning of Sanskrit, Arabic, and indigenous sciences was banned. For Macaulay had compared investment in indigenous knowledge systems to "wasting public money; for printing books that are of less value than the paper on which they are printed while it was blank; for giving artificial encouragement to absurd history, absurd metaphysics, absurd theology; for raising up a breed of scholars who find their scholarship an encumbrance and a blemish" (Macaulay, 1972: 250).

The contest over the English language has not been confined to India. Mandal (2000) details the role played by English in the contest over cultural globalization in Malaysia. Likewise, Macaulay has not been the only "world leader" whose pronouncement has changed the course of a people's organizational history. Ivan Illich (1981) documents the way in which a speech made by President Harry Truman in 1945 marked the unleashing of the whole concept of "development" on the world whereby it became the founding principle of all "aid"-related interactions between the "developed" and the "developing" nations. The proponents of development exhibited as much sensitivity to indigenous knowledges as did Macaulay, as can be evidenced by this communiqué from the United Nations Department of Economic Affairs in 1951 (quoted in Escobar, 1994: 3):

> There is a sense in which rapid economic progress is impossible without painful adjustments. Ancient philosophies have to be scrapped; old social institutions have to disintegrate; bonds of caste, creed and race have to burst; and large numbers of persons who cannot keep up with progress will have to have their expectations of a comfortable life frustrated.

The ethnocentricity of this view apart, it points toward the way in which the exercise of structural reform, be it colonial or modernist, sought to create a certain kind of subject. Thompson (1966) chronicles the manner in which the working class was constructed in Britain; similar processes were being enacted on a global scale, where the colonial workforce was being produced, theorized as a particular cultural artifact, and subjected to material and organizational practices based on these myths (Said, 1978).

Colonial Concepts, Organizational Practices

Many organizational scholars and organizational historians contend that what we understand to be default organizational structures and processes (such as the M-form enterprise, contract-based organizational relationships, or the market for corporate control) owe their construction to peculiarities of historical and political events (Kaufman, Zacharias, & Karson, 1995). Similarly, many organizational structures/processes owe much to the colonial process that took place overseas. For instance, the first joint stock company was formed by Genoan merchants to run plantations (Verlinden, 1970). The first instance of a joint venture between a government and a private entrepreneur was between Queen Elizabeth I and a slave trader (Rodney, 1974: 83). The East India Company, which was active in a number of nations in the eighteenth century, was organized into national subsidiaries reminiscent of a geographically specialized multinational corporation. Essentially, many organizational forms as we know them were experimented upon in the regimes of colonialism.

Ideologies of Colonizing, Ideologies of Organizing

One of the driving ideologies of the euromodern organization has been that of "reality as resource," whereby existing social and economic arrangements are appropriated for competitive advantage. Critiques of this ideology have been launched from a variety of standpoints, such as the environmental perspective (Shrivastava, 1996) that critiques anthropocentric ontologies, the Marxian perspective (Marglin, 1974) that critiques the conflation of exploitation and wealth creation, or the feminist perspective (Charrad, 2001; Pearson, 1986) that identifies the way in which traditional sex-roles have been used in labor deployment. The ideology of reality-as-resource was manifested very strongly in colonial practices, be it the overt use of slave labor (Williams, 1944), or the covert process of forced migrations (Tinker, 1974). Manning (1982) recounts the manner in which the use of labor in Benin by French organizations was sustained by ideological discourses of sustaining local life patterns, and Lord Curzon, the famous colonial administrator, was frank in his admission that "administration and exploitation go hand in hand" (quoted in Dutt, 1970: 129). Just as colonial power materially masks the situated nature of industrialization, the uncritical emphasis that management historians place on "decontextualized techno-economic decision making" marks an ideological position, for it neglects to consider the manner in which imperial policy determined seemingly independent market forces (Fieldhouse, 1981).

Colonial Governance, International Governance

One thing that colonial systems excelled in was the development of relational structures between private enterprise and government systems. For instance, the physical and military security of the East India Company was underwritten by the British Army. Headrick (1988: 379) points to the fact that "trade did not follow the flag as come wrapped in it." Between 1520 and 1820, Spain's Central American colonies were administered by private enterprise, and once the United States supplanted Spain in Central America (vide the Monroe Doctrine of 1823), U.S. troops were sent 36 times to this region between 1822 and 1964 to support the interests of U.S. corporations (Faber, 1993). In the modern organizational scheme, international regimes like those of the WTO have often been seen as attempts to bring structural and procedural congruence to global trade and economy, but they need to be constantly reevaluated in light of allegations that such regimes are primarily geared toward supporting multinationals at the expense of local industry (Zinn, 2000).

Postcolonial Theory: An Introduction

As we have seen, it is important to be introspective about the manner in which euromodern organizing and control systems represent a way in which multiplicities of organizational and economic realities have been denied, and singular systems have been installed as being the most efficient. Unless we find, identify, and try to understand other ways of organizing and control, we are in danger of perpetuating organizations and organizing systems that will sustain and exacerbate the power imbalances and systems of exploitation that have already created their own logic, epistemology, and justification; a cycle that will sooner or later come back to haunt all of us, irrespective of our location and our affiliation.

We have sought to embark on this exercise by subjecting the current logic of euromodern organizing to scrutiny, and the methodological tool we use for this purpose is that of postcolonial theory. Postcolonial theory, like all theories that have the word "post" prefixed to them, is amorphous and defies neat definitions. However, we may operationally describe postcolonial theory under two heads. The first is as a device, which has emerged in recent scholarship—notably in literary and historical theory—and that may be described as an attempt to "provincialize" the current practices of Western epistemology and question its right to theorize "its particular-organic empirical reality into a cognitive-epistemic formula on behalf of the entire world" (Radhakrishnan, 1994: 308). The second is as an attempt to directly engage with the colonizing propensities of our institutions and challenge their right to do so, by articulating different practices that have existed in societies before the advent of colonialism, or the manner in which the colonial forces have been subverted and rechannelized by violent practices (Cabral, 1994). Both of these offer important conceptual possibilities that we propose to explore. In what follows, we begin by concentrating on the first aspect of postcolonial theory, that is, on its role as a contextualizing element in cultural, political, and organizational arenas, and then subject various theories of organizational control to critique through its lens.[4] Thereafter, we offer a brief vignette as a pointer toward imagining a "different" practice in postcoloniality.

Postcolonial Theory as Critique

The postcolonial perspective is not amenable to easy definition (Lewis, 2000; Manlove, 2000). There has been a notorious tendency observed in the academic canon to loosely prefix the term "post" to a variety of discursive formations in an attempt to free some space for ideas that exist at the margins of these discourses. This may sometimes have a profoundly negative effect, in that a teleological and temporal linearity is assumed in the discourse where there might be none. However, given the institutionalization of terms such as postmodernism and post-structuralism, this tradition has founded for itself an uneasy precedent. In a similar vein, postcolonialism may be seen as a theoretical position that, while acknowledging its debts to postmodernism/post-structuralism, expresses a point of divergence from the latter on grounds of the kind of politics such positions seem to entail. The critique of postmodernism/poststructuralism[5] that is mounted from the postcolonial viewpoint may be summarized as follows:

1. Most postmodern/post-structuralist thought results from an extremely self-referential view of the West, which is then presented to the world as a universal viewpoint; to that extent, it obscures the intimate, and often violent dialogue that is taking place between Western and non-Western economies on a variety of contested terrains, such as modernity, industrialization, and ways of knowing.

2. The tendency of the postmodernist/post-structuralist viewpoints to be overoccupied by practices of representation often leads to the ignoring of the vital and physicalistic nature of phenomena. For example, some postmodernist/post-structuralist accounts of events such as wars tend to view them more as representational issues than as acts of extreme violence and destruction (Baudrillard, 1995).

3. Situated as it is in the context of a late capitalist society, postmodern/post-structuralist thought discards categories that may have outlived their utility from a Western standpoint (e.g., nationalism). In so doing, it primarily denies agency to those subjectivities who may not be willing to reject those categories.

4. Postmodernist/post-structuralist thought, despite its critique of logocentrism, derives most of its theories from the articulation of dualistic, binary oppositions. To that end, it privileges this logocentric thought over all else, including systems of knowing that may not be logocentric or dualistic in character.[6]

In the world of organizational theory too, we are witnessing a distressing contestation of activist spaces in the name of emancipatory postmodernism. In the wake of the glib assertion by Foucault and Deleuze (1977) that "representation is dead," we have well-known critical organizational scholars like Stewart Clegg announce that critique is dead. According to Clegg, "to the extent that the notion of critique allies with essentialist positions of one kind or the other, I think we should abandon the notion of critique" (cf. Jermier & Clegg, 1994: 5). With due respect and understanding of the important contributions of such scholars, it is perhaps crucial for us to contextualize these statements as having been made from the perspective of late capitalist, post-industrial societies. For while it may be possible for the Western scholar to issue a "grand obituary notice regarding the death of representation and narrative voice" (Radhakrishnan, 1994: 312), the Third World scholar still has to acknowledge that "the subaltern cannot speak" (Spivak, 1988: 308) and that the duty of representation is not something one can afford to discard with a flourish. In a sense, postcolonialism joins voice with marginal subjectivities within postmodernist traditions, such as postmodern feminists (Irigaray, 1994; Mohanty, Rousseau, & Torres, 1991), who seek venues of agency and activism, and discover that subjectlessness is not a firm enough anchor for any form of voice.

What would happen to the identity of the once-colonized subject if the world were to be defined purely by postmodernist epistemology? Is it possible for the subjects of the Third World to participate in any form of knowledge sharing unless their knowledges are accorded some sort of epistemological status within the canon? Indeed, the entire way in which the postmodern argument has been framed leads one to suspect that postmodernism offers a mere chimera of an epistemological break while furthering the domination of Western epistemology. As Radhakrishnan (1994: 309) remarks, "if canonical anthropology's message to pre-modern societies was 'I think, therefore you are,' postmodern orthodoxy takes the form of 'I think, therefore I am not.' You are 'I am not.' "

How then, can one articulate a postcolonial space for activism? Postcolonial theory operates in two distinct ways. First, it seeks to identify a space of activism for non-Western subjectivities that, while acknowledging the political nature of all meta-narratives, advocates a position of *strategic essentialism*, where a subject position (say nationalism or feminism) is assumed to open up a space for activism, despite the acknowldgment of the constructed and contested nature of such a subject position. This perspective, while acknowledging the hierarchical relations between various subjectivities such as race, gender, and class, chooses definite subject positions with a view to confronting the ethnocentricity imbedded in various discourses. However, it considers the telos of such identity politics as an attempt to transcend the very subject position it has chosen for itself, and to render that position unremarkable. For example, even when we know that a term like "race" is socially constructed, we can organize around it to fight racism. Despite knowing that "nation" is a constructed term, it can be used as a strategic category to fight colonialism. The final task of principled theorists/activists is that when the political goal is achieved, they must transcend the term. So if racial equality has been achieved in society, the category of "race" can be dismantled. Until then, this category is indispensable to the racial minority, even if it is a constructed category.[7]

Second, postcolonialism seeks to contextualize the modernist and colonial experience as being but one part of the histories of colonized societies. Therefore, despite the loss and subordination of knowledge systems that resulted from the contact with euromodernity, there still exist, in however fragmented a form, enduring carry-overs of various knowledge systems, belief systems, systems of spirituality and connectedness with nature that need to be articulated, and examined. These systems are not invulnerable to critique, nor does the postcolonial critic seek to invest an automatic emancipatory possibility to all local narratives. However, to the extent that incommensurability with the hegemonic narratives of logocentricity and positivism do not disqualify a theory, postcolonialism seeks to make a politico-epistemological case for the politics of representation. For instance, it seeks to unmask the links between technology and capitalism, but without necessarily endorsing a Luddite position; it argues in favor of an ecocentric approach to regimes of accumulation, but views it as more of an issue of the consumption of natural resources within the West and the co-optation of Third World elites into a partnership with Western elites in a program of environmental degradation; and it recognizes the global nature of industrial phenomena, while asserting the right of nation states to decide the pace at which they will allow foreign capital to enter their country.

It must be stated very clearly at this juncture that the postcolonial critique of mainstream theory shares a lot that is in common with specific strands of the radical position. The political positions assumed by scholars such as Marx, Foucault, and Gramsci resonate powerfully within postcolonial theory. In particular, Foucauldian ideas such as the production of the subject (Foucault, 1980), governmentality (Foucault, 1991), and dividing practices (Foucault, 1977) represent some of the epistemological cornerstones of the postcolonial argument. Also, the post-structuralist techniques of literary analysis such as deconstruction and "reading against the grain" represent some of the more formidable weapons in the postcolonial arsenal. The critical (pun intended) difference between post-structuralist and postcolonial theories however, is not in their choice of mode of analysis, but rather in the *site* of their analysis. In the face of the mystifying reluctance on the part of most radical scholars to acknowledge the imbedded and sedimented nature of global imperialism, their somewhat shocking lack of knowledge about non-Western subjectivities, and the manner in which postmodern/post-structuralist authors render phenomena that profoundly impact the Third World as issues of mere representation, their lofty analyses need to be subjected to critique and recontextualization.

In the next section, we examine various theories of organizational control in light of the postcolonial position, and suggest that whether related to dominant or resistant positions, modernist theories of organizational control are deficient in the attention they pay to the context in which they are imbedded.

Theories of Organizational Control

While the notion of organizational control has been theorized from a variety of divergent perspectives, we may think of the various theories as being loosely grouped under the following two heads: (a) the "mainstream" narratives, which posit control mechanisms as being the drivers of normatively desired organizational goals, and (b) the "radical" perspectives, which seek to view control either as a process of whimsical reality creation by dominant groups, which then gets paraded as the normative truth, or as an alienating mechanism designed to render organizational constituents vulnerable to domination. In this chapter, it is contended that both the mainstream and the radical perspectives, despite their obvious disagreements, emerge from a similar set of Eurocentric assumptions regarding the apparent universality of their positions. In effect, they seek to impose a default view of organization upon the world, and deny some of the fundamental contestations about modernity and industrialization that exist between the Western and the non-Western ("restern") world.

Mainstream Theories of Organizational Control

The mainstream views seek to study organizations as apolitical entities that emerge as a result of rational choices made by rational constituents from a variety of possibilities. These choices are defined as being based on the organizational need to maximize its output. Each of the examined mainstream ideas of organizational theory is accompanied by a specific idea of the nature and the goal of control mechanisms within the organizational realm. Control arrangements herein are seen as devices for ensuring the survival and viability of the organization. Upon examining a variety of disparate theories of organization, and the control arrangements they espouse, we identify six different perspectives on organizational control—rationalization, superordination, habituation, adaptation, dialogue, and efficiency maximization—which are discussed in the following sections.

Control as Rationalization

Informed in large part by what we now refer to as "classical organizational theory," this view is theoretically influenced by the Tayloristic (1911) idea of scientific management, and its incorporation into theory by Gulick and Urwick's (1937) principles of administration, where individual tasks were fragmented and procedures standardized. Managerial control in such a case is maintained by systems of reward and punishment that channel collective tasks in a particular direction.

Such a notion of control has come under severe attack for its "Social Darwinism" (Perrow, 1986: 54), and for rendering workers as mere adjuncts to machinery (Braverman, 1974). These valid critiques, however, fail to emphasize one crucial point of this exercise. Taylor's gift was to perpetuate a process of appropriating indigenous knowledge that had marked industrialization since its beginning and continues even today. In Taylor's own words, "managers assume . . . the burden of gathering together all of the traditional knowledge which in the past has been possessed by the workmen and then of classifying, tabulating, and reducing this knowledge to rules, laws, and formulae" (Taylor, 1911: 36). In modern times, this same process of "incorporating" local knowledge into global knowledge, and then discrediting local knowledge, is evident in many arenas. Take, for example, the controversies over patent laws and their applicability to life forms. On one hand, biotechnology firms have sought to patent herb-based products that are derived from local knowledge systems, such as extract of the neem plant from India. On the other hand, indigenous agricultural methods are derided as inefficient, and "modern" products, such as "terminator" seeds are sought to be marketed to local farmers thus rendering them perennially dependent on the multinational-controlled market for seeds (Shiva & Holla-Brar, 1993). This arrangement, of course, is mediated by international institutions such as the WTO, the designated control agents of this process.

Control as Superordination

Advocated primarily by the Human Relations School pioneered by Mayo (1933) and Roethlisberger and Dickson (1939), and furthered by the humanistic tradition of Argyris (1957), Bennis (1966), Herzberg (1968), McGregor (1960), and many others, this notion of control is based on the fact that the personal aspirations of workers also need to be addressed by organizational processes. These theorists argue for organizational processes that take the "higher order needs" of the workers into account. The organization visualized by the humanists contains both a formal as well as an informal organization, and control arrangements seek to align the two, or at least to manage the conflict that arises between them. The notion of control thus acquires a superordinate status insisting that the control and supervision of the worker, at least within the "zone of indifference" (Barnard, 1938), is necessary for the good of the organization and its members. Such a notion of control has spawned a variety of subfields like organizational development (OD) and organizational psychology, and a variety of techniques such as quality circles and self-managed work teams.

However, this notion of control has not been spared scrutiny from critical scholars. As Clegg contends, "Mayo developed Human Relations as a therapeutic cooling-out of the worker, a way of not listening to the accounts the worker proffered, or of systematically reconstructing them and representing them in terms other than those in which they were produced" (cf. Jermier & Clegg, 1994: 7).

Control as Habituation

Associated most directly with the works of March and Simon (1958), decision theory made a direct case for rendering the workers habituated to working within a finite set of possible actions. The argument was that workers were "boundedly rational" in their judgments, and therefore their responses needed to be simplified. Simon (1957: 102–103) identifies five mechanisms of organizational influence, namely: work division, establishment of standard practices, systems of authority and influence, channels of communication, and indoctrination. All of these may be conceived as creating routines for control, which are managed not by the coercive intensity of the rationalization process, but by withholding "irrelevant" information from organizational constituents. Thus, decision theorists view habit as an "important mechanism that assists in the preservation of good behavior"(Simon, 1957: 88). Of course, the possibility of the development of the worker in order to expand the boundaries of their rationality is entirely evaded in this conversation.

What is crucial here is not just the secrecy and lack of decision-making authority, but the premises on which these are enacted. The worker does need to be manipulated by the control system, as long as the premises of the workers decisions can be determined by the context. Marglin (1990) points out how industrialization acted to divest workers of their decision premises. Contemporary evidence of this process can be seen in the plush, computerized atmosphere of the global subsidiaries of multinational corporations where the organizational atmosphere of relatedness have been replaced by isolated workstations peopled by isolated individuals, with a precarious and deskilled existence (Appadurai, 1990).

Control as Adaptation
If the organization can be viewed as a part of the social environment, or as a system in interaction with other social systems (Katz & Kahn, 1966), buffering itself against organizational uncertainties becomes one of its primary tasks (Thompson, 1967). Control in such an environment is achieved only through developing continuities between organizations and systems around them. Apart from systems theory, such a notion of control also informs evolutionary theories of the organization (Hannan & Freeman, 1977), wherein the diminished value of organizational choice in an atmosphere of environmental determinism dictates that adaptation is the only guarantor of survival. Both theories, that is, systems theory and population ecology, draw substantially upon the work of Talcott Parsons, who viewed organizations as goal-oriented systems (Whyte, 1964). In such a theory, since the external environment is the primary controlling mechanism, the only method of ensuring survival is through adaptation.

Such an argument evidently prefers continuity to change, and thereby profoundly negates the possibility of any transformative processes in organizations. Indeed, the Parsonian view has come under a variety of attacks, for its negation of the role of conflict (Clegg & Dunkerley, 1977), its inability to theorize social change (Van den Berghe, 1973), and its overreliance on the organization–society interface at the expense of intra-organizational processes (Whyte, 1964).

Control as Dialogue

Yet another mode of control has been the notion of dialogue. Linked to constructivist notions of reality and organization (Srivastava & Cooperrider, 1990), it views the process of dialogue, or conversation, as crucial to building healthier and better organizations. It has been advocated as essential to the learning organization, as crucial to the democratized corporation (Flood, 1999), and as the basic resource for global corporations to become more socially productive and less exploitative (Gergen, 1995). It can even be seen as a key link to the development of stakeholder policies. This restores rationality and participation to multiple participants in organizations and proffers easy ways to create mutually beneficial control systems.

While such a perspective is indeed far more humanizing and cognizant of human potential than most other mainstream theories, one is tempted to ask, is not this the great quest of euromodernity? To find ways to reduce the incommensurability of humanity and reality so that we can all connect easily and painlessly? Such a quest implies a fear of not being connected (Berman, 1990; Marcuse, 1966), a fear that makes the *theorizing of differences* almost impossible. And even if we grant this desire for epiphanic togetherness its due, the truth is that in the global organizational setting, dialogue demands that incommensurabilities be dealt with (Mir, Calás, & Smircich, 1999). The debate between the Ogoni tribe and Shell in Nigeria is unlikely to be resolved by dialogue. For the subaltern subject, in a world mediated by unequal social/resource relations, attempts at full communication lead to the, slightly inexorable, reign of the panopticon. The desire for disclosure and communion by certain people in this standoff inevitably leads to their inclusion by the dominant group, leading to their marginalization in their own group, and a sense of inferiority compared to the co-opting group (Brendan, 2000; Said, 1978). It is no wonder then, that determined activists invest not in collaboration, but in secrecy, in dissensus (Lyotard, 1984), in the processes of invalidating (Guha, 1983) or even more soulfully, in non-engagement (Gandhi, 1962), as techno-economic elites are stripped of their pretensions that they can lead others. Ultimately, while cooperation and dialogue is important, it is far more important that dispossessed people create their own agendas that others can be invited into (Pena, 1995).

Control as Efficiency Maximization

Organizational theorists, frustrated by neoclassical economics' refusal to recognize the firm as anything but an atomized entity in a price mechanism, add two economic theories to their arsenal. Transaction cost theory views firms as being the creation of the failure of the price mechanism to ensure the fulfillment of contracts, while agency theory sees organizations as engaged primarily in an attempt to eliminate the dissonance between principals and agents caused by moral hazard and information insufficiency. In both these cases, the preferred mode of control is through the formation of contracts, which carry punitive actions if not fulfilled. Even intra-organizational relations are meant to be governed by a contract; indeed, agency theorists view a firm as being nothing more than a nexus of contracts (Fama, 1980), and Williamson (1985) calls these contractual arrangements "the economic institutions of capitalism."

Such a view can be best summarized by Banuri's (1990: 74) *impersonality postulate*: "impersonal relationships are inherently superior to personal relations." This again, is a peculiar and parochial notion, one unique to the constellation of disembedded epistemologies that form euromodernity. This view in particular must be critiqued for the environmental and societal havoc it wreaks globally. It leads to the formulation of oxymorons like sustainable development that offer technocratic control to the few over the many, the essence of the colonial endeavor.

Radical Theories of Organizational Control

There are, of course, other critiques within the system, and it is to these we turn in our exploration of radical theories of control. Just as the mainstream perspective is predicated upon a *sociology of regulation*, radical theories are defined as those that subscribe to a *sociology of change* (Burrell & Morgan, 1979), where the power imbalances in society are viewed as a cause for concern and redress. Upon examining a variety of theories that we may consider radical, we identify three different perspectives on the issue of organizational control, namely domination, disciplinarization, and alienation.

Control as Domination

Informed primarily by Marxist and neo-Marxist theory, but incorporating other more nuanced perspectives such as radical environmentalism and radical feminism as well, this view suggests that organizations are capable of social, cultural, and economic havoc, often in combination with the modern state (Morgan, 1986). Such organizations rely on transparently coercive and intimidatory means of control, literally bringing Weber's "iron cage" metaphor to life. Workers in such organizations are viewed as adjuncts of machines (Braverman, 1974), and organizational discipline is maintained primarily through control mechanisms that are punitive and freedom threatening. This narrative has been critiqued on account of the fact that it visualizes control relationships as being created to foster the private appropriation of socially produced goods (Althusser, 1969; Glucksman, 1974). Such a perspective tends to be parochial in that it focuses on the interests of workers within hyper-consuming societies and is inadequately contexualized in the global social and ecological realities.

Control as Disciplinarization
Most controlling processes in organizations seem to have achieved considerable success in preempting the potential tensions and crises of distributional imbalances. One way in which organizational processes have sustained themselves is through the creation of a docile and manageable workforce, one that views the demands made of it as perfectly normal practice. This approach to control owes a lot to the work of Foucault, who theorized control as the creation of "normal" disciplined subjects. According to Foucault, the control relationship is not a coercive arrangement, but often is a productive arrangement; in his words, "power produces; it produces reality; it produces domains of objects and rituals of truth" (Foucault, 1977: 194). Moreover, Foucault (1980) contends that power and control arrangements not only produce rituals of truth, they actually produce the worker.

As is common in most postmodern analyses, this proposition tends to be very subjective. As Marglin (1990) points out, it is primarily the eviscerated sense of work culture propounded by euromodernity that offers workers no cultural sources of resistance. Moreover, such a perspective implicitly negates all value systems as being produced, thereby ironically insulating the values of modernity from critique. Indeed, one wonders with Gayatri Spivak (1988: 271) how "some of the most radical critique coming out of the West today is the result of an interested desire to conserve the West as a subject."

Control as Alienation
Despite their complicity in the production of the subject, control systems are plainly alienating. Not only are they materially alienating, they also produce a form of discursive alienation, where organizational constituents may feel disconnected from their reality. A radical interpretation of control as habituation would reveal that such practices, which seek to shield organizational constituents from the complexity (and potential richness) of live problems, represent both controlling and alienating arrangements.

Alienating practices in organizations include the commodification of work and identity, the reduction of the workplace to a unidimensional entity, and the absence of systems of community. The phenomenon of discursive alienation therefore reflects a deep-set dissonance between organizational and individual reality. While most organizational research on alienation has reduced it to simplistic terms such as "dissatisfaction" (Kakabadse, 1986), some more incisive theorists have articulated the finely nuanced nature of alienation. Jermier (1985) makes a distinction between the Marxist notion of alienation, according to which alienation is historically produced as a result of the tension between social forces of production and private appropriation of capital, and the view of critical theorists that alienation is better conceptualized as a loss of awareness of the worker and a loss of connectedness with the work.

However, alienation as a construct is inadequate to understand the global condition where euromodern processes are replacing all epistemes, societies, and traditions with their own scientist notions of truth and value. This kind of disconnectedness is barely touched upon in current constructs of alienation, which have few ways to understand once-colonized societies. As a consequence while the notion of alienation makes sense in the euromodernized enclaves of many societies, it is useless in most institutional systems of the world where the concept of social citizenship is far less individualized. As Prasad and Prasad (1993: 178–180) comment, an alternative to alienation can only be produced by "the decommodification of work and identity... building community and connectedness... and questioning the reified logic of organizations."

Commonalities in the Mainstream and the Radical Perspectives
Upon studying both the mainstream and radical schemes from a postcolonial perspective, we find that while oppositional in a variety of ways, they share a number of common perceptions (Mir, Calás, & Smircich, 1999: 274–278):

1. They both generalize from the Western experience to universal human rules.
2. While differing in issues of how wealth needs to be distributed, they seldom differ on how it must be accumulated; for example, they are both predicated upon human conquest of nature.
3. They assume bureaucracy as the default organizational structure.
4. They employ logocentric and dualistic means of understanding organizational processes (e.g., markets/hierarchies, managers/workers).

It becomes doubly important for the postcolonial scholar, therefore, to attempt to articulate a position of organizational control that moves beyond the assumptions and binary dualities that characterize this perspective. However, in order to do that, it may be necessary to abandon the language of rationality and logocentricity, as we proceed on exploratory journeys.

Control as Liberation: A Story from the "Small Voice of History"[8]

Rather than summarize our argument, we would like to end with a brief story of what may represent a postcolonial possibility for organizational control. While myriad stories of postcolonial organizing are possible, we would like to share this one not as a detailed case study, but as a vignette for understanding and celebrating different ways in which control can be reconceptualized. This vignette will by necessity be brief,[9] and does not represent an empirical study per se, but is more a pointer toward such studies of postcolonial understanding

Grameen Bank: Control through Trust and Collective Responsibility

Literally meaning "rural bank," the Grameen Bank[10] has been an astonishing success story of nontraditional banking. Conceived of as a way of distributing money to the rural poor in Bangladesh, this bank, in its first 15 years, disbursed over a quarter of a billion dollars to over eight hundred thousand people, predominantly women with little or no material collateral (Canadian Broadcasting Corporation, 1991). Started in 1983 by a single individual named Muhammad Yunus, the Grameen Bank began by offering loans to bamboo workers who had not been recognized by the government as worthy of agricultural or industrial loans, and whose only source of capital had been exploitative private moneylenders. It now supports a variety of agricultural and small-scale industrial activities throughout Bangladesh. Unlike conventional banking systems, the securities needed to borrow from the Grameen Bank are not derived from traditional collateral, but from nonfinancial sources such as guarantees from village councils, guarantees from established borrowers, and at times, no guarantees at all. Despite such "flimsy" guarantees, and contrary to the opportunism postulate, the recovery rate is 98 percent, which is substantially higher than that of any bank in Bangladesh. By May 2001, for instance, the bank had over 1000 branches serving over 40,000 villages, and it had distributed loans equivalent to 3.4 billion U.S. dollars. This amount is of course modest compared to the loan outlay of several large banks all over the world. What is distinctive and impressive about the Grameen Bank is that this amount was distributed among over 4.5 million members. The loans contributed to the building of over half a million houses, showing that capital can be stretched to include a large number of potential recipients.

This is not to say that the Grameen Bank represents the romantic *noblesse oblige* of the Bangladeshi poor. It uses a variety of control systems to sustain its recovery rate. For example, the bank rarely gives loans to individuals. If a person wishes to approach the bank for a loan, she is asked to form a group of five prospective applicants and apply en masse. The bank then gives loans to two out of the five applicants (chosen from amongst the five internally), with a promise that others in the group will be given loans subject to non-delinquency on the part of the first two. This cyclical practice of loans and repayments can be sustained perpetually if the group exhibits sustained conscientious repayment. Default by one hurts the group as a whole, and rarely occurs.

Once several groups are formed in a single village, the bank sets up a "center" in the village, which is managed in consultation with senior group members. The basis of setting up the center is that the bank should go to the people rather than the people coming to it, and is aimed at reducing the feeling of powerlessness and anxiety that rural folk experience when they are asked to interact with urban institutions.

Predictably, the bank's practices have rendered it more than a mere economic institution, its influence has seeped into various aspects of rural life. For instance, Grameen Bank does not lend to people who accept dowry payments for their sons, conducts mass marriages, engages in tree planting in deforested areas, sells vegetable seeds to combat malnutrition, and helps run local schools. In a patriarchal society, 90 percent of its clients are women, and despite severe opposition from a disgruntled elite and suspicious government, the bank has forged its way into the forefront of rural life in Bangladesh, based on a simple principle that control systems based on trust and collective responsibility beget trust and collective responsibility in return.

Of course, institutions such as Grameen Bank should not be held immune from rightful critique. Microcredit, in its conceptual form, continues to be interpellated with some of the key ideologies of larger social systems, which continue to be exploitative and patriarchal. As Fernando (1997: 1) observes in his critique of institutions such as Grameen Bank, "the intervention of NGOs reproduces and sustains the very institutions that they aspire to transform." However, we believe that institutions such as Grameen Bank, despite their shortcomings, represent impressive and innovative ways to re-imagine the way in which organizations control individuals.

The vignette serves as a good conclusion, because it manifests a few dimensions of postcoloniality that are relevant to re-creations of the organizing sciences. First, in its conception, it offers a critique of the different euromodern theories of being and becoming. The second dimension is the empirical observation of postcolonial systems at work; the subjects of the bank are those who have traditionally been the inheritors of a difficult and oppressive colonial legacy. The job of the institution here is one of renewal; similarly, we express our job as scholars to explore the stories and fables of postcolonial renewal. Whether in industrial or nonindustrial settings, the key feature of this renewal is the manner in which modernist systems are re-appropriated for emancipatory ends, and the innovative control systems employed to regulate both the environment and organizational constituents. Finally, this story allows us to identify the space and time of the multiple local and grand traditions that carry on, living and creating and working in ways that include euromodernity but are not determined by it.

Viewed in light of our earlier critiques of control, the enumeration of liberatory possibilities is in danger of appearing as a classic example of Orwellian newspeak. However, we would be naive if we did not recognize that control is a normative and integrative aspect of a collectivity. It is only when the collectivity is illegitimate, and thus uses force as the primary means of control, that it is colonizing. There are nonviolent, and liberatory aspects of control that we need to invoke, learn about, and celebrate. This is what we seek to do by inviting the organizational sciences to join us in the global threshold of postcoloniality. Of the myriad uses of the prefix "post" that float around the intellectual landscape, this is probably the most appropriate. Globally, it is the most relevant. We live in a world with many mechanisms of domination and hegemony, but we also live in a world where we can recreate our presents and futures. Thus in speaking of the postcolonial we do not speak of what has happened, but of what is happening. Our emphasis here is on describing an alive, spontaneous, and planned set of processes and events that comprise this revolution of possibilities. We speak of the sites of struggle that are all multiply determined, but unswervingly inviolate. For the postcolonial is a growing and developing way of being and becoming, a way of deliberately and recalcitrantly reclaiming our presents from euromodernity. It is a process with many products and a constant inventiveness. It has a tradition, beginning with those who never did give up even when enslaved and despoiled. And above all, it has a proud and diverse today, which we seek to articulate and share. Beyond the epistemes of control common to euromodern knowledge lie stories as hieroglyphics, as a "written figure that is both sensual and abstract, both beautiful and communicative" (Christian, 1990: 38).

Notes

1. We use the term "euromodern" in this paper to contextualize the term "modern" as used in social sciences in Western societies. Such a usage does away with many of the spatial dualities (such as Orient/Occident, North/South, modern/traditional, First World/Third World, etc.) that are used in essentialist discourse, and opens possibilities to understand how societies create their own modernities.

2. We use the term "eurolimited" in place of the traditionally used "eurocentric" because if scholarship had been merely eurocentric, other realities would have gained at least some peripheral status. In eurolimited discourses, these realities are denied, and even eradicated (Davies, Nandy, & Sardar, 1993; Nandy, 1983; Todorov, 1984).

3. See Kiely (2000) and Werbner (2001) for some recent empirical investigations on this issue.

4. For an introduction to postcolonial theory and some of the prominent arguments that it advances, see Williams and Chrisman (1994).

5. In this paper, we have used the terms "postmodernist" and "post-structuralist" together for purposes of simplicity. However, we do acknowledge that there are myriad subtle (and not so subtle) differences between the two positions.

6. This despite Derrida's constant reminders against the perils of binary dualisms (see Derrida, 1987).

7. See Ray (2000) for a discussion of gender issues in Third World environments.

8. The term is borrowed from Guha (1983).

9. For a more detailed, and indeed, a more traditional reading of this vignette, see Holcombe (1995).

10. A very rich source of information on Grameen Bank can be found at their website (http://www.grameen-info.org/).

References

Althusser, L. 1969. *For Marx* (B. Brewster, Trans.). New York: Pantheon Books.

Appadurai, A. 1990. Technology and the reproduction of values in rural western India. In F. A. Marglin & S. Marglin (Eds.), *Dominating knowledge: Development, culture and resistance* (pp. 186–216). Oxford: Clarendon Press.

Argyris, C. 1957. *Personality and organization: The conflict between system and the individual.* New York: Harper.

Banuri, T. 1990. Modernisation and its discontents: A cultural perspective on the theories of development. In F. A. Marglin & S. Marglin (Eds.), *Dominating knowledge: Development, culture and resistance* (pp. 73–101). Oxford: Clarendon Press.

Barnard, C. I. 1938. *The functions of the executive.* Cambridge, MA: Harvard University Press.

Baudrillard, J. 1995. *The gulf war did not take place.* Bloomington, IN: Indiana University Press.

Bennis, W. G. 1966. *Changing organizations: Essays on the development and evolution of human organization*. New York: McGraw-Hill.

Berman, M. 1990. Coming to our sense: Body and spirit in the hidden history of the West. Bantam Books: New York.

Braverman, H. 1974. *Labor and monopoly capital: The degradation of work in the twentieth century*. New York: Monthly Review Press.

Brendan, T. 2000. The illusion of a future: Orientalism as traveling theory. *Critical Inquiry, 26* (3), 558–583.

Burrell, G., & Morgan, G. 1979. *Sociological paradigms and organisational analysis: Elements of the sociology of corporate life*. London: Heinemann.

Cabral, A. 1994. National liberation and culture. In P. Williams & L. Chrisman (Eds.), *Colonial discourse and post-colonial theory: A reader* (pp. 53–65). New York: Columbia University Press.

Castle, G. 2001. *Postcolonial discourse*. London: Blackwell Publications.

Canadian Broadcasting Corporation. 1991. Interview with Mohammed Younus of Grameen Bank. CBS IDEAS Transcripts.

Cannella, A. A., & Paetzold, R. L. 1994. Pfeffer's barriers to the advancement of organizational sciences: A rejoinder. *Academy of Management Review, 19*, 331–341.

Chandler, A. D. 1962. *Strategy and structure: Chapters in the history of the American enterprise*. Garden City, New York: Doubleday.

Chandler, A. D. 1977. *The visible hand: The managerial revolution in American business*. Cambridge, MA: Belknap Press.

Charrad, M. 2001. *States and women's rights: The making of postcolonial Tunisia, Algeria, and Morocco*. Berkeley, CA: University of California Press.

Chaturvedi, V. 2000. *Mapping subaltern studies and the postcolonial*. New York: Verso Books.

Chodos, R., & Murphy, R. 1974. *Let us prey*. Toronto: J. Lorimer.

Christian, R. C. 1990. *From the bottom up*. Chicago: Jeff Spritz.

Clegg, S. R., & Dunkerley, D. (Eds.). 1977. *Critical issues in organizations*. London: Routledge.

Davenport, T., & Prusak, L. 1998. *Working knowledge: How organizations manage what they know*. Boston, Mass: Harvard Business School Press.

Davies, M. W., Nandy, A., & Sardar, Z. 1993. *Barbaric others: A manifesto for western racism*. London: Pluto Press.

Derrida, J. 1987. *Psyche: Inventions de l'autre*. Paris: Galilee.

Dutt, R. P. 1970. *India today*. New Delhi: Navjivan Press.

Escobar, A. 1994. *Encountering development*. Princeton, NJ: Princeton University Press.

Faber, D. 1993. *Environment under fire: Imperialism and the ecological crisis in Central America*. New York: Monthly Review Press.

Fama, E. F. 1980. Agency problems and the theory of the firm. *Journal of Political Economy, 88*, 288–307.

Fernando, J. 1997. *Disciplining the mother: Microcredit in Bangladesh. Ghadar, 1* (1), 1.

Fieldhouse, D. 1981. *Colonialism 1870–1945: An introduction*. New York: St. Martin's Press.

Flood, R. L. 1999. *Rethinking the fifth discipline: Learning within the unknowable*. London: Routledge.

Foucault, M. 1977. *Discipline and Punish: The birth of the prison*. New York: Pantheon Books.

Foucault, M. 1980. *Power/knowledge: Selected interviews and other writings*. (C. Gordon, Ed.). Brighton: Harvester Press.

Foucault, M. 1991. Governmentality. In G. Burchell, C. Gordon, & P. Miller (Eds.), *The Foucault effect: Studies in governmentality*. Chicago: University of Chicago Press.

Foucault, M., & Deleuze, G. 1977. A conversation. In M. Foucault, *Language, counter-memory, practice: Selected essays and interviews* (pp. 205–217). Ithaca: Cornell University Press.

Gandhi, M. K. 1962. *Hind swaraj*. Ahmedabad: Navjivan Press

Gergen, K. 1995. Global organisation: From imperialism to ethical violence. *Organization 2*, 519–533.

Glucksman, M. 1974. *Structuralist analysis in contemporary social thought: A comparison of the theories of Claude Levi-Strauss and Louis Althusser*. London: Routledge.

Gran, G. 1983. *Development by people: Citizen construction of a just world*. New York: Praeger.

Guha, R. 1983. *Elementary aspects of peasant insurgency in colonial India*. New Delhi: Oxford University Press.

Gulick, L. H., & Urwick, L. 1937. *Papers on the science of administration*. New York: Institute of Public Administration.

Hannan, M. T., & Freeman, J. 1977. The population ecology of organizations. *American Journal of Sociology, 82*, 929–964.

Headrick, D. 1988. *The tentacles of progress: Technology transfer in the age of imperialism*. New York: Oxford University Press.

Herzberg, F. 1968. *Work and the nature of man*. Cleveland: World Publication Company.

Holcombe, S. 1995. *Managing to empower: The Grameen Bank's experience of poverty alleviation*. London: Zed Books.

Illich, I. 1981. The delinking of peace and government. *Gandhi Marg, 3*, 257–265.

Irigaray, L. 1994. *Thinking the difference: For a peaceful revolution*. New York: Routledge.

Jermier, J. M. 1985. When the sleeper awakes. *Journal of Management, 11*, 67–80.

Jermier, J. M., & Clegg, S. R. 1994. Crossroads: Critical issues in organization science: A dialogue. *Organization Science, 5* (1), 1–13.

Jermier, J. M., Knights, D., & Nord, W. (Eds.). 1994. *Resistance and power in organizations*. New York: Routledge.

Kakabadse, A. 1986. Organizational alienation and job climate: A comparative study of the structural conditions and psychological adjustment. *Small Group Behavior, 17*, 458–471.

Katz, D., & Kahn, R. 1966. *The social psychology of organizations.* New York: Wiley.

Kaufman, A., Zacharias, L., & Karson, M. 1995. *Managers vs. owners: The struggle for corporate control in American democracy.* New York: Oxford University Press.

Kiely, R. 2000. Globalization: From domination to resistance. *Third World Quarterly, 21* (6), 1059–1070.

Korten, D. 1995. *When corporations rule the world.* Hartford, CT: Kumarian Press.

Kozul-Wright, R. 1995. Trans-national corporations and the nation state. In J. Michie & J. Smith (Eds.), *Managing the global economy* (pp. 135–171). Oxford: Oxford University Press.

Lewis, G. 2000. *Race, gender, social welfare: Encounters in a postcolonial society.* New York: Polity Press.

Lyotard, J. F. 1984. *The postmodern condition: A report on knowledge.* Minneapolis: The University of Minnesota Press.

Macaulay, T. B. 1972. A minute on Indian education. In T. B. Macaulay, *Selected writings* (pp. 237–251). Chicago: The University of Chicago Press.

MacKerron, C., & Cogan, D. (Eds.). 1993. *Business in the rainforests: Corporations, deforestation, and sustainability.* Washington DC: Investor Responsibility Research Centre.

Manning, P. 1982. *Slavery, colonialism, and economic growth in Dahomey, 1640–1960.* Cambridge: Cambridge University Press.

Mandal, S. 2000. Reconsidering cultural globalization: The English language in Malaysia. *Third World Quarterly, 21* (6), 1001–1012.

Manlove, C. T. 2000. Towards a dialectic of identity and economy in postcolonial studies. *College Literature, 28* (2), 198–206.

March, J., & Simon, H. 1958. *Organizations.* New York: Wiley.

Marcuse, H. 1966. *One-dimensional man: Studies in the ideology of advanced industrial society.* Boston: Beacon Press.

Marglin, S. 1990. Losing touch: The cultural conditions of worker accommodation and resistance. In F. A. Marglin & S. Marglin (Eds.), *Dominating knowledge: Development, culture and resistance* (pp. 217–282). Oxford: Clarendon Press.

Marglin, S. 1974. "What do bosses do?" The origins and functions of hierarchy in capitalist production, Part I. *Review of Radical Political Economics 6* (2), 60–112.

Mayo, E. 1933. *The human problems of an industrial civilization.* New York: The Macmillan Company.

McGregor, D. 1960. *The human side of enterprise.* New York: McGraw-Hill.

Mintz, S. 1985. *Sweetness and power: The place of sugar in modern history.* New York: Penguin.

Mir, R., Calás, M., & Smircich, L. 1999. Global technoscapes and silent voices: Challenges to theorizing global cooperation. In D. Cooperrider & J. Dutton (Eds.), *Organizational dimensions of global change* (pp. 270–290). London: Sage Publications.

Mohanty, C., Russo, A., & Torres, L. (Eds.). 1991. *Third world women and the politics of feminism.* Bloomington: Indiana University Press.

Morgan, G. 1986. *Images of organization.* Beverly Hills: Sage Publications.

Nandy, A. 1983. *The intimate enemy: Loss and recovery of self under colonialism.* New Delhi: Oxford University Press.

Nandy, A. (Ed.). 1993. *Science, hegemony and violence: A requiem for modernity.* Tokyo and Delhi: United Nations University and Oxford University Press.

Pearson, R. 1986. Multinational corporations and the sexual division of labour: A historical perspective. In A. Teichova (Ed.), *Multi-national enterprises in historical context* (pp. 339–350). Cambridge: Cambridge University Press.

Pena, M. 1995. *Theologies of liberation in Peru: The role of ideas in social movements.* Philadelphia, PA: Temple University Press.

Perrow, C. 1979. *Complex organizations: A critical essay.* Glenview, Ill.: Scott, Foresman.

Perrow, C. 1986. *Complex organizations: A critical essay* (2nd ed.). New York: Random House.

Pfeffer, J. 1993. Barriers to the advance of organizational science: paradigm development as a dependent variable. *Academy of Management Review, 18,* 599–620.

Polanyi, K. 1957. *Trade and market in the early empires: Economies in history and theory.* Glencoe, IL: Free Press.

Prasad, A., & Prasad, P. 1993. Reconceptualizing alienation in management inquiry: Critical organizational scholarship and workplace empowerment. *Journal of Management Inquiry, 2* (2), 169–183.

Radhakrishnan, R. 1994. Postmodernism and the rest of the world. *Organization, 1* (2), 305–340.

Ray, S. 2000. *En-gendering India: Woman and nation in colonial and postcolonial narratives.* Durham: Duke University Press.

Rodney, W. 1974. *How Europe underdeveloped Africa.* Washington DC: Howard University Press.

Roethlisberger, F., & Dickson, W. 1939. *Management and the worker.* Cambridge, MA: Harvard University Press.

Said, E. 1978. *Orientalism.* New York: Pantheon Books.

Shiva, V., & Holla-Brar, R. 1993. *Intellectual piracy and the neem patents: The neem campaign.* Dehradun, India: Research Foundation for Science, Technology and Natural Resource Policy.

Shrivastava, P. 1996. *Greening business: Profiting the corporation and the environment.* Cincinnati, OH: Thomson executive Press.

Simon, H. 1957. *Administrative behavior: A study of decision-making processes in administrative organization.* New York: Macmillan.

Spivak, G. C. 1987. *In other worlds: Essays in cultural politics.* New York: Methuen.

Spivak, G. C. 1988. Can the subaltern speak? In C. Nelson & L. Grossberg (Eds.), *Marxism and the interpretation of culture* (pp. 271–313). Urbana: University of Illinois Press.

Srivastva, S., & Cooperrider, D. 1990. *Appreciative management and leadership: The power of positive thought and action in organizations.* San Francisco: Jossey-Bass.

Taylor, F. 1967. *The principles of scientific management.* New York: Norton [originally published in 1911].

Thompson, E. P. 1966. *The making of the British working class.* New York: Vintage.

Thompson, J. D. 1967. *Organizations in action: Social science bases of organization theory.* New York: McGraw-Hill.

Tinker, H. 1974. *A new system of slavery: The export of Indian labour overseas, 1830–1920.* New York: Oxford University Press.

Todorov, T. 1984. *The conquest of America: The question of the other.* New York: Harper and Row.

Van de Berghe. 1973. Dialectic and functionalism: Toward a cultural synthesis. In W. J. Chabliss (Ed.), *Sociological readings in the conflict perspective* (pp. 41–61). Reading, MA: Addison Wesley.

Verlinden, C. 1970. *The beginnings of modern colonization* (Y. Freccero, Trans.). Ithaca, NY: Cornell University Press.

Werbner, P. 2001. The limits of cultural hybridity: On ritual monsters, poetic licence and contested postcolonial purifications. *Journal of the Royal Anthropological Institute, 7* (1), 133–152.

Weick, K. 1979. *The social psychology of organizing.* Reading, MA: Addison-Wesley.

Whyte, M. K. 1964. Parsons' theory applied to organizations. In M. Black (Ed.), *The social theory of Talcott Parsons* (pp. 250–267). Englewood Cliffs, NJ: Prentice Hall.

Williams, E. 1944. *Capitalism and slavery.* Chapel Hill, NC: University of North Carolina Press.

Williams, P., & Chrisman, L. (Eds.). 1994. *Colonial discourse and post-colonial theory: A reader.* New York: Columbia University Press.

Williamson, O. 1985. *The economic institutions of capitalism.* New York: Harcourt Brace.

Zinn, H. 2000. A Flash of the Possible. *The Progressive, 64* (1), 12.

CHAPTER 3

Managing Organizational Culture and Imperialism

Bill Cooke

I n *Culture and Imperialism* (1994), Edward Said sets out to reconnect cultural forms, notably the novel, "with the imperial processes of which they were manifestly and unconcealedly a part" (1994: xv). Thus he famously identifies allusions to the slave-based Caribbean sugar industry in Jane Austen's 1814 *Mansfield Park*, resituating our understanding of Austen's narrative within British imperialism of the time. Culture in Said's sense includes not just art forms like the novel and opera, but "the specialized forms of knowledge in such learned disciplines as ethnography, historiography, philology and literary history" (1994: xii). In this vein, Bishop (1990) has, for example, explored Western mathematics as a secret weapon of cultural imperialism, and Rabasa (1993) re-presented Mercator's Atlas as a Eurocentric imposition of meaning upon the World. This chapter, titled in homage to Said,[1] presents the management of organizational culture (MOC) as another such cultural form. This form is perhaps more mundane than the novel, opera, Western mathematics, or Mercator's atlas. As the basis for interventions in the working lives of employees in the United States and the United Kingdom, particularly from the 1980s onwards (Burnes, 1996; French & Bell, 1998) MOC is however particularly pernicious.

Slemon (1994) notes that there is a "remarkably heterogeneous" set of critical projects associated with postcolonialism. Of the eight critical possibilities he lists, this chapter is postcolonialist in the sense that it challenges the claims to authority of a Western historiography (in this case of MOC) that has written out colonialism and empire. It does so by taking two of MOC's central techniques, *action research* and *group dynamics*, and demonstrating that both have a history, hitherto unacknowledged by their orthodoxy, as responses to the struggle against imperialism. That this history has been suppressed (consciously or otherwise) is all the more telling given the particular claims made for these techniques as empowering, and giving voice to the powerless (e.g., Reason & Bradbury, 2001a). MOC is consequently revealed as one of the "...ways of perceiving, organizing, representing and acting upon the world which we designate as 'modern' [which] owed as much to the colonial encounter as they did to the industrial revolution, the Renaissance and the Enlightenment" (Seth, Gandhi, & Dutton, 1998: 7).

This chapter deals with events, which took place about 50–60 years ago (particularly leading up to 1946) in the United States. These temporal and spatial locations may appear to make the linkage with colonialism problematic. The great European empires began to disintegrate more or less around that time; and the United States never was, it is claimed, an imperial power in the same sense (Chen, 2001). Both claims can be challenged on their own terms, of course. Temporally, some nations did not achieve independence until the 1960s and 1970s and beyond, and indeed attempts to impose rule from the metropolitan centers of the United States, Britain, and France continued throughout the twentieth century (Cooke, 2001a). But more importantly, postcolonialism here is not seen as primarily referring to an era, but to a relatively distinct epistemology and methodology. As understood in this chapter, in part, postcolonial theory is—as Seth et al. make it clear—about revealing the debt to empire in *contemporary* ways of knowing and acting in the world.

Chen (2001), drawing on Kaplan (1993), argues that postcolonialists have not taken the United States as seriously as they should as an imperial power because of the peculiarities of U.S. imperial expansion, particularly its use of commerce rather than formal territorial acquisition and, in Asia, its post-1945 assumption of Japan's imperial role. The United States did, in any case, hold formal imperial possessions in Asia and Latin America. Moreover, its very creation as a nation required the colonialist oppression of its indigenous population, and of millions of enslaved Africans and their descendants (LaFeber, 1993), and it is these two colonial engagements in particular that this chapter deals with. Space permitting, an extended case for describing them as colonial could be made. For example in the postcolonial canon, notwithstanding Chen, the position of African Americans with respect to global processes of imperialism and colonialism has been the subject of complex analysis and theorizing. Bhabha (1994) presents nuanced arguments regarding, for example, hybridity, consciousness, and identity, whereas Gilroy (1993) identifies a Black Atlantic diaspora, in work that has overt links to the early and mid-twentieth-century Pan-Africanism of W. E. B. Dubois.

From this latter position, the fight of Africans and of African Americans against racism, colonialism, and its modern manifestations, has always been in many (but not all) respects a common struggle. However, not only is the presentation of this case not possible, space-wise; it is not necessary. This is because the two key individuals involved in the invention of action research and group dynamics, John Collier and Kurt Lewin, themselves made explicit the relationship between colonialism and their own work.

Following this introduction, I will in the next brief section explain the central part played by action research and group dynamics in MOC. The section following that begins by setting out the significance attributed to Kurt Lewin (1890–1947) as the inventor of group dynamics, action research, and other key change management ideas, and identifying the moment of their invention in 1946 in New Britain, Connecticut, U.S.A. It then goes on to explore the genuine ambivalence surrounding Lewin and New Britain in relation to imperialism. Lewin's position on U.S. imperialism provides a personal link to a consideration of John Collier, who was the Commissioner of the U.S. Bureau of [American] Indian Affairs (BIA) from 1933 to 1945. Collier's advocacy of a version of colonial administration known as indirect rule and its relation to the invention of action research is discussed. In the conclusion, I explore the implications of this chapter's analysis for current theorizing and practice in two domains, (a) action research/group dynamics/ MOC and (b) Critical Management Studies (CMS). Inasmuch as it demonstrates MOC's role in sustaining a particular set of power relations, this chapter (like others in this volume) might be seen to fall within CMS (see Grey & Fournier, 2000). At the same time, its particular postcolonialist understanding sheds new light on CMS itself.

Action Research and Group Dynamics in the Management of Culture Change

Changing Organizational Culture

Organizational culture is variously defined as shared values, attitudes, assumptions, beliefs, and so on (Morgan, 1997). Beneath this diversity of definitions, however, a single managerialist assumption seems to exist. This is that workers' behavior is determined by their "culture," and can be changed—"improved"—by changing this culture (see, famously, Peters &

Waterman, 1982). The field of Organization Development (OD), a planned approach to organizational change, is where this concern with MOC initially achieved its greatest coherence (see French & Bell, 1998). The two ideas of action research and group dynamics, which this chapter addresses, might at one stage in the history of management have been solely associated with OD. Now, however, group dynamics and action research are also important in other approaches to MOC, for example, Total Quality Management (TQM). Action research also has a life of its own in management and organizational studies, and in the social and behavioral sciences more generally. Recent years have also seen the production of an extensive literature in the field (as exemplified, for instance, by the forty-five separately authored chapters in Reason & Bradbury, 2001b). This chapter therefore also provides some (very limited) balancing of this largely acritical output.

Action Research

Action research brings four key principles to MOC. The first—of action being informed by data collection and research—is evident in both OD and TQM implementation processes (see Cooke, 1992). The second—of a sequential and often iterative sequence of intervention steps—is manifested in models of planned change and of organizational consultancy processes in general (famously in Lippitt, Watson, & Westley, 1958), and in OD and TQM processes aimed at culture change in particular.

The third principle is the requirement of a collaborative/participative relationship between the change agent (i.e., the researcher) and client (i.e., the researched). The claims for empowerment associated with action research have their roots in this very collaboration. The argument, in short, is that the participants' participation gives them otherwise unavailable control over events, and that the very process of participation extends their problem-solving capabilities (exemplified in Schein, 1987a,b). The fourth principle is the need for a shared change agent/client understanding of the need for change. The third and fourth principles together are also taken to engender a sense of "ownership" of the change process amongst employees it affects. They offer a socialization process that leads to an internalization of, and commitment to, both the need to change an organization's culture, and to the new form that that culture is to take. Both principles are particularly evident in the literature on change agency and culture change, for example, in Lippitt and Lippitt's (1978) standard text on the consultancy process, and in Schein's equally important volumes on Process Consultation and OD (Schein, 1987a, 1988).

Group Dynamics

Theories of group dynamics address the social psychological processes within small groups of people. Managerial uses of group dynamics first emerged in the 1950s and 1960s fad for T-(training) groups, also known as laboratory or sensitivity training. Trainees' analyses[2] of the group dynamics in the T-group in which they were participating were intended to provide insights into their own interpersonal behavior, and into the values and beliefs upon which this behavior was founded. These insights were often, ultimately, supposed to lead to changes in attitudes, and hence, in an organizational setting, to culture change. T-groups seem to have been unfashionable for a while (Pettigrew, 1985), although there are consultancies that still offer them. There has, however, been a permanent managerial interest in the use of teamwork and teambuilding as a component of culture-change programs, and as a means for improving organizational effectiveness (see, e.g., Wilkinson, 1990; and Grint, 1994, in relation to TQM and Business Process Reengineering (BPR), respectively); and as Kleiner (1996) and Hanson and Lubin (1995) have argued, managerial teambuilding processes are built on theories of group dynamics.

We may conclude this section by noting that the central position that these two sets of ideas have within MOC is mutually reinforcing. They are, as I will show, often represented as having been developed in conjunction with one another, and often tend to overlap. Thus, for instance, in action research processes in organizations, it is often group dynamics processes that are the focus of research.

Situating the Invention of Group Dynamics and Action Research

Lewin the Father

In the management orthodoxy, Kurt Lewin (1890–1947) stands as the most important individual in the history of change management, and in MOC. For Burke he is "the theorist amongst theorists" (1987: 37). Kleiner claims that "nearly every sincere effort to improve organizations from within can be traced back to him" (1996: 30). For Schein (1980: 238) "there is little question that the intellectual father of contemporary theories of applied behavioral science, action research and planned change is Kurt Lewin." According to Burnes (1996: 180), action research was a "term coined by Lewin (1946) in an article called *Action Research and Minority Problems.*" Likewise Lewin is credited as the inventor not just of the idea of group dynamics, but of the actual term (Marrow, 1969).

Lewin has other inventions to his name, for example, force field analysis, a change management problem-solving technique, and the three-stage "unfreeze/change/refreeze" model of change management. He is also seen as important for his determination to apply research rigors—indeed science—to real-world problems, embodied in his aphorism, "there's nothing so practical as a good theory" (cited in Marrow, 1969: ix). Moreover, it is clear that Lewin inspired a generation of his students and collaborators who were, after his death, to become leading figures and theorists of OD and MOC in their own right, for example, Ronald Lippitt, Kenneth Benne, and Leland Bradford. In the introduction to their change-management classic, *The Dynamics of Planned Change*, which is dedicated to Lewin's memory, Lippitt, Watson, and Westley (1958: vii) claim to have been "greatly stimulated by the ideas and example of Kurt Lewin." More recently, Chris Argyris, currently a guru of organizational learning, has claimed Lewin as an important influence (interviewed in Pickard, 1997).

In Cooke (1999), I argued that orthodox histories of change management had written out Lewin's left politics. This was evident, among other things, in his membership and then presidency of the Society of Psychologists for the Study of Social Issues (SPSSI). During this presidency in 1941–1942, SPSSI activist Goodwin Watson and a colleague were accused by Representative Dies, Chair of the House Un-American Activities Committee, of being "federal employees whose activities were proven to be interwoven with communist front organizations" (Sargent & Harris, 1986: 49). Although the Supreme Court ruled in Watson's favor, his post was nonetheless abolished by the Congress. Watson (who was to become the first editor of the *Journal of Applied Behavioral Science* in 1962) then went to work with, among others, the American Jewish Congress's Commission on Community Inter-relations (CCI), founded by Lewin in 1944 (Marrow, 1969). It is when we turn toward the CCI and its group dynamics and action research work that we begin to notice some ambivalence with respect to imperialism/colonialism. This ambivalence requires more than a dichotomous identification of Lewin and this work as either anti- or pro-imperialist/colonialist. Lewin's work can clearly be described as antiracist, and by his own word, anti-imperialist. However, as will become clear, this is not the only possible interpretation.

The New Britain Workshop

If Lewin is the founding father, then the single defining event in the history of change management and MOC is a workshop conducted by the CCI in 1946, in New Britain, Connecticut. This workshop, which came to be known as the "New Britain workshop," was set up by Lewin at the request of the Connecticut State Interracial Commission and staffed, among others by Bradford, Benne, and Lippitt (see Lippitt, 1949). Here, it is claimed, the learning and potential for achieving attitude change through reflective feedback on intrapersonal, interpersonal, and group processes as they happened first became apparent. According to Burke (1987: 26, quoting Carl Rogers), "this interactive mode of learning, which had its beginnings that summer in Connecticut was to become 'perhaps the most significant social invention of the [twentieth] century.'" The New Britain workshop led to the establishment, soon after Lewin's death, of what became the National Training Laboratory (NTL). NTL developed the T-groups from which the managerial applications of group dynamics sprang.

I have previously argued (Cooke, 1999) that, with few exceptions (e.g., Bell, 2001), the point is rarely made that the CCI workshop of 1946 was about relationships between ethnic groups. Neither is it acknowledged in the management literature that 29 percent, the largest proportion, of the forty-one community activist delegates at New Britain were African Americans. Twenty-five percent were Jewish American, 23 percent English American, 13 percent Irish American, 5 percent Canadian American, and 5 percent Italian American. This at a time when the United States was an apartheid state, when segregation was legal, where African Americans were denied the vote, and lynchings of African Americans were frequent (see Paterson, 1996). In the context of this chapter, it is important to recognize that in his account of the workshop (in *Action Research and Minority Problems*), Lewin aligned the antiracist struggle within the United States with a global struggle against imperialism. Lewin here must in fairness be quoted verbatim (1946: 45–46):

> Inter-group relations in this country will be formed to a large degree by the events on the international scene, and particularly by the fate of the colonial peoples. . . . Are we . . . to regress when dealing with the United States' dependencies to that policy of exploitation which has made colonial imperialism the most hated institution the World over? Or will we follow the philosophy which John Collier has developed in regard to American Indians and which the Institute for Ethnic Affairs is proposing for the American dependencies? This is a pattern which leads gradually to independence, equality and cooperation. Whatever the effect of a policy of permanent exploitation would be on the international scene, it could not help but have a deep effect on the situation within the United States. Jim-Crowism on the international scene will hamper tremendously progress of intergroup relations within the United States and is likely to endanger every aspect of democracy.

Lewin's position is therefore apparently close to that of, for example, Dubois in that he aligns the internal processes of the United States with those of colonialism and imperialism globally. This has to be seen as a courageous statement on Lewin's part, given his personal experiences of Nazism and of the House Un-American Activities Committee, and the fragility of his status as an exile (although by then he was a U.S. citizen). However, in his praise of John Collier—who is addressed in his own right later in this chapter—and by using the word "gradually" in the quoted statement, Lewin adopts a position that is far removed from the Pan-Africanist calls of the time for immediate independence. Moreover, once New Britain is situated within the history of African American opposition to racism, rather than that of MOC, a quite different, and more problematic, understanding of its relation to the consequences of empire emerges.

New Britain and an Old Struggle

In "Action Research and Minority Problems" Lewin claims that in terms of intergroup relations "one of the most severe obstacles in the way of improvement seems to be the notorious lack of confidence and self-esteem of most minority groups ..." (1946: 44). Certainly, African Americans could find themselves the subject of vicious punishment if their behavior did not meet the standards of deference demanded by many white Americans. However, the extent of African American organization and struggle in the years surrounding the New Britain workshop seems to suggest that lack of confidence and self-esteem was not the problem. A more or less contemporary account of that struggle, which does not figure in histories of action research and group dynamics, can be found in John Hope Franklin's 1947 classic, *From Slavery to Freedom*.[3]

Franklin shows both the pervasiveness of institutional racism within what Roosevelt had called "The Arsenal of Democracy", and the determination of African Americans to oppose it, while still fighting fascism overseas. For example, the African American newspaper, *The Pittsburgh Courier*, "waged a 'Double-V' campaign, victory at home as well as abroad" (1947: 579). Franklin also describes how A. Philip Randolph, President of the International Brotherhood of Sleeping Car Porters, set in motion a plan for 100,000 men to march on Washington D.C. in 1941, in response to which Franklin Roosevelt issued Executive Order 8802, which sought to end segregation in the defense industries. Elsewhere, Savage (1999) shows how African Americans between 1938 and 1948 sought to challenge racism not through the micro-processes of group dynamics but through the mass medium of radio dramas, documentaries, and political programming. In her introduction, Savage warns against the homogenization of the African American struggle, pointing out that there were differing political positions, organizations, and strategies, and that the tactics pursued varied over time and in different parts of the United States.

According to Kryder (2000), however, the fact that a unified, coherent Black liberation movement did not emerge was not just because of the heterogeneity of the struggle. It was also because U.S. government officials developed a range of responses to defuse and address African American unrest on a case-by-case basis. Some of these responses were new. Thus Kryder speaks of innovation in "the field of surveillance..." where a "more complex repertoire of measures" (2000: 250) was developed. Even though New Britain took place after the war's end, the workshop, and consequently group dynamics and this application of action research, can be read as exemplars of these measures.

We need to recall here that the New Britain workshop was run by the CCI at the request of the Connecticut State Interracial Commission. Of such Commissions generally from 1944 onwards, Wynn notes that they were often established to try and forestall riots, and that they often "centered their attentions on building goodwill" (1976: 108) rather than on addressing fundamental problems such as poverty, or discrimination in housing and employment. Typical, in this respect, Wynn suggests, was the work of the American Council of Race Relations. Lewin mentions this Council positively, if only in passing, in "Action Research and Minority Problems." He also appears to anticipate Wynn's critique:

> ...let us examine the way...intergroup relations are handled. I cannot help feeling that the person returning from a successful goodwill meeting is like the captain of a boat who somehow feels that his ship steers too much to the right and therefore has turned the steering wheel sharply to the left. Certain signals assure him that the rudder has followed the mover of the steering wheel. Happily he goes to dinner. In the meantime of course, the boat moves in circles. In the field of intergroup relations all too frequently action is based on observations made "within the boat" and all to seldom based on objective criteria regarding to the relations of the movement of the boat to the objective to be reached. (Lewin, 1946: 38)

Alfred Marrow notes that this was a matter of dispute in the CCI (1969: 197), and that there was debate about whether its goal should be institutional change (e.g., the removal of racist discrimination in universities, housing, and employment), or rather, to change attitudes. Marrow does not say how this dispute was resolved. But the outcomes of the New Britain suggest, notwithstanding Lewin's warning, that the workshop did worse than merely focus on, as Lewin had it, what was happening "within the boat," and downplay a broader struggle. Rather, the evidence, supplied by Lippitt (1949: 193), demonstrates that the emphasis on personal feelings and group dynamics at New Britain actually shifted participants' desires for action to this *micro level*, and away from the broader agenda of antiracist social change. What was invented there, then, was a method that had precisely the effect that Wynn identified, namely of focusing on "goodwill" (1976: 108) to the exclusion of issues such as employment, housing, poverty, and opposing racism per se.

Amongst the tables in Lippitt's 1949 report is empirical data that seem to confirm this. To illustrate, goals of "improving employment opportunities" were reported by 24 percent of participants before the workshop, and by only 8 percent after it. The figures for "improving housing conditions, decreasing discrimination in housing" were 20 percent before and 7 percent after. Thirteen percent of participants made "statements about improving equality" ("vague," according to Lippitt) before the workshop, none made such statements after. However, the proportion with the goals of bringing groups together in "cooperative working relations" increased from 20 to 27 percent, of re-educating attitudes and behaviors from none to 16 percent. Sixteen percent had mentioned "education to improve inter-group understanding" purely in the classroom context before the workshop. After the workshop, 30 percent had this goal, apparently in a more general sense (all figures from Lippitt, 1949: 193). Lewin's assertions against Jim Crow suggest that this occurred despite the best of intentions on the part of Lewin and his collaborators. It must also be remembered, of course, that "Action Research and Minority Problems" was published after the New Britain workshop, and that Lewin's "in the boat" warnings may be a sign that Lewin himself had reservations about its process.

John Collier: Action Research, Colonial Administration, and Indirect Rule

John Collier is mentioned in very few histories of MOC, all of which track back to French and Bell (1998), where he is said to have invented action research simultaneously with, but "independently" of Lewin. Collier was Commissioner of the [U.S.] Bureau of [American] Indian Affairs under Roosevelt, after which, in 1945, he founded the Institute of Ethnic Affairs (IEA), of which Lewin was a vice-president. In his autobiography, Collier describes how the then Israeli ambassador, Eliahu Elath, and Kurt Lewin met at his home in 1946 to plan "an action-research institute, or an ethnic affairs institute for the Middle East" (1963: 334). This plan was cut short, according to Collier, by the war that soon followed, and by Lewin's untimely death.[4]

There is, therefore, at least some suggestion that Lewin and Collier did not invent action research independently of one another (see also Cooke, 1998, 1999). Moreover, in an article published in 1945 Collier claims, and is supported by evidence elsewhere (Philp, 1977), to have been carrying out action research from the 1930s onwards. In this article, Collier (1945: 275) lists a number of principles that underpinned his time with the BIA. Principle seven (also cited by French & Bell):

> ... I would call the first and the last; that research and then more research is essential to the program, that in the ethnic field research can be made a tool of action essential to all the other tools, indeed that it ought to be the master tool.... We had in mind research impelled from central areas of needed action.... since the finding of the research must be carried into effect by the administrator and the layman, and must be criticized by them through their experience, the administrator and the layman must participate creatively in the research, impelled as it is from their own area of need.

One action-research success Collier identifies was a land reform/soil conservation project with the people of Acoma, where (1945: 285)

> ... no divorce was created by the old lasting life, its consecrations, its hopes, and the new life; instead, the old life created the new, and no dichotomy arose at all, no split in the community organization, no conflict between fundamentalism and science, and no conflict between world views.

What Collier does not mention is that those being invited to engage with modernity while maintaining their "old world view" often saw themselves as belonging to sovereign nations with relationships to the United States defined by binding treaties. From this position, action research was an impugning of sovereignty and autonomy (see Costo, 1986). Moreover, some of my own earlier work on Collier was remiss in failing to take note of Hauptmann's (1986) revelation of Collier as a self-described "colonial administrator." Particularly telling, Hauptmann shows that Collier's espousal of American Indian self-government was always within the limits prescribed by the British model of colonial administration known as "indirect rule." Collier claimed to be inspired by indirect rule, the principles of which were most famously set out in the British colonial administrator Lord Lugard's, *The Dual Mandate in British Tropical Africa* (1922).

Lugard argued that British colonial rule could only be sustained "indirectly" by co-opting (and in reality, often creating) "native" (*sic*) institutions. Hence the idea of indirect rule, the essential feature of which is that "native chiefs are constituted as an integral part of the machinery of the administration," however, the "chief himself must understand that he has no right to place and power unless he renders his proper services to the [imperial] state" (Lugard, 1965: 207). Hence also, for instance, Mamdani's account of a "separate but subordinate state structure for natives" (1996: 62). Mamdani also notes the pejorative and offensive nature of the terms "native" and "tribes," and argues that the investing (not to mention invention) of "chiefs" with administrative power led to forms of decentralized despotism.

Following Lugard, indirect rule was subsequently endorsed by, among others, the British liberal imperialist Huxley, who states in *Africa View* (1931: 103):

Indirect rule, in fact, means the employment of the existing institutions of the country for all possible purposes to which they are adequate, their gradual molding by means of the laws made and taxes imposed by the Central [i.e. colonial] Government and of the guidance given by administrative officers, into channels of progressive change, and the encouragement within the widest limits of local traditions, local pride and local initiative, and so of the greatest possible freedom and variety of local development within the territory.

This paragraph is cited *approvingly* in Collier's memoirs (Collier, 1963: 345), which also discusses British indirect rule in Fiji, India, and Africa. While Collier is far from uncritical of certain manifestations of indirect rule, not least its manipulation by white settlers, he was unquestionably an advocate. Hauptmann also states that Collier made *Africa View* required reading for BIA employees. Collier's position on decolonization, endorsed by Lewin in "Action Research and Minority Problems" was the British liberal imperialist view that fulfillment of "British responsibility to the Africans will take a century" (Hauptmann, 1986: 367). Hauptmann also cites a BIA employee in Collier's time stating that Collier set up participatory experiments because "he believed that students of group activities among exotic peoples might demonstrate some skill in *manipulating* them" (1986: 371, italics added).

Compared to both his predecessors and successors Collier was a comparatively liberal figure, and a debate continues about his real significance. Biolsi (1992), referring specifically to the Lakota, sees Collier's legacy as paradoxical. Under his rule, BIA actions actually contradicted its official discourse of empowerment, through the use of what Biolsi describes as various technologies of power and surveillance. Nonetheless, Biolsi argues that Collier changed the way in which power was represented, "opening up the political space for all Lakota people of all political stripes..." (1992: 85), and that the "postcolonial culture of Indian affairs is [an] important legacy of... [Collier's] Indian New Deal". Moreover there can be no doubt that Collier, like Lewin, was of the political left (Cooke, 1999), and that some of the criticisms aimed at Collier—arguably, for example, those of Costo (1986)—were partly prompted as reactions to this left politics. It is nonetheless incontrovertible that action research emerged in an institution of colonial rule, albeit rule exercised within U.S. continental boundaries. It did so under the leadership of an individual committed to a particular form of colonial administration, indirect rule. This provided for an appearance of autonomy (as does action research) as an alternative both to the more obvious tyranny of direct rule, and to the immediate over-throw of imperial power. Moreover, Kurt Lewin, the "official" inventor of action research and group dynamics, apparently supported Collier in this respect.

Discussion and Conclusion

This chapter has challenged the very foundation of the claims for collaboration, participation, and empowerment associated with MOC in general, and action research and group dynamics in particular. Thus far, historiographies of this field have been presented primarily from a narrow, technocratic and managerialist standpoint. That view has been challenged here by one that attempts to foreground African American and Native American "participants," and that seeks to understand their involvement with the project of action research and group dynamics mostly in terms of their response to the impact of colonialism, imperialism, and racism on their lives. What emerges as a result is a recognition that the invention of action research and group dynamics may be viewed as an outcome of a state-sponsored U.S. attempt to manage, contain, and shape challenges to existing political, economic, social, and cultural order. Ironically, action research, group dynamics, and consequently MOC are revealed as products of an imperial resistance to change, rather than facilitators of genuine social change.

This is not to suggest that the liberal intentions of Lewin and his colleagues, and of Collier, were anything but genuine. As this chapter has made clear, both Collier and Lewin were more critical of U.S. imperialism than was generally the case in the white politics of the time. Collier should also at the very least be commended for his public and repeated argument that the U.S. state's relationship to Native Americans was as colonialist as that of traditional European imperial powers to those in their colonies. That MOC at its very beginning was such a problematic enterprise, however, is cause for some concern now, six decades later, in relation to two current areas of theorizing and practice. The first, not surprisingly is action research/group dynamics and MOC; the second is Critical Management Studies.

Action Research, Group Dynamics, and MOC

Central to the literature on action research and group dynamics, and MOC more generally, are calls for a deep and genuine reflexivity on the part of the practitioner. The underlying argument, that the practitioner must be conscious of his or her own embedded cultural assumptions before changing those of others, is both practical and ethical. Interventionists' cultural biases will frame their understanding of "clients" cultures and how they should change. In instrumental terms, unacknowledged biases may impinge on the success of a culture-change project, by, for example, making it difficult for the practitioner to step outside his or her own cultural assumptions the better to understand the other. Ethically, it is seen as wrong to subject someone else's culture to deep scrutiny and adjudge it in need of change without doing the same for oneself (see, e.g., Schein, 1987b, 2001; Lippitt & Lippitt, 1978).

What this chapter has shown is how shallow, self justifying, and deceiving that reflexivity has actually been. The story of the invention of action research and group dynamics plays an important—indeed foundational— part in the construction of MOC as a body of theorizing and practice, and in providing the consequent interventions in people's working lives with some legitimacy (at least in the eyes of the interventionist and those who pay them). In writing that story from the point of view of the interventionist, rather than the participant, theorists of action research and group dynamics have not only been hypocritical on their own terms (because of the evident falsehood of the claim to give voice to the powerless); they have served to conceal from themselves, and from their clients, the extent to which their practices have, from the very start, been more about manipulation (unwitting though it may be) rather than emancipation.

The other consequence of privileging the interventionist in the MOC narrative is that the assumption that he or she is right, and has the right, to intervene in other people's social organizations, goes unchallenged. The uncomfortable question for those of us on the left, and/or with liberal/progressive aspirations, is whether this assumption is valid. Some writers on MOC (see again Schein, 1987b) have made the obvious point that social interventions influence power relations, and that interventionists must be prepared to accept the consequences of their action. It follows, therefore, that this chapter (as a case study) demonstrates the need for a far more sophisticated and nuanced understanding of the political and institutional dynamics in which an interventionist operates. Also required for intervention would be an awareness of the colonialism inherent in the particular ways of knowing and acting associated with MOC. This is most evident currently in the World Bank's use of the language and processes of MOC in the imposition of neoliberal social and economic policy on Third World nations, and in the apparent complicity of MOC practitioners in this (see Cooke, 2002; Marshall & Woodroffe, 2001). The danger is that the glaring nature of this replication of the uses of MOC to sustain indirect rule (Cooke, 2001a) shades the day-to-day quasi-colonialist practices in MOC's workplace usage.

A greater danger still is that in presenting this call for a better—more nuanced, more institutionally and geo-politically aware—version of MOC, I continue to privilege its status by assuming that MOC should continue. The alternative to the argument of the previous paragraph is to halt all action research, group dynamics, and MOC interventions. As Uma Kothari and I have argued in the context of participatory international development (Cooke & Kothari, 2001; see also Cooke, 2001b), a genuinely open minded reflexivity must surely include a willingness to abandon particular practices if required. That requirement is suggested here both by MOC's roots in colonial/imperial manipulation, and in the very denial thereof. This denial is all the more startling in that MOC, group dynamics, and action research are, on the one hand, far from under-researched (e.g., Reason & Bradbury, 2001a), and on the other, that the interpretation of events here is based not on extensive archival inquiry in the United States, but on fairly straightforward published-literature-based-research conducted in the United Kingdom. Metaphorically speaking, writers on MOC have had to look quite hard in the other direction in order to *avoid acknowledging their colonialist heritage.*

Critical Management Studies (CMS)

There are, of course, critiques of managerial attempts to shape organizational culture, which have preceded this chapter, particularly those associated with

CMS. Action research and group dynamics have been seen as important tools (Cooke, 1999) in what Alvesson and Willmott (1996: 31) have called "the strategic re-engineering of employee norms and values" in line with those "identified by top management or their consultants and legitimized by academics." An associated long-standing critique is that MOC focuses on the mechanics of organization change and ignores the historical and immediate contexts of change (Pettigrew, 1985; Wilson, 1992). Wilson also points out that this is reinforced by the immediacy of the "here and now" ("in the boat," as Lewin would have had it). It is also widely argued that participatory approaches to management, which action research and group dynamics exemplify, are used to try to co-opt otherwise resistant workers into supporting managerial agendas—in other words that participation in the workplace can be a technique, to use to Kryder's (2000) term, to "defuse" workplace unrest (Alvesson & Willmott, 1996; Willmott, 1993).

In a way, this chapter can just be seen as an addition to this genre, contributing the irony that these problems with MOC have existed ever since it was first invented, albeit not in the context of work organizations, but in that of the struggle against the consequences of colonialism/imperialism and racism. But it should also give CMS cause for concern on its own terms. That this truth has been missed signals a conceptual gap in CMS's understandings of management. This gap relates to the organizational and managerial processes and complexities of imperialism. At the risk of oversimplifying, management ideas and practices are identified in CMS as emerging from the need to get workers to engage with (initially) U.S. and European industrialization, and (more recently) with the global spread of post-Fordism (e.g., Clegg, 1990). Insofar as CMS depicts management as a consequence of capitalism alone, it is not all that far from the managerialist orthodoxy (e.g., Chandler, 1977). Empire, in other words, is absent from CMS; yet imperialism was *organized*, and it was *managed*.

Thus this particularly narrow version of the history of capitalist development completely ignores the role of imperialism and colonialism (and subsequently neo-colonialism and neo-imperialism) as its driver (Hobsbawm, 1968). In that this kind of analysis goes as far back, inter alia, as Lenin in 1917 (cf. Lenin, 1947), this absence can hardly be explained by the relative novelty of postcolonialism. Not that, we may note in passing, novelty is an acceptable explanation in any case, given CMS's proclaimed theoretical eclecticism (Grey & Fournier, 2000), and the enthusiasm for postcolonialism elsewhere in the academy, characterized by Slemon as the *Scramble for Postcolonialism*. Given the claims that CMS makes for itself, this absence of empire is therefore as telling as the equivalent absence from MOC/action research/group dynamics. Until the present volume, CMS too seems to have been looking hard in the other direction. This suggests that the approach followed in this chapter—which puts the idea of capitalist development to one side, and looks for the contribution of imperialism per se to the development of management—is required, at the very least, as a remedy to this strange oversight on the part of CMS. Cooke (forthcoming), which presents managerialism's debt to modern American slavery, and Raza Mir, Ali Mir, and Punya Upadhyaya's, and Denis Kwek's chapters in this volume are starters in this direction. Together we point to a need for a thoroughgoing postcolonialist revision of management history.

Notes

1. Not the first such. "Organizational Culture and Imperialism" is a subheading in Mills and Helms Hatfield's (1999) chapter on the continuities between imperialism and globalization.
2. "Facilitated" by a trainer.
3. Now in its 8th edition, with CD ROM.
4. This, in turn, may be seen as pointing to Lewin's Zionism (cf. e.g., Marrow, 1969). This would be a very important issue for this chapter to consider if there were more evidence available of the consequences of this for the development of action research/group dynamics. However, at the moment, any such consideration would be mostly speculative.

References

Alvesson, M., & Willmott, H. C. 1996. *Making sense of management.* London: Sage.

Bell, E. A. 2001. Infusing race into the US discourse on action research. In P. Reason & H. Bradbury (Eds.), *The action research handbook.* London: Sage.

Bhabha, H. 1994. *The location of culture.* London: Routledge.

Bishop, A. J. 1990. Western mathematics: The secret weapon of cultural imperialism. *Race and Class, 32* (2), 51–65.

Biolsi, T. 1992. *Organizing the Lakota.* Tucson: The University of Arizona Press.

Braverman, H. 1974. *Labor and monopoly capital.* New York: Monthly Review Press.

Burke, W. W. 1987. *Organization development—A normative view.* Reading MA: Addison Wesley.

Burnes, B. 1996. *Managing change.* London: Pitman.

Chandler, A. D. 1977. *The visible hand: The managerial revolution in American business.* Cambridge: Belknap.

Chen, K-H. 2001. America in East Asia: The Club 51 syndrome. *New Left Review, 12* (November/December), 73–87.

Clegg, S. R. 1990. *Modern organizations.* London: Sage.

Collier, J. 1945. United States Indian Administration as a laboratory of ethnic relations. *Social Research, 12* (May), 265–303.

Collier, J. 1963. *From every zenith.* Denver: Sage.

Cooke, B. 1992. Quality, culture and local government. In I. Sanderson (Ed.), *Management of quality in local government.* Harlow: Longman.

Cooke, B. 1998. "Participation", "process" and "management": Lessons for development in the history of organization development. *Journal of International Development, 10* (1), 35–54.

Cooke, B. 1999. Writing the left out of management theory: The historiography of the management of change. *Organization, 6* (1), 81–105.

Cooke, B. 2001a. *From colonial administration to development management.* Paper presented at Academy of Management Conference, Washington DC, August.

Cooke, B. 2001b. The social–psychological limits of participation. In B. Cooke & U. Kothari (Eds.), *Participation: The new tyranny?* London: Zed Books.

Cooke B. 2002. Managing the neo-liberalization of the Third World: The case of development administration and management. *Management in Development Paper 3,* Manchester, Institute for Development Policy and Management.

Cooke, B. (forthcoming). The denial of slavery in management studies. *Journal of Management Studies.*

Cooke, B., & Kothari, U. 2001. The case for participation as tyranny. In B. Cooke & U. Kothari (Eds.), *Participation: The new tyranny?* London: Zed Books.

Costo, R. 1986. Contribution to chapter 2, Federal Indian Policy 1933–1945. In K. R. Philp (Ed.), *Indian self rule: First hand account of Indian–White relations from Roosevelt to Reagan.* Salt Lake City: Howe Brothers.

Franklin, J. H. 1947. *From slavery to freedom: A history of American Negroes.* New York: Knopf.

French, W. L., & Bell, C. H. 1998. *Organization development: Behavioral science interventions for organizational improvement.* Englewood Cliffs: Prentice Hall.

Gilroy, P. 1993. *The Black Atlantic: Modernity and double consciousness.* London: Verso.

Grint, K. 1994. Reengineering history: Social resonances and business process reengineering. *Organization, 1* (1), 1–20.

Grey, C., & Fournier, V. 2000. At the critical moment: Conditions and prospects for critical management studies. *Human Relations, 53* (1), 7–32.

Hanson, P. G., & Lubin, B. 1995. *Answers to questions most frequently asked about organization development.* Thousand Oaks: Sage.

Hauptmann, L. M. 1986. Africa view: John Collier, The British Colonial Service and American Indian Policy, 1933–45. *The Historian, 48* (3), 359–374.

Hobsbawm, E. 1968. *Industry and empire.* Harmondworth: Pelican.

Huxley, J. 1931. *Africa view.* London: Chatto & Windus.

Kaplan, A. 1993. Left alone with America: The absence of empire in the study of American culture. In A. Kaplan & D. Pease (Eds.), *Cultures of United States imperialism.* Durham: Duke University Press.

King, D. 1995. *Separate and unequal: Black Americans and the US federal government.* Oxford: Oxford University Press.

Kleiner, A. 1996. *The age of heretics.* London: Nicholas Brealey.

Kryder, D. 2000. *Divided arsenal: Race and state during World War II.* Cambridge: Cambridge University Press.

LaFeber, W. 1993. *The Cambridge history of American foreign relations (Vol. II): The American search for opportunity, 1865–1913.* Cambridge: Cambridge University Press.

Lenin V. I. 1947. Imperialism: The highest stage of capitalism. In V. I. Lenin, *The essentials of Lenin in two volumes* (Vol. 1). London: Lawrence and Wishart.

Lewin, K. 1946. Action research and minority problems. *Journal of Social Issues, 2* (4), 34–46.

Lewin, M. 1992. The impact of Kurt Lewin's life on the place of social issues in his work. *Journal of Social Issues, 48* (2), 15–29.

Lippitt, R. 1949. *Training in community relations.* New York: Harper.

Lippitt, R., & Lippitt, G. 1978. *The consulting process in action.* La Jolla: University Associates.

Lippitt, R., Watson, J., & Westley, B. 1958. *The dynamics of planned change.* New York: Harcourt Brace.

Lugard, F. D. 1965. *The dual mandate in Tropical Africa* (5th ed.). London: Frank Cass & Co.

Mamdani, M. 1996. *Citizen and subject: Contemporary Africa and the legacy of late colonialism.* Princeton: Princeton University Press.

Marrow, A. 1969. *The practical theorist.* New York: Basic Books.

Marshall, A., & Woodroffe, J. 2001. *Policies to roll back the state and privatize? Poverty reduction strategy papers investigated.* London: World Development Movement

Mills, A. J., & Helms Hatfield, J. C. 1999. From imperialism to globalization. In S. Clegg, Ibarra-Colado, & Bueno-Rodriquez (Eds.), *Global management: Universal theories and local realities.* London: Sage.

Morgan, G. 1997. *Images of organization.* London, Sage.

Morris, B. 1994. *1948 and after.* Oxford: Oxford University Press.

Patterson, J. T. 1996. *Grand expectations: The United States, 1945–1974.* New York: Oxford.

Peters, T. J., & Waterman, R. H. 1982. *In search of excellence: Lessons from America's best run companies.* New York: Harper and Row.

Pettigrew, A. 1985. *The awakening giant.* Oxford: Blackwell.

Philp, K. R. 1977. *John Collier's crusade for Indian reform, 1920–1954.* Tucson: University of Arizona Press.

Pickard, J. 1997. Profile: Chris Argyris. *People Management,* 6 March, 34–35.

Rabasa, J. 1993. *Inventing A-M-E-R-I-C-A: Spanish historiography and the formation of Eurocentrism.* Norman, Oklahoma: University of Oklahoma Press.

Reason, P., & Bradbury, H. 2001a. Preface. In P. Reason & H. Bradbury (Eds.), *The action research handbook.* London: Sage.

Reason, P., & Bradbury, H. (Eds.). 2001b. *The action research handbook*. London: Sage.

Said, E. 1994. *Culture and imperialism*. London: Penguin.

Sargent, S. S., & Harris, B. 1986. Academic freedom, civil liberties and SPSSI. *Journal of Social Issues, 42* (1), 43–67.

Savage, B. D. 1999. *Broadcasting freedom: Radio, war and the politics of race, 1938–1948*. Chapel Hill: The University of North Carolina Press.

Schein, E. H. 1980. *Organizational psychology*. Englewood Cliffs: Prentice Hall.

Schein, E. H. 1987a. *Process consultation* (Vol. 2). Reading MA: Addison Wesley.

Schein, E. H. 1987b. *The clinical perspective in fieldwork*. London: Sage Publications.

Schein, E. H. 1988. *Process consultation* (Vol. 1). Reading MA: Addison Wesley.

Schein, E. H. 2001. Clinical Inquiry/Research. In P. Reason & H. Bradbury (Eds.), *The action research handbook*. London: Sage.

Seth, S., Gandhi, L., & Dutton, M. 1998. Postcolonial studies: a beginning . . . *Postcolonial Studies, 1* (1), 7–11.

Slemon, S. 1994. The Scramble for postcolonialism. In C. Tiffin & A. Lawson (Eds.), *De-scribing empire: Postcolonialism and textuality*. London: Routledge.

Wilkinson, A. 1990. Managing human resources for quality. In B. G. Dale (Ed.), *Managing quality*. Hemel Hempstead: Prentice Hall.

Willmott, H. C. 1993. Strength is ignorance; slavery is freedom: Managing culture in modern organizations. *Journal of Management Studies, 30* (4), 515–552.

Wilson, D. C. 1992. *A strategy of change*. London: Routledge.

Wynn, N. A. 1976. *The Afro-American and the Second World War*. London: Paul Elek.

CHAPTER 4

The Empire of Organizations and the Organization of Empires: Postcolonial Considerations on Theorizing Workplace Resistance[1]

Anshuman Prasad and Pushkala Prasad

> Be extremely subtle, even to the point of formlessness. Be extremely mysterious, even to the point of soundlessness.
>
> Sun Tzu, *The Art of War*
>
> When the sign ceases the synchronous flow of the symbol, it also seizes the power to elaborate . . . new and hybrid agencies and articulations.
>
> Homi K. Bhabha, *The Location of Culture*

ecent management and organizational research has frequently noted the complex nature of workplace resistance, and commented upon the difficulties attending scholarly efforts to theorize resistance in organizations (Hodson, 1995; Jermier, Knights, & Nord, 1994a; Prasad & Prasad, 1998, 2000, 2001). The objective of this chapter is to explore the limits/margins of current management scholarship on workplace resistance by means of drawing upon certain aspects of resistance theory that have received attention in postcolonial theory and criticism. In so doing, the chapter seeks to direct scholarly focus toward new—and hitherto relatively unexplored—areas of complexity that may surround management researchers' endeavors aimed at theorizing resistance in organizations. Toward that end, the chapter especially looks at two features often found in postcolonial theoretic meditations on resistance—(a) the notion of "unconscious resistance," and (b) ideas of ambivalence, mimicry, hybridity, and so on and their significance for resistance—and examines the questions, issues, concerns, and dilemmas that they seem to raise for organizational scholars engaged in researching workplace resistance.

Broadly speaking, past research on workplace resistance appears to have followed three major avenues of inquiry. Early organizational research on resistance (e.g., Lawrence, 1969) mostly tended to be managerialist in nature, and was guided by a desire to "overcome" worker resistance to managerial efforts aimed at furthering management's control of the workplace. Subsequent years, however, saw the emergence of a critical stream of research on workplace resistance, which was driven by an emancipatory concern for advancing workers' autonomy (e.g., Braverman, 1974; Burawoy, 1979). For the most part, this stream of research conceptualized worker resistance as acts of organized opposition that attempted to alter the structure of control at the workplace. While so doing, this stream of research sought also to identify the wider structural or ideological forces that might constrain worker resistance. During more recent years, several organizational researchers (Ezzamel, Willmott, & Worthington, 2001; Hodson, 1991; Jermier et al., 1994a; Prasad & Prasad, 2000, 2001) have turned their attention toward "subtle" and everyday forms of resistance with a view to emphasizing the ordinariness and pervasiveness of workplace resistance.[2] This chapter proposes to discuss how certain postcolonialist positions with respect to unconscious resistance, on the one hand, and ambivalence, mimicry, and so on, on the other, raise some important issues for researchers of workplace resistance.

It may be useful to note here that current workplace resistance research is mostly premised on the belief that resistance necessarily means/implies *conscious* resistance; that is, people engaging in resistant actions must be aware and conscious that they are resisting. In contrast, several postcolonial theorists argue that resistance can be either conscious or unconscious (e.g., Bhabha, 1994; Haynes & Prakash, 1991; Nandy, 1983). As we shall see, this relative lack of concern (on the part of postcolonial theory) with self-consciousness raises troubling questions for organizational researchers. Similarly, consider the noted postcolonial theorist, Homi Bhabha's (1994) theorization of colonial ambivalence, mimicry, hybridity, and so on.[3] In the colonial context, mimicry, for instance, has usually been seen as an effect of the colonizer's power and authority, which requires the colonized to internalize the norms and values of the colonizer. Conventionally, therefore, mimicry has been regarded as one more "proof" of the colonizers' hegemony. In a classic act of reinterpretation, however, Bhabha theorizes mimicry as a space for resistance that frustrates the colonizer's desire for hegemony. In sum, Bhabha's theorizations of ambivalence, mimicry, and so on raise intriguing questions for workplace resistance research.

In this chapter, we will analyze the aforementioned aspects of post-colonialist theorizations of resistance, and ponder over the questions and concerns that postcolonialism raises for management researchers interested in studying workplace resistance. To begin with, however, an overview of management and organizational research on workplace resistance may be in order.

Workplace Resistance in Management and Organizational Research

Workplace resistance has attracted the attention of scholars for a long time (Hodson, 1991, 1995, 1999, 2001; Jermier et al., 1994a; Prasad & Prasad, 1998, 2000, 2001). Past research on worker resistance has used the term, resistance, in several senses and under diverse contexts. While seeking to understand past scholarship on workplace resistance, however, a useful distinction may be made between: (a) the relatively new and innovative approaches focusing upon "subtle" and "everyday forms" of resistance, and (b) the more conventional works, which conceptualize resistance some-what differently. In turn, the latter category of research may be seen to comprise two broad groups: (a) managerialist and (b) critical (Nord & Jermier, 1994).

Managerialist versus Critical Research on Workplace Resistance

As we know, the concept of managerialism emerged in the context of theorizations about the rise of the "modern corporation" (Berle & Means, 1932) and the "managerial revolution" (Burnham, 1941; Chandler, 1977), which argued that control in modern firms had passed from owners to professional managers. Gradually, however, managerialism came to be understood as a philosophical orthodoxy or ideology (Deetz, 1992). As a philosophy, managerialism tends to endorse the labor–management dichotomy, and regards management's concern with rationalization and control of work, efficiency and predictability of task performance, and obscuring of organizational conflict, and the like as inherently valuable (Deetz, 1992).

Managerialist researchers mostly tend not to question the preceding (primarily control-oriented) goals of management. These researchers' interest in workplace resistance, hence, mainly surfaces in those situations in which workers oppose and resist managerial efforts to change the arrangement of work with the aim of furthering management's control of the workplace. This research interest, moreover, is explicitly driven by a concern to *overcome* such worker resistance to change efforts initiated by management. Thus, under the rubric of "overcoming resistance to change," managerialist researchers have long studied workplace resistance engendered by such factors as technological change, changes with respect to policy, organizational change efforts stemming from shifts in the external environment, and so on (Child & Smith, 1990; Lawrence, 1969; Pava, 1983). In brief, as Nord and Jermier (1994: 398) note, managerialist researchers hold a "pejorative view" of worker resistance, according to which, resistance is an "undesirable" *problem* for organizations, and their research is primarily guided by a desire to cure or subdue such resistance. Generally seen as starting with Lawrence's (1969) *Harvard Business Review* piece, research in this tradition has continued to prosper. Some recent examples of resistance research in the managerialist tradition include Herbold's (2002) study of overcoming resistance to centralized initiatives in the Microsoft Corporation, Kirkman and Shapiro's (2001) inquiry into the mediating role of employee resistance in assessing the impact of national cultures on job satisfaction and commitment, Schraeder's (2001) analysis of predictors of employee resistance to corporate mergers, Stanley's (2002) ruminations on managing organizational change, Wargin and Dobiey's (2001) essay identifying reasons for employee resistance to change and offering advice on how to deal successfully with such resistance, and so on.

In contrast to managerialist researchers' focus upon facilitating management's control of the workplace (and upon overcoming worker resistance to enlargements of managerial control), the critical stream of resistance research (e.g., Braverman, 1974; Burawoy, 1979; Edwards, 1979; Gordon, Edwards, & Reich, 1982) claims to be motivated by an emancipatory concern for advancing workers' autonomy and interests. Conventional critical research on worker resistance is mostly informed by Marxist and neo-Marxist theories, and is marked (either explicitly or implicitly) by a longing for worker revolution, and radical transformations of prevailing politico-economic structures.

During much of the 1970s and the 1980s, this group of critical researchers was troubled by the fact that working-class revolutions (which had been predicted by orthodox Marxism as occurring with the inevitability of the laws of nature) had failed to take place in the West. These researchers believed that the nonoccurrence of proletarian revolutions in the West implied that workers, as a group, were failing to engage in meaningful acts of resistance. Hence, one of the important research interests of these scholars involved a search for explanations that may account for the workers' failure to revolt, and the political quietism of the working class.

Theorizing the Limits to Workplace Resistance

The critical stream of research concerned with understanding the *absence* of meaningful workplace resistance often seeks to analyze how worker resistance is constrained by wider structural, cultural, and ideological forces. In many respects, this stream of research may be said to have been inaugurated by Harry Braverman's (1974) influential study, *Labor and Monopoly Capital.* Principally, Braverman sought to advance the thesis that macro-structural changes during the late twentieth century exhibited an overall tendency toward the *real* subordination of labor to capital. In brief, Braverman (1974: 113) argued that by "divorc(ing) conception from execution," by rendering "labor process...independent of craft, tradition, and the workers' knowledge," and by planning and executing the division of labor at the most minute of levels, management was in a position of asserting total control over labor. Braverman's (1974) analysis of the labor process, thus, mostly focused upon management's control to the virtual exclusion of worker resistance.

Not surprisingly, Braverman was widely criticized for painting capital in the image of a monolithic and unstoppable juggernaut, for rendering the worker a passive pawn of capital, and for neglecting working-class subjectivity and resistance (Edwards, 1979; Elger, 1979). Notwithstanding such criticisms, post-Braverman studies of the labor process mostly continued to focus upon managerial strategies for the *control* of the worker (and upon how such control constrained worker resistance), rather than upon workplace resistance as such (Burawoy, 1979; Gordon et al., 1982).

A case in point is Michael Burawoy's (1979) important study, *Manufacturing Consent.* In some respects, Burawoy (1979) offers his study in opposition to Braverman's (1974) coercive and constraining account of the labor process, and as an attempt to salvage worker subjectivity. Burawoy (1979: xi) asks himself the question: "Why do workers work as hard as they do?" The answer, he says, is to be found not in coercion, but in the mechanisms through which worker *consent* is produced at the point of production. Following participant observation in a machine shop, Burawoy (1979) proposed that such consent was constructed through the game of "making out," that is, maximizing incentive pay linked to piece-rate (p. 46 ff.). Burawoy (1979: 81) argued that the game of "making out" "insert(ed) the worker into the labor process as an individual rather than as a member of a class distinguished by a particular relationship to the means of production," leading to "voluntary servitude," that is, consent on the part of the worker.

Burawoy's (1979) work is noteworthy for being one of the earliest attempts to restore subjectivity to workers. However, the image of worker subjectivity that emerges from his study is a highly constrained one: it is a subjectivity, which is easily inveigled into the game of "making out," which naively gives full and willing consent to its own domination. As a result, Burawoy (1979) came under extensive criticism (cf. Jermier, Knights, & Nord, 1994b), mainly for not examining the implications of his analysis for worker resistance.

As Burawoy (1979: xii) himself acknowledged, his analysis of the production of consent in the workplace was inspired by the writings of Antonio Gramsci (1971), one of the most prominent of the Western (or Hegelian) Marxists. Western Marxism emerged during the early parts of the twentieth century as a critical response to the economic determinism of orthodox Marxism, and emphasized the importance of understanding culture, consciousness, and subjectivity not as simple reflections of the economic "base," but as relatively autonomous spheres of the wider social reality. Western Marxism, thus, was an important force in restoring the role of subjectivity in radical scholarship.

It is important to remember, however, that, as a group, the Western Marxists too worked within a broad historical context that was largely defined by the failure of the working class to revolt in the West. Frequently, therefore, Western Marxism's investigations of subjectivity became meditations on socio-cultural *impediments* to the emergence of revolutionary consciousness. For example, the Frankfurt School's (e.g., Adorno, 1967; Adorno & Horkheimer, 1979) analyses of commercial culture mostly argued that the culture industry so thoroughly saturated people's consciousness that all possibilities of resistance were erased. Similarly, Lukacs (1971) used such concepts as "reification" and "false consciousness" to account for the ideological domination of the proletariat. And Gramsci (1971) developed the idea of "hegemony" to characterize a social order in which people voluntarily offered their submission (to the dominant groups) without being subjected to coercive force. Even while attempting to restore proletarian subjectivity, therefore, Western Marxism theorized a somewhat constrained subjectivity for the working class, which limited the potential for resistance. As Burawoy's (1979) study shows, the influence of such theorizing was felt among workplace scholars as well, who, as a result, tended to develop a somewhat narrow and incomplete view of worker resistance.

The Turn to "Everyday Forms" of Workplace Resistance

Thus, for the most part, post-Braverman exhortations for studying workplace resistance appear to have spurred more research on managerial control than on resistance to such control. Nevertheless, influenced in part by analyses of "micro practices" of resistance in peasant communities (Scott, 1976, 1985), and by the entreaties of "new social history" (Hobsbawm, 1974) to produce a people's history (or "history from below") focusing upon working-class culture and experience, a significant segment of *critical* scholarship on worker resistance gradually turned toward the study of "everyday forms" of resistance. Studies of everyday forms of workplace resistance focus *not* upon overt and head-on clashes between labor and management, but upon such covert and subtle acts of worker opposition as slowdowns and work-to-rule, foot dragging and work avoidance, whistle blowing and harassing supervisors, impression management and duplicitous conformity, silent protests and withdrawal of cooperation, stealing, theft and pilferage of company property, rumors and gossip, humor, jokes and horseplay, as well as wastage, vandalism and sabotage (e.g., Collinson, 1988; Hodson, 1991, 1995; Jermier, 1988; Martin, 1986; McFarland, 1980; Tucker, 1993). In the main, studies of everyday resistance seek to highlight the facts that (a) managers' control of workers is far from being total, and (b) that worker subjectivity frequently expresses itself in highly creative ways with a view to maintaining its own autonomy and self-worth, and for purposes of constructing an oppositional culture at the workplace.

Organizational scholars' turn toward everyday forms of resistance was occasioned mainly by their uneasiness with a number of limitations of past research. For instance, according to several scholars (Hodson, 1991, 1995; Jermier et al., 1994b; Prasad & Prasad, 1998, 2000, 2001), past research is frequently grounded in an artificial distinction between (a) "real" or "genuine" resistance and (b) everyday forms of resistance. Based as it is upon the Marxist teleology of a proletarian revolution *finally* overthrowing capitalism, this schema considers only those acts (of worker opposition) that are fully informed by class consciousness as belonging to the category of "real" resistance; oppositional activities not informed by such class-consciousness are not regarded as "genuine" acts of workplace resistance. Critics point out that such a distinction between "real" and everyday resistance is arbitrary, and hence, epistemologically unsound. This separation of "real" and everyday resistance may also be seen as partly linked to previous researchers' tendency to regard overt and dramatic expressions of resistance as resistance per se, and to mostly ignore subtle and covert forms of resistance. A major consequence of such exclusive concern with dramatic clashes alone is a serious undercon-ceptualization of resistance in workplace research (Hodson, 1995).

Another limitation of conventional research is exhibited in its propensity to see resistance (or the absence of resistance) as manifesting worker pathol-ogy (Nord & Jermier, 1994). As already alluded to, if managerialists view the presence of worker resistance as an abnormality, critical researchers consider the absence of class-conscious resistance as being an indication of the deeper problems of workers' passivity, division, resignation, and anaesthetization, which are viewed as resulting from structural controls and/or ideological saturation. Thus, both managerialist and critical scholars seem to regard workers' behaviors as symptoms of a deeper pathology, rather than as sensi-ble choices made by knowing men and women. Hence, according to some critics (e.g., Nord & Jermier, 1994: 400), both of these approaches are "pro-foundly elitist." For the critical researcher, moreover, this approach soon leads to the conclusion that full-fledged capitalism destroys all resistance, which results in highly pessimistic theorizing. Such pessimism, however, may not be warranted in the face of ample evidence that points to the unreality of absolute managerial control of the workplace (Ezzamel et al., 2001; Juravich, 1985).

Furthermore, researchers note, traditional scholars' tendency to approach resistance in terms of "universal and totalizing oppositions to capitalism" also leads to an "all or nothing conception of resistance" (Jermier et al., 1994b: 3). The "all or nothing" understanding of resistance seems to be based on the logic that as long as capitalism continues to survive, worker resistance must be missing (Hodson, 1995: 82), and argues, in effect, for recognizing the presence of resistance only in those situations where oppositional activities lead to a thorough overhauling of existing relations of power. Such a dichoto-mous view, however, may ignore the complex nature of resistance. Scholars point out that worker cooperation is frequently accompanied by resistant behavior as well, so that it may be more profitable to view cooperation/adap-tation and resistance as parts of the same continuum, rather than as two binary polarities where the presence of one presupposes the absence of the other (Hodson, 1991; Martin, 1986).

Organizational scholars' dissatisfaction with conventional resistance research stems also from the latter's relative neglect of workers' consciousness and subjectivity (Martin, 1986). Such neglect of subjectivity may be said to derive from two contrasting images of the worker held in traditional work-place research (Martin, 1986). The first of these two images sees workers as "finally" transforming society as a result of their *structural* position within capitalism. For those who subscribe to this image of the worker, it is unnecessary to understand workers' subjectivity, because "the dictatorship of the proletariat is inevitable" (Martin, 1986: 259). In contrast, the second image of workers regards them as "fully incorporated or bought off" by capitalism, with the result that worker subjectivity is treated as marginal because it is seen as lacking "transformative political significance" (Martin, 1986: 259). Coupled in some ways with such neglect of working-class consciousness, traditional research seems to suffer also from a somewhat limited understanding of the worker as an active subject, that is, of worker agency (Hodson, 1991; Nord & Jermier, 1994; Prasad & Prasad, 2000, 2001). If, for managerialism, workers are mere objects of manipulation, for much of past critical research, workers are structurally constrained and/or victims of ideology. Critics contend that, as a result of such *a priori* theoretical images of the worker, conventional research is often undiscerning of diverse forms of actual instances of worker resistance, creativity, and agency.

In a large measure, therefore, the turn toward everyday forms of resistance may be seen as a critical response to past researchers' preoccupation with analyzing the *limits* of workplace resistance. Notwithstanding such criticism of the "limits to resistance" theorizing, several organizational scholars (e.g., Clegg, 1989, 1994; Knights & Morgan, 1990) continue to show interest in understanding the limits placed on worker resistance under contemporary capitalism. Relying upon Michel Foucault's analysis of power, for instance, some researchers (e.g., Knights & Morgan, 1990) have sought to understand the constitution of the so-called 'self-disciplined worker,' which seemingly limits workplace resistance and makes direct management control unnecessary. Similarly, Clegg (1989, 1994) focuses upon the phenomenon of organizational "outflanking" which may minimize worker resistance.

Key Tendencies in Critical Workplace Resistance Research

As the preceding overview suggests, a significant section of critical organizational scholarship has increasingly sought to incorporate greater complexity in its formulations of resistance. This implies, among other things: (a) rejecting a dichotomous notion of control and resistance, (b) emphasizing the significance of subjective consciousness as a mediatory mechanism, and (c) recognizing the existence of a dynamic dialectic between structure and agency in which neither structure nor agency is seen as unidirectionally determining the other. The result, in part, is that resistance has come to be seen as a multidimensional phenomenon (Hodson, 1991), and the earlier binarism between cooperation (or, adaptation) and opposition has been rendered problematic. Concomitantly, resistance has come to encompass *both* overt and covert acts, both head-on clashes as well as subtle acts of worker defiance and creativity.

Along with the aforementioned, scholars of worker resistance also display a tendency to eschew "grand narratives" of class struggle and revolution, and to move toward developing a more local, situational, and context-specific understanding of resistance (cf. Jermier et al., 1994a). Reflecting a general trend in social theory, organizational scholarship has increasingly become somewhat skeptical of grand theories and sweeping generalizations. One important result of such recognition of the limits of grand theory is the heightened attention paid to localized analyses of workplace resistance.

According to some scholars (e.g., Nord & Jermier, 1994), the disaffirmation of grand theory and shift toward localized forms of resistance also imply a greater concern with understanding resistance "in its own terms" (p. 401). For Nord and Jermier (1994), this involves seeking to grasp the subjective meanings that participants *themselves* attach to their oppositional activities. Hence, researchers like Jermier et al. (1994b) are critical of "the tendency of researchers to *impose*, rather than *investigate*, the meaning that subjects themselves attribute to their actions" (pp. 10–11, italics in the original), and stress the importance of taking participants' own words and descriptions seriously. Closely related to such concern with subjective meanings, is the entire realm of how actors' subjectivities are constituted in the first place (e.g., Clegg, 1994; Rofel, 1992).

In sum, the tendency among several contemporary critical researchers of workplace resistance is to emphasize: (a) a more complex and expanded conceptualization of resistance, (b) the importance of understanding local and everyday forms of resistance, (c) the significance of worker consciousness, including a focus upon subjective meanings, the role of consciousness as a mediatory mechanism, and the structure agency dialectic, and (d) investigating the constitution of participants' subjectivity. Closely linked to the above-mentioned tendencies is the critical organizational scholarship's increased recognition of the worker as an active agent. We will now turn our attention toward understanding how certain postcolonial notions seem to raise some vexing questions for researchers of workplace resistance.

Theorizing Unconscious Resistance

One of the important tenets of current management research on workplace resistance is the belief that "resistance requires consciousness" (Clegg, 1994: 295). In other words, for an action to be categorized as resistance, the person or persons engaging in such action must be aware of the oppositional nature of such action. Management and organizational researchers allow that such personal awareness (or consciousness) of the oppositional nature of the action may be high or low, but they insist that there must be "a minimum of some such reflexivity" (Clegg, 1994: 297). In contrast, however, several postcolonial theorists argue that resistance can be either conscious or unconscious (e.g., Haynes & Prakash, 1991; Nandy, 1983). As Nandy (1983: 98) puts it: "Defiance need not always be self-conscious." Or, as Haynes & Prakash (1991: 3) elaborate:

> Resistance, we would argue, should be defined as those behaviors and cultural practices by subordinate groups that contest hegemonic social formations, that threaten to unravel the strategies of domination; *"consciousness" need not be essential to its constitution.* Seemingly innocuous behaviors can have unintended yet profound consequences for the objectives of the dominant or the shape of a social order (italics added).

By way of providing an example of resistance that may not be self-conscious, Nandy (1983) offers the case of a bank clerk who secretly writes poetry. Let us take this example in directions that Nandy (1983) himself may or may not have intended, and try to delineate the conditions under which this worker's action may, arguably, become an act of resistance. Let us imagine that this worker[4] is so fond of writing poetry that he must write poetry even while at work. Let us imagine further that this worker has no conscious complaints against his employer, that he does not consider his activity to be a gesture of defiance against the bank, and that he may even feel somewhat guilty about not putting in an honest day's work because of his fondness for writing poetry. Can this worker's action be considered an act of resistance? According to a significant section of management scholars currently working in the area of workplace resistance, the answer to this question must be in the negative. The answer of several postcolonial theorists, on the other hand, will likely be: 'Whether or not this worker's action may be categorized as an act of resistance depends upon the material and symbolic context and consequences of his action' (cf. Haynes & Prakash, 1991: 4).

In order to better understand the difference between the two perspectives on theorizing resistance (one from within management scholarship and the other postcolonialist), let us further expand on the example of the poetry-writing bank clerk. Let us consider, for instance, the following scenario. What if this clerk had the responsibility for certain key activities in the bank, and as a result of his secret preoccupation with poetry, he neglected his work and, as a result, the bank lost a huge sum of money? Furthermore, what if this loss occurred in the context of an ongoing management–union battle? And, finally, what if, as a result of this huge loss, the bank's management was forced to capitulate in this ongoing labor dispute and to relinquish some significant aspect of its control of the workplace? We then clearly have a situation in which the bank clerk's poetry writing (an action that the clerk himself does not regard as oppositional) has profound consequences for the structure of control within the bank. Several postcolonial theorists, therefore, may categorize this act as an act of resistance. For management and organizational researchers, however, the absence of self-consciousness on the part of the clerk implies that, notwithstanding the profound reshaping of the structure of control as a result of the clerk's action, his action may not be regarded as an act of resistance.[5]

With the preceding as the backdrop, we will now seek to explore some of the questions, issues, and dilemmas that the postcolonial theorization of unconscious resistance poses for management researchers studying workplace resistance. Several observations seem to be in order here. First of all, when the categorization of an act as resistance is linked to (or is contingent upon) the worker[6] being aware of the oppositional nature of his/her act, an important question that arises is: "How do we as researchers successfully and accurately determine whether or not the worker in question was truly aware that his/her action was resistant?" For instance, do we ask the worker himself/herself? Do we take the worker's self-report at its face value? How do we know whether or not the worker is answering our question truthfully? Or, do we ask others (e.g., the worker's peers and colleagues, or supervisor, or manager) for an insight into the worker's state of mind? How do we know for sure that these peers/supervisors/managers have a correct and immaculate understanding of the worker's state of mind?

Second, imagine that a worker engages in Act A, and believes Act A to be resistant in nature. In which case, is the worker's belief about the resistant nature of Act A the necessary and sufficient condition for Act A to be categorized as resistance? For instance, let us imagine that a worker comes to work on time in the morning, works hard the entire day, and then goes home, but he is convinced that he was engaging in genuine resistance. Does that qualify the worker's action to be categorized as resistance? Faced with this scenario, the likely response of the management researcher will be: "No. We must take the consequences of the worker's action in consideration. Only when an act materially or symbolically disrupts (or threatens to disrupt) the accomplishment of control at the workplace, can we categorize the act as resistant." This, according to postcolonialist resistance theory, is true enough. However, the management researcher will insist that, in order for any disruptive act to be categorized as resistance, the worker must be aware of the potentially disruptive nature of the act.

In which case, let us consider the following scenario: the worker arrives late for work, hardly does any work throughout the day, goes home early, and the worker's behavior sets up a chain reaction of similar behavior among her fellow workers that results in the management relaxing a number of control devices. But the worker in question does not believe that she was engaging in resistance. In such a case, the management researcher must conclude that this worker was not engaging in resistant behavior. We would like to suggest, however, that what is more likely in this situation is that the management researcher will refuse to believe that the worker is being truthful. In other words, the management researcher would do his/her best to "prove" that, "in reality," the worker "knew" all along that she was engaging in disruptive behavior. In which case, we are back to our initial dilemma: "How do we ensure that we have a correct knowledge of the worker's state of mind?"

In some ways, this problem is similar to the one commonly faced by judges and juries all the time, namely, how to determine whether or not a crime was premeditated and with malice aforethought? In the context of crime and punishment, the idea of determining whether or not a criminal act was premeditated, may seem to make some sense (inasmuch as, for instance, the severity of punishment can then be linked to the degree and extent of premeditation). For instance, to the extent that a society's response to crime includes the element of punishment, it does make some sense to determine whether Person A killed Person B accidentally/unintentionally, or whether the killing was planned and intentional. However, the question that we (as scholars) need to consider is whether or not we are serving any useful purpose by importing such a logic of crime and punishment into the field of workplace resistance research. It is possible to argue that, to the extent the system of control at the workplace includes recourse to punishment, it may be useful for a superior to determine whether or not any (potentially) disruptive act by a subordinate was done self-consciously. In which case, it would seem that the idea of linking resistance to self-consciousness would be useful mostly to managerialist researchers alone, whose research is motivated by a desire to subdue workplace resistance. But what about non-managerialist researchers? Does the idea of linking resistance to self-consciousness serve some useful purpose for non-managerialist researchers as well?

Arguably, in linking resistance to self-consciousness, the thinking of non-managerialist organizational researchers may be seen as being conditioned by notions of logical consistency. In other words, non-managerialist researchers might believe that simply by virtue of the fact that the logic of premeditation/self-consciousness is employed in the legal system, the same logic must be employed when studying workplace resistance because we must be consistent in our application of logical principles across different spheres of human activity and behavior. In that event, at least three, somewhat related, questions come to mind: (a) Is the notion of logical consistency an absolute "good" so that it must be privileged over other competing considerations? (b) Are the two contexts (viz. the context of the legal system on the one hand and of workplace resistance on the other) similar enough so that it makes sense for us to be consistent in applying the same logic under both these contexts? and (c) What about the argument that our primary concern should not be with logical consistency per se but with the consequences of such consistency? (In other words, that we should be consistent in our application of logical principles across different human spheres only to the extent that the consequences/effects of such consistency are ethically desirable and/or acceptable.)

These are important questions for workplace researchers to ponder over. Moving on in a slightly different (though not altogether unrelated) direction, however, this paper would now like to consider the argument that there may well be more to management scholars' commitment to linking resistance to self-consciousness than mere faith in the unconstrained value of logical consistency. Could it be the case that the shadow of Hegel's philosophy looms large here in more ways than one? To briefly recapitulate some of the well-known conclusions of Hegelian philosophy as developed during the course of his *Phenomenology of Mind* and *Philosophy of History*, according to Hegel (1900, 1967): (a) the teleological end of History is reached when the *Geist* (i.e., the Universal Mind or the Universal Spirit) achieves Absolute Knowledge in the form of self-awareness (in other words, Absolute Knowledge is synonymous with, and nothing other than, self-knowledge), and, moreover, (b) that "Europe [i.e., 'the West'] is absolutely the end of History" (Hegel, 1900: 163). For Hegel, of course, History came to an end in the Europe of his own times; indeed, as Singer (1983: 71) notes, History ended with the writing of the concluding few pages of Hegel's own *Phenomenology of Mind*.

Be that as it may, it is important to emphasize here that Hegelian philosophy embodies the claim not only that Europe/West represents the teleological conclusion of Universal History, but also that such a conclusion to History must necessarily be arrived at: (a) in the cultural space of Europe/West, and (b) that this conclusion can only be arrived at by way of the *Geist* achieving self-consciousness. These are powerful claims with enormous consequences for a number of things, including the cultural valence of the notion of self-consciousness in the West (because, with Hegel's philosophy, self-consciousness now becomes synonymous with Europe's dutiful role as the end of History).

Now as we are well aware, Hegel's philosophy has played an important part in the crafting of the legitimating narratives of European/Western colonialism with its attendant hierarchical binaries of center–periphery, superior–inferior, civilized–savage, developed–backward, the vanguard–the led, and so on and so forth. Partly by the way of these binaries, moreover, Hegelian philosophy has played an active part in constituting the European/Western subjectivity. Indeed, as the contemporary discourses of development, democracy, and the like suggest, Hegelian philosophy continues to remain important to the constitution of the European/Western subjectivity. Could it be that the Western management scholars' commitment to linking workplace resistance to self-consciousness reflects a (witting or unwitting) desire on their part to rescue Hegelian philosophy, and in so doing, to safeguard the aforementioned Western subjectivity that this philosophy has partly helped constitute? On the other hand, could it be the case that the desire for linking worker resistance with self-consciousness is a symptom of a romantic quest for the class-conscious worker who may help usher in the long-awaited proletarian revolution?

Ambivalence and Resistance

As we may recall, a significant section of postcolonial critique is rooted in a recognition of the deep *ambivalence* that invests colonial discourse (Bhabha, 1994). For example, colonial discourse is ambivalent inasmuch as it simultaneously speaks the language of bringing light and civilization to the colonized on the one hand, and of savagery and rapaciousness, on the other; or that even as this discourse talks of "the Rights of Man," it also inscribes unspeakable violence on the colonized. Hence, scholars like Bhabha, for instance, insist that what characterizes colonial discourse is not monolithic homogeneity; quite to the contrary, this discourse is characterized by heterogeneity, fragmentation, contradictions, cracks, fissures, fractures, incongruities, and inconsistencies. Consequently, colonial discourse forever fails in establishing *hegemonic* control and, as a result of such failure, there opens up a space for resistance on the part of the colonized. Bhabha's theorizations of "sly civility," "mimicry," "hybridity," and so on seek to adumbrate the resistance that emerges in this oppositional space.

We noted earlier in this chapter that an important section of current critical research on workplace resistance similarly rejects the idea that contemporary organizations are characterized by regimes of hegemonic control. Indeed, recognizing the worker as an active agent, critical researchers emphasize that the organizational realm is not a domain of worker passivity and inertness, but a turbulent space where worker agency exerts constant pressure on the smooth functioning of managerialist discourse. In firmly rejecting the idea of the triumph of hegemony, these organizational researchers may clearly be seen as theorizing in tandem with those postcolonial scholars who deny the colonizers' hegemony.

Despite such conceptual affinity or parallel, however, so far there does not seem to have been much effort on the part of critical management scholars to seriously engage with the issues that come up during the course of postcolonialist theorizations of ambivalence and resistance. In view of the distinctly ambivalent nature of managerial discourse—seen, for instance, in its celebration of worker autonomy and empowerment, while it simultaneously seeks to inscribe further strategies of surveillance and control at the workplace—such a theoretical engagement would clearly seem warranted. Accordingly, our intention here is to combine/articulate workplace resistance research with postcolonial theoretic ideas of ambivalence, mimicry, and so on, with a view to inviting organizational scholars to examine certain nuances and complexities of (researching) resistance that seem to have remained mostly unexplored in management and organization studies.

Let us consider ambivalence first. Following Bhabha, one may argue that the ambivalence of managerialist discourse (e.g., as noted above, with respect to worker autonomy and empowerment) "threatens the authority of... [managerial] command" (1994: 97). However, as Bhabha himself seems to point out, ambivalence may also be seen as a calculated "strategy of... [domination] and exploitation" (1994: 98). For instance, in the organizational context, the trope of worker empowerment may also be seen as a strategically deployed ideological device, designed to render managerial control more secure. Indeed, several organizational scholars (e.g., Harley, 1999; Sewell, 2001) appear to be making precisely the very point that the project of worker empowerment mostly operates as an ideological instrument.

At the organizational site, however, this would seem to create a situation laden with uncanny ambiguity for, after launching the project of empowerment, the top echelons of the organization would forever remain uncertain as to whether the workers might be "buying" the ideology (resulting in greater managerial control), or whether the workers could possibly be "seeing through" the ruse (potentially leading to increased challenges to managerial authority).[7] In the colonial situation, notes Bhabha, one of the results of such ambiguity is "a vigorous *demand for narrative*" (1994: 98, italics in the original), whereby the colonizer commands the colonized other to authorize the colonizer's self. Rendering Bhabha into the idiom of management, one could say that, faced with the kind of ambiguity spoken of above, the manager seeks "feedback" from the worker with a view to ascertaining how the project of "empowerment" might be faring at the workplace.

It is while discussing the colonizer's aforementioned "demand for narrative" (or feedback) that Bhabha comes to view "sly civility" and "evasions"— which often pepper the feedback provided by the colonized—as acts of resistance (1994: 99).[8] "Sly civility" and "evasions" mark those seemingly ambiguous responses (provided by the colonized) that fail to satisfy the colonizer. Bhabha argues that the colonizer's demand for narrative represents a "narcissistic, colonialist demand that it should be addressed directly, that the Other should authorize the self, recognize its priority . . . and still its fractured gaze" (1994: 98). When—by resorting to sly civility and evasions—the colonized subject addresses the colonizer only obliquely and not directly, and thereby refuses to fulfill the colonizer's wish for unambiguous affirmation, the result is, first, an anxious questioning on the colonizer's part about his[9] own relevance (and about the meaning of the wider colonial enterprise), and, next, a sense of paranoia through which the refusal of the colonized to provide direct answers comes to be "reinscribed as implacable aggression" (Bhabha, 1994: 100). Sly civility, thus, triggers a powerful inner pressure within the colonizer, and appears to have serious consequences for his psychic well-being. It seems to make sense, therefore, to view sly civility as an act of resistance.

Such a perspective could open new avenues of inquiry in workplace resistance research. For the most part, evasive responses by a worker during the "feedback" process are likely to be treated by current management scholarship as survival strategies on the worker's part, or as failures of trust/communication. Such framings have a legitimate place in management research. However, management scholars may also need to focus upon the aspect of resistance embedded in evasions and sly civility, widening in the process the overall extent of workplace resistance research.

Similarly, postcolonial theorizations of mimicry have the potential of further expanding the scope of workplace resistance research. As noted earlier in this chapter and elsewhere,[10] for a number of postcolonial theorists, the imitation of the colonizers by the colonized is "not the familiar exercise of *dependent* colonial relations" (Bhabha, 1994: 88, italics in the original) through which supposedly ideologically saturated colonized subjects become mere replicas of their masters, but rather an act of resistance that constantly menaces and frustrates colonial authority. The applicability of this perspective to workplace resistance research appears to be fairly straightforward.

Imagine, for instance, that a worker arrives at work one day suddenly wearing clothes that are identical to the clothes her/his superior commonly wears. Is this an instance of ideological saturation? Or, do we have here a worker who, by mocking and parodying the superior officer, obstructs the accomplishment of order at the organizational site? And what about acts of mimicry that might not be as blatant or transparent as the one in this example? For instance, what about imitations of "micro" behavior like style of speech, style of dress/demeanor/deportment, or even lifestyle elements (e.g., food, music, art, aesthetics, etc.)? Could these work as acts of opposition too? It would appear that there could be a whole realm of worker mimicry waiting to be investigated for its potentially resistant and subversive implications and consequences. This is a realm that, for a variety of reasons, does not seem to have been explored thus far by researchers of workplace resistance.

In a similar vein, the concept of hybridity would seem to have important implications for workplace resistance scholarship. The notion of hybridity is used in postcolonial theory (e.g., Bhabha, 1994; Nandy, 1983) to refer to a process of cultural "translation" by the colonized—a process in which (because of the relative incommensurability of the *categories* that constitute the different cultural worlds of the colonizers and the colonized) translation across the two worlds leads to "mistaken reading" (Spivak, 1999) or "inappropriate appropriation" (Gandhi, 1998: 150)—that produces uncanny distortions and transformations of the colonizers' original message/command/ discourse. Postcolonial theory regards hybridity as resistance because, by distorting the colonizers' commands, hybridity often thwarts the achievement of their intentions and objectives, and because hybridity "turns the [colonizing] West into a reasonably manageable vector within the traditional worldview" of the colonized (Nandy, 1983: xiii).

Researchers of workplace culture (e.g., Alvesson, 1993; Martin, 1992) have pointed out that organizational cultures frequently consist of multiple subcultures that may exhibit considerable differences with respect to key categories, values, beliefs, stories, myths, and so on. The existence of such cultural differences implies the possibility, within individual organizations, of the kind of "mistranslation" that postcolonial scholars of hybridity have theorized as a form of resistance. This would appear to open a whole new area of inquiry for workplace resistance research. For instance, management researchers might investigate the ways in which differences (e.g., of cultural categories, their meanings, their prioritization, etc.) across organizational subcultures often distort processes of planned organizational change, employee socialization, and so on, and examine how such distortions would operate to block the fulfillment of managerial objectives with a view to assessing the oppositional consequences of hybridity in the organizational realm. In these and other ways, postcolonial notions of ambivalence, mimicry, and so on may have the potential of considerably expanding the ambit of workplace resistance.

Conclusion: The Ethics/Politics of Knowledge

Postcolonial theory is seriously given to the idea that research and scholarship are acts of ethical engagement with the larger world in which we live. Hence, from the postcolonial perspective, research primarily tends to get judged in terms of its ethical/political effects and consequences. As a result, for the postcolonial scholar, research becomes a responsible response (to localized situations as well as to wider socio-cultural and political conditions); a response for which the researcher assumes responsibility. Seen from this viewpoint, when we as management researchers enter a research site (e.g., a corporation), the output of our research must respond responsibly (i.e., in an ethically informed manner) not only to the situation of the corporation at hand, but also to that of the wider context. Research, thus, comes to take the form of ethically informed critique, local as well as global. Moreover, following Mahatma Gandhi (1927, 1951, 1962), we would submit that such an ethical imperative requires, on the part of the (management) researcher, a commitment to *Ahimsa*, or nonviolence (cf. Bilgrami, 2002; Parekh, 1995, 1997). In other words, the "knowledge" that we produce when we study power, control, resistance, and other phenomena at the workplace, or when we as researchers decide to classify certain behaviors as acts of resistance or otherwise—in so far as the effects and consequences of such knowledge are concerned—must support and facilitate *Ahimsa*, and oppose *Himsa* (violence) in all the latter's various guises, including political, economic, cultural, epistemological, and so forth.[11]

Related in some ways to the preceding, what also needs to be emphasized here is that when we categorize a worker's action as resistance or otherwise we are, in many respects, engaging in an exercise in hermeneutic interpretation and understanding—in other words, we are attempting to understand and interpret the "text" that is the worker's action (Prasad, 2002). When management scholars demand that the categorization of a worker's action as resistance be dependent upon the worker's self-awareness of the resistant nature of such action, these scholars, in essence, are insisting that our interpretation of the meaning (or meanings) of the "text" that is the worker's action must be guided by the author-intentional theory of meaning. In this connection, as several hermeneutic philosophers (e.g., Gadamer, 1975, 1976, 1989) have noted, the author-intentional view of meaning relies upon an untenable subject–object dichotomy that sees a radical separation between the "text" (i.e., the object) and the reader–interpreter (i.e., the subject). On the contrary, Gadamer and other hermeneutic philosophers point out that interpretation always proceeds through a participative enmeshment between the text and the interpreter, with the result that the meaning of the text is never tied to authorial intentions, but only emerges through a dialogue and "fusion of horizons" between the text and the interpreter. Interpretation, hence, is an interested activity, in which the interpreter's personal history and ethics/politics play important roles.[12] The implication of these hermeneutic insights is that, as management researchers, we need to recognize that the very act of categorizing/interpreting an action as workplace resistance or otherwise has an in-built ethical/political dimension or aspect. In many respects, therefore, the important question, in the context of categorizing an action as workplace resistance or otherwise, may not necessarily be whether or not the worker in question was self-conscious about the resistant nature of his/her action, but what could be the ethical/political effects, consequences, and implications of categorizing a particular act as resistance. Indeed, posing this question may well be the first important step in the direction of ethically informed knowledge production.

In attempting to develop an articulation between workplace resistance research and postcolonialism, it is not our intention to suggest that power relations existing within all contemporary organizations necessarily match the violence of colonial power relations. There are, of course, several cases where today's organizations continue to be implicated in the oppressive dynamics of neocolonialism. Examples of this kind of organizations may be found, for instance, in companies operating in the Mexican *maquiladoras* (Goldsmith, 1996), in the U.S. meat-packing industry (Schlosser, 2002), in Shell Oil's Nigerian subsidiary (Young, 1999), and so forth. In cases such as these, organizations serve as instruments of neocolonialism, and organizational processes may frequently be seen as clear stand-ins for (neo-)colonial processes. In such cases, insights of postcolonial theory have very obvious applicability.

Can it be claimed with sufficient reason, however, that postcolonial theoretic insights may have relevance even for examining power relations within a merchant bank's offices in London, or at an insurance company's headquarters in Mumbai, or in the offices of a government ministry in Beijing? Clearly, by no stretch of imagination can one responsibly claim that everyday power relations in these organizational settings *precisely* replicate those existing under colonial conditions. Nevertheless, postcolonialism's insights might be of use even in these organizational situations, in part because we inhabit a postcolonial world.[13] Postcolonial theory, moreover, has made highly innovative contributions in such areas, among others, as power, resistance, and the ethics of knowledge production, and this chapter reflects our belief that certain aspects of postcolonial meditations on power, resistance, and so on could fruitfully be employed in management and organization studies with a view to catalyzing inquiry in new and productive ways. While so doing, however, it becomes our responsibility—as ethical management researchers—not to collapse all organizational situations into the colonial ones, and to remain alive to the differences that might exist between the colonial theater and the arena of contemporary organizations, as well as to the heterogeneities across different organizational sites.

Notes

1. Earlier versions of this paper were presented at the International Crossroads in Cultural Studies Conference, Birmingham, U.K. (June 2000), and the International Conference on Critical Management Studies, Manchester, U.K. (July 2001).
2. See Prasad and Prasad (1998) for an overview of research on everyday forms of workplace resistance.
3. See also, in this connection, discussions of Bhabha in Prasad's chapter, and in the chapter by Priyadharshini, both in the present volume.
4. Since the worker in Nandy's (1983) example is a man, we will be using the masculine pronoun for referring to this worker.
5. We would like to note here that even if our poetry-writing clerk's action did not have the kind of "tangible" consequences detailed in the scenario discussed above, his action could still be considered an act of resistance. Nandy (1983) has pointed out that structures of authority seek to reorder our original cultural priorities—and, thereby, reconstitute our subjectivity—with a view to rendering control more secure and stable. The bank clerk's *continued* poetry writing is a demonstration that the clerk has effectively resisted the attempt to reorder his original cultural priorities (which presumably continue to place greater value on the aesthetic pursuit of poetry than on the bureaucratic and narrowly analytical activities of a bank employee). The clerk in question, thus, seems to have successfully blocked the bank's attempts to reconstitute his subjectivity.
6. For simplicity, we are framing most of our discussion of workplace resistance in terms of workers resisting managers. However, workplace resistance need not be seen as limited to this frame alone, and may take place along other relationships of asymmetric power.

7. Here, we could be said to be somewhat simplifying (and inflecting) Bhabha for our own use.
8. It is useful to note here that, for Bhabha also, resistance may be conscious as well as unconscious. "Resistance," Bhabha argues, "is not necessarily an . . . act of political *intention*" (1994: 110, italics added).
9. Although Western men as well as women took part in the project of colonization, it is possible to argue that, in some ways, men were, by far, the more active participants in the violence of this enterprise. Accordingly, we have decided to employ the masculine pronoun when referring to the colonizer.
10. See the introductory chapter by Prasad.
11. For a discussion of the notion of epistemic violence, see Spivak (1999: 131 ff., 205 ff., 234 ff., 266 ff.).
12. See in this connection, Gadamer (1989) for his important notion of the interpreter's "historically effected consciousness"—*Wirkungsgeschichtliches Bewusstsein*—as an element that facilitates interpretive "fusion of horizons." See also, Prasad (2002).
13. On this issue, see the introductory chapter by Prasad. Also, it is important to keep it in mind here, as the Prasad chapter points out, that although the entire world is indeed postcolonial, different sites may well be postcolonial *in different ways*.

References

Adorno, T. W. 1967. *Prisms*. London: Spearman.
Adorno, T. W., & Horkheimer, M. 1979. *Dialectic of Enlightenment*. London: Verso.
Alvesson, M. 1993. *Cultural perspectives on organizations*. Cambridge: Cambridge University Press.
Berle, A. A., & Means, G. C. 1932. *The modern corporation and private property*. New York: Macmillan.
Bhabha, H. 1994. *The location of culture*. London: Routledge.
Bilgrami, A. 2002. Gandhi's integrity: The philosophy behind the politics. *Postcolonial Studies, 5*, 79–93.
Braverman, H. 1974. *Labor and monopoly capital: The degradation of work in the twentieth century*. New York: Monthly Review Press.
Burawoy, M. 1979. *Manufacturing consent: Change in the labor process under monopoly capitalism*. Chicago: University of Chicago Press.
Burnham, J. 1941. *The managerial revolution*. Harmondsworth: Penguin.
Chandler, A. D. 1977. *The visible hand: The managerial revolution in American business*. Cambridge, MA: Harvard University Press.
Child, J., & Smith, C. 1990. The content and process of organizational transformation. In R. Loveridge & M. Pitt (Eds.), *The strategic management of technological innovation* (pp. 311–337). Chichester: Wiley.
Clegg, S. 1989. *Frameworks of power*. London: Sage.

Clegg, S. 1994. Power relations and the constitution of the resistant subject. In J. M. Jermier, D. Knights, & W. Nord (Eds.), *Resistance and power in organizations* (pp. 274–325). London: Routledge.

Collinson, D. 1988. Engineering humor: Masculinity, joking and conflict in shop-floor relations. *Organization Studies, 9,* 181–199.

Deetz, S. A. 1992. *Democracy in an age of corporate colonization.* Albany, NY: State University of New York Press.

Edwards, R. 1979. *Contested terrain.* New York: Basic Books.

Elger, T. 1979. Valorization and "deskilling": A critique of Braverman. *Capital and Class, 7,* 58–99.

Ezzamel, M., Willmott, H., & Worthington, F. 2001. Power, control and resistance in the "factory that time forgot." *Journal of Management Studies, 38,* 1053–1079.

Gadamer, H-G. 1975. *Truth and method* (G. Barden & J. Cumming, Trans.). New York: Seabury Press.

Gadamer, H-G. 1976. *Philosophical hermeneutics* (D.E. Linge, Trans.). Berkeley: University of California Press.

Gadamer, H-G. 1989. *Truth and method* (2nd Rev. ed.). (J.Weinsheimer & D. G. Marshall, Trans. Rev.). New York: Continuum.

Gandhi, L. 1998. *Postcolonial theory.* New York: Columbia University Press.

Gandhi, M. K. 1927. *An autobiography: Or the story of my experiments with Truth.* Ahmedabad: Navajivan.

Gandhi, M. K. 1951. *Non-violent resistance (Satyagraha).* New York: Schocken Books.

Gandhi, M. K. 1962. *Hind swaraj.* Ahmedabad: Navajivan.

Goldsmith, A. 1996. Seeds of exploitation. In J. Mander & E. Goldsmith (Eds.), *The case against the global economy* (pp. 267–272). San Francisco: Sierra Club Books.

Gordon, D. M., Edwards, R., & Reich, M. 1982. *Segmented work, divided workers.* Cambridge: Cambridge University Press.

Gramsci, A. 1971. *Selections from the prison notebooks* (Q. Hoare & G. Nowell-Smith, Trans.). London: Lawrence and Wishart.

Harley, B. 1999. The myth of empowerment: Work organization, hierarchy, and employee autonomy. *Work, Employment, and Society, 13,* 41–66.

Haynes, D., & Prakash, G. 1991. Introduction: The entanglement of power and resistance. In D. Haynes & G. Prakash (Eds.), *Contesting power* (pp. 1–22). Berkeley, CA: University of California Press.

Hegel, G. W. F. 1900. *Philosophy of history* (J. Sibree, Trans.). New York: P. F. Collier.

Hegel, G. W. F. 1967. *The phenomenology of mind* (J. B. Baillie, Trans.). New York: Harper & Row.

Herbold, R. 2002. Inside Microsoft: Balancing creativity and discipline. *Harvard Business Review, 80,* 72–79.

Hobsbawm, E. J. 1974. Labor history and ideology. *Journal of Social History, 7,* 371–381.

Hodson, R. 1991. The active worker: Compliance and autonomy at the workplace. *Journal of Contemporary Ethnography, 20,* 47–78.

Hodson, R. 1995. Worker resistance: An underdeveloped concept in the sociology of work. *Economic and Industrial Democracy, 16,* 79–110.

Hodson, R. 1999. Organizational anomie and worker control. *Work and Occupations, 26,* 292–323.

Hodson, R. 2001. Disorganized, unilateral, and participative organizations: New insights from the ethnographic literature. *Industrial Relations, 40,* 204–230.

Jermier, J. 1988. Sabotage at work: A rational view. In N. DiTomaso & S. B. Bacharach (Eds.), *Research in the Sociology of Organizations, 6,* 101–134. Greenwich, CT: JAI Press.

Jermier, J., Knights, D., & Nord, W. (Eds.). 1994a. *Resistance and power in organizations.* London: Routledge.

Jermier, J., Knights, D., & Nord, W. 1994b. Introduction: Resistance and power in organizations: Agency, subjectivity and the labor process. In J. Jermier, D. Knights, & W. Nord (Eds.), *Resistance and power in organizations* (pp. 1–24). London: Routledge.

Juravich, T. 1985. *Chaos on the shop floor.* Philadelphia: Temple University Press.

Kirkman, B., & Shapiro, D. 2001. The impact of cultural values on job satisfaction and organizational commitment in self-managing work teams: The mediating role of employee resistance. *Academy of Management Journal, 44,* 557–569.

Knights, D., & Morgan, G. 1990. Management control in sales forces: A case study from the labour process of life insurance. *Work, Employment and Society, 4,* 369–390.

Lawrence, P. 1969. How to deal with resistance to change. *Harvard Business Review,* Jan–Feb, 37–45.

Lukacs, G. 1971. *History and class consciousness.* London: Merlin.

Martin, J. 1992. *Cultures in organizations: Three perspectives.* New York: Oxford University Press.

Martin, R. 1986. Sowing the threads of resistance: Worker resistance and managerial control in a paint and garment factory. *Humanity and Society, 10,* 259–275.

McFarland, J. 1980. Changing modes of social control in a New Brunswick fish packing town. *Studies in Political Economy, 4,* 99–113.

Nandy, A. 1983. *The intimate enemy.* Delhi: Oxford University Press.

Nord, W., & Jermier, J. 1994. Overcoming resistance to resistance: Insights from a study of the shadows. *Public Administration Quarterly, 17,* 396–409.

Parekh, B. 1995. *Gandhi's political philosophy* (1st Indian ed.). Delhi: Ajanta Publications.

Parekh, B. 1997. *Gandhi.* Oxford: Oxford University Press.

Pava, C. 1983. *Managing new office technology: An organizational strategy.* New York: Free Press.

Prasad, A. 2002. The contest over meaning: Hermeneutics as an interpretive methodology for understanding texts. *Organizational Research Methods, 5,* 12–33.

Prasad, A., & Prasad, P. 1998. Everyday struggles at the workplace: The nature and implications of routine resistance in contemporary organizations. *Research in the Sociology of Organizations, 15,* 225–257.

Prasad, A., & Prasad, P. 2001. (Un)willing to resist? The discursive production of local workplace opposition. *Studies in Cultures, Organizations and Societies, 7*, 105–125.

Prasad, P., & Prasad, A. 2000. Stretching the iron cage: The constitution and implications of routine workplace resistance. *Organization Science, 11*, 387–403.

Rofel, L. 1992. Rethinking modernity: Space and factory discipline in China. *Cultural Anthropology, 7*, 93–114.

Schlosser, E. 2002. *Fast food nation.* New York: Perennial/HarperCollins.

Schraeder, M. 2001. Identifying employee resistance during the threat of a merger. *The Mid-Atlantic Journal of Business, 37*, 191–203.

Scott, J. C. 1976. *The moral economy of the peasant: Subsistence and rebellion in Southeast Asia.* New Haven: Yale University Press.

Scott, J. C. 1985. *Weapons of the weak: Everyday forms of peasant resistance.* New Haven: Yale University Press.

Sewell, G. 2001. What goes around, comes around: Inventing a mythology of teamwork and empowerment. *Journal of Applied Behavioral Science, 37*, 70–89.

Singer, P. 1983. *Hegel.* Oxford: Oxford University Press.

Spivak, G. C. 1999. *A critique of postcolonial reason.* Cambridge, MA: Harvard University Press.

Stanley, T. 2002. Change: A common-sense approach. *Supervision, 63*, 7–9.

Sun Tzu. 1988. *The art of war* (T. Cleary, Trans.). Boston: Shambhala Publications [originally written during sixth century B.C.].

Tucker, J. 1993. Everyday forms of employee resistance. *Sociological Forum, 8*, 25–45.

Wargin, J., & Dobiey, D. 2001. E-business and change. *Journal of Change Management, 2*, 72–82.

Young, R. 1999. Dangerous and wrong: Shell, intervention and the politics of transnational companies. *Interventions, 1* (3), 439–464.

CHAPTER 5

Decolonizing and *Re*-Presenting Culture's Consequences: A Postcolonial Critique of Cross-Cultural Studies in Management[1]

Dennis Kwek

People...must know how to resist a diversity of representational practices that would traverse them, claim their time, control their space and their bodies, impose limitations on what can be said and done, and decide their being.

R. Ashley and R. Walker, *Speaking the Language of Exile*

The discovery of the plurality of cultures is never a harmless experience.

P. Ricoeur, *Civilization and National Cultures*

With businesses steadily increasing their international exposure and interaction, the past decade has seen an unparalleled interest in the cross-cultural aspects of management. Multinational and transnational firms are rapidly becoming the norm, bringing to the forefront a myriad of organizational and management issues ranging from international human-resource management practices to governance and control, from multinational organizational structures to managing cultural diversity. The international context is reflected in attempts by many management schools to "internationalize" their faculties and curricula, as well as in the increasing emphasis on cross-cultural management studies in both theoretical and practical arenas. It is against this emergent backdrop of concerns that the recent spate of cross-cultural management studies was initiated.[2]

Cross-cultural management studies center around understanding the similarities and differences across management practices situated in different cultural contexts. It was, arguably, Geert Hofstede's widely cited study, *Culture's Consequences* (1980), which ignited cultural sensitivity and awareness among theorists and practitioners alike. For that alone, his work must be seen as an important contribution. However, this chapter contends that Hofstede's *substantive* contributions to our understanding of cultural differences must not be viewed uncritically. In particular, the chapter argues that Hofstede's theorizations need to be understood as *cultural products* of a Eurocentric mindset. Hofstede's scholarly contributions, moreover, must be viewed in the context of the historical power-relationships that existed between East and West during colonialism, and that allowed the East to be *defined* by the West. From this point of view, theories of cross-cultural difference (and the frequent attempts by such theories to typologize cultures into universalistic dimensions), may be seen as implicitly claiming privileged access to the *meta-language* of cultural definitions, and in so doing to collude, wittingly or unwittingly, in the ongoing reproduction of (neo-)colonial domination.

The purpose of this chapter, accordingly, is to critically examine contemporary cross-cultural management studies. Using postcolonial theory—especially Edward Said's *Orientalism* (1978)—I, therefore, attempt to *decolonize* cross-cultural management studies by sifting through its implicit assumptions to reveal the underlying *representationalistic* logics that create objects of cultural knowledge separate from any actual reality. I argue that the cultural dimensions typified in such studies *impose* their representations upon the very reality they seek to describe, subsequently permitting actors to mold their behaviors, understandings, and strategies based upon such representations. Such studies, moreover, become Western tools for colonization of thought—yet another method of homogenizing our ways of thinking. Cross-cultural studies, therefore, can be seen also as pre-emptively preventing other cultures from having a voice in their own representation.

Central to the understanding of postcolonial theory—and to the task of revealing the organizing logics of cross-cultural management studies—is an examination of the nature of representation and its authoritative claim to possess some truth or epistemological value. By critically investigating the concept of representation and focusing on its constitutive properties, this chapter shifts attention to the *ideology of representation*, and representational systems can then be explored as apparatuses of power. In other words, here I am less interested in what representations *say* than in what they *do*. This gives questions of culture and cultural differences a formative, not merely an expressive, place in the constitution of social, cultural, and political life. Hence, cultural representations need to be examined as an integral part of the social processes of differentiation, exclusion, incorporation, and rule. Drawing attention to the complex matrix of ideological relations that determine dominant conceptions of cultural analysis and discourse exposes the ways in which domination and subjugation are inscribed within the representational systems of the West. Representation is not neutral, nor can it ever be so; it is an act, arguably the founding act, of the will to power.

Cross-Cultural Management Research

A survey of literature on cross-cultural studies in management reveals two broad research approaches, namely: (a) quantitative, survey-based studies, and (b) qualitative, ethnographic ones (Usunier, 1998). However, the main corpus of Western cross-cultural management research is located largely in the snapshot-based, taxonomic, universalizing, nomothetic, grand theoretic approach[3] (Redding, 1994; Roberts & Boyacigiller, 1996). Two main assumptions are made in such studies: (a) that there are some universal traits (usually defined in the form of cultural dimensions) inherent in cultures, which can be excavated from empirical research data, and (b) that the tools, methodologies, and languages used to investigate different cultures are objective, value-free, and culture-neutral.

The most widely known research that compares national cultures in terms of broad value differences is the pioneering work of Hofstede conducted during the 1970s and 1980s (Hofstede, 1980, 1991, 2001a; Hofstede & Associates, 1998). From statistical analyses of survey questions drawn from over fifty countries, Hofstede initially identified four central and independent dimensions of value differences that, according to him, define the cultural landscape we live in: (a) large/small power distance, (b) high/low uncertainty avoidance, (c) individualism/collectivism, and (d) masculinity/femininity. A fifth dimension—Confucian dynamism (subsequently renamed short-term/long-term orientation)—was subsequently "discovered" (Hofstede & Bond, 1988). Others have refined, modified, or extended these five dimensions (e.g., Hampden-Turner & Trompenaars, 1997, 2000; Schwartz & Bilsky, 1990).

Interestingly, it seems that Hofstede's work may be important not necessarily because of its accuracy, but on account of its *popularity*; his framework is considered superior because it can be easily replicated, extended, and confirmed (Sondergaard, 1994), and its cultural dimensions have been codified into acceptable management vocabulary. Gannon and Audia (2000) note how easily understandable Hofstede's framework is to both researchers and laypersons, and the strength of his dimensions is said to rest in their ability to explain and predict behavior on a comparative basis. However, Earley and Singh (2000) have argued that a consequence of this framework is a certain "laziness" in the discipline, because most research continues to be an extension of Hofstede's theory at the expense of other likely conceptual models. It is this comment that, in some ways, foregrounds the typical essentializing representationalism inherent in such approaches. While different sets of dimensions may be posited by different researchers, their underlying assumption is similar, namely that different cultures, howsoever disparate, are defined and characterized by certain shared dimensions that are waiting to be discovered and utilized. This attitude serves to perpetuate a colonizing process that seeks to homogenize, reduce, and silence other cultures. To better understand such a process of colonization, it is necessary to examine the nature of representation and its ideological function.

Representation

It was Man's unique ability to create and manipulate signs that led Aristotle to claim that representing is an inherently human activity, and representation the definitive human process: "Man learns his first lessons by representing things" (Mitchell, 1990: 11). Thereafter, Descartes' notion of knowing as possessing correct representations in the mind resulted in a fracture between external reality and internal representations, with the result that from the seventeenth century, knowledge became internal, representational, and judgmental. Richard Rorty, however, has noted that epistemology as the study of mental representations was a distinctly European development that rapidly became the "quest for certainty over the quest for reason" (1979: 61). The pursuit was not so much for a theory of knowledge as "a desire to find 'foundations' to which one might cling, frameworks beyond which one must not stray, objects which impose themselves, representations which cannot be gainsaid" (Rorty, 1979: 315). Epistemological concerns then, says Rorty (1979: 3), involved the clarification and judgment of the subject's representations:

> Philosophy's eternal concern is to be a general theory of representations, a theory which will divide culture up into the areas which represent reality well, those which represent it less well, and those which do not represent it at all (despite their pretense of doing so).

Typically, our beliefs are grounded in a reality that is apprehended via a logical progression from "appearance" to "mental representations" to "reality." Ian Hacking, however, argued that the order should be reversed, since it is the invention and subsequent practice of representation that allows for the concept of reality, "a concept which has content only when there are first-order representations" (Hacking, 1983: 136). The conceptualizing of reality is therefore the direct consequence of determining whether representations are "real or unreal, true or false, faithful or unfaithful" (Hacking, 1983: 136). This resonates with Martin Heidegger's (1977) argument that the modern age is the age of representation whereby the world is increasingly made to resemble its representations, not the inverse. According to Heidegger, everything that exists does so only in/through representation, with the implication that the world exists only in/through a subject who believes that s/he is producing the world in producing its representation. Therefore, the ultimate goal is for Man to "be that particular being who gives the measure and draws up the guidelines for everything that is" (Heidegger, 1977: 134). This raises the problem that representation is ultimately, always, a re-*presentation*. Unfortunately, such an understanding is marginalized by the primacy of "realism" especially when it comes to the so-called objectivity of scientific knowledge.

Representationalism

Representationalism, or the ideology of representation, is the belief that theories are attempts to accurately describe and represent reality as it is in itself (Chia, 1996; Tsoukas, 1998; Woolgar, 1988). When such accurate mirroring of reality is achieved, theories are deemed to be true and therefore carry the full weight of scientific authority with them. However, universality of application can only be achieved through systematically undermining, marginalizing, and removing competing views—in other words, the presentation of an objective "fact" about the world is the product of contestation where strength has prevailed. Representationalism is therefore axiomatic not just to the practice of science, but also to other practices that lay claim to capturing some essential features beyond the object itself. In this context, science, despite its privileged status, must be seen as a highly institutionalized and visible manifestation of the ideology of representation (Woolgar, 1988).

The act of representing requires a reduction of the distance between the signifier and the signified such that the two mirrored each other, an act that, while often associated with notions of accuracy, proof, and truth, still characterizes the representationalist agenda in the natural and social sciences.

However, as the link that enables the signifier to represent the signified is an arbitrary one, it is problematic to insist that particular words or theories can be essentially linked to a piece of reality. Ultimately, the act of representing is not merely an attempt to "copy" an external reality, but enables us to grasp and manipulate "difficult or intransigent material into a form that facilitates control" (Cooper, 1992: 255). It is through the organizing logics of representationalism that the practice of representation derives its substantive ability to control and define reality.

Properties of Representation

Various properties of representation serve to constitute the organizing logics of representationalism, some of which are isolated here as heuristic devices since not all properties are present in every representational form and, moreover, they frequently overlap and intertwine and cannot fully be disentangled from one another.

Circularity may be understood as referring to the mutually constitutive and formative role that representations perform, an understanding that is entrenched in the notion of difference as something that mediates between and in so doing, holds apart while holding together, or "in-one-anotherness" (Cooper, 1983). Such a "double reference" serves to signify as much as it creates, as can be observed in Stuart Hall's notion of cultural identity: "Identity is a structure of representation that only achieves its positive through the narrow eye of the negative. It has to go through the eye of the needle of the other before it can construct itself" (1991: 21). *Containment* is often required to achieve the mutually defining role that circularity plays; it creates precise borders that includes/excludes one from the other, despite the intricate relationship between one/other. It is through containment that ideas and understandings can be represented, and ultimately objectified, reduced, and displaced. Consequently, through the process of *substitution*, the very act of representing allows objects to be controlled remotely by making present that which is absent, and bringing close while simultaneously distancing (Cooper, 1992). Such *control at a distance* produces a form of *displacement* whereby the representation is always a re-presentation of the object and never the object itself.

Perhaps the most crucial property is that of *essentialization*. Representation is an effort to essentialize, to reproduce objects of the world in a limited and miniaturized form so that they can be more easily engaged. For example, Chia (1996) draws attention to the etymology of Chinese characters. These underwent progressive reductions that increasingly amplified their explanatory power, facilitating manipulation and control, while requiring minimal time and effort to utilize them. Critical to essentialization is the fact that economy and control is achieved through *reduction*, a process that requires omission of salient properties and characteristics of the represented objects. For example, the cultures of colonized peoples were often reduced only to certain aspects that facilitated the colonial political and commercial agenda. This selective loss or deliberate *absence* of characteristics can therefore turn out to be a largely political process. Combined, the dual acts of essentializing and displacing to achieve control create representations that become *fixed* in space and time in order to facilitate transportation and control.

A fundamental condition of representation is its *transparency*, which designates a perfect equivalence between reality and its representation; in other words, the signifier and signified come to mirror each other. But such representational transparency can be achieved only through a strategy of concealment. There is, therefore, a need to render visible the implicit, invisible strategies whereby representation achieves its putative transparency. Importance lies not so much in what representation reveals, but in what it conceals. Finally, the goal of any representation is the *proprietorship* of the representation. As Heidegger noted, representation is appropriation through a "laying hold and grasping," a "making-stand-over-against, an objectifying that goes forward and masters" (Heidegger, 1977: 149–150). Marin (1980) likewise argues that whoever represents the world, appropriates reality for him/herself, and by appropriating it, dominates it, thereby constituting it as an apparatus of power. As Marin (1980: 301) notes:

We may understand this process as one by which a subject inscribes himself as the center of the world and transforms himself into things by transforming things into his representations. Such a subject has the right to possess things legitimately because he has substituted for things his signs, which represent them adequately—that is, in such a way that reality is exactly equivalent to his discourse.

Postcolonial Theory

Postcolonial theory is an increasingly important device for analyzing the cultural dynamics of control, resistance, and representation in the process of colonialism and its purported aftermath. It is inherently difficult to characterize postcolonial theorizing, in part because of the multiplicity of interdisciplinary linkages that have influenced its formation. The term, postcolonial, is traditionally seen as a chronological marker that points to the period following colonialism—a view that raises controversial questions such as when, if ever, did colonialism end? A better approach to understanding post-colonialism, therefore, may be to move away from the emphasis on its chronological implications, and toward a more processual understanding that emphasizes a "coming-into-being" of resistances, tensions, and struggles against the many guises and effects of colonialism (Quayson, 2000). Such a focus emphasizes examining the epistemological interdependencies between the West and its Others, especially in light of the formative role representations play in their constitution. The process of postcolonializing should, therefore, be seen as the critical process of relating modern-day events, phenomena, and knowledge systems to their explicit, implicit, or even potential relationships. This process involves not just the "postcolonial" areas of the world, but, more generally, the world shaped at numerous interrelated levels by the effects of the colonial legacy. Whilst postcolonialism engages with, resists, and seeks to deconstruct the effects of colonialism in the material, historical, political, pedagogical, discursive, and textual domains, it is cultural colonization that is often at the center of academic critiques. Emphasizing the importance of such a focus, Pennycook (1998), for instance, has argued that "although the economic exploitation and political rule of colonialism should of course never be downplayed since they have had very real material effects on the colonized people, the cultural effects of colonialism need to be given equal weight, not as mere rationalizations or products of social and economic relations but rather as a significant site of colonialism in their own right" (1998: 16).

Edward Said's *Orientalism*

Arguably the most influential work in postcolonial theory, Edward Said's *Orientalism* (1978) raised a critical question highly relevant to this chapter's endeavor: how to study other cultures from a "non-repressive and non-manipulative perspective" (Dallmayr, 1996: xvii). Said's argument was that Orientalism needed to be understood "as a discourse...by which European culture was able to manage—and even produce—the Orient politically, sociologically, militarily, ideologically, scientifically, and imaginatively during the post-Enlightenment period" (1978: 3). *Orientalism* marked a significant paradigm shift from examining the material factors governing empire, to an analysis of representation and its role in the formation and consolidation of imperial power. Its most important contribution lies in investigating various aspects of the politics of representation that exposes the connection between knowledge and power, thereby revealing how Western systems of knowledge and representation are complicit in the West's material and political subordination of the non-Western world.

Said is interested in the relationship between the West and the East, and the particular discourse that mediates this relationship—a discourse which he calls Orientalism. For him, the central concern is that all Western discourses about the East are determined by the will to dominate Oriental territories and peoples. Orientalism, therefore, must be seen as a "corporate institution for dealing with the Orient—dealing with it by making statements about it, authorizing views of it, describing it, by teaching it, settling it, ruling over it: in short, Orientalism as a Western style for dominating, restructuring, and having authority over the Orient" (Said, 1978: 3). The pursuit of knowledge therefore cannot be "disinterested," first because the relationship between cultures is an unequal one, and second because such knowledge, whether of the languages, customs, or religions of the colonized, is consistently appropriated to serve the colonial powers (Dallmayr, 1996).

In Said's view, Orientalism operates in the service of the West's hegemony over the East primarily by producing the East discursively as the West's inferior "Other," a maneuver that constructs and strengthens the West's self-image as a superior civilization. By distinguishing and essentializing the identities of East and West through a dichotomizing system of representations typically embodied in the regime of stereotypes, the construction of difference between Western and Eastern parts of the world can be accomplished. Yet, in constructing and accentuating differences, *circularity* is achieved in this representational act: the West produces and creates the cultural constructs of the East/Other and in so doing helps to perpetuate them. Simultaneously, the West knows itself only by taking the position of the Other through which it comes back to itself. The discourses of colonization and the West are thus fundamentally dependent upon the construction of an ontological Other. Furthermore, in the process of defining the West as the Orient's "contrasting image, idea, personality, experience," the discourse of Orientalism, Said asserts, produces and institutionalizes an elaborate series of hierarchical binary polarities (1978: 2). The Orient, for instance, is often characterized as voiceless, sensual, female, irrational, and backward. By contrast, the West is represented as masculine, democratic, rational, moral, dynamic, and progressive. What is significant about such definition is the *static historicity* of the constructed product, independent of context and time: the Orient is represented as ahistorical, temporally fixed, unmoving and unchanging, inferior, and always in direct contrast to the West's increasing pace of colonization and development. Such a discourse ultimately reifies culture as a *fixity* (of ideas and values) that simply "exists" out there.

Orientalism, therefore, problematizes the essentializing strategies of the colonizer, by means of which the alien Other is reduced to a timeless essence that pervades, shapes, and defines the significance of the people and events that constitute it. Such a representationalist maneuver strategically selects only those attributes of the Other that the West deems acceptable and relevant for itself, particularly traits that heighten the differences between the West and the East while simultaneously excluding the "deviant" ones. For Said, this immediately raises the issue of the questionable relationship between the representation and the real. Hence, Said's (1978: 272–273) observation that:

> . . . we must be prepared to accept the fact that a representation is *eo ipso* implicated, intertwined, embedded, interwoven with a great many other things besides "truth," which is itself a representation. What this must lead us to methodologically is to view representations (or misrepresentations—the distinction is at best a matter of degree) as inhabiting a common field of play defined for them, not by some inherent common subject matter alone, but by some common history, tradition, universe of discourse.

Orientalism is a project that reveals three aspects of the way Western culture forms the East. It refers to the primary representations of the East and the other peoples that have circulated in Western discourse since classical times and whose characteristics are embodied in the West's knowledge of the East. It also refers to the style in which such representations are conceived, presented, imagined, and used, raising questions of political positionality. Finally, it describes the systems of scholarship and the cultural and disciplinary institutions that refine, comment upon, and circulate these representations.[4]

Decolonizing Cross-Cultural Management Studies

Postcolonial analyses can provide an important perspective for gaining critical understanding into management studies, particularly cross-cultural studies (Calás & Smircich, 1999; Mohan, 2001; Prasad, 1997a). Such analyses alert us to the fact that the imperialist lens that greatly influenced the West's perception of the non-West during the colonial era is, arguably, still actively shaping and controlling the non-West in numerous domains today. Postcolonial studies are likewise concerned with issues of subjectivities and representations, particularly the ways in which "Western scholarship creates categories of analysis that, even at their most critical, are blind to their own ethnocentrism" (Calás & Smircich, 1999: 661). Such studies can help re-evaluate the narratives of "origins" in Western theories by giving voice to alternative histories of the Other that will shed light on the West's relation-ship to its Other. Furthermore, postcolonial critiques can examine the con-figurations of Western theories and institutions as a "politics of knowledge" in addition to "offering analytical categories and representational approaches for the others to represent themselves in 'their own terms'" (Calás & Smircich, 1999: 661). Finally, useful insights can be gained into the intrica-cies of social and cultural marginality, especially in the context of discussions of center and periphery, with the borderlands that interweave these two act-ing as a locale for resistance. Such insights can help us understand the per-vasiveness of the dominant discourse in its ability to marginalize and silence, especially in cross-cultural management studies that have engendered a method of *representing* and *interpreting* the other cultures to the Western management disciplines. The postcolonial perspective highlights the dangers of such representationalism, its inadequacies and undesirable consequences. Moreover, by directing attention to inequities in modes of representation, the postcolonial project aims to correct such representational imbalances.

As such, there are several vectors of analysis that are opened up by a post-colonial examination of cross-cultural management studies, all of which interweave and impact upon one another (Kwek, 2003). Four strands, in particular, are pertinent to our critique. These relate to: (a) the pervasive reductionist ideology and self-proclaimed neutrality of modern science and its scientific method, (b) the methodological problems of positivistic cross-cultural research with reference to their essentializing and exclusionary agenda, (c) the representationalism of cross-cultural knowledge, and (d) the colonizing and disciplinary effects of such knowledge and the complicity of academic institutions in these dynamics.

Modern Science

Explicitly and/or implicitly, cross-cultural studies in management continue to valorize modern science as humanity's chosen instrument for grasping Truth. A generalized critique of modern science, hence, may be helpful in highlighting some of the shortcomings—at a fundamental level—with such studies. Modern science is often seen as a system of knowledge elevated above all other belief and knowledge systems by its supposed universality and value-neutrality, and by the ability of its logical method to allegedly produce objec-tive claims about the world. Yet modern science is a particular response of a particular group of people—it is a specific project of Western Man that came into being during the fifteenth through seventeenth centuries as the much-vaunted "Scientific Revolution." It is only recently that researchers from postcolonial and feminist backgrounds have begun to recognize that the dominant science system emerged as an emancipating force not for all of humanity (though it legitimized itself that way) but as an imperial and patriarchal project that necessarily entailed the subjugation of other cultures and women (Harding, 1998; Nandy, 1988; Prasad, 1997b; Shiva, 1988). The intimate relationship between modern science and colonization cannot be disputed—the development of modern science in Europe is often followed by the decline of local indigenous knowledge systems not only in the colonies, but in other parts of the world as well. This has led Sandra Harding (1998) to argue that the universality of Western science is a direct consequence of European expansion and not a product of valid epistemological claims.

Science's legitimizing power derives from a number of assumptions and strategies that authenticate it as the only valid method and knowledge system. Even though almost every civilization and culture has produced its own science, Western science established itself as distinct and separate from all other sciences and traditions. It did this by assuming a reductionist strategy of representational separateness: separability of observer/observed, parts/whole, man/nature, mind/matter, science/religion. Breaking a system into discrete and atomistic constituents means it can be studied in a way that is unique to Western civilization, typified by the experimental methods of Bacon, the father of modern Western science (Nandy, 1988). Another strategy is to define only that which can be measured as real. Ideas, notions, phenomena for which no experimental or observational evidence could be discovered are deemed irrational and unscientific, and dismissed. This was easily and immediately linked with the imperial project because it effectively excluded non-Westerners from being experts and owners of knowledge; holistic ways of knowing that include cultural and natural complexities and interconnectedness were also excluded from being scientific. The non-West was therefore written out of scientific history.

Vandana Shiva (1988) points out a more insidious function of modern scientific knowledge—that it is increasingly a source of violence and destruction. This is reflected in four different ways. First, violence is implicated in the separation of experts and nonexperts since it converts the nonexperts into non-knowers, even though they are active users and practitioners of their local knowledges. Second, by essentializing and reducing the objects of knowledge, such objects are violated because they are no longer seen holistically. The clearest violation at this level is the ecological crisis around the world. Third, violence is inflicted upon the supposed beneficiaries of scientific knowledge—people. The poor in particular are the worst victims. Finally, Western science uses suppression and falsification of facts to legitimize its own mode of knowing as the only mode, hence violating knowledge itself. An example of this exclusionary practice is the outlawing of Islamic medicine in the Middle East during the era of colonial expansion. Another is the witch-hunting hysteria during the Scientific Revolution aimed at destroying women in Europe because they were knowers of and experts on knowledge deemed heretic (in other words, nonscientific). Hence, modern Western scientific methodology achieves a threefold exclusion (Shiva, 1988): (a) at the *ontological* level, other properties that may be important are marginalized, (b) at the *epistemological* level, other ways of knowing are not recognized as legitimate, and (c) at the *sociological* level, nonexperts are divested of their right to knowledge, both access to it and the ability to judge it.

There is also the issue of the value of neutrality in modern science. This is particularly ironic because even if it is possible to be neutral in any political or cultural sense, the value-neutrality itself can be seen as a distinctively European concern. In other words, trying to maximize neutrality, as well as claiming it, expresses a culturally specific value. As Harding points out: "Most cultures do not value neutrality; they value their own Confucian, or indigenous American, or Islamic, or Maori, or, for that matter, Judaic or Christian values. So one that does value and maximize apparent neutrality is easily identifiable" (1998: 61). It is therefore clear that the notion of scientific neutrality is itself a reflection of a specific ideology. Ultimately, modern science's ideology (of objectivity, neutrality, and progress) has to be seriously questioned. By hiding its own ideology, science has sought to elevate itself to the position of a superior and universal knowledge system, one that is not open to critique, one that is inflicted on all culture, gender, and classes so that these Others may be subjugated and controlled. The preceding critique of science alerts us to the limitations that invest cross-cultural management studies as a result of the latter's largely unquestioning commitment to the ideological system of science.

Methodology

The preceding issues have a significant bearing on the scientific methodologies utilized by cross-cultural management researchers. While a number of researchers have voiced problems with the positivistic approach of measuring a concept such as culture (e.g., Smelser, 1992), or even with the concept itself (e.g., McSweeney, 2002), few have questioned the methodological aspects of reducing and dimensionalizing culture. Tayeb (2001) however has argued that dimensionalizing a culture results in an understanding that is too simplistic and over-essentializing. Urgently insisting that we need to "move on" (2001: 104), Tayeb (2001: 93) notes:

> ... by putting culture into neat, sometimes unconnected, little boxes we are in danger of losing sight of the big picture. National culture cannot really be simplified and reduced to a handful of boxes into which some nations are placed and from which others are excluded. To do this will give one only a myopic and incomplete picture of a nation. Neither is it possible to attribute a certain degree of cultural characteristics to a nation and their opposites to others and then pigeon-hole them there for ever.

Furthermore, such an approach encourages a minimalist view of conducting cross-cultural research, whereby researchers exclude information on the studied cultures on the assumption that Hofstede already offers a definitive account of culture. McSweeney (2002) condemns this tendency by observing that "the on-going unquestioning acceptance of Hofstede's national culture research by his evangelized entourage suggests that in parts of the management disciplines the criteria for acceptable evidence are far too loose" (2002: 112).

An analogy can be made between Hofstede's work and the "science" of craniometry exemplified by Samuel George Morton's *Crania Americana* (1839). Morton claimed to have empirically proved that skull sizes are directly linked to the mental capacities of different races, thereby creating a hierarchy of racial intelligence with the modern Caucasion race at the top and the Negro race at the bottom (Gould, 1997). Although the positivistic mechanisms used were arguably accurate, the underlying assumptions (e.g., the relationship between skull size and intelligence) were flawed, and there were more sinister undertones at work: a colonial justification of the will-to-power.

Western scientific culture propounds a clear hierarchy of knowledges that places quantifiable, statistically testable knowledge above all other forms (Sibley, 1999). The power of statistical method resides in this privileged position and in its ability to filter out and refine the heterogeneity and complexities of the sociocultural world into an orderly one. More often than not, it uses a set of highly rational procedures and instruments to *confirm* the existence of such order. However, it achieves order (and "truth") through distancing the subject—keeping the observer and observed apart—as well as by retreating from lived experiences. Both these practices serve to reduce anxieties about disorder and threats posed by differences. Differences, particularly within cultures, are thus subjugated, homogenized, and essential-ized, simply because they *threaten boundaries*. Statistical analysis, therefore, has the power to silence and marginalize other representations deemed dif-ferent from the dominant ones, rendering them invisible in the subsequent "authoritative" construction of the world. Often, this is achieved through essentialism—by conflating the values, worldviews, and practices of some socially dominant groups with those of "all members of the culture." Such essentialism continues to inform most cross-cultural studies in management. Yet, paradoxically, at the between-culture level, differences are accentuated in the form of binary cultural dimensions that provoke an "insistence of Difference" (Narayan, 2000: 82):

> The discursive reiteration of such "essential differences" operates in a manner that helps construct the senses of cultural identity that shape the self-understandings and subjectivities of different groups of people who inhabit these discursive contexts. . . . Discourses about "difference" often operate to conceal their role in the production and reproduction of such "differences," presenting these differences as something pre-given and prediscursively "real" that the discourses of difference merely describe rather than help construct and perpetuate.

In addition, statistical analysis in its essentializing mode has the ability to control at a distance. As Cooper (1992) points out, it is only through statis-tical representation that researchers can manage a large amorphous mass from afar. The vast magnitude of national cultures means, in a sense, that human masses are remote; their sheer number makes them physically unmanageable. Before they can be organized and managed, such populations have to be re-presented through remote control, displacement, and reduc-tion. This kind of control is sought to be achieved in cross-cultural manage-ment studies through statistical analysis coupled with a reductionist metaphysics of culture, which uses the device of cultural *dimensions* to impose an arbitrary order on the chaos that may be said to fundamentally inhere in complex cultures. This is analogous to Bentham's Panopticon that facilitated the reductive representation of the physical world in classes, num-bers, and names. Finally, the statistical methods such as inference are them-selves value-laden. When statisticians test a scientific hypothesis, they determine its truth or falsity in terms of a "confidence level." As Ravetz (1988: 35) has noted, "Whether the limit is 95 of 99 percent depends on the values defining the investigations, the costs and importance placed to social, environmental or cultural consequences."

Representationalism

It may be useful to recall here that representations of cultural difference (of the sort receiving our attention here) are produced by Western projections onto the Other. This puts into place sets of cultural institutions that refine, comment upon, and circulate these primary representations. By controlling the language of discourse, cross-cultural management studies are responsible for propagating colonial (and colonizing) ways of thinking in a manner similar to imperialistic control of the Orient's perception of itself. Furthermore, by governing the definitions of cultural dimensions, researchers like Hofstede may be seen as controlling the very definition of identity for *other* peoples and cultures. The representationalistic logics of Hofstede's framework, therefore, create sense-making constructs that produce for other cultures essentialized, taxonomized understandings of what is appropriate, normal, and reasonable. These logics both prompt and constrain human actors at multiple levels, and influence the kinds of social roles, actions, and strategies that come to be constituted as conceivable, efficacious, and legitimate in any cultural setting. Such representationalism actually *shapes* the world and becomes a tool for acting in it. As Tsoukas (1998: 792) notes:

> The models through which we view the world are not mere mirrors upon which the world is passively reflected but our models also help constitute the world we experience.... The knowledge generated within a representational epistemology is not so much a representation of how the world is, but is rather a tool for shaping it.

Hofstede's research defines, for example, how the Chinese are perceived to behave, and subsequently how non-Chinese *should* behave toward them. Robert Burns's (1998) book, *Doing Business in Asia* (which is particularly popular in Singapore) uses Hofstede's dimensions to understand and prescribe negotiations with Singaporeans thus (pp. 136–137):

> The Chinese business people tend to be tough negotiators and you may find yourself pressured into making concessions, however negotiations will proceed fairly rapidly. Don't be misled by Western-dressed, Western-educated Singaporeans who speak excellent English. They are still Asian in mindset and attitude, relatively conservative and focused on the long-term perspective... Should you need to point out errors or disagree, you should do it discreetly in private to prevent loss of face. Criticism focussed at a person is considered highly personal and

objectionable. Conversely, avoid handing out excessive compliments, for these (and by implication you) will be perceived as insincere. The culture extols modesty and humility.

Discussing the "collectivistic" and "paternalistic" nature of Singaporeans and drawing on Confucian values, Burns argues that "while families may live apart, the smallness of the island has helped retain an underlying strong Asian culture of collectivism and high power distance; elderly members of families are highly respected and patriarchies flourish in business" (1998: 132). What this image ignores is the fact that in Singapore (and in some other "collectivistic" countries in Asia), old age discrimination in employment, for instance, is rife (Chiu, Chan, Snape, & Redman, 2001). The "reality" (generated from essentialized constructs) that Burns talks about, does not stand up to closer scrutiny in Singapore's case. The examples of indigenous researchers using Hofstede's dimensions and even reifying them for their own cultures do not stop here. Malaysian researcher Asma Abdullah's *Going Glocal* (1996), uses Hofstede's cultural dimensions and even extends them with some "locally generated" dimensions. Thereby, Abdullah unwittingly internalizes such constructs, all the while seeming to remain completely unaware of their constitutive or ideological effects (Abdullah, 1996). Another popular book about Asia, *China Business: The Rule of the Game* by Carolyn Blackman (2000), describes the collectivistic and Confucianistic nature of China. It paints China as backward, corrupt, difficult to manage, stubborn, and inferior to the West (Blackman, 2000). This work reveals the static historicity of such representations, which seek to temporally and spatially fix the properties of the culture in question. Such a strategy ignores the effects of cultural change as well as the impact that noncultural factors may have on culture (Tayeb, 2001). Ultimately, however, the fact that research with such strong colonial and representationalist themes exists and is being produced today is a constant reminder that we are still living in an imperial age.

Discipline

A crucial feature of most cross-cultural studies is that they emerge out of metropolitan centers, seeking to add value to the "raw material" of research imported from non-Western cultures. The categories devised to "discover" cultures are constructs specified (legislated?) by Western thought and developed by the dominant (Western) culture in the world of management research. Seen in this light, the cultural dimensions stipulated by Hofstede and others are quintessentially Western. For example, Hofstede has been very vocal in denouncing the universal applicability of American theories, and he even questions the ethnocentric tendencies of researchers who utilize his dimensions (Hofstede, 2001b). But what he does not question is the ethnocentric origins of his own dimensions or methodology, nor the implications of such tools for marginalizing other knowledges. While the Confucian Dynamism dimension (Hofstede & Bond, 1988) was excavated using research designed with "a deliberate non-Western bias" (Hofstede, 1991: 161), the research was merely an extension of Hofstede's existing methodology. Hofstede's dimensions were repeatedly deemed to be universal, objective, and value-free, seemingly validated by the fact that *Culture's Consequences* has now appeared in its second edition (Hofstede, 2001a). Supported by Soondergard's (1994) review of how his work had been used, Hofstede added that replications and extensions to his work "confirmed the dimensions; the few cases of dis-confirmation of particular dimensions could be accounted for by chance" (2001b: 13). Even in recent work on international management, while David Thomas, for instance, is mindful of the limitations of such frameworks, he nevertheless insists that "these problems do not render the systematic descriptions of cultural variation useless" (2002: 67). He certainly does not seem to be aware of the colonizing mechanisms that inform the power/knowledge nexus in such descriptions.

Postcolonial theory calls upon us to focus our attention on opening up new productive spaces for others to "speak back"—spaces that would include knowers and cultural experts from other cultures who hold unique knowledges, but have been silenced so far. Such marginalized knowers derive their understandings of culture from their local, lived experiences of cross-cultural encounters or from the collective sociocultural memories of the peoples—knowledges that are deemed unscientific, overly subjective, and emerging from people with no scientific training or expertise. To resist the hegemony of the dominant style of cross-cultural theorizing, we therefore need to ask the following questions. What other theories are there, or should there be? Which groups of peoples are written out of current theories and what are the consequences of such marginalization (Calás & Smircich, 1999)? Is the West ready to accept potentially strange knowledges, not as alternatives but as equals? If given the chance, would the Others choose to resist or continue to follow the West? Are the Others able to create their own voices external to the discourses of the West? And to repeat the poignant concluding remark of Mir, Calás, and Smircich, "is the West ... even capable of listening?" (1999: 290).

Unfortunately, the absence of alternative voices is an authentic concern. Pointing to the dearth of an Australian management corpus, Clegg, Linstead, and Sewell lament that "Australian organizational thought literally seems not to exist—Australia is merely another field experiment in the global laboratory of universalizing US management theory" (2000: 109). Jaya (2001) engages directly with Western organizational hegemony by encouraging her students to critically re-examine the Eurocentric assumptions and biases inherent in much contemporary management discourse. Others (often in the East) find the postcolonial rhetoric and styles of engaging with Western management dominance too "exotic" and "antagonistic," as one academic discovered when he submitted a postcolonial critique of contemporary management to a prominent Asian conference in the field of management. The anonymous reviewers' comments complained that the paper had an "advocacy tone in its counter-rhetoric," that postcolonial discourse is "too controversial," and that it does not "move the field of management" in any practical sense. It is comments such as these that seem to allude to the unwillingness of the Other to shirk off the West's stranglehold. In a self-sustaining loop, the circularity of this marginalization process passes through management theorists from Asian cultures, who are not only frequently "seduced" by the imperialistic authority of such cross-cultural studies, sometimes they are even required to authenticate their voices through Western discourses so that their knowledge may be recognized as *legitimate* knowledge. As noted Asian scholar Wang Gung-Wu (1998: 16) comments:

> Many [Asian] societies respect their scholars more if they keep close links with their teachers and colleagues in the West than if they work with other Asians. . . . What is fresh and stimulating and worthy . . . [seemingly] comes from the successful West.

Alternatives

Strategies of Resistance

How do we challenge such seeming dominance of Western theories? Cultures are often reduced and essentialized as if they are natural, neatly distinct, entities existing in the world. These representations erase the fact that boundaries are human constructs—arbitrary and shifting designations linked to political agendas that differentiate one culture from another for a purpose. One useful maneuver would be to restore history and politics to this otherwise ahistorical picture of cultures. Such historical and political sensitivity would then raise awareness of the processes by which values, traditions, or practices have come to be seen as fundamental constitutive components of a culture (Kwek, 2003). In addition, cultures are understood better when they are not viewed as simplistic dimensional binaries but in terms that do not diminish the fluid, multilayered complexities that culture encapsulates. We need to resist representationalistic simplifications by pointing to the internal plurality, dissension, and contestation over values, and the ongoing changes occurring in virtually all cultures. Appadurai (1994), for example, uses the idea of the "fractal" boundaries and the dialectic "polythetic" overlapping of cultures to highlight their inherent heterogeneity. This would challenge the worldview that cultures can be classified into neat, internally consistent, and monolithic categories.

Another mode of resistance comes from a small (but hopefully increasing) number of research voices appearing from the horizons of marginality that challenge and engage with Western management thought. Such voices bring to the center of mainstream knowledge production alternative understandings that set up a location for decolonization and the development of counter-hegemonic ways of knowing and being. A recent example originates from New Zealand and introduces Maori research that may offer radically different conceptualizations that do not fall into clear "qualitative-quantitative, or positivist-interpretive-critical categorizations" (Henry & Pene, 2001: 238). Likewise, Chinese philosophical approaches can create the potential to generate alternative ways of understanding cultures. For example, Western thought has traditionally tended to view the *self* as a fixed essence that renders humans distinct from nature and from all other living beings, and to subscribe to a model of the self as a fundamentally permanent and stable seat of power and cognition. Eastern philosophies offer an alternative perspective: the self is seen not as given but constructed, not stable and permanent but painfully fractured—all is in a state of constant flux and all is relational. Cross-cultural studies, originating in the West, give ontological primacy to a historically individuated self whose values and meaning systems guide actions and behavior. By assuming this notion of self to be universal, such studies prevent investigations of interesting alternative approaches. Confucianism, however, brings forward the *relational* self that can be a pointer to a non-Western approach to cross-cultural understanding (Marsella, Devos, & Hsu, 1985). By situating the self not in terms of what goes on inside the individual, but in terms of the larger whole that draws from and is affected by the individual's relations and transactions with her/his fellow humans, such a conception can serve as a different basis for understanding cross-cultural behavior.

Consider, for example, Tu Wei-Ming's (1994) notion of a Cultural China. Tu defines China not in terms of geo-politico-national boundaries, but in terms of a continuous interaction between three symbolic constellations.

The first consists of societies populated predominantly by cultural and ethnic Chinese (such as Hong Kong, Singapore, Taiwan). The second consists of the Chinese diaspora, communities throughout the world who have settled far from their ancestral homeland. The third consists of individual men and women such as scholars, teachers, industrialists, businesspeople, and writers who try to understand China intellectually and bring their conceptions of China to their own communities. How would our grasp of culture and cultural differences be transformed if we started from such a conceptualization of culture? An Eastern way of examining culture defined in such a relational manner could contribute towards a radically different understanding of cultures, as well as critically engage (and interrogate) cross-cultural studies from the Other side.

Positions

Peruvemba Jaya (2001: 228) writes of her own positionality in the Western academic sphere (a situation I can empathize with):

> … here I am, writing and speaking in the language of the West in a location for knowledge production circumscribed by the western academy. Moreover, I am of the diaspora, yet, while I was at "home," I supported the hegemony of the colonizer by embodying the elitist possession of knowledge of a certain language. Even now, as I begin to question the western foundation of knowledge that I am imparting in business and management education, why, in order to be heard, must this critique come from within the dominant metropolitan location and be voiced in the language of the western majority?

The fact that I write in the dominant language situated in the privileged spaces of Western scholarship should not undermine the more crucial fact that postcolonial critiques of cross-cultural studies have the potential to open up imaginative spaces for other knowledges to appear and engage with Western discourses. I believe that as a postcolonial researcher, it is necessary to be reflexive in one's own text, a position that requires critical sensitivity toward the numerous issues and perspectives that contest, negotiate, and legitimize the interdisciplinary boundaries of both postcolonial and management knowledge. We have a responsibility to not only state, but constantly question our own biases and assumptions as much as, if not more than, those that we are critiquing: after all, any discourse based on the questioning of boundaries must never stop questioning its own.

Finally, Ato Quayson points to a tension felt by many postcolonial researchers between an activistic engagement for solutions in the real world, versus a more distanced mode of participation via textual, visual, and discursive analyses whose purpose "seems to be to rivet attention permanently on the warps and loops of discourse" (2000: 8). I would argue that any productive postcolonial critique of cross-cultural studies would need to strike a careful balance between these tensions while recognizing the ideological practices inherent in both "sides." Consequently, a theoretical encounter between postcolonial processes and the discourses of a Eurocentric, largely positivist, cross-cultural management theory can only help to shed a critical light on the nature of representing cultures as well as mark the end of the innocent notion of the essential cultural Others, with its attendant political consequences. It is necessary to remember that it is precisely at the frontier between what can be represented and what cannot that the postcolonial operation is staged, aiming not to transcend representation but to expose the system of power that authorizes certain representations while excluding, silencing, and invalidating others. What is ultimately at stake is the recognition of the diversity of subjective positions, cultural experiences, and identities that compose the various cultures. It is only after those in cross-cultural management studies acknowledge that other cultures are, in important ways, politically and culturally *constituted*, that progress can be made toward the recognition of the immense diversity and differentiation of the historical and cultural experiences of other cultures. This may necessarily and potentially result in a weakening or even fading of the notion of "culture" and certainly cultural *dimensions* as applied in cross-cultural management studies. This essay, therefore, may appropriately be concluded by recalling David Spurr's (1993: 185) remarks in *The Rhetoric of Empire*:

> The first step towards an alternative to colonial discourse, for Western readers at least, has to be a critical understanding of its structures; and this understanding would be an insider's because we read the discourse from a position already contained by it.

Notes

1. The author thanks Robert Chia, Joyce Heng, Anshuman Prasad, Nidhi Srinivas, and Teng Siao See for their comments, criticisms, and encouragement.
2. See, for example, Clegg, Ibarra-Colado, and Bueno-Rodriquez (1999), Earley and Singh (2000), Hampden-Turner and Trompenaars (1997, 2000), Hofstede (1980, 1991, 2001a), Jackson and Aycan (2001), and Thomas (2002).

3. One reason for the lack of extensive ethnographic research is the difficulty of attributing scientific validity and objectivity to such qualitative work. Another reason is that, more often than not, researchers rarely interact across the quantitative – qualitative divide as a result of their substantially different methodological paradigms as well as occasional deep-seated antagonism between members of the two camps (Usunier, 1998).

4. Said's understanding of representation and its connection to power and knowledge is the basis of this research. However, I am attentive to the criticisms made against *Orientalism*, including the charges that this book tends to essentialize both the West and the non-West into monolithic images (Young, 2001), and that it ignores interrelated issues of resistance and involvement of the colonized with the forms of knowledge produced about them (Quayson, 2000). Furthermore, *Orientalism* also seems to exhibit signs of some epistemological ambivalence. However, while such critiques do exist, Young (2001) points out that there is surprisingly little work that attempts to re-theorize the colonial discourse framework set up by Said.

References

Abdulla, A. 1996. *Going glocal: Cultural dimensions in Malaysian management.* Kuala Lumpur: Malaysian Institute of Management.

Appadurai, A. 1994. Disjuncture and difference in the global cultural economy. In P. Williams & L. Chrisman (Eds.), *Colonial discourse and post-colonial theory: A reader.* London: Harvester Wheatsheaf.

Ashley, R., & Walker, R. B. J. 1990. Speaking the language of exile: Dissident thought in international studies. *International Studies Quarterly, 34* (3), 259–268.

Blackman, C. 2000. *China business: The rules of the game.* New South Wales: Allen & Unwin.

Burns, R. 1998. *Doing business in Asia: A cultural perspective.* Melbourne: Addison Wesley Longman.

Calás, M. B., & Smircich, L. 1999. Past postmodernism? Reflections & tentative directions. *Academy of Management Review, 24* (4), 649–671.

Chia, R. 1996. *Organizational analysis as deconstructive practice.* Berlin: Walter de Gruyter.

Chiu, W. C. K., Chan, A. W., Snape, E., & Redman, T. 2001. Age stereotypes & discriminatory attitudes towards older workers: An East-West comparison. *Human Relations, 54* (5), 629–661.

Clegg, S. R., Ibarra-Colado, E., & Bueno-Rodriquez, L. 1999. *Global management: Universal theories & local realities.* London: Sage.

Clegg, S. R., Linstead, S., & Sewell, G. 2000. Only penguins: A polemic on organization theory from the edge of the world. *Organization Studies, 21,* 103–117.

Cooper, R. 1983. The other: A model of human structuring. In G. Morgan (Ed.). *Beyond method: Strategies for social research.* London: Sage.

Cooper, R. 1992. Formal organization as representation: Remote control, displacement and abbreviation. In M. Reed & M. Hughes (Eds.), *Rethinking organization: New directions in organizational theory & analysis*. London: Sage Publication.

Dallmayr, F. 1996. *Beyond orientalism*. New York: State University of New York Press.

Earley, P. C., & Singh, H. 2000. *Innovations in international and cross-cultural management*. London: Sage.

Gannon, M. J., & Audia, P. G. 2000. The cultural metaphor: A grounded method for analyzing national cultures. In P. C. Earley & H. Singh (Eds.), *Innovations in international and cross-cultural management*. London: Sage.

Gould, S. J. 1997. *The mismeasure of man*. London: Penguin.

Hacking, I. 1983. *Representing & intervening*. Cambridge: Cambridge University Press.

Hall, S. 1991. The local & the global: Globalization & ethnicity. In A. King (Ed.), *Culture, globalization and the world system*. London: Macmillan.

Hampden-Turner, C., & Trompenaars, F. 1997. *Mastering the infinite game: How East Asian values are transforming business practices*. Oxford: Capstone.

Hampden-Turner, C., & Trompenaars, F. 2000. *Building cross-cultural competence: How to create wealth from conflicting values*. Chichester: John Wiley.

Harding, S. 1998. *Is science multi-cultural? Postcolonialisms, feminisms and epistemologies*. Indianapolis: Indiana University Press.

Heidegger, M. 1977. The age of the world picture. In *The question concerning technology* (W. Lovitt, Trans.). New York: Harper & Row.

Henry, E., & Pene, H. 2001. Kaupapa Maori: Locating indigenous ontology, epistemology and methodology in the academy. *Organization, 8* (2), 234–242.

Hofstede, G. 1980. *Culture's consequences: International differences in work-related values*. London: Sage.

Hofstede, G. 1991. *Cultures and organizations: Software of the mind*. New York: McGraw Hill.

Hofstede, G. 2001a. *Culture's consequences: Comparing values, behaviors, institutions and organizations across nations*. London: Sage.

Hofstede, G. 2001b. Culture's recent consequences: Using dimension scores in theory and research. *International Journal of Cross-Cultural Management, 1* (1), 11–16.

Hofstede, G. & Associates. 1998. *Masculinity & femininity: The taboo dimension of national cultures*. London: Sage.

Hofstede, G., & Bond, M. 1988. The Confucius connection: From cultural roots to economic growth. *Organizational Dynamics, 16* (4), 5–21.

Jackson, T., & Aycan, Z. 2001. International journal of cross-cultural management – Towards the future. *International Journal of Cross-Cultural Management, 1* (1), 5–9.

Jaya, P. S. 2001. Do we really "know" and "profess"? Decolonizing management knowledge. *Organization, 8* (2), 227–233.

Kwek, D. 2003. *Representing culture: A postcolonial critique of cross-cultural and indigenous management studies*. Unpublished Doctoral Thesis, Colchester: University of Essex.

Marin, L. 1980. Toward a theory of reading in the visual arts: Poussin's The Arcadian Sheperds. In S. R. Suleiman & I. Crosman (Eds.), *The reader in the text: Essays on audience and interpretation*. Princeton: Princeton University Press.

Marsella, A. J., Devos, G., & Hsu, F. L. K. 1985. *Culture and self: Asian and Western perspectives*. New York: Tavistock Publications.

McSweeney, B. 2002. Hofstede's model of national cultural differences and their consequences: A triumph of faith; a failure of analysis. *Human Relations, 55* (1), 89–118.

Mir, R. A., Calás, M. B., & Smircich, L. 1999. Global technoscapes & silent voices: Challenges to theorizing global cooperation. In D. L. Cooperider & J. E. Dutton (Eds.), *Organizational dimensions of global change: No limits to cooperation*. London: Sage.

Mitchell, W. J. T. 1990. Representation. In F. Lentricchia & T. McLaughlin (Eds.), *Critical terms for literary study*. Chicago: University of Chicago Press.

Mohan, G. 2001. Beyond participation: Strategies for deeper empowerment. In B. Cooke & U. Kothari (Eds.), *Participation: The new tyranny*. London: Zed Books.

Morton, S. G. 1839. *Crania Americana or, a comparative view of the skulls of various aboriginal nations of North and South America*. Philadelphia: John Pennington.

Nandy, A. (Ed.). 1988. *Science, hegemony and violence: A requiem for modernity*. Delhi: Oxford University Press.

Narayan, U. 2000. Essence of culture and a sense of history: A feminist critique of cultural essentialism. In U. Narayan & S. Harding (Eds.), *Decentering the center: Philosophy for a multicultural, postcolonial and feminist world*. Bloomington: Indiana University Press.

Pennycook, A. 1998. *English and the discourses of colonialism*. London: Routledge.

Prasad, A. 1997a. The colonizing consciousness and representations of the other: A postcolonial critique of the discourse of oil. In P. Prasad, A. J. Mills, M. Elmes, & A. Prasad (Eds.), *Managing the organizational melting pot: Dilemmas of workplace diversity*. London: Sage.

Prasad, A. 1997b. Provincializing Europe: Towards a post-colonial reconstruction: A critique of Baconian science as the last stand of imperialism. *Studies in Cultures, Organizations & Societies, 3* (1), 91–117.

Quayson, A. 2000. *Postcolonialism: Theory, practice or process?* Cambridge: Polity Press.

Ravetz, J. R. 1988. Science, ignorance and fantasies. In Z. Sardar (Ed.), *The revenge of Athena: Science, exploitation and the Third World*. London: Mansell.

Redding, S. G. 1994. Comparative management theory: Jungle, zoo or fossil bed? *Organization Studies, 15* (3), 323–359.

Ricoeur, P. 1965. Civiliz ation and national cultures. In C. A. Kelbley (Ed.), *History and truth*. Evanston: Northwestern University Press.

Roberts, K. H., & Boyacigiller, N. A. 1996. Cross-national organizational research: The grasp of the blind men. In A. Inkeles & M. Sasaki (Eds.), *Comparing nations and cultures*. Englewood Cliffs, NJ: Prentice-Hall.

Rorty, R. 1979. *Philosophy and the mirror of nature*. Oxford: Blackwell.

Said, E. W. 1978. *Orientalism*. London: Routledge & Kegan Paul.

Schwartz, S., & Bilsky, W. 1990. Toward a theory of the universal content & structure of values: Extensions and cross-cultural replications. *Journal of Personality and Social Psychology, 58*, 878–891.

Shiva, V. 1988. Reductionist science as epistemological violence. In A. Nandy (Ed.), *Science, hegemony and violence: A requiem for modernity*. Delhi: Oxford University Press.

Sibley, D. 1999. Untouched by statistics: Representing and misrepresenting other cultures. In D. Dorling & S. Simpson (Eds.), *Statistics in society: The arithmetic of politics*. London: Arnold.

Smelser, N. J. 1992. Culture: Coherent or incoherent. In R. Munch & N. J. Smelser (Eds.), *Theory of culture*. Berkeley: University of California Press.

Sondergaard, M. 1994. Research note: Hofstede's consequences: A study of reviews, citations and replications. *Organization Studies, 15* (3), 447–456.

Spurr, D. 1993. *The rhetoric of empire: Colonial discourse in journalism, travel writing, and imperial administration*. Durham: Duke University Press.

Tayeb, M. 2001. Conducting research across cultures: Overcoming drawbacks and obstacles. *International Journal of Cross-Cultural Management, 1* (1), 91–108.

Thomas, D. C. 2002. *Essentials of international management*. London: Sage.

Tu, W. M. 1994. Cultural China: The periphery as the center. In W. M. Tu (Ed.), *The living tree: The changing meaning of being Chinese today*. Stanford: Stanford University Press.

Tsoukas, H. 1998. The word and the world: A critique of representationalism in management research. *International Journal of Public Administration, 21* (5), 781–817.

Usunier, J-C. 1998. *International and cross-cultural management research*. London: Sage.

Wang, G. 1998. World view: Academic blind spot in Asia. *Times Higher Education Supplement*, 5th June 1998, 16.

Woolgar, S. 1988. *Science: The very idea*. Sussex: Ellis Horwood.

Young, R. J. C. 2001. *Postcolonialism: An historical introduction*. Oxford: Blackwell.

PART III

Current Issues and Empirical Investigations

CHAPTER 6

The Return of the Native: Organizational Discourses and the Legacy of the Ethnographic Imagination[1]

Pushkala Prasad

...the problem of the native is also the problem of modernity and modernity's relation to "endangered authenticities."

Rey Chow, *Writing Diaspora:*
Tactics of Intervention in Contemporary Cultural Studies

One of the arguably "scholarly" by-products of the West's era of high imperialism was *ethnography*—the institutionalized practice of studying indigenous (non-Western) peoples through a process of extended cultural immersion. While ethnography for the most part tends to be strongly identified with the anthropological subfield that engages in cultural depictions of "other," its own cultural influence extends way beyond its immediate academic location. Indeed, something that might well be called an "ethnographic imagination" (Evans, 1999; Herbert, 1991) is very much present in many realms of Western society. As di Leonardo (1998: 29) has astutely observed, "anthropology as trope has long been an element of American [and Western] cultural baggage."

It is this chapter's contention that long after the "official" demise of colonialism, the ethnographic imagination has lingered on as a throbbing collective impulse seeking fulfillment in innumerable walks of life. Organizations in contemporary post-industrial and fast-capitalist societies, moreover, are active and ambitious players in the rush to cater to this impulse in institutional fields as diverse as education, retailing, and tourism. Such organizational efforts only serve to further institutionalize the ethnographic imagination, reproducing identities and relationships that are vividly reminiscent of colonial dynamics. With the help of postcolonial theory, this chapter closely examines this process with a view to appreciating its wider discursive consequences.

Colonialism and the Emergence of Ethnography

As the vanguard methodological opposition to die-hard positivism, ethnography in organization studies has acquired a somewhat marginal and rebellious image. Within organization studies, ethnographers have been most responsible for restoring subjectivity to scholarly inquiry (Atkinson & Hammersley, 1994), for taking native standpoints seriously (Gregory, 1983), and for privileging local meanings over universal social pronouncements (Young, 1989). It would be a mistake, however, to believe that ethnography occupies a similarly marginal position in symbolic anthropology (where it first developed as an academic genre). Far from being marginal, ethnography has always been virtually synonymous with the symbolic anthropological tradition, and is the methodology of choice for most scholars in that discipline.

Early "amateur" ethnographies were written by European participants in the first stages of the global colonial enterprise. Explorers, adventurers, traders, settlers, missionaries, colonial governors, and administrators often maintained diaries and logs, or wrote extensive reports providing detailed personal accounts of "native" (non-European) cultures that they encountered in Asia, Africa, and the so-called New World. These documents were of enormous value to colonial administrators back home for they offered rich portraits of customs, taboos, and ways of life among people who were in the process of being subjugated and exploited by systematic colonial rule.

In course of time, ethnography's usefulness to the colonial home front became so well recognized that the leading imperial powers of the day—Britain, France, and the Netherlands—actively began sponsoring academic ethnographic missions in various parts of the world. By the end of the nineteenth and well into the twentieth century, European scholars interested in studying exotic natives could count on considerable governmental and other institutional support in their home countries. This was also the period that witnessed the formation of various ethnological societies in Europe and North America with an interest in the "scientific" study of native peoples.

Ethnological societies were founded in Paris in 1839, in New York in 1842, and in London in 1843 (Stocking, 1985). Along with many newly founded anthropological departments in leading universities, these ethnological societies also cosponsored a number of ethnographic field projects that would add to the European knowledge base of native societies. In the United States (a settler-colony where somewhat different vectors of colonialism received emphasis), ethnographers received enormous support from the Bureau of Indian Affairs and the Smithsonian Institute so that they might supply information about the various indigenous native societies that were steadily being destroyed by the westward frontier expansions (Vidich & Lyman, 1994).

Adding to this impressive array of institutional sponsors were the anthropological or ethnographic museums such as the National Museum of Ethnology in Leiden, the *Musee de L'homme* in Paris, and the Peabody Museum at Harvard (Stocking, 1985), all strongly supporting ethnographic projects that were expected to return with large quantities of native cultural artifacts for museum displays. In France, ethnography was also regarded as an important art, of great use to the colonial administrator in his dealings with the natives. In fact, novice administrators who were soon to be dispatched all over the French empire were required to attend a course on ethnography offered by the celebrated French ethnographer, Marcel Griaule at the *Institut d'Ethnologie* (Clifford, 1988).

Ethnography's immense functional value to colonial rule was threefold. First and foremost, ethnographers provided supposedly "authentic" cultural portraits of native ways, and thereby facilitated a better understanding of the people who were in the course of being conquered, subjugated and even, on occasion, exterminated. The ethnographer stood at the threshold of two worlds—the recognizable European or Western one, and the unknown mysterious world of the natives. Through persistent, systematic, and even intrusive methods of participant observation, the ethnographer was believed to have acquired a mastery over native cultures which was most useful for the purposes of colonial rule and domination.

Second, the practice of ethnography in the nineteenth and early twentieth centuries kept museums and universities in Europe and North America well-stocked with an endless stream of native artifacts that were eventually displayed in the enormously popular exhibitions and museum shows of the time. Indeed the line between the collection of ethnographic details for writing the ethnographic account and the collection of material objects was incredibly fine. Professional ethnographers incessantly *collected* native objects—whether they were bronzes from Benin, rugs from the Middle East, or masks from Tanganyika to refurbish their own accounts and to add to museum and other institutional collections (Coombes, 1994). Some ethno-graphic projects were, in fact, unabashedly intended to supply home institutions with an array of native artifacts. The famous French Mission Dakar-Djibouti is a noteworthy illustration of this practice. Under the leadership of the renowned anthropologist, Marcel Griaule, the several-year-long expedition eventually yielded no less than 3500 objects for the *Musee de L'homme* in Paris (Clifford, 1988). Between 1879 and 1904 alone, the Smithsonian's Bureau of Ethnology collected at least 41,500 objects, many of them being the fruit of ethnographic expeditions among various native societies in America (Evans, 1997). The ethnographic passion for collecting extended in some cases to native bodies themselves. Men and women from different parts of Africa and Asia were periodically shipped back to the West for the entertainment and edification of home audiences.

In sum, ethnographic research accounts and ethnographic collections jointly constituted the "native" as a primitive and exotic subject (Gidley, 1992; Root, 1996), a simultaneous source of abhorrence (Youngs, 1992) and excitement. It is important to note that the Western discursive constitution of the native was primarily characterized by a profound ambivalence. The native represented crude primitivism, noble savagery, exotic sensuality, degeneracy, luxuriance, passivity, mysterious danger, and sublimity (Benz, 1997; Root, 1996). At the same time, the native also stood out as the embodiment of *difference*—biological, cultural, and intellectual. In a word, then, the native was cast as the exotic other, a simultaneous source of dangerous fantasy and intense pleasure (Prasad & Prasad, 2002a). Yet, the native's position as an inferior (albeit exciting) subject also served to legitimize colonial rule and domination over native cultures. And ethnography, along with many other discursive instruments, reinforced the moral righteousness of European conquest and domination.

The Rise of the Ethnographic Imagination

By the early twentieth century, ethnography had clearly emerged as a professionalized academic practice serving multiple institutional interests. However, it is important to also understand how ethnography took powerful hold of the popular imagination in both Europe and North America. In fact, the rise of something that could well be described as an *ethnographic imagination* (Evans, 1999; Herbert, 1991) is a striking feature of the times. Ethnographic texts were not only consumed by literary and scholarly societies, but were also translated into less academic versions that appeared in magazines such as *Harpers Monthly* and the *Century Illustrated Monthly* in

America. A number of prominent ethnographers even became celebrated public figures eliciting considerable admiration from a growing educated, middle-class public who eagerly consumed narratives of exotic cultures that were presented by academic experts who had traveled extensively among the natives.

Well-known anthropologists such as Bronislaw Malinowski, Marcel Griaule, and Frank Hamilton Cushing emerged as heroic and adventurous figures who returned from exciting ethnographic sojourns to tell stories of strange and exotic native cultures. The rise to celebrity status of Frank Hamilton Cushing is a particularly interesting case in point. Cushing, who spent close to 20 years among the Zuni, becoming a native shaman in the process, was cast as a glamorous and romantic adventurer in several magazines of the times. While professional anthropologists frequently derided Cushing's style of "gone-native" ethnography (Prasad & Prasad, 2002a) for its lack of distance and detachment, the very same techniques gained him a wide and admiring public audience. In one of the 1882 issues of the *New Century Illustrated* magazine, Cushing is visually portrayed in the full native regalia of a Zuni war priest and extolled for his adventures among the natives. Several years later, Margaret Mead (who was an even more controversial figure) also achieved close to celebrity status for her stories of sexual escapades among the Samoan natives.

At the heart of the ethnographic imagination was the ethnographer him/herself—a colorful, adventurous personality willing to immerse him or herself in exotic and unknown cultures. In many ways, the ethnographer was an archetypical colonial persona with a commitment to gathering information about native cultures. Ethnographers also played active roles in organizing cultural exhibitions that were popular at that time. Innumerable fairs and exhibitions of considerable magnitude were organized in the latter part of the nineteenth and early twentieth centuries. The exhibits that drew the most crowds were often the ethnographic ones displaying native "specimens" or groups of natives working on some task or the other.

One of the more infamous instances of human display was that of Ota Benga, the African "pygmy" who was brought to the United States by missionary ethnologist, Samuel Phillips Vermeer and displayed as a native exhibit in the St. Louis World Fair of 1904 (Bradford & Blume, 1992). After being subjected to the public gaze in St. Louis, Ota Benga was placed in the Monkey House in the Bronx zoo to demonstrate the closeness between primitive people and primates. Nearly 30 years earlier, the Centennial Exhibition in Philadelphia celebrating one hundred years of American independence had displays of "wild children" from Borneo (Slotkin, 1985).

One of the most popular exhibitions at the Philadelphia Exposition was the Japan Pavilion, which included Japanese craftsmen building a tea-house. While the spectators were in general captivated by the Japanese Pavilion, a frequent complaint was that the workmen were often in Western dress (Harris, 1990). To viewers already under the spell of the ethnographic imagination, natives were expected to be exotically dressed. Anything else was likely to be disappointing.

In probably the most shameful examples of native body displays, a woman called Sarah Bartman from the Hottentot tribe—better known to the world as the "Hottentot Venus"—was publicly exhibited in London in 1810 to illustrate the Black woman's primitive anatomy which was believed to be responsible for her animal-like sexual behavior. After Bartman's death in 1815, her body was dissected and sections of her genitalia also put on display to illustrate the source of her so-called primitive sexual appetites (Gilman, 1985).

In Britain, native artisans from India were part of a live ethnographic display at the Colonial and Indian Exhibition held in London in 1886 (Mathur, 2001) where they "performed" the daily life of craftwork in an Indian village. Many individuals from Africa, such as the Batwa people of the Congo, were also shipped to London by Colonel James Harrison in 1905 so that they could be displayed live or photographed for various museum displays of physiognomy (Coombes, 1994). European and American publics were increasingly captivated by the sight of natives themselves (rather than texts or images) serving as the medium of ethnographic representations in which they, in some sense, performed *themselves* in the public gaze (Kirshenblatt-Gimblett, 1998).

Altogether, ethnographic texts and narratives, images of heroic ethnographers, collections of native artifacts, and organized displays of the natives themselves jointly fueled the ethnographic imagination—a mindset that anticipated and enjoyed encounters with native cultures to fulfill a sense of adventure, as an intellectual pursuit, and for erotic and aesthetic stimulation. It is possible to argue that the ethnographic imagination was the product (at different moments) of three distinct but overlapping discourses: *primitivism, orientalism,* and *tropicalization.* The term discourse is being used here in the broadest sense and is close to Foucault's (1972: 49) notion of "practices that systematically form the objects of which they speak." According to Foucault, any discourse (e.g., managerial, medical, or literary) offers pronouncements about reality, truth, aesthetics and so on that become an unquestioned part of our everyday lives. From this perspective, discourse is much more than speech or written texts and is best understood as "an ensemble of ideas, concepts and categorizations that are produced, reproduced and transformed in a particular set of practices through which meaning is given to social realities" (Hajer, 1995: 44). Discourses emerge out of institutionalized practices at various levels of society and are "ways of constituting knowledge together with the social practices, forms of subjectivity and power relations which inhere in such knowledges and the relations between them" (Weedon, 1997: 105).

At their core, all three discourses mentioned above—primitivism, orientalism, and tropicalization—actively participated in constituting the ethnographic imagination by carving out identities of the Western self and the non-Western Other, and by delineating relationships between them through a series of hierarchical oppositional categories. While the three discourses do have much in common, they are also distinctive in nuanced ways. Broadly speaking, while primitivism dominates the ethnographic imagination about Africa, orientalism is concerned mainly with Turkey and the Middle East, and tropicalization deals with Latin America and the Caribbean.

Primitivism

The discourse of primitivism primarily centers on the dichotomy of civilized (Western) and savage (non-Western) cultures. Primitivism is at the same time an *avant-garde* (Coombes, 1994) artistic movement and a state of mind that regards certain native populations as savage, childlike, tribal, libidinous, irrational, fecund, close to nature, innocent, and clearly underdeveloped (Torgovnick, 1990). Even when so-called "primitive" native art was much admired in the late nineteenth century, it was simultaneously represented as "lower" and inferior to Western art (Clifford, 1988). Part of primitivism's appeal lay in the evolutionary notion that primitive societies represented an earlier stage of human development, that had long been transcended by European cultures. To ethnographers like Malinowski (1929) therefore, the task of studying primitive societies was essential to understanding human nature in its original pristine form before it had been influenced by civilizing forces.

Primitivism, for the most part, plays into that part of the ethnographic imagination that is preoccupied with Africa, and exhibits two dominant discursive tropes. The first trope is that of cultural underdevelopment and the second is that of danger. The so-called primitive societies hold the appeal of both innocence and savagery at the same time. Their location at the lowest rung of the civilizational ladder gives them the charm of innocence while their closeness to nature turns them into unpredictable sources of irrational violence. In other words, the tribalesque discourse of primitive societies, which was romanticized as being enviably close to nature, also meant that primitive natives could turn in an instant from innocent children into cannibalistic savages. In sum, primitivism cast the native as a figure from the Western self's distant past, a time before the birth of civilization itself. It is worth noting here that while most of Africa was recruited for the discourse of primitivism, Egypt—whose legacy of a "civilized" past was taken to mean that Egypt rightfully could only belong to the Middle East, rather than to Africa—became a prime candidate for the discourse of orientalism.

Orientalism

While few readers will need an introduction to orientalism, a brief discussion may be in order. The term first came into prominence with Edward Said's (1979) masterly work, *Orientalism*, which closely examined the West's preoccupation with and representation of the so-called "orient." According to Said (1979: 2), orientalism is "...a style of thought based upon an ontological and epistemological distinction made between the Orient and (most of the time) the Occident." For Said, orientalism was simultaneously a structure of thought and a set of discursive practices that repeatedly constituted the orient (i.e., Turkey and the Middle East) as a place of despotism, cruelty, splendor, and sensuality, and the oriental native as untruthful, illogical, passive, malleable, and cunning. Some of the dominant tropes in the discourse of orientalism were decline, degradation, and decadence (Dirks, 1992), and this discourse overflowed with such images as that of the despotic and degenerate sultan, and of harems filled with sensuous and exquisite women, who sometimes also carried a hint of danger about them (Richon, 1985).

Within this discourse, the orient and the occident are no longer merely words, but symbolically charged terms constituting both Western and oriental cultural identities. As Richon (1985: 1) points out, "...the Occident as a category cannot exist without the Orient. And inversely, the Orient will then only exist from a Western vantage point." Orientalism eventually took concrete shape through literary, scholarly, and artistic mediums. Paintings, novels, and scholarly texts in tandem created an "Orient" that primarily existed in the European imagination as a place of barbaric splendor, haunting beauty, extreme cruelty, and sensuality. An elaborate set of hierarchical binary oppositions (e.g., passive versus active, archaic versus modern, etc.) distinguishing the orient from the occident is at the heart of this discourse (Prasad & Prasad, 2002b).

Tropicalization

Tropicalization may be understood as the counterpart of orientalism and primitivism with respect to the imagination and representation of Latin

America and the Caribbean in Western consciousness. The discourse of tropicalization creates a vast ontological separation between temperate (Anglo and North European) and tropical cultures (Aparicio & Chavez-Silverman, 1997). The term, "tropics" was first used by Spanish conquerors upon their arrival in the New World and was popularized centuries later by the French anthropologist, Claude Levi-Strauss in his well-known work, *Tristes Tropiques*. From the original encounters between Europe and the New World and right up to contemporary times, the tropics have been discursively constituted in literature, travel writings, scholarly texts, and the media as an exotic, heathenish, and luxuriant place—a virtual Eden of surpassing beauty and simultaneous lurking menace (Benz, 1997).

On the one hand, the discourse of tropicalization represents the tropics as a lush earthly paradise, full of exotic flora and fauna. On the other hand, this Edenesque abundance is simultaneously held responsible for the lethargy and idleness of tropical natives. In fact, as Benz (1997) notes, the discourse of tropicalization can be reduced to a single formula—tropical lands are desirable but the natives (while exotic and sexually stimulating) are inferior and undesirable. Describing the Honduras in 1896, for instance, the American writer Richard Harding Davis marvels at the country's mineral wealth and luxuriant forests while castigating its natives as "a gang of semi-Barbarians in a beautifully furnished house" (Davis, 1896: 147). By and large, tropicalization cast the natives as corrupt, charming, indolent, exotic, and unclean and the tropics themselves as a place of exotic pleasures and fatal decadence (Castillo, 1997). To the temperate sojourner, the tropics were simultaneously attractive and repellent—a land of Carmen Mirandas, dark bandits, and Aztec violence.

The ethnographic imagination is clearly undergirded by orientalism, primitivism, and tropicalization—all discourses of considerable ambivalence toward native cultures that were repeatedly constituted as despicable and desirable at the same time. The ethnographic imagination can therefore be conceptualized as a mindset that developed around a set of fantasies (Zantop, 1997) governing the Western self's relationships to the native others under conditions of colonialism. I suggest here that the ethnographic imagination is very much a product of that imperial mindset that derived immense pleasure from so-called "authentic" experiences with native cultures (Root, 1996). In many ways, the ethnographer was the quintessential colonial archetype—journeying courageously into mysterious and unknown lands, becoming intimate with savage natives and returning with trophies in the form of native art and artifacts, and stories about native cultures that were invaluable to colonial governing apparatuses in the home country. The ethnographer was thus simultaneously an adventurer, a storyteller, a collector, a scientist, and sometimes even a voyeur (e.g., Malinowski, 1929), engaged in spying on the sexual practices of the natives. It is not surprising, therefore, that ethnographers like Margaret Mead, Frank Hamilton Cushing, Bronislaw Malinowski, and Marcel Griaule—all of whom communicated a heroic vision of ethnography as a romantic, exciting, and scientifically demanding enterprise—should become such celebrated figures in the public imagination (Clifford, 1988; di Leonardo, 1998).

The Ethnographic Imagination in a Post-Colonial World

The ethnographic imagination did not automatically evaporate with the official demise of colonialism. Like many of colonialism's other cultural by-products, the ethnographic imagination has lingered in the Western consciousness and finds expression in many diverse situations. This, as Root (1996) points out, is not really surprising. The colonial period was one in which the white male subject was (or certainly believed himself to be) in total *command* over another culture and its natives. The colonies were often regarded as territorial properties and playgrounds to be used at the will and pleasure of colonial rulers. Colonial administrators (even at lower levels of the bureaucratic hierarchy) could demand a level of civic and sexual compliance from native subjects that might not have been possible at home because of social conventions and their own social (including class) locations. In many ways, therefore, the colonies represented a place of unbridled pleasure and control for the colonizer, and memories of them fueled a nostalgia for colonial rule long after colonialism was being practiced.

Alongside this nostalgia for a colonial-type control is the nostalgia for the purity of the primitive existence (di Leonardo, 1998; Torgovnik, 1990). The daily frustrations and alienation of industrial and post-industrial societies trigger a longing for an idealized sense of community found in tribal or pre-modern societies, where life is believed to be lived in a more "authentic" manner. In part, this nostalgia for the authenticity and simplicity of primitive existence is so resilient because it also seems to reassure the West of the complexity and advancement of its own society, which, for all its disadvantages, is still seen as being "superior" to tribal societies.

The attraction of the primitive is also strengthened by the aura of exoticism that clings to it. Native bodies, frequently imagined in sparse clothing and in various stages of semi-nudity, have been systematically constituted as erotic objects of desire. From the elemental passion of the African jungle lover to the smoldering charms of the Latina and the veiled seductiveness of the harem inmate, the native is relentlessly inscribed in the Western imagination as the essence of sexuality and desire. Over time, these images have contributed to the emergence of a sensibility which Mario Vargas Llosa describes as the *sed de exotisimo*—a thirst for the exotic—that has outlived colonialism, and lives on as a part of the contemporary ethnographic imagination.

Another nostalgia that surfaces again and again is the nostalgia for the "White Man's Burden," a missionary longing for engaging in the conversion of souls and the salvation (both spiritual and material) of the natives (Cannizo, 1998). One of the colonial period's most enduring heroes was David Livingstone, the celebrated explorer renowned for his adventures among African natives as well as for his missionary work among them. Livingstone himself constantly emphasized that Christianity was a necessary condition for the exploitation of African land and resources (Brantlinger, 1985). To him, the conversion of natives to Christianity could only improve their social and spiritual conditions, thereby making them "fit" for trade and commerce with the civilized world (Spurr, 1993). The celebration of the missionary adventurer also reinforced the West's image of itself as the harbinger of progress and true faith in native cultures, and legitimized the colonial powers' role as the "custodians" or trustees of heathen societies. Remnants of such thinking in our own times continues to place "civilized" Christian countries in the role of moral guardians over less enlightened societies.

These fantasies of absolute power over native subjects, the nostalgia for the simplicity and innocence of the pre-modern, and the glow of a missionary-like crusade all contribute to the endurance of the ethnographic imagination long after the official proclamation of colonialism's end. While the term, ethnography, in its strictest sense refers to specific forms of fieldwork in anthropology, the ethnographic *imagination* is a collective sensibility that derives much of its inspiration from scholarly ethnography with all its colonialist imprints. I am arguing here that the valorization of ethnographers and ethnography triggered a collective longing in the West for a share in these ethnographic adventures. This longing, moreover, continues to be reflected in the demand for more popular contemporary narratives of adventures among different "natives." Hunter Thompson's (1981) risky stint with the Hells Angels, Lisa Dalby's (1983) excursion into the world of Japanese geishas, and Tobias Schneebaum's (1969) sojourn among the natives of the South American rain forest are ethnographic stories that have attracted a wide audience. In all these writings, the ethnographer-protagonists venture into foreign cultural territory, become intimate with the natives and return with exhilarating stories of adventure among them.

Popular ethnographies are only one way of delighting the ethnographic imagination. In a society where consumption is an overriding preoccupation, natives and their cultures are quickly *commodified* for instant consumption. From the Navajo motifs gracing the clothing and jewelry offered by Coldwater Creek (a somewhat upscale, chi-chi catalogue company in the United States) to the Body Shop's cosmetic line that is supposedly inspired by the "tribal wisdom" of the Amazon Indians, the romance of native cultures continues to thrill (albeit in a slickly packaged form) the ethnographic imagination. As several writers remind us (Clifford, 1988; di Leonardo, 1998; Root, 1996), the *native*—that despised yet enticing creation of colonial discourse—remains an indispensable figure in the ethnographic fantasies of today's Western subject.

This discursive return of the native is almost entirely orchestrated by a number of organizations in diverse institutional fields including those of education, retail, the media, travel, and art. The inscription and institutionalization of the contemporary native and her/his culture is, therefore, very much an *organizational act* enacted by organizational players in organizational settings. Moreover, while earlier discourses of the native were primarily influenced by the logic of imperialism, current discursive practices are more driven by the imperatives of consumerism intersecting with specific memories and fantasies of colonialism. The result is the representation of the native in a form that reproduces and reaffirms the legacy of colonialism for both the West and the non-West. In much the same way as feminists have scrutinized organizational discourses for traces of patriarchy (Ferguson, 1984; Maier, 1987), the remainder of this chapter will examine routine organizational commodifications of the native with a view to understanding their role in perpetuating forms of *latent colonialism* (Zantop, 1997).

In general, organizations engaged in catering to the ethnographic imagination produce discourses emphasizing those elements (e.g., authenticity, sensuality, etc.) that provide maximum enjoyment of native cultures under conditions of minimum risk. In other words, the trick is to supply the excitement of cultural difference without any of its physical or emotional dangers. To make this a possibility, organizations in diverse institutional fields appropriate specific elements of cultural otherness corresponding to specific moments of the ethnographic imagination and offer them for public consumption (Root, 1996). Two different institutional fields are briefly considered here. They are tourism in Third World destinations and ethnographic museums.

Third World Tourism: Deep Play among the Natives

Celebrated anthropologist, Margaret Mead, made most famous by ethnographic accounts of her own sexual antics with the Samoan natives beneath the palm trees (Mead, 1928), is a glamorous if controversial character in the ethnographic imagination. While Mead's playfulness is notorious for its sexual timbre, other ethnographic heroes like Frank Hamilton Cushing and Tobias Schneebaum, whose adventures are of the more spiritual and ritualistic kind, also sparked a longing for free and authentic (though probably risky) experiences with natives. Today, no set of institutional players seems to recognize the urgency and market potential of this longing as clearly as the tourism industry, which is systematically engaged in producing images of sexual, racial, and ethnic difference in order to promote different native worlds (i.e., Third World and Aboriginal) as desirable travel destinations (Britton, 1979; Enloe, 1989). Travel agencies, hotels, tour operators, cruise lines and the like design and market a set of experiences that supposedly provide opportunities for close and playful encounters with exotic native cultures (Prasad & Prasad, 2002b).

While native sexuality may not be the sole motif in this discourse, it is certainly one of its more prominent ones. At one extreme, we are privy to the availability of sex tours in Thailand where outrageously young girls are brazenly offered for the gratification of the (mainly) Western tourists' erotic fantasies. For the most part, however, the sexuality of native women is more decorative—found, for instance, in travel brochures depicting the charms of Hawaii where attractive native maidens cater to diverse tourist wants, or in advertisements for the Bahamas where voluptuous and scantily-clad waitresses bring a nice mix of sex and servility as they serve daiquiris to tourists lounging on Caribbean beaches.

In other discursive productions of Third World tourism destinations, the land itself is constituted as a source of excitement with mountains to be climbed, wild animals to be photographed, and jungles to be "penetrated." Within these adventurous locales, natives are typically inscribed as safari guides, helpers, and sherpas, cast in a multitude of roles in which they introduce tourists to the delights of the land and protect them from the perils of untamed nature. Once cast in these roles, today's natives bear a strong resemblance to anthropology's "informants"—trusted subordinates who translated a number of cultural practices and helped ethnographers gather information about native ways of being. However, whether contemporary native cultures are constituted as languorous Edens or exciting tropical terrains, their representation seems to be inspired by those moments of the ethnographic imagination that celebrate the ethnographer as an adventurous adolescent. In his discussion of British imperialist literature in Africa and India, Brantlinger (1985) astutely highlights the distinctly *adolescent* quality that pervades much of it. The writings of Kipling and Rider Haggard, for instance, share a sense of boyish adventure and exhilaration with the explorer-ethnographer narratives of David Livingstone and Marcel Griaule. In both genres, when the natives are not playing villainous characters, they are little more than shadowy and insubstantial figures at the behest of the European protagonists.

While tourism is frequently held to be beneficial for the economic health of Third World countries, it is important to point out that a pernicious form of *latent colonialism* (Zantop, 1997) is very much at work here. As tourism discursively constitutes native cultures as sources of exotic pleasures and adventurous thrills, it still continues to reproduce former colonial relationships of Western dominance in different ways. Crick (1989) for instance, argues that in systematically constituting the Caribbean as an earthly paradise at the disposal of Western tourists, its inhabitants are invariably reduced to occupying subordinate, sexualized and servile positions in the drama of global tourism. Similar arguments can easily be proposed on behalf of natives playing their designated roles in Thailand, Polynesia, and sections of Africa. Moreover, the discursive effects of such representations have implications not only for individual identities, but also spillover into wider terrains such as development and international relations (Enloe, 1989) where they shape the discourses of policy planning and implementation.

Museums: Natives in Glass Cases

Few institutional forms have been so closely intertwined historically with colonialism in general and the ethnographic imagination in particular as museums. From their genesis as spaces in which material objects satisfying the European curiosity about the native other were displayed, museums have gone hand in hand with the colonial enterprise. Museums such as the Smithsonian Institute and France's *Musee del'homme* were strong supporters of ethnographic forays into native cultures, and immediate beneficiaries of the expeditions that returned laden with native artifacts for their collections (Clifford, 1988; Evans, 1997). As ethnography moved further and further away from the ranks of avid amateurs and became an institutional subfield of professional anthropology, museums in both Europe and North America redoubled their efforts to stand by the ethnographic enterprise. By the early twentieth century, some museums (notably those in the American Southwest) had become entirely dependent on ethnographers for stocking their collections. In referring to the museum therefore as "the institutional homeland of anthropology," Lurie (1981: 181) merely highlights the existing connections between the ethnographic imagination and the museum.

Museums primarily resonate with those moments of the ethnographic imagination that are absorbed with the "scientific" collection, organization, and presentation of natives and their cultures. As our earlier discussion has shown, native bodies and cultural artifacts have long been coveted as collectibles to be placed under the Western gaze—a gaze which, under the guise of science, systematically objectified and dehumanized them. During the period of high-colonialism, there can be little doubt that museums helped legitimize colonial rule at home by serving as a showcase for the spoils of colonialism, and by holding elaborate exhibitions in which different native cultures were dehumanized through a scientific system of classification and display. It is tempting to believe that with the passing of colonialism, museums would cease to participate in any kind of colonialist discourse. Two things, however, need to be kept in mind. First, the cultural effects of colonialism rarely died a swift death in its immediate aftermath. And second, as Stocking notes, museums' position as *archives* of material culture ties them firmly to the past and prevents a serious overhaul of their ongoing practices. In short, for Stocking (1985: 4), "museums...are institutions in which the forces of historical inertia (or cultural lag) are profoundly, perhaps inescapably, implicated."

While several museums in recent years have attempted to grapple with the problematic legacy of the ethnographic imagination, many of their structural arrangements and everyday discursive practices continue to perpetuate a form of latent colonialism. First of all, the fundamental separation of museums and their collections into two categories—art museums (e.g., the Louvre), and folk or ethnographic museums (e.g., the Museum of Northern Arizona, or the Tropean Museum in the Netherlands)—has created, and continues to reproduce, a relatively unquestioned hierarchical division between "high" art and "folk" or native artifacts. That this institutional dichotomy is symbolically and materially loaded is without doubt. As Coombe (1993) notes, it has successfully produced two diverse and separate art worlds, the world of art museums that house so-called *authentic masterpieces* created by talented and artistic individuals, and the world of ethnographic museums that house *authentic native artifacts* representing the efforts of collective craftsmanship.

This enduring distinction between "high" and "native" art has many problematic consequences. The structure and discourse of museums constitute high art as representing the virtuosity and creativity of individual genius, and has made it overwhelmingly the province of Western artists (Clifford, 1988). Native art, on the other hand is rarely presented as the work of talented individuals even though this may well be the case. Rather it tends to be represented as emblematic of a generic form of craftsmanship such as Hopi earthenware, Bhambra masks, or Persian carpets. Native art, therefore, is of interest to the Western audience mainly as "ethnographic specimens" (Clifford, 1988) representing an entire culture rather than the creative impulses of an individual or group. Not surprisingly then, native arts under the confined gaze of the museum are largely *undifferentiated*, reproducing an older colonial discourse in which Western art is appreciated for its variation and nuances, while native art is valued for its capacity to symbolize certain broad cultural patterns.

The logic of the ethnographic museum is also tied up with the preservation of cultures that are believed to be extinct or on the verge of extinction. For Root (1996: 108), ethnographic museums are "large edifices containing...the paraphernalia of cultures believed to be dead or dying, all organized according to current scientific theory." Put differently, many of these institutions have little interest in vibrant contemporary native cultures given their romantic preoccupations with preserving supposedly dead ones. In their zeal to ensure cultural preservation, some institutions such as the Museum of Northern Arizona have been actively involved in even preventing artistic innovations in traditional southwest native arts and crafts (Wade, 1985). As one of the largest single consumers of native artifacts, the museum was able to systematically play a regulatory role in disallowing the use of non-traditional shapes and techniques in the production of Hopi earthenware and blankets.

In other words, within the sphere of the ethnographic imagination, the native is of interest only as an exotic other who typifies a "pristine" non-Western state *uncontaminated* by the effects of change and modernity. The work of contemporary native artists tends to be exhibited in museums only when they are regarded as bearing the hallmarks of ethnicity. For many native artists in the southwest, this implies that they are forced to permanently float between the lower institutional tiers of "fine art" and the nostalgic world of folk crafts (Wade, 1985).

The ethnographic imagination has also been instrumental in the formation of an institutional space (i.e., museums) in which natives and their cultural trappings could be routinely exhibited to an interested public. While museums originally served to mainly satisfy the simple curiosity of Western audiences, they soon began to strongly resonate with the scientific-scholarly moments of the ethnographic imagination, devoted to ordering, classifying and cataloguing natives and their cultures. Museums soon turned themselves into respectable repositories of scientific knowledge about the other. By the mid-nineteenth century, many museums in England and the continent had turned into "imperial archives" (Richards, 1993) in which "the procession of objects from peripheries to center symbolically enacted the idea of London [and other metropolitan centers] as the heart of empire" (Barringer & Flynn, 1998: 11). Museums quickly developed into cultural formations, which were: (a) authoritative institutions producing knowledge about (native) cultures, and (b) imperial centers that could legitimately command the movement of native goods of value from colonial outposts to their own enclaves.

In effect, the ethnographic imagination endowed museums with two vital and interlinked roles governing their relationships to native others. One was that of the *expert* over native cultures and the other was that of responsible *guardian* over valuable material objects from these cultures. This mantle of expert stewardship over native cultures is not easily discarded by museums whose very *raison d'etre* often derives from this role. Expert stewardship also allows museums to claim ownership rights over innumerable native objects including totem poles, ivory carvings, bronze masks and potlatch blankets from a multitude of different cultures. This taken-for-granted custodial right has increasingly been challenged beginning with the 1970 controversy over the New York State Museum at Albany's possession of Iroquois wampum belts (Stocking, 1985). When confronted with such claims, museums are typically unyielding, arguing that they are likely to be the most suitable custodians of material objects since they would be unlikely to subject these objects to the wear and tear of any kind of ritual or functional use. So caught up are museums and their advocates in the discourse of the ethnographic imagination that they fail to realize that the utility value of an object (whether sacred or secular) can have a cultural significance that far exceeds that of scientific display and exhibition.

The main point here is that museums can still be enmeshed within a particular discourse of the ethnographic imagination where natives are preserved and enjoyed at a scientific distance. Museums render the exoticism of natives pleasurable by freezing them in time and place, thereby diffusing their more dangerous and resistant tendencies. It is worth noting here that the widespread institutionalized practice of displaying native cultures in glass boxes is exclusive to the West and is coterminous with the rise of colonialism. While one can often come across collections of Western "Art" in the museums and galleries of Cairo and Shanghai, one does not ever witness exhibitions of everyday Western cultural practices (e.g., Belgian bankers or American cheerleaders) in the museums of Bombay or Baghdad. The idea of quotidian cultural practices being of interest to the public gaze is indeed something that grew out of the ethnographic imagination in the West.

Conclusion

This chapter has traced the connections amongst colonial practices, the ethnographic imagination and contemporary organizational discourses in the fields of tourism and museums. While the discussion here has been necessarily limited to these two fields, this by no means implies that the ethnographic imagination has not left its footprints on other institutional fields as well. The yearning for natives and their cultures is routinely exploited by retail organizations like the Banana Republic selling dreams of safari adventures through their apparel line (de Leonardo, 1998), by management consultants hawking "spirituality" in the workplace by invoking native religious rituals and ceremonies (Elmes, 2001), and by Western management trainers proselytizing native managers in Eastern Europe and Latin America in order to raise their levels of capitalist and entrepreneurial consciousness.

Three things stand out in all these discourses. First, the *cultural footprints* of colonialism continue to linger in a multitude of organizational/institutional locations long after the occurrence of *political decolonization*. Second, these colonial constitutions of the native other are markedly characterized by *ambivalence* rather than by one-dimensionality where otherness is almost invariably cast in both pejorative and pleasurable images. And third, the enjoyment of natives requires that they and their cultures be domesticated and *pacified*, purged of their more unpredictable and fearsome elements. In sum, through a combination of primitivism, orientalism and tropicalization, otherness is transformed into a desirable cultural commodity that continues to be constituted primarily on the West's own terms.

More to the point, all this is of increasing relevance in a world of accelerated globalization. Beneath its seductive veneer of free trade and informatization, globalization can also serve as a process of expanding neocolonialism in economic and cultural spheres (Larrain, 1994). Even as native cultures are liberalized, opened up, and marketed in the West (supposedly for their own economic well-being), they are also often re-constituted in keeping with the fantasy worlds of the ethnographic imagination. Within these fantasy worlds, native personas are represented as attractive and desirable while culturally inferior to the Western self. Even as globalization purportedly tears down national boundaries and expands the channels of communication between First and Third World nations, organizations in diverse fields are actively engaged in confining natives within these discursive prison houses of exoticization. Yet, through some mysterious oversight, most scholars within mainstream and critical management studies have remained oblivious to these tendencies and appear incapable of acknowledging the legacy of colonialism on contemporary organizational discourses. Like many other pieces in this volume, this chapter also hopes to initiate a cultural critique of organizations that is not confined to the parameters of labor process theory, managerial elitism or hegemonic capitalism.

An analysis like the one in this chapter might well lead one to believe that latent colonial discourses have such a tight grip on contemporary imaginations that escape from them is not really possible. It is far from my intent to suggest that this might be the case. Resistance to the ethnographic imagination, while often less apparent, is always at hand. From the artful burlesquing of "ethnic tourists" by Pueblo Indians during their ritual dances (Sweet, 1989), the boycotting of tourism-related occupations in parts of the Caribbean to the diverse challenges mounted by Third World and aboriginal governments to the property rights of museums (Coombe, 1993), the discourse of the ethnographic imagination is frequently under assault and contestation. In detailing the connections between contemporary organizations and this specific variant of colonialist discourse, this paper joins these various attempts in resisting the lingering cultural legacies of colonialism.

Note

1. My thanks to Sven Andersson for first drawing my attention to the notion of *tropicalization*. Thanks also to Carol Batker for her encouragement of the ideas in this chapter.

References

Aparicio, F. R., & Chavez-Silverman, S. 1997. Introduction. In F. R. Aparicio & S. Chavez-Silverman (Eds.), *Tropicalizations: Transcultural representations of Latinidad*. Hanover, NH: University Press of New England.

Atkinson, P., & Hammersley, M. 1994. Ethnography and participant observation. In N. K. Denzin & Y. Lincoln (Eds.), *Handbook of qualitative research* (pp. 248–261). Thousand Oaks, CA: Sage Publications.

Barringer, T., & Flynn, T. 1998. The South Kensington Museum and the colonial project. In T. Barringer & T. Flynn (Eds.), *Colonialism and the object: Empire, material culture and the museum* (pp. 11–27). London: Routledge.

Benz, S. 1997. Through the tropical looking glass: The motif of resistance in U.S. literature on Central America. In F. R. Aparicio & S. Chavez-Silverman (Eds.), *Tropicalizations: Transcultural representations of Latinadad* (pp. 51–66). Hanover, NH: University Press of New England.

Bradford, P. V., & Blume, H. 1992. *Ota Benga: The pygmy in the zoo*. New York: St. Martin's Press.

Brantlinger, P. 1985. Victorians and Africans: The genealogy of the myth of the Dark Continent. In H. L. Gates (Ed.), *"Race", writing and difference* (pp. 185–222). Chicago: University of Chicago Press.

Britton, R. A. 1979. The image of the third world in tourism marketing. *Annals of Tourism Research, 6*, 18–28.

Cannizo, J. 1998. Gathering souls and objects: Missionary collections. In T. Barringer & T. Flynn (Eds.), *Colonialism and the object: Empire, material culture and the museum* (pp. 153–166). London: Routledge.

Castillo, D. A. 1997. The tropics of the imagination: Quetzelcoatl and all that. In F. R. Aparicio & S. Chavez-Silverman (Eds.), *Tropicalizations: Transcultural representations of Latinidad* (pp. 67–98). Hanover, NH: University Press of New England.

Clifford, J. 1988. *The predicament of culture: Twentieth century ethnography, literature and art*. Cambridge, MA: Harvard University Press.

Coombe, R. J. 1993. The properties of culture and the politics of possessing identity: Native claims in the cultural appropriation controversy. *Canadian Journal of Law and Jurisprudence, 6*, 249–285.

Coombes, A. E. 1994. *Reinventing Africa: Material culture and the popular imagination in late Victorian and Edwardian England*. New Haven: Yale University Press.

Crick, M. 1989. Representations of international tourism in the social sciences: Sun, sex, sights, savings, and servility. *Annual Review of Anthropology, 18*, 307–344.

Dalby, L. 1983. *Geisha*. Berkley, CA: University of California Press.

Davis, R. H. 1896. *Three Gringos in Venezuela and Central America*. New York: Harper.

di Leonardo, M. 1998. *Exotics at home: Anthropologies, others, American modernity*. Chicago: University of Chicago Press.

Dirks, N. 1992. Introduction. In N. Dirks (Ed.), *Colonialism and culture* (pp. 1–25). Ann Arbor, MI: University of Michigan Press.

Elmes, M. 2001. Moved by the spirit: Contextualizing workplace empowerment in American spiritual ideals. *Journal of Applied Behavioral Science, 37*, 33–50.

Enloe, C. 1989. *Bananas, beaches and bases: Making feminist sense of international politics*. London: Pandora.

Evans, B. 1997. Cushing's Zuni sketchbooks: Literature, anthropology and American notions of culture. *American Quarterly, 49*, 717–745.

Evans, B. 1999. *The ethnographic imagination in American literature: A genealogy of cultures, 1865–1930*. Unpublished Ph.D. dissertation, University of Chicago.

Ferguson, K. E. 1984. *The feminist case against bureaucracy*. Philadelphia: Temple University Press.

Foucault, M. 1972. *The archaeology of knowledge*. London: Tavistock.

Gidley, M. 1992. *Representing others: White views of indigenous peoples*. Exeter: University of Exeter Press.

Gilman, S. L. 1985. Black bodies, white bodies: Toward an iconography of female sexuality in late 19th century art, medicine and literature. In H. L. Gates, Jr. (Ed.), *"Race", writing and difference* (pp. 223–261). Chicago: University of Chicago Press.

Gregory, K. 1983. Native-view paradigms: Multiple cultures and culture conflicts in organizations. *Administrative Science Quarterly, 28*, 359–376.

Hajer, M. A. 1995. *The politics of environmental discourse: Ecological modernization and the policy process.* Oxford: Clarendon Press.

Harris, N. 1990. *Cultural excursions: Marketing appetites and cultural tastes in modern America.* Chicago: University of Chicago Press.

Herbert, C. 1991. *Culture and anomie: Ethnographic imagination in the nineteenth century.* Chicago: University of Chicago Press.

Kirshenblatt-Gimblett, B. 1998. *Destination culture: Tourism, museums and heritage.* Berkeley, CA: University of California Press.

Kostera, M. 1995. The modern crusade: The missionaries of management come to Eastern Europe. *Management Learning, 3*, 331–352.

Larrain, J. 1994. *Ideology and cultural identity: Modernity and the third world presence.* Oxford: Polity Press.

Lurie, N. 1981. Museumland revisited. *Human Organization, 40*, 180–187.

Maier, M. 1997. "We have to make a management decision: Challenger and the dysfunctions of corporate masculinity. In P. Prasad, A. Mills, M. Elmes, & A. Prasad (Eds.), *Managing the organizational melting pot: Dilemmas of workplace diversity* (pp. 226–254). Thousand Oaks, CA: Sage Publications.

Malinowski, B. 1929. *The sexual life of savages: An ethnographic account of courtship, marriage and family life among the natives of the Trobiand Island, British New Guinea.* New York: Harcourt, Brace and World.

Mathur, S. 2001. Living ethnological exhibits: The case of 1886. *Cultural Anthropology, 15*, 492–524.

Mead, M. 1928. *Coming of age in Samoa.* New York: American Museum of Natural History.

Prasad, A., & Prasad, P. 2002a. Otherness at large: Identity and difference in the new globalized organizational landscape. In I. Aaltio & A. Mills (Eds.), *Gender, identity and the culture of organizations* (pp. 57–71). London: Routledge.

Prasad, P., & Prasad, A. 2002b. Casting the native subject: The ethnographic imagination and the (re)production of difference. In B. Czarniawska & H. Hopfl (Eds.), *Casting the other: The production and maintenance of inequality in organizations* (pp. 185–204). London: Routledge.

Richards, T. 1993. *The imperial archive: Knowledge and fantasy of empire.* London: Verso.

Richon, O. 1985. Representation, the despot and the harem: Some questions around an academic orientalist painting by Lecomte-du-Nouy. In F. Barker, P. Hulme, M. Iversen, & D. Loxley (Eds.), *Europe and its others* (Vol. 1, pp. 1–13). Colchester: University of Essex Press.

Root, D. 1996. *Cannibal culture: Art, appropriation and the commodification of difference.* Boulder, CO: Westview Press.

Said, E. 1979. *Orientalism.* New York: Vintage Books.

Schneebaum, T. 1969. *Keep the river on your right.* New York: Grove.

Slotkin, R. 1985. *The fatal environment: The myth of the frontier in the age of industrialization, 1800–1890.* New York: Atheneum.

Spurr, D. 1993. *The rhetoric of empire: Colonial discourse in journalism, travel writing and imperial administration.* Durham, NC: Duke University Press.

Stocking, G. 1985. Essays on museums and material culture. In G. Stocking (Ed.), *Objects and others: Essays on museums and material culture* (pp. 3–14). Madison, WI: University of Wisconsin Press.

Sweet, J. 1989. Burlesquing "the other" in Pueblo performance. *Annals of Tourism Research, 16,* 62–75.

Thompson, H. 1981. *Hells Angels.* New York: Ballantine.

Torgovnick, M. 1990. *Gone primitive: Savage intellects, modern lives.* Chicago: University of Chicago Press.

Vidich, A. J., & Lyman, S. M. 1994. Qualitative methods: Their history in sociology and anthropology. In N. K. Denzin & Y. Lincoln (Eds.), *Handbook of qualitative research* (pp. 23–59). Thousand Oaks, CA: Sage Publications.

Wade, E. L. 1985. The ethnic art market in the American Southwest, 1880–1980. In G. Stocking (Ed.), *Objects and others: Essays on museums and material culture* (pp. 167–191). Madison, WI: University of Wisconsin Press.

Weedon, C. 1997. *Feminist practice and poststructuralist theory.* Oxford: Blackwell.

Young, E. 1989. On the naming of the rose: Multiple meanings as elements of organizational culture. *Organization Studies, 10,* 187–206.

Youngs, T. 1992. The medical officer's diary: Travel and travail with the self in Africa. In M. Gidley (Ed.), *Representing others: White views of indigenous peoples* (pp. 25–36). Exeter: Exeter University Press.

Zantop, S. 1997. *Colonial fantasies: Conquest, family and nation in precolonial Germany, 1770–1870.* Durham, NC: Duke University Press.

CHAPTER 7

Reading the Rhetoric of Otherness in the Discourse of Business and Economics: Toward a Postdisciplinary Practice

Esther Priyadharshini

[Certain texts are given] the authority of academics, institutions, and governments...Most important, such texts can create not only knowledge but also the very reality they appear to describe. In time such knowledge and reality produce a tradition, or what Michel Foucault calls a discourse, whose material presence or weight, not the originality of a given author, is really responsible for the texts produced out of it.

Edward Said, Orientalism

The circular relationship among texts, knowledge, and reality, each involved in the production of the other, has been the focus of much post-structural and postcolonial theorizing. This chapter, which is a postcolonial critique of a selection of texts widely read by the business and management communities, also works on the same principle. Arguing that these texts are premised on neocolonial representations of Others, the paper moves through a circuitous route, introducing first, the idea that the rhetoric of otherness contained in these texts is based on a particular way of representing the *political* and *economic* features of these Others. This is in contrast to the emphasis on racial and cultural differences more usually attributed to such rhetoric in postcolonial theory. It then goes on to examine some issues that may arise while attempting to practice a pedagogy which pays attention to these political and economic dimensions within the business and management classroom. It concludes by raising questions about some of the D/disciplinary boundaries that currently define "management studies" and the need to more closely examine its relationship with global economics and politics.

To examine the texts in question, I have used the concepts of Knowing and Representation as discussed in postcolonial theory and criticism. Edward Said's work *Orientalism* (1978) exposed how the project of "Knowing" the Other was central to the establishment and maintenance of colonial rule. In the colonial era, the process of knowing was engineered through a systematic collection of information by agents within the colonial apparatus, who measured, described, and classified other peoples, their cultures, histories, geographies, bodies, and so on. From Foucault (1980) we learn that such practices had come to be seen as an integral part of the governance of modern states in Europe and as such were not particular to colonial government. However, the difference from the European situation was that in the colonies, this mode of knowing became one of the ways through which colonial subjects were encouraged to know themselves as inferior to European race, thought, literature, art, and the like. Through this strategy of hierarchization, colonial discourse was able to construct the colonial subject through "an articulation of forms of difference—racial and sexual" (Bhabha, 1994: 67). This "negative" difference became the basis for the process of Othering which justified colonial rule and its racial and cultural hierarchies.

Focusing on the persistence of this mode of knowing in contemporary history is an integral part of the postcolonial project.[1] For instance, with regard to academic knowledge, it has been pointed out that, "virtually all branches of European knowledge and science have grown with the confident conviction that the world is knowable only through those categories of knowledge that have been developed in Europe—indeed that the world may even *exist* only in and through such categories of European modernity" (Prasad, 1997a: 94, italics original; see also, Chakrabarty, 1992). Most legitimized epistemologies work on the same principle. As the other contributions to this book reveal, this is largely the case with the fields of economics and management as well. In fact, in recent times there has been a renewal of the colonialist mode of knowing the Other in areas that fall within the ambit of their academic domains. Undoubtedly, the phenomenon of globalization has provided much of the impetus for such developments. In the early 1950s, with the end of the "formal" colonial era, many of the newly independent countries of Asia and Africa looked for greater economic independence and self-reliance, and it was common practice for national governments to frame economic policies that protected local industry and kept foreign firms, capital, and influence away. By the turn of the century, however, we have a very different picture—a global economy with greater interdependence between countries, organizations spanning several continents, and national economic policies being urged toward greater integration. With the opening up of formerly regulated or protected economies and the lowering of trade and investment barriers, the need for greater knowledge about hitherto unavailable or restricted markets has become vital—hence an increased momentum in the collection, comparison, classification, and representation of a host of variables. Typically, these have included national economic policies, laws, customs, and traditions, "consumer" behaviors, interests, desires, habits, lifestyles, and other intimate aspects of groupings defined by class, gender, nationality, geography, ethnicity, and so on. Such developments are also noticeable in the growth of "corporate anthropology" by businesses that wish to expand their operations overseas (Suchman, 2000).

Apart from such anthropological research, one of the most convenient ways of obtaining the "latest" knowledge about both familiar and unfamiliar market environments is through published secondary sources like that of business journalism—the genre contained in business and economics magazines and newspapers. This genre is ubiquitous, noticeable at newsstands everywhere and in both public and academic libraries. The increasing importance of this source can also be attested by their prominent appearance on approved and informal reading lists for students of business, management, or economics courses around the world. In some cases, they fashion academic debate and influence curriculum design lending credence to the idea that "such texts create not only knowledge but also the very reality they appear to describe." This chapter is, in part, a reaction to such developments that I encountered as a student in India and more recently as a researcher in the United Kingdom. Thus far, academic communities seem to have paid little attention to the content or construction of texts in this genre[2] or to its relationship with institutionalized academic disciplines.

The texts that I have chosen for analysis here are those that relate to the Indian economy, some of which I read as a student in the early 1990s. They were published in issues of *The Economist*[3] (in 1991, 1995, 1997) and in the *Newsweek*[4] in 1997. The timing of these publications is in itself revealing—1991 is seen as the landmark year of economic liberalization[5] and 1997 was marked, with a certain degree of fanfare, as the fiftieth anniversary of Indian independence. The flurry of articles bracketed by these two events reveals how the construction of knowledge about the global economic present is often contingent on the postcolonial nature of the political nation-state. To interpret these texts, I have drawn on some key concepts offered by post-colonial theory. Of particular use have been the concepts of mimicry, ambivalence, and stereotyping as theorized by Homi Bhabha (1994).

Mimicry, Ambivalence, and the Stereotype

Bhabha explains how mimicry can be the result of a narcissistic demand made by the colonizer on the colonized to mimic the habits, values, speech, institutions, cultures, and so on, of the colonizer. Based on the Lacanian con-cept of mimicry as camouflage—as identification based on an image outside the self—it is the desire for a reformed, palatable Other, who would be recognized as "almost the same, but not quite." Therefore, the discourse of mimicry always exhibits an ambivalence—it "appropriates" the Other through reform, regulation, and discipline while at the same time, it is also the sign of the inappropriate, because of its difference from the "original" and "authentic." Hence authorized versions of otherness like the "mimic men" or the "brown sahib," are also inappropriate colonial subjects who "menace rather than resemble," "repeat rather than re-present" the colonizer. According to Bhabha, this grotesque doubling, by reflecting an alienating "Other" image gazing back at the looker, ultimately threatens the certainty of the origin and de-authorizes colonial authority.

This ambivalence also haunts the discursive strategy of the stereotype which, in colonial discourse is essentially a problem of representing the Other. Bhabha takes care to point out that "the stereotype is not a simplifi-cation because it is a false representation of a given reality. It is a simplifica-tion because it is an arrested, fixed form of representation…" (1994: 75) That is, the stereotype is a reductive way of seeing the Other because it denies the complexities and the play of difference within that Other.

Because it is an arrested form of representation, the stereotype also allows for a form of multiple, contradictory belief. As Bhabha (1994: 82) explains, "The black is both savage (cannibal) and yet the most obedient and dignified of servants (the bearer of food); he is the embodiment of rampant sexuality and yet innocent as a child; he is mystical, primitive, simple-minded and yet the most worldly and accomplished liar, and manipulator of social forces." Such contradictory beliefs can be held simultaneously, to facilitate explana-tion in different contexts. They also supported the argument that under the right conditions, the native could be reformed into civilized ways, which in turn, justified the colonial "civilizing" mission. It was by "knowing" the Other on stereotypical terms that "discriminatory and authoritarian forms of political control" could be considered legitimate. The colonized thus come to be fixed as both the cause and the effect of the colonial system, "imprisoned in the circle of interpretation" (Bhabha, 1994: 83). Since *knowing* and *representation* are central to the exercise of colonial power, they also become the main concepts of analysis in the critique of colonial discourses.

In this chapter, I have used these same concepts on texts within the genre of business journalism that typically divide their attention between the political and economic environments within which businesses operate. All the texts studied interweave the representation of the economic and the political, quite often collapsing the two, perhaps revealing in the process, how "capitalism is being re-territorialized as democracy" (Spivak, 1995: 177). I have chosen to look at these two aspects individually, starting with the political, through an examination of what can be identified as the "democracy discourse."

The Democracy Discourse

I hope to reveal here how the discursive representation of the Indian political system is characterized by the ambivalence that typically accompanies the stereotype. Indian democracy becomes simultaneously the object of both extravagant praise and abuse, being lauded and reviled in turns. This is possible through a process of comparative evaluation in which two levels of comparisons are made.

First, overt comparisons are drawn between the *political* systems of similarly placed *economies*—in this case, between India, Pakistan, and China. By this practice, the economic-material is conflated with the political-cultural and, a contingent link is established between economic poverty (usually defined in GDP terms) and political deficiency (defined by "universalistic" notions of democracy). This is best illustrated by the following statement from *The Economist's* 1997 survey:

> ... India's democracy for all its flaws is real. People are free to say what they like and do so with relish. Governments rule by popular consent. When they lose that consent, they are replaced and peaceably. Of how many of the world's *comparably poor* countries could the same be said? (1997: 3, italics added)

Second, one can also detect a covert comparison of "Third World democracy" being made against the ideal of an original "Democracy," located elsewhere in the "First World," against which all of these countries fail. Whenever Indian democracy passed, it was chiefly because it was contrasted in a favorable manner against its neighbors. It seemed to have escaped classification as Communist, militaristic, or fundamentalist. As the world's largest democracy with 600 million voters (at the time of the magazine's publication), its miraculous survival through the famine of the 1960s, the emergency of the 1970s and the wars with China and Pakistan, was lauded. Borrowing from Amartya Sen's work,[6] Indian democracy was also given credit for rooting out famine—the free press and the opposition forced the Indian government to act toward a better distribution of food while China reeled under the 1958–1960 famine because of the absence of similar democratic apparatuses. Also in comparison with China, India's failures in areas of health, education, sanitation, and poverty alleviation were highlighted. However, since it is capitalism that is being re-territorialized as democracy, the article refrains from directly crediting China's achievements on these fronts to her communist system.

In this discursive representation, we see a key difference from the earlier manifestations of colonial discourse. Then, race with "skin" as signifier was often the point of difference. Now, the political system of democracy, already identified as a mimicry of an original located Westwards, occupies this space. The concept of "Democracy" working within the Indian context is seen to produce several shortcomings from the mythical original. This reinforces certain irreducible differences that render the Indian version, and by extension, Indians, "almost the same but not quite." For instance, in several of the articles analyzed, there is a celebration of the fact that democracy, with its inclusive agenda allowed the complex Indian society to "reconcile conflicting claims." At the same time, many references are made to the fact that being a democracy is often held up as an excuse for not taking "courageous" or "difficult" decisions that may offend certain minority interests. For this, it blames the

> ... anarchistic individualism of Indians all of whom think they deserve a say. Indians are an opinionated lot, and no great respecters of authority. This does not help things to happen quickly. (*E*, 1995: 7)

While one could do a number of "takes" on this comment, it is particularly interesting to bear in mind that the "things that need to happen quickly" refers primarily to economic liberalization. It is also less easy to dismiss this as a piece of opinionated journalism or even sophistic reporting if we remember the notion of the "fixity" of stereotype—not as a false representation of a given reality but as an arrested, fixated form of representation that denies the play of difference and thus constitutes a problem for the representation of the subject/object. In denying the scope for difference within the concept of "democracy," there is a containment of its very definition that only allows for a narrow conceptualization and representation. More crucially, there are subject-forming effects to this discourse when the shortfalls of Indian democracy are extended to the citizens within such a state. I will return to the implications of this in later sections of this chapter. For now, I want to point out other instances where this play of ambivalence becomes visible. For example, in discussing the nature of coalition governments, one article in *The Economist* laments that a "strong leadership" necessary to push ahead with further economic reforms is absent (*E*, Aug. 1997: 11). In another, it points out that "weak" governments led by unobtrusive politicians have been known to unexpectedly usher in reforms through the backdoor (*E*, Feb. 1997: 26). Similarly, narrow regional movements are said to lack vision (*E*, Aug. 1997: 20) while the same dissension and divisiveness is believed to prevent "dangerous mass enthusiasms" (*E*, Jan. 1995: 30).

Such discursive representations show the Indian democracy as operating simultaneously from two extreme points, some examples of which I have presented in table 7.1.

Thus the call to mimic Western style democratic arrangements is strong but the results are always less than satisfactory, the "grotesque doubling" falling short of the authentic original resulting in ambivalent, multiple, and contradictory representations.

The interpretation of Indian democracy as a "rare flower in the Third World" that has nevertheless "taken deep root" (*E*, Aug. 1997: 19) exposes this predicament and highlights the confluence of the political and the economic in this discourse. This also naturalizes the act of comparing countries located on the same rung—leaving out those too far below (sub-Saharan Africa) or those too far ahead (First World nations), allowing the formation of a formidable "double difference"—a negative difference from the more "liberalized," "progressive" economies and a positive difference from the "closed," "backward" ones. Thus a linear, progressive continuum is established in which every point works to stabilize a larger global hierarchy.

Jungle Book Economics

Moving on to the discourse of economics, one finds a glaring yet surprisingly under-examined feature of this discourse—the use of animals as metaphors to imagine economies. The most common ones are wild or mythical animals like elephants, tigers, and dragons used to describe the economies of South

Table 7.1   Discursive Descriptors of the Indian Political System in
The Economist (1991–1997)

Democracy vibrant, not a sham, real, genuine, has taken deep root in India (May 1991: 3; Feb. 1997: 3; Aug. 1997: 11, 19)	Volatile, uncertain, fragile, flawed, not genuine, blemished, corrupt, superficial (May 1991: 3; Jan. 1995: 29; Feb. 1997: 18)
Democracy suits India, it allowed room for dissension and thus preserved the union of states; its divisiveness has prevented dangerous mass enthusiasms (Jan. 1995: 30; Aug. 1997: 19)	Anarchistic individualism of Indians an impediment, they are too opinionated and everyone wants to have a say (Feb. 1997: 7)
New loose federation of states, less centralized, closer to people, gives expression to heterogeneity (Jan. 1995: 30)	Coalition of thirteen losers, an ill-matched grouping, many narrow regional movements, growing secessionism. (Aug. 1997: 11, 20)
Weak, unobtrusive politicians can usher in reforms. Political uncertainty served the country better. Nonentities cannot become dictators (Feb. 1997: 26)	Lack of strong leadership and direction; unsettled, ineffective, unambitious coalitions; din of political turbulence detrimental for the economy (May 1991: 6, 18; Aug. 1997: 11)

and South East Asia. These metaphors are so ubiquitous that they have now passed into everyday language as conventional descriptors.

The scrutiny of metaphors to explicate the relations among language, thought, and reality has been done most famously by Derrida in his essay *"White Mythology"* (1974). Metaphors are now more overtly recognized as crucial to our perception and conception of reality. Alvesson (1993) shows how metaphors can be ambiguous as they are essentially created by carrying over terms from one system or level of meaning into another. He reveals metaphors to be seductive, appealing to fantasy, and triggering off associations that can lead to the formation of pictures that may not correspond with the meaning intended by the author. As a result, simple metaphors used to convey a sharp and coherent picture or image of an object, could end up conveying a broad range of different images. This is explained through the idea of second-level metaphors that lie behind explicit metaphors. These second-level metaphors are usually visible only upon close readings of the larger body of literature by which they are created and sustained, which can then reveal the partiality of the information provided by the espoused metaphors.

The tiger metaphor is a classic example that can take up many hours of deciphering. What appears at first glance as flattering—the tiger (economy) as dynamic? powerful?—begins to look less complimentary on closer examination—as dangerous? uncivilized? less than human? threatening? uncontrollable? volatile? and so forth. Indeed, with the near collapse of some of the "tiger" economies of East Asia in the late 1990s, they were referred to as "wounded tigers" that were more "dangerous" than before (CNBC television advertisement aired in December 1998)!

While even a cursory pause before the "tiger" reveals the discrepancies between the meanings at the multiple levels at which the metaphor can be read, it grows more ludicrous when applied to any of the First World economies.[7] The use of allegory, metaphors, and tropes in colonialist discourse has been widely examined with respect to colonial discourse (see McClintock, 1995; Sharpe, 1993; Shohat & Stam, 1994). Shohat and Stam explain how "animalization" or rendering the colonized as wild beasts has been a favorite colonialist trope. They point out that the role of animalization within discourse is connected to "the larger, more diffuse mechanism of naturalization: the reduction of the cultural to the biological, the tendency to associate the colonized with the vegetative and the instinctual rather than with the learned and the cultural." (Shohat & Stam, 1994: 138). Within the discourse of globalization, the use of the tiger metaphor to represent "developing" economies replays this colonialist logic in the economic-material dimension as well. However, in relation to the process of liberalization, there is a more overt role that the tiger metaphor plays.

The *Economist*'s May 1991 survey of India carried the title, "Caged," illustrated with the picture of a tiger behind bars (figure 7.1). The article says,

Indians are fond of saying that whereas Japan, South Korea and the other thriving economies of East Asia are tigers, their own country is an elephant: immense, cautious, slow-moving, but also sure-footed, strong, purposeful. (It is a comforting image in another way: Ganesh, the Hindu god of good fortune, has the form of an elephant.) The idea is as false as the Hindu rate of growth. If a zoological metaphor is desired, a better one is this: India is a tiger caged. This tiger, set free, can be as healthy and vigorous as any in Asia. . . . The challenge is political. The government must dismantle an unbelievably complicated system of restraints and rewards that, over the past four decades has securely enclosed every aspect of Indian life. The first and necessary

Figure 7.1 The Indian Economy: Caged.
Source: Economist—Survey of India, May 4, 1991.

step is to see these restraints and rewards as the cage that they are. Depressingly, India is far even from realizing that. (*E,* May 1991: 5)

In the first few lines, we catch a glimpse of the close relationship between discourse and subject formation; and of how subject positions based on a hierarchization of economies could be naturalized and internalized. The more explicit point being made though is that the economy is the tiger and the rules and regulations that govern it, the confining and restrictive cage.

Continuing the same logic, the title of the post-reform 1995 survey was, "The Tiger Steps Out." It carries the photograph of a tiger emerging from a thicket (figure 7.2). Two years later, in February 1997, apparently disappointed with the lack of momentum in the reform process, the title of yet another Survey of India says, "Time to let go" and carries on the cover, a drawing in the Mughal miniature style (figure 7.3).

Figure 7.2   The Indian Economy: The Tiger Steps Out.
Source: *Economist—Survey of India*, January 21, 1995, reprinted by permission of
Chuck McDougal/ARDEA London Ltd.

In figure 7.3, a tiger has been let out of its cage, it rears to clear the pit in
which it finds itself but is held back by a rope around its neck that is still
tethered to the cage. The August issue of the same year, brought out to coin-
cide with India's 50 years of independence, carries the subtitle, "Of tigers and
elephants," and claims that if the economy was fully reformed, it might grow
at a "tigerish" 8 or 9 percent a year (*E*, 1997: 11). A few pages away, another
article points out that "muddled" reform had produced growth averaging
only 7 percent.

> That is well below India's potential, and means Indians will remain far
> poorer than they deserve to. Yet, 7% is not to be sniffed at. India may be
> less than a tiger, but it is no longer a bumbling centipede. (*E*, 1997: 19)

Figure 7.3 The Indian Economy: Time to Let Go.
Source: *Economist—Survey of India*, February 22, 1997, © Matilda Harrison/ARENA.

From slow elephants and caged tigers to bumbling centipedes, substantial metaphoric ground is being covered, in many ways reminiscent of the literature and images of the Raj.[8]

Clearly, the dominant theme of the articles is to highlight the need for faster "reform" or "liberalization" of the economy. Collectively, this genre seems to suggest that even if India was a recognizable democracy, it was a flawed one since government bureaucracy and economic regulations stifled its economic freedom and prosperity. Here again, Spivak (1995: 184) has pointed out the difference in language when describing phenomena in the North and in the South. While in the North, "privatization" is the preferred choice, in the South, the process is labeled "liberalization"—another example of capitalism being re-territorialized as democracy. The articles play on the imagery of the cage and claim that whenever Indians have traveled abroad, out of their "economic prison," they have done exceedingly well (*E*, 1991: 3; *E*, 1997: 4). Yet, in *The Economist*'s 1991 (pre-reform) survey of India, substantial sections of the Indian population, including the government, the political rulers and civil servants, ministers and lesser politicians (p. 5), academics and journalists (p. 5), the educated elite (p. 4), the intellectuals (p. 7, 8), the middle class (p. 6), the unions (p. 12) and the priviligentsia, that is, established business families benefiting from the regulations (p. 15), are either berated for being critics of reform or for their lack of will to reform the economic system. Apparently, the only "glimmer of hope" to push for greater reforms were "a few economic dissidents inside the bureaucracy" and "India's managers and entrepreneurs" (p. 5).[9]

Linear Progress and Development

For all my critique of the ideology, tone and style of the articles, there might be some merit in the criticisms they level against Indian economic policy. Arguably, the articles point out some of the nonviable features of the pre-1991 economy, for example, tariff protection for inefficient industries, a restrictive licensing regime, and so on, all of which might have contributed to inflation and balance-of-payments troubles (*E*, Feb. 1997: 4). However, equally indefensible is the idea that the mixed bag of processes lumped together in these articles under the label of "economic reforms" would somehow magically translate as "progress and liberty" for all segments of the larger Indian society.

The idea of "progress" has been labeled as "one of the most tenacious tropes of colonialism" by McClintock, who observes that in "colonial discourse...space is time and history is shaped around two, necessary movements: the 'progress' forward of humanity from slouching deprivation to erect, enlightened reason. The other movement presents the reverse: regression backwards from (white male) adulthood to a primordial, black 'degeneracy' usually incarnated in women" (1994: 253). The fact that the call for economic reforms is also underpinned by faith in the idea of linear historical progress, of a forward movement from darkness to light, is clear from the titles and subtitles of these articles—*Work in progress; Better late than never; Faster, faster; Keep going; Far to go; The road ahead; The next 50 years; India in the Sunlight; Out of the Dark Ages; Daylight's children; From the Old to the New; A Passage from the Past; One more push.*

This marriage of "development/progress" with "economic reform" is a potent cocktail in any "Third World," postcolonial context. However, what is offered as a logical link between the two on closer examination does not always hold. Some of them, like the *Baywatch* argument, are particularly ludicrous: according to *Newsweek* (August 1997), economic growth coupled with the media revolution (20 million cable and satellite TV connections established in two years) is

> ...working a revolution among many millions...of India's poor....
> As the vision of "Baywatch" filters through Bihar, so even the poorest of the poor finally begin to rise from the depths of rotted isolation. And so does poor, old India. (*N*, 1997: 17)

This is all the more surprising since Bihar is often referred to as India's "basket case,"

> ... with stagnant pools of humanity..., the hopeless heart of a subcontinent where the squalid villages might remind you of sub-Saharan Africa—except that the poorest Africans fare better than the destitute of Bihar. (*N*, 1997: 15)

Yet, further on, in the same page, the article states,

> ...now satellite TV has come to Bihar, and so has Coke; health and education will one day follow. (*N*, 1997: 15)

What is on offer is the "fairy tale of unlimited technological and capital growth" (McClintock, 1995: 393) and the unfounded hope that the free market would bring in its wake, social welfare, and political health. Another example of a similar liberal argument would be the claim that India's "rural awakening" will be more than just a marketing opportunity (*N*, Aug. 1997: 18). It claims that liberalization will mean that farmers will increase exports of their agricultural products and that this would transform them into proponents of foreign trade. Since globalization's benefactor will be the rural farmer as much as the urban industrialist, its benefits will extend from the managers, entrepreneurs, and industrialists to the poorest below the poverty line. The always tenuous link between free market reforms and prosperity for the masses is re-presented as a given by the neo-liberal discourse of global economics.

Mimic Economies, Mimic Wo/men

So far, the hegemonic ideology that has driven globalization (and the bulk of management and economic studies) is the neo-liberal one, defined by Hoogevelt as having belief in the idea that "private property and accumulation are sacrosanct and that the prime responsibility of governments is to ensure 'sound finance': they must 'fight inflation' and maintain an attractive 'business climate' in which, amongst other things, the power of unions is circumscribed. These ideas both underpin, and are the result of, the 'structural power' of capital that is so internationally mobile that the investment climate of each country is continually judged by business with reference to the climate which prevails elsewhere" (2001: 149). This brings us full circle to the modes by which economies are known, represented, and placed in a hierarchy—*according to other investment climates.*

If the integrationist imperative of global capital as driving force allows for little difference from the imaginary ideal, this explains why, in the rhetoric of neo-liberalism,

India has seemed strangely out of tune with the times around it . . . India was the exception. But exceptionalism did not build prosperity, and since prosperous nations stand a better chance of happiness than poor ones, when India stood apart, it stunted the life chances of its people. Those days are over. The India that now sets out into the sunlight is changing fast. It is becoming more like the rest of the world (which does not mean that it will be quite like anywhere else). (*N*, 1997: 12)

Thus, "becoming more like the rest of the world" will always precede and contain "not quite like anywhere else" in parentheses. However, the call to mimic Western economic regimes at the national policy level is also a call to mimic Western lifestyles and consumerism. Here, the subject forming effects of discourse are even more obvious. *The Economist* says,

> In India, programmes that glamorise western lifestyles—especially those that happen to display desirable goods as well as desirable bodies—have an unexpectedly high educational content. All this means more competition and a growing army of more demanding consumers. (*E*, Feb. 1997: 9)

Since the market cannot flourish without enrolling consumers willing to behave in specific ways, the discourse needs to work on the subjectivities of the population at large. This is a frustratingly tall task:

> Consumerism is a troublesome idea for a country whose hero liberated his country wearing a loin cloth, and spent his leisure hours toiling at a spinning-wheel. Not that Gandhi invented asceticism: Hinduism preaches self-purification through the denial of desires. (*E*, Jan. 1995: 4)

This is the same population earlier described as "ambitious" and "materialistic" (*E*, 1991: 3)—so once more, the ambivalence of stereotype raises its head. It is at this juncture where capitalism, democracy, discourse, and subject formation meld that we seem to reach the limits of contemporary literary theorizations of mimicry as resistance. The concept of mimicry within this economic-geopolitical arena cannot seem to deliver the destabilizing, subversive potential identified within sections of postcolonial literary and psychoanalytic theory. Faced with the "integrationist imperatives" of global capitalism, the agency located in mimicry seems both woefully shaky and annoyingly inadequate. While this could be read as a case of the "necessary lack of fit between discourse and example, the necessary crisis between theory and practice" (Spivak, 1996: 145) or perhaps, even just a case of expecting too much from the concept of mimicry, there are implications for what this means to the everyday trade of academics in management and business studies. Implicated as we are in a neo-liberal system, how can we best teach students of business and management to attempt a critical reading of the (con)texts that have been handed to us? This seems to me to indicate a disciplinary predicament that cannot be addressed without adopting a postdisciplinary approach.

Postdisciplinary Readings in the Management Classroom

In the interest of forging closer links between theory and practice, research and teaching, I return to the management classroom by examining the implications for practicing a critical, postdisciplinary pedagogy. In this final section, I also explain why a postdisciplinary pedagogy is not simply a multi or interdisciplinary approach to management education. But first, a look at the issues confronting critical pedagogues in management studies.

In order to evade the trap of "globalocentrism" (Bergeron, 2001), by which global capitalism is presented as a force that determines all outcomes (economic, political, or cultural), it is important to focus on accounts of disruptions and resistances as well (Sassen, 1998). One way to initiate critical readings of "traditional" texts in the classroom is by illuminating the gaps within dominant disciplinary discourses. Spivak has written about the critical reading practice of diagnosing what a piece does not say as "something like a collective ideological *refusal*. This would open the field for a political-economic and multidisciplinary ideological reinscription of the terrain" (1988: 286). This could be done by locating alternative readings offering different perspectives and reading them in opposition to the dominant ideology. For example, even within the same genre of journalism, there is the tale of farmer unrest—the other face of rural awakening—and the story of the widening gap between the rich and the poor. Accounts of the 50,000 Indian farmers who staged a rally against legislation on plant genetic resources in 1992 and the burning of the office of the seed giant Cargill in 1993 (*The Observer, 1997*) are available from other perspectives. *The Observer* article points out that "economic liberalization since 1991 had meant a 'severe setback' to poverty reduction . . . In nearly every (Indian) state, rural poverty was worse in 1992 than in 1989–90." A juxtaposition of such disparate accounts of the same processes can reveal the instability of neo-liberal logic and denaturalize the link between the mixed bag of reforms advocated, the promise of "economic freedom" and an improved quality of life for the general masses.

Apart from journalistic accounts, there is also a vast body of literature by Third World, postcolonial, feminist, and environmentalist critics on "development and progress" (e.g., Jackson & Pearson, 1998; Salazar, 1998; Sassen, 1996; Sittirak, 1998; Visvanathan, Duggan, Nisonoff, & Wiegersma, 1997) that can inform our readings of mainstream knowledge. Also available are more recent theorizations of why globalization is not necessarily an inevitable "package deal" (Othman & Kessler, 2000), and how resistance, agency, and politics can be theorized in more nuanced ways in the post-Seattle world (Kiely, 2000; Patomaki, 2000).

Of course, such pedagogical practices necessitate the crossing of disciplinary boundaries with the danger of perhaps losing credibility within our primary professional audiences/communities. This is not an easy task especially given the weight of tradition bearing down on most business schools and their academics around the world—a tradition which is sustained by the active policing of academia's many disciplinary boundaries, movements across which can be experienced as an illegal trespass. Particularly notorious in this respect are the disciplines of economics and management where, at least in the United Kingdom, academics are restricted in their publishing efforts to a select list of journals "in the field" for the Research and Assessment Exercise (RAE). In this instance, because of the financial, not to mention cultural, clout of this exercise, the RAE becomes the institutional mechanism for maintaining disciplinary parochialisms. However, the problems with such conventions are painfully clear. As Robert Cox and Sinclair state,

> Academic conventions divide the seamless web of the...social world into separate spheres, each with its own theorizing;...[But] such a conventional cutting up of reality is at best just a convenience of the mind... Subdivisions of social knowledge thus may roughly correspond to the ways in which human affairs are organized in particular times and places. They may, accordingly, appear to be increasingly arbitrary when practices change. (1996: 85)

In the case of management and economics, academic compartmentalization has resulted in a de-contextualized understanding of the myriad global economic processes, and theories rooted in one or the other discipline cannot seem to offer adequate explanations for them. This results in current academic practices (and texts) actually "nursing the ignorance" (Ferro, 1997: 351) around global economics. "Globalization," notwithstanding its standardizing, time-space compression effect (Giddens, 1991; Harvey, 1989), often has a very specific, localized effect (Escobar, 2001). Lata Mani's (1990) idea that "Western" ideological and political presence operating within indigenous institutions, discourses, histories, and practices results in refractions from the "original" underscores this point. But an inadequate grounding of global processes within the contexts of their operation can contribute to a foggy understanding of the workings of global capital and economics.

It can also be argued that because of the lack of a postdisciplinary approach within both postcolonial and business studies, those branches of management that are seen to be more amenable to the influence of postcolonial theory do not go *far enough* with their critique. For instance, the branch of International Management often takes on board lessons from cultural criticism but glosses over the economic differences between countries like those in labor markets that form the basis for an international division of labor. There is an obvious neglect in accounting for the workings of geo-political power (seen as the subject of International Relations) in the study of business and economics.[10]

Similarly, issues of identity and subjectivity that have been dealt with fairly rigorously within postcolonial studies have rarely included the eco-nomic or geopolitical angle. There is a need to take a closer at look at issues of identity and subject formation through these coordinates as well. For example, what are the implications when some communities are described predominantly as "investors" or "consumers" and others mainly as "produc-ers" or "laborers"? What is the impact of geopolitical identities on individual subjectivities when tiger, dragon, or elephant metaphors are used to imagine economies given that there is usually a conflation of the economic, political, and social stereotypes in the process? What kinds of relationships exist amongst regional/national currencies, exchange rates, and identities? What kinds of impacts do these relationships have on workers in transnational organizations who are situated in different geographical locations: on travel-ers, tourists, "foreign" students? These questions, rather obliquely, raise ques-tions about the "worth" of individuals, of how people are valued economically and perhaps even, morally (Sayer, 2001).

By cutting across traditional disciplinary concerns, these questions point to a need for a redefinition of the subject and scope of study of both man-agement and economic studies, as well as postcolonial theory. But they also reveal that multi or interdisciplinarity will not be sufficient. Sayer (1999) points out the problem with interdisciplinarity:

> Interdisciplinary studies... at worst... provide a space in which mem-bers of different disciplines can bring their points of view together in order to compete behind a thin disguise of cooperation, so the researchers don't actually escape from their home disciplines—at best they merely offer the prospect of such an escape.

On the other hand, ideally speaking,

> Post-disciplinary studies emerge when scholars forget about disciplines and whether ideas can be identified with any particular one; they iden-tify with learning rather than with disciplines.

For sure, the conditions of possibility for such "forgetting" and "identify-ing" may not yet be manifest, but as co-creators of these conditions, the responsibilities for attempting to construct them lie squarely with practicing academics. Which perhaps explains why this essay—which began with a critical reading of certain texts popular within management studies—has moved full circle to return to everyday academic practice as the site for critical, postdisciplinary interventions.

Notes

1. The bulk of this paper focuses on the macro level implications of "knowing" and "othering." For an analysis of these phenomena at a more intimate micro level, see Ahmed (2000).
2. An exception is Prasad's (1997b) paper on the treatment of OPEC countries in Western media and the implications for diversity management in organizations.
3. Henceforth, *E*.
4. Henceforth, *N*.
5. Very briefly, the changes that marked liberalization in India included the devaluation of the rupee, deregulation of administered prices, increasing of food and fertilizer prices, opening the economy to greater foreign investment and de-licensing industry. Some of these measures were said to be voluntary and others "imposed" to meet conditions for obtaining loans from the IMF and the World Bank.
6. For a critique of Sen's brand of "pragmatic neo-liberalism," which allows his arguments to be appropriated by free market advocates, see Sandbrook (2000).
7. It is interesting to observe that among Western nations, it is the Irish economy that has been labeled "the Celtic Tiger." The lowly position of the "Celtic race" in colonial discourse has not escaped notice within postcolonial studies (McClintock, 1995; Wills, 1991).
8. Interestingly, the Economist's 1999 survey is a joint survey of India and Pakistan in their new status as nuclear powers. In spite of (or because of?) their more "dangerous" status, in the cover image the tiger(s) have morphed into humans—members of the Indian and Pakistani national teams playing cricket in white flannels, the symbols on their caps signifying their nationality. The title is "Not Cricket" and here, the chiding, colonial overtones are inescapable. The tone of this article though seems marginally more sympathetic and less disdainful, with even the chaos of Indian democracy being described as a "Creative Chaos" (1999: 16)!
9. See Vanita Shastri (1997) for an explanation of how policy elites (bureaucrats in alliance with like-minded political leaders) influenced by a new set of ideologies were able to effect radical changes in long established economic policies.
10. As a corrective to this tendency in accounting, see Neu's chapter in this volume.

References

Ahmed, S. 2000. *Strange encounters: Embodied others in postcoloniality*. London and New York: Routledge.

Alvesson, M. 1993. The play of metaphors. In J. Hassard & M. Parker (Eds.), *Postmodernism and organizations* (pp. 114–131). London: Sage.

Bergeron, S. 2001. Political economy discourses of globalization and feminist politics. *Signs: Journal of Women in Culture and Society, 26* (4), 983–1006.

Bhabha, H. 1994. *The location of culture.* London: Routledge.

Chakrabarty, D. 1992. Postcoloniality and the artifice of history: Who speaks for "Indian" pasts? *Representations, 37* (Winter), 1–26.

Cox, R., & Sinclair, T. 1996. *Approaches to world order.* Cambridge: Cambridge University Press.

Derrida, J. 1974. White mythology: Metaphor in the text of philosophy. *New Literary History, 6* (1), 5–74.

The Economist. 1991. A Survey of India. May 4.

The Economist. 1995. A Survey of India. January 21.

The Economist. 1997. A Survey of India. February 22.

The Economist. 1997. Vol. 344 (8030). August 16–22.

The Economist. 1999. A Survey of India and Pakistan. May 22.

Escobar, A. 2001. Culture sits in places: reflections on globalism and subaltern strategies of localization. *Political Geography, 20,* 139–174.

Ferro, M. 1997. *Colonization: A global history.* London: Routledge.

Foucault, M. 1980. Governmentality. *Ideology and Consciousness, 7,* 5–21.

Giddens, A. 1991. *Modernity and self-identity.* Cambridge: Polity.

Harvey, D. 1989. *The condition of postmodernity.* Oxford: Blackwell.

Hoogevelt, A. 2001. *Globalisation and the postcolonial world: The new political economy of development* (2nd ed.). London: Macmillan Press.

Jackson, C., & Pearson, R. 1998. *Feminist visions of development.* London and New York: Routledge.

Kiely, R. 2000. Globalization: From domination to resistance. *Third World Quarterly, 21* (6), 1059–1070.

Mani, L. 1990. Multiple mediations: Feminist scholarship in the age of multinational reception. *Feminist Review, 35* (Summer), 24–41.

McClintock, A. 1994. The angel of progress: Pitfalls of the term "postcolonialism". In F. Barker, P. Hulme, & M. Iverson (Eds.), *Colonial discourse/postcolonial theory* (pp. 253–266). Manchester: Manchester University Press.

McClintock, A. 1995. *Imperial leather: Race, gender and sexuality in the colonial context.* London and New York: Routledge.

Newsweek. 1997. Vol. CXXX (5) August 4.

*The Observer.*1997. New colonial pyre lit for India. Business Section, Sunday 3, August.

Othman, N., & Kessler, C. 2000. Capturing globalization: Prospects and projects. *Third World Quarterly, 21* (6), 1013–1026.

Patomaki, H. 2000. The Tobin tax: A new phase in the politics of globalization? *Theory, Culture and Society, 17* (4), 77–91.

Prasad, A. 1997a. Provincializing Europe: Towards a postcolonial reconstruction. *Studies in Cultures, Organizations & Societies, 3* (1), 91–117.

Prasad, A. 1997b. The colonizing consciousness and representations of the other: A postcolonial critique of the discourse of oil. In P. Prasad, A. J. Mills, M. Elmes, & A. Prasad (Eds.), *Managing the organizational melting pot: Dilemmas of workplace diversity* (pp. 285–311). Thousand Oaks, CA: Sage.

Said, E. 1978. *Orientalism.* New York: Vintage Books.

Salazar, M. 1998. The peso: National currency as rhetoric. *Visible Language, 32* (3), 280–293.

Sandbrook, R. 2000. Globalizations and the limits of neo-liberal development doctrine. *Third World Quarterly, 21* (6), 1071–1080.

Sassen, S. 1996. *Losing control? Sovereignty in an age of globalization.* New York: Columbia University Press.

Sassen, S. 1998. *Globalization and its discontents.* New York: New Press.

Sayer, A. 1999. *Long live postdisciplinary studies! Sociology and the curse of disciplinary parochialism/imperialism* (draft). Department of Sociology, Lancaster University. [www.lancaster.ac.uk/sociology/soc025as.html]

Sayer, A. 2001. What are you worth? Recognition, valuation and moral economy. Department of Sociology, Lancaster University. [www.comp.lancs.ac.uk/sociology/soc069as.html]

Sharpe, J. 1993. *Allegories of empire: The figure of woman in the colonial text.* Minneapolis and London: University of Minnesota Press.

Shastri, V. 1997. The politics of economic liberalization in India. *Contemporary South Asia, 6* (1), 27–56.

Shohat, E. & Stam, R. 1994. *Unthinking eurocentrism: Multiculturalism and the media.* London and New York: Routledge.

Sittirak, S. 1998. *The daughters of development: Women in a changing environment.* London and New York: Zed Books.

Spivak, G. C. 1988. Can the subaltern speak? In C. Nelson & L. Grossberg (Eds.), *Marxism and the interpretation of culture* (pp. 271–313). Basingstoke: Macmillan Education Ltd.

Spivak, G. C. 1995. Teaching for the times. In J. N. Pieterse & B. Parekh (Eds.), *The decolonization of imagination: Culture, knowledge and power* (pp. 177–202). London: Zed Books.

Spivak, G. C. 1996. *The Spivak reader: Selected works of Gayatri Chakravorty Spivak.* (D. Landry & G. Maclean, Eds.). New York and London: Routledge.

Suchman, L. 2000. Anthropology as "brand": Reflections on corporate anthropology. Department of Sociology, Lancaster University [www.comp.lancs.ac.uk/sociology/soc0581s.html]

Visvanathan, N., Duggan, L., Nisonoff, L., & Wiegersma, N. 1997. *The women, gender and development reader.* London and New Jersey: Zed Books.

Wills, C. 1991. Language, politics, narrative, political violence. In R. Young (Ed.), Neo-colonialism, *The Oxford Literary Review, 13*, 21.

CHAPTER 8

Accounting for the Banal: Financial Techniques as Softwares of Colonialism

Dean Neu

banal–adj. devoid of freshness or originality; hackneyed or trite
Random House Dictionary

In *Eichmann in Jerusalem*, Hannah Arendt develops the notion of the banality of evil as a situation in which a perfectly normal person does horrendous things because his culture tells him that what he is doing is right. She points out that this is caused by thoughtlessness and the abdication of moral judgement. She also shows, however, that the banality of evil does not invalidate free will, and that there will always be those who are willing to choose the right when everyone around them does wrong.

Knapp, 1998: 1

Techniques of accounting, accountability, and finance are ubiquitous in modern-day society. Universities, colleges, and a variety of other institutions offer courses on accounting, financial planning, and finance for people who wish to pursue related career paths. The popular press and even public broadcasters regularly report accounting-based information on corporations. As a result terms such as annual reports, earnings per share calculations, profit and loss numbers, price-earnings ratios, and earnings forecasts have entered the public lexicon. Likewise on a personal level, the notions of accounting and accountability are central to "income tax planning," "retirement planning" and to the annual ritual of submitting an income tax form.

The ubiquitous nature of financial information results in a certain taken-for-grantedness surrounding such techniques. On one level, this taken-for-grantedness helps to construct an image of accounting as a neutral and objective practice—one that is concerned with the "identification, measurement, and communication of financial information about economic entities to interested persons" (Kieso, Weygandt, Irvine, Silvestre, & Young, 1991). Indeed, the metaphor of the "map" has been used to describe the apparent neutrality and objectivity of accounting information (Solomons, 1991). However on another level this taken-for-grantedness has also implicitly defined the field and scope of accounting—accounting is thought to be a series of techniques which measures and reports information about corporate activities. While these techniques occasionally impact on individuals via income taxes or retirement planning, accounting is thought to be primarily a corporate activity.

This chapter also starts from the notion that techniques of accounting and finance are ubiquitous. However, rather than suggesting that such techniques are simply commonplace, I propose that such techniques are banal where banal is taken to mean unoriginal, partisan, and thoughtlessly utilized and reproduced. Following from Arendt's discussion of the banality of evil, something can be commonplace without necessarily being banal:

> For me, there is a very important difference: "commonplace" is what frequently, commonly happens, but something can be banal even if it is not common. Banal does not presuppose that the evil has a common place in everyone. (Arendt, quoted in Assy, 1998: 1)

This chapter builds upon Arendt's insights to propose that, within the colonial context, not only are techniques of accounting/finance banal (i.e., lacking originality, partisan, and unthinkingly utilized) in that they sustain colonialism but also that colonialism itself is banal in terms of being a continuing pattern of exploitative relations.

More specifically, in this chapter I argue that the scope of accounting is much broader than conventional understandings in that accounting techniques serve to structure and reproduce social relations. Furthermore, globally, the relations that are structured and reproduced tend to be those of imperialism/colonialism. In contrast to assertions that accounting is a series of neutral techniques, I suggest that both the conventional definition and the scope of accounting implicit within this definition are rhetorical techniques to deflect attention from the partisan role played by accounting within colonial processes. Second, accounting/finance is banal but banal in a very specific sense: accounting/finance techniques help to translate colonial objectives into practice in a manner that obscures both the partisan nature of the translations and the (often genocidal) consequences for the groups targeted by these practices.

The section following this introduction suggests that accounting/finance techniques be viewed as a software of colonialism, which helps to translate colonial policies into practice. This theoretical framing is then used to examine three "moments" of colonial practice by way of highlighting the role of such techniques within colonialism. Mini case studies of: (a) Canada, (b) Chiapas, Mexico, and (c) Ghana, Africa illustrate not only the differing ways in which accounting/finance techniques reproduce colonialism but also the continuity of these techniques over the last century. Implicit within this chapter is the belief that such softwares of colonialism have played and continue to play a significant role in supporting and rationalizing the exploitative relations upon which colonialism is predicated.

Theoretical Framing

Like other social constructs, the notion of accounting is itself contested. Conventional definitions stress the identification, measurement, and communication of financial information to interested parties. However this information is usually assumed to relate to the activities of corporations and the interested parties are usually assumed to be investors and creditors. This definition, while highlighting certain aspects of the social practice we call accounting, obscures other aspects (Burchell, Clubb, Hopwood, Hughes, & Nahapiet, 1980). In particular, this definition downplays both the broader functioning of such techniques and the ways in which such techniques both operationalize and re-produce relations of power and domination. Thus my preferred definition of accounting explicitly acknowledges these aspects. Accounting here refers to the mediation of relations between individuals, groups, and institutions through the use of numerical calculations and monetarized techniques, and includes the accountability relations that arise from these social interactions.

Implicit within this definition is the acknowledgment that power relationships are also measured and rationalized by accounting techniques (Tinker, 1980); that the use of numerical and representational techniques rationalizes unequal social relationships by "inciting" action through the construction of incentive schemes and funding relations (Preston, Chua, & Neu, 1997); that numerical techniques encourage action at a distance and bring home distant knowledges to centers of calculation (Miller & Rose, 1990).

Note that this definition does not contradict the more conventional notion that accounting is the "identification, measurement, and communication of financial information about economic entities to interested persons" (Kieso et al., 1991). Instead it emphasizes not only the broader nature and functioning of accounting techniques and calculations (Burchell et al., 1980), but also that what counts as accounting is historically contingent (Miller & Napier, 1993).

In thinking about the broader functioning of accounting and the way in which accounting techniques mediate social relations, the literature on governmentality is useful. Foucault (1991: 102) proposes that we view government as an "ensemble of institutions, calculations and tactics" that attempt to arrange things in order to attain specific ends. Furthermore, the mode of control exercised by and through the state is not singular; rather, through a diversity of forces and groups government in heterogeneous ways seeks to regulate the lives of individuals. However, this regulation is often directed at "populations" of individuals (Foucault, 1991), furthermore, "hierarchies of populations" exist in that different techniques are used and sanctioned depending on the populations to be governed (Neu, 2000a).

One of the heterogeneous ways in which state power is exercised is through mundane and indirect mechanisms such as accounting. Miller & Rose (1990: 8) refer to these mechanisms as *technologies of government* because they are "actual mechanisms through which authorities of various sorts have sought to shape, normalize, and instrumentalize the conduct, thought, decisions and aspirations of others in order to achieve the objectives they consider desirable."

Although these techniques of government have been and are used by most governments since the late 1800s (Burchell, Gordon, & Miller, 1991), their usage within colonial contexts is particularly interesting. Specifically, I would like to suggest that accounting techniques have provided imperial powers with a method of translating imperial objectives into practice, thus such techniques should be viewed as part of an ongoing process of colonialism/imperialism. Imperialism, here, is taken to mean "the practice, the theory, and the attitudes of a dominating metropolitan center ruling a distant territory" and "colonialism, which is almost always a consequence of imperialism, is the implanting of settlements on a distant territory" (Said, 1993: 8).

Thus imperialism/colonialism is a set of processes and practices that make it possible for imperial powers to continue to dominate both the colonized territory and its inhabitants.

Prior research on imperialism has often distinguished between the hardwares and softwares of imperialism. Hardwares refer to technologies such as steam gunboats and breech-loading guns that provide the means for imperial expansion, technologies that facilitate the use of force (Headrick, 1981). Softwares of imperialism refer to disciplinary knowledges such as accounting, anthropology, geography, and medicine that complemented these hardwares, making it possible to govern from a distance (Bell, Butlin, & Heffernan, 1995).

As a software of imperialism, accounting techniques help imperial powers come to "know" distant territories and their inhabitants. Accounting is a method of indirect societal governance, a micro-process enabling action at a distance, thereby facilitating indirect rule. For example, Miller and Rose (1990) note that accounting, similar to the maps used by eighteenth-century navigators, allowed for the colonization of distant territories "because, in various technical ways, these distant places were 'mobilized' and brought home to centers of calculation." Furthermore, accounting techniques are part of the dialectic of control in that accounting techniques gather information, which is used to construct knowledges that are used for control at a distance: "knowledge gives power, more power requires more knowledge, and so on in an increasingly profitable dialectic of information and control" (Said, 1979: 36).

This view of accounting emphasizes the informational aspects; however, the incentive aspects are also salient. Incentive mechanisms and funding relations encourage certain types of behaviors on the part of individuals, agents, and institutions in distant locales. Governments might use direct incentives to encourage certain behaviors on the part of peoples in distant territories. For example, colonial powers in Canada instituted the practice beginning in the 1600s of distributing yearly presents to indigenous peoples. Initially, the types of presents distributed were clothing, ammunition, and objects adapted to gratify a savage taste, but in later periods the nature of the payment was changed to encourage farming activities and the containment of indigenous peoples on reservations (Neu, 2000a,b). Such techniques are intended to change behaviors by influencing the minutiae of daily life (cf. Foucault, 1991).

Incentive relations do not have to be direct, however. Governments can provide *indirect* incentives to third parties or they can change accountability mechanisms, which impact upon third parties as a way of encouraging certain actions directed at colonized territories and peoples (Neu, 2000b).

For example, during the initial colonization of North America, colonial powers provided bounties for the scalps of indigenous peoples. In 1749, the Governor of Nova Scotia, Lord Cornwallis, issued a proclamation stating that a bounty would be paid of "ten Guineas for every Indian Micmac taken or killed, to be paid upon producing such Savage taken or his scalp" (quoted in Paul, 1992: 108). Over the course of three years, this policy resulted in a reduction of the Micmac population by 80 percent (Paul, 1992: 114). And in the United States these types of bounties continued until the late 1800s (Churchill, 1994). More recently, changed accountability mechanisms along with financial incentives have been used throughout the Americas to encourage transnationals to develop resource extraction industries on or near aboriginal territories (cf. Churchill, 1994; Galeano, 1997).

While these techniques of governmentality have become increasingly popular, one difference between the colonial and other contexts is the use of force and the manner in which force is threatened and/or used against "inferior" populations. Fanon (1963) comments that force is part of the history of colonial relations and forms the backdrop for current colonial relations. In the Americas, the "implication of force" forms the backdrop for government policies directed toward indigenous populations in ways which would not occur for "white" or ladino populations (Menchú & Wright, 1998). Therefore, the combination of hierarchies of population in colonized territories, along with the continued presence of force, suggests a much more ambiguous, yet dynamic, relationship between techniques of governance and techniques of force within the colonial context.

The preceding has suggested that accounting functions as a technology of government that helps imperial powers to translate abstract objectives into concrete practices. Furthermore, I have proposed that accounting techniques fulfill both informational and incentive roles, and that incentives can be of a direct or indirect nature. But is it appropriate to refer to accounting as a banal technique?

Arendt develops her notion of the banality of evil in the context of the trial of Otto Adolf Eichmann in Israel in 1961 where she was in attendance as a reporter for the *New Yorker*. Her first reaction to Eichmann "the man in the glass booth," was—*nicht einmal unheimlich*—"not even sinister" (Arendt quoted in Young-Bruehl, 1982: 329). "The deeds were monstrous, but the doer...was quite ordinary, commonplace, and neither demonic nor monstrous" (Arendt quoted in Assy, 1998: 1). Arendt concludes that it was thoughtlessness that was the defining feature of Eichmann:

> Eichmann's ordinariness implied in an incapacity for independent critical thought: "...the only specific characteristic one could detect in his past

as well as in his behavior during the trial and the preceding police examination was something entirely negative: it was not stupidity but a curious, quite authentic inability to think." Eichmann became the protagonist of a kind of experience apparently so quotidian, the absence of the critical thought. Arendt says: "When confronted with situations for which such routine procedures did not exist, he [Eichmann] was helpless, and his cliché-ridden language produced on the stand, as it had evidently done in his official life, a kind of macabre comedy. (Assy, 1998: 1)

Adherence to technique replaced thought and moral judgment. And although Arendt does not identify accounting as one of these techniques, subsequent research has suggested that in the case of the holocaust it was bureaucratic routines and accounting techniques that allowed bureaucrats to deal in numbers and statistics, thereby erasing the individuals affected by the techniques (Funnel, 1998).

From this vantage point, techniques such as accounting are banal in that they help governments to translate abstract policies into practice while permitting government bureaucrats to be unthinking about the consequences. Furthermore, such techniques are clearly partisan in that they are directed toward targeted populations. Finally, these techniques serve to reinforce and reproduce the exploitative social relations upon which the use of the techniques is initially predicated. Thus, in applying the term banal to accounting, I am not only arguing that banal can be used as an adjective to describe the use of these techniques but also that these techniques, while perhaps not evil, are partisan, and facilitated consequences, which were dysfunctional and/or genocidal for the targeted populations. The next sections provide a series of empirical examples to illustrate the scope, continuity, and consequences of such technologies of government.

Empirical Examples

Canada

Said (1993: 5) remarks that imperialism means thinking about, settling on, and controlling land that you do not possess, that is distant, that is lived on and owned by others. In the case of Canada, Britain issued a Royal Proclamation in 1763 indicating that land not already ceded by indigenous peoples would be "purchased," also implying that relations between the British crown and indigenous peoples would be on a nation-to-nation basis (Milloy, 1983). The Proclamation was an attempt to formalize relations between the British government and indigenous peoples in the period following the fall of New France (Milloy, 1983: 56). The crown hoped that the Proclamation would ensure the continued loyalty on the part of indigenous peoples (Tobias, 1983: 40).

Although the Royal Proclamation ostensibly set out and defined relations between the British (and subsequently the Canadian) government and indigenous peoples, since the mid-1800s accounting technologies of government have been used to restructure these relations. Initially *direct incentives* were used to encourage the containment of indigenous peoples on reservations so as to not interfere with settlement activities. For example, during the mid-1830s, the issue of whether to change the nature of annuity payments (which were called "presents") from implements used for hunting to either money or other goods was extensively discussed (cf. Neu, 2000a). Initially, government officials considered whether to distribute money as opposed to goods since this would economize on the monetary costs of annuity payments. However, this was apparently rejected because the payment of money would lessen government control over indigenous peoples. Instead, officials decided to change the nature of the goods distributed in an attempt to simultaneously decrease costs associated with annuity payments while increasing the level of control.

The modified annuity payments sought to encourage farming, schooling, and to discourage not only less civilized pursuits such as hunting but also idleness (cf. Neu, 2000b). Instead of providing clothing, blankets and hunting supplies, agricultural implements and raw materials for clothing were distributed. Likewise it was recommended that a portion of the yearly distribution now expended in the purchase of stores and presents, (be directed) to the erection of school houses, the purchase of elementary books, and the payment of resident school-masters, for the benefit of the Indian tribes (RAIC, 1845, S.1: 10) and that prizes be distributed to indigenous children who did well in school to stimulate their exertions (p. 10). Thus, through the careful consideration as to the type of yearly distribution, government bureaucrats hoped to influence the minutiae of daily life.

Around the time and subsequent to the Canadian confederation in 1867, federal legislation containing financial carrots and sticks became a preferred method of translating government policies toward indigenous peoples into practice. For example, the 1860 Act for the Management of Indian Lands stated:

> The Governor in Council may, subject to the provisions of this Act, direct how, and in what manner, and by whom the moneys arising from sales of Indian Lands, and from the property held in trust for the

Indians, shall be invested from time to time, and how the payments to which the Indians may be entitled shall be made, and shall provide for the general management of such lands, moneys, and property, and what percentage of proportion thereof shall be set apart, from time to time, to cover the cost of, and attendant upon, such management under the provisions of this Act.... (SC, 1860: c. 151)

Despite the legalese in which the statute is written, the implications are clear (Neu, 2001). The Governor in Council would decide *how* the proceeds from land sales would be invested and spent. He would decide "*which* Indians" would receive a portion of the proceeds. And he would decide *what* "administration fee" would be deducted from the proceeds to cover the costs associated with his administration of indigenous monies. The provisions contained in this Act found their way into the 1868 Act pertaining to the management of Indian lands and then into the 1876 Indian Act.

In 1876, the Indian Act was introduced as a method of consolidating prior legislation pertaining to indigenous peoples into a single Act (Bartlett, 1978: 585). The premise of the Act as outlined in the 1876 Annual Report was that: "our Indian legislation rests on the principle, that aborigines are to be kept in a condition of tutelage and treated as wards or children of the state" (Bartlett, 1978: xiii). Over the next 100 years, a series of amendments to the Act were introduced, which sought to either tighten control over indigenous finances or to facilitate the expropriation of indigenous land or resources by the federal government (cf. Neu, 2001). Over time, layers of financial regulation were introduced to govern various aspects of indigenous behavior that not only stripped indigenous people of agency but also served to confirm bureaucratic sentiments regarding the inability of the indigenous to "manage" their own affairs.

Beginning in the late 1800s, the federal government began the process of providing incentives to third parties as a way of influencing indigenous peoples. Noteworthy amongst these initiatives was the use of missionary societies to provide residential schooling (Milloy, 1999). Government bureaucrats believed that residential schooling was a preferred method of translating government assimilation objectives into practice. A report commissioned by the federal government in 1883 recommended the development of residential schools, operated by third parties such as religious orders (Grant, 1996: 64). The government would provide a set amount of funding to the religious orders to operate the schools while the government would maintain an inspection system to ensure uniformity. To encourage assimilation, attendance at residential schools was compulsory; the schools themselves were located long distances from the reservation (even though many treaties spec-ified the provision of on-reserve schooling); and the use of Indian languages was forbidden under the threat of corporal punishments (Grant, 1996: 189–190; Nuu-chah-nulth Tribal Council, 1996: 42). By the end of the 1800s, residential schooling had become an important part of government policy with over 35 percent of total government appropriations being spent on residential schooling (Department of Indian Affairs, 1900).

Although a complete analysis of the residential school initiative is beyond the scope of this chapter (see Miller, 1996; Milloy, 1999), residential schools were important in several respects. First, residential schooling represented one of the first movements within Canadian government-indigenous peoples relations to the use of third-party agents. Through the use of specific finan-cial incentives and specific accountability mechanisms, the federal govern-ment attempted to translate assimilation into practice through the use of missionary societies. However, more importantly, the residential school expe-rience demonstrates the genocidal consequences that often result from the use of such techniques. A funding mechanism, which emphasized cost min-imization along with not only the absence of adequate inspection mecha-nisms but also the unwillingness of government bureaucrats to intervene, resulted in mortality rates in some residential schools approaching 50 percent as a result of disease (Milloy, 1999). Furthermore, charges of sexual, physi-cal, and emotional abuse of indigenous children in the residential schools continue to make their way through the Canadian justice system. At present, the churches responsible for administering the residential schools are on the brink of bankruptcy as a result of the number of lawsuits that they are facing.

More recently, government policy has used changed accountability mech-anisms as a method of encouraging a "new-style" colonialism (Davis & Zannis, 1973; Neu, 2000b). The extraction of resources from around or on traditional indigenous territories has become increasingly important (Churchill, 1994). Through both the provision of financial incentives and the downgrading of environmental standards, the Canadian (and U.S.) gov-ernments have sought to facilitate the appropriation of land-based wealth. Direct financial subsidies to multinationals is one method used by govern-ments to encourage the exploitation of the indigenous land base. These sub-sidies are often packaged with decreased accountability relations to encourage multinational involvement (Neu, 2000b). For example, in the case of the Grassy Lake Ojibwa's, the Ontario provincial government pro-vided a multinational corporation operating a pulp mill with a financial escape hatch that allowed it to escape liability for the mercury contamination of the English-Wabigoon River: a contamination that resulted in the closure of commercial fisheries and sport fishing guiding operations run by the Ojibwa's along with significant mercury poisoning of Ojibwa peoples (Shkilnyk, 1985). At the same time that the Ojibwa's were pressuring the multinational for compensation, the provincial government was providing the involved multinational with over $50 million in subsidies.

Chiapas, Mexico

The preceding case highlighted the way in which accounting and accountability mechanisms have been utilized to translate government policies into practice. The case of indigenous peoples in Chiapas, Mexico is similar but different. While techniques of financial governance have been important, the implication of force is much more visible. This is not to say that violence has not been implicated in the Canadian case, as the early examples of bounties for indigenous scalps, and the confrontations during the 1990s between the Canadian military and indigenous peoples, amply illustrate. Rather it is to suggest that the role of the military has been both more visible and constant in Chiapas. The case that follows illustrates the intersection between the hardwares and the financial softwares of colonialism.

Following the arrival of the Spanish, native peoples in Chiapas experienced declining populations due to the introduction of new diseases and to the erosion of community lands by colonial courts and the clergy (Harvey, 1998). Like Canada, religious orders were entrusted by the Spanish Crown to convert the native population to Christianity and to civilize it (Neu & Heincke, in print). However the legacy of religious orders seems more ambiguous in that the Dominicans lobbied the Crown to establish laws against the slavery of Indians and forced labor. New laws introduced in 1542 permitted indigenous authorities to control their community affairs, *if* their behavior responded to the Crown and Church mandates. Unfortunately indigenous peoples continued to live in misery, tortured by ladinos, and under the threat of losing their communal land (Russell, 1995; Villafuentes et al., 1999).

At the beginning of the nineteenth century, the interests of the business class, merchants, and owners clashed with the royal government in Chiapas, and in the second decade, Chiapas became an independent Mexican State. However, independence did not improve the living conditions of aboriginals; rather, processes of internal colonialism (cf. Churchill, 1994) resulted in the imposition of practices which benefited the elites. By 1850, liberal policies and constitutional reforms had resulted in the increased privatization of church and communal indigenous lands and the accumulation of wealth and land in *caciques* (Harvey, 1998: 44–45).

Resistance by indigenous peoples invariably resulted in the use of military force. For example, the Ladino response to the 1867 insurrection was the use of military force (Ruiz, 1993). After the insurrections were defeated, technologies of government once again became the preferred method of governance. Examples of such technologies included the introduction of new laws during the 1890s that both increased taxes and reduced the authority/ autonomy of indigenous communities. New regulations forced indigenous peoples to participate in the market economy by being employed at different times of the year (Harvey, 1998: 47).

The beginning of the twentieth century saw an emphasis on modernization reforms, including the establishment of new laws and policies encouraging "economic development." These reforms increased foreign investment, brought new technologies, and incorporated parts of Chiapas into the international economy, while at the same time centralizing the political and economic control of the elites—with the result of increasing the financial dependence of the peasantry (Villafuentes et al., 1999: 70). Incentive mechanisms were used to translate modernization into practice as macro government policies provided transnationals with incentives to locate in Chiapas (Neu & Heincke, in print). However, these policies simultaneously decreased subsistence activities as land was taken over by the multinationals. The result was that, in the absence of subsistence activities, indigenous peoples were forced to work on the newly created plantations. As Galeano (1997) suggests, this type of financial incentive-induced enclosure movement has occurred at various junctures throughout Latin America.

If macro financial policies encouraged the movement of indigenous peoples into the market economy, micro financial policies ensured that indigenous peoples remained captives of the transnationals. Payment for wage labor was received in tokens, which could only be spent in company stores known as *tiendas de atarralla*. However, since the payment was not enough to cover minimum expenses, indigenous peoples were obligated to acquire loans from the employer or *patron*, thereby resulting in a lifelong commitment and dependence. Like the example of "presents" in the Canadian context, the use of pseudo monies on the part of governments and transnationals allowed for the continued control of indigenous peoples. This combination of macro incentives provided to transnationals, along with the micro incentives used by the transnationals, effectively structured indigenous behaviors by displacing them from communal lands and by enrolling them in the plantation market economy.

The pattern of financial incentives to transnationals, indigenous resistance, partial government attempts at land reform, and the subversion of these reforms by the landed elites continued throughout the twentieth century (Harvey, 1998). This pattern changed slightly around 1950, when the natural resource wealth of Chiapas became increasingly important to the Mexican economy. These natural resources, when combined with the history of internal colonialism in Chiapas, encouraged the federal government to treat Chiapas as an extractive region, producing income without costs. While Chiapas was a major source of Mexican hydroelectricity, gas and petroleum reserves, coffee, banana, corn, cacao, and beef production (EZLN, 1994; Ruiz, 1993; Russell, 1995), Chiapas remained the least electrified, least schooled, least literate, and most agricultural state in the country (Harvey, 1998).

Throughout the 1960 to 1980 period, indigenous and poor peasants of Chiapas pressured the government to solve some of the pressing issues facing the rural poor. And while the government was often initially sensitive to these concerns, the introduced policies were either overridden when economic circumstances changed or circumvented by local elites (Neu & Heincke, in print). For example, in the 1960s, the government decided to clear the Lacandona forest and to encourage the indigenous and peasant population to relocate. Financial incentives were offered to encourage relocation in the form of expenditures on infrastructure (schools and hospitals) and market guarantees. However the consequence was that the local elites once again ended up acquiring the most productive parts of the Lacanadona forest. Furthermore, at a later date the government attempted to expropriate indigenous land within the Lancandona forest and to give it to 66 families in order to exploit reserves of flint. The expropriation was supported by a violent army attack to expel the peasants (Harvey, 1998: 78).

These trends of government indecision/reversals continued throughout the 1980s. The "debt crisis" of the early 1980s encouraged the Mexican government to further develop large oil exploration and hydroelectric projects in Chiapas as a way of generating income (Stephenson, 1995). Consequently, subsistence activities of indigenous peoples were further reduced when 200,000 hectares of land was flooded for the hydroelectric dam. Ironically, when oil prices dropped in 1982, thereby making oil exploration and production less viable, the government was forced to reduce its support for agriculture in an attempt to balance its budget (Russell, 1995).

The Chiapas mini-case illustrates the intersection of the softwares and hardwares of colonialism. Although macro and micro financial incentives were used to translate economic development policies into practice, it was both the backdrop and the use of force that was used to buttress these techniques. Thus while financial techniques did impact the day-to-day activities of indigenous peoples by eliminating subsistence possibilities and by coercing them into the market economy, force was used to quell any resistances to these policies. Furthermore, the case highlights that when techniques of financial governance were introduced, which attempted to improve the position of indigenous peoples vis-à-vis local elites, local elites were able to change or circumvent the techniques in order to maintain or improve their own social position. Certainly with respect to the governance of elites, techniques of financial governance are eternally optimistic and perpetually failing (Miller & Rose, 1990).

Ghana, Africa

The two preceding cases highlight the manner in which governments use techniques of financial governance to translate colonial policies into practice. The case of Ghana illustrates the ways in which first-world governments along with international organizations such as the World Bank support and buttress colonial practices in other countries through the use of techniques of financial governance.

In 1961, the newly independent government of Ghana established a state-owned electricity company called Volta River Authority (VRA) (Rahaman & Lawrence, 2001a). The VRA's principal asset was to be the world's largest man-made lake and hydroelectric dam. The Ghanaian government believed that an adequate supply of electricity was a precondition to economic development in this African country (Rahaman & Lawrence, 2001b). At the time that the VRA was established, large portions of Ghana lacked electricity.

Lacking sufficient financial resources to construct the dam, the Ghana government was forced to enlist external financiers. Discussions between the governments of Ghana, United States, and Britain along with the World Bank were initially unsuccessful in that the Ghanaian government was unable to demonstrate a sufficient demand for electricity within Ghana to provide an adequate return on investment (Rahaman & Lawrence, 2001b). This prompted the parties to search for a transnational corporation that might be willing to locate in Ghana and, in return for "cheap" electricity, commit to taking a percentage of the generated electricity. Rahaman, Lawrence, and Roper (in print) explain the process as follows:

> Following recommendations of a committee commissioned by the government, it was agreed that an aluminium smelter be established to guarantee that electricity generated from the Volta Project would be fully utilised. While such a project was within the government's plans for integration of the aluminium industry, the additional capital requirement made it difficult for the government to invest in such a smelter.

Thus a way around the problem was to invite private enterprises to build the smelter for this purpose. After a series of negotiations, agreements were signed between the Government of Ghana (acting on behalf of VRA) and Valco,[1] guaranteeing the supply of a minimum amount of electricity to the smelter at a rate that was fixed in the early 1960s at 2.625 mills/kwh without any provision for escalation for a thirty-year period and subject to an additional twenty-year period if Valco opted to continue its operations in Ghana.

Once Valco committed to purchasing a portion of the generated electricity, negotiations continued on the financing for the dam and the related infra-structure. As Rahaman et al. (in print) state:

> Although the entire cost of building the dam, power station and trans-mission lines was estimated at 70 million pounds sterling, the project was completed under budget at a cost of 56 million pounds sterling... The government of the newly independent Ghana provided 35 million pounds sterling representing over half of the total cost of the project... In addition the Ghana government also provided about 7.5 million pounds sterling for the necessary infrastructure including the construction of roads for access to the dam and housing and to resettle the people dis-placed by the project... The other parties then provided the remaining funding for the project almost in equal proportions. However, the World Bank has been a major provider of subsequent funding for various proj-ects that VRA has undertaken since it started its operations in 1966.

The preceding extracts suggest that the entire initial cost of the dam and related infrastructure was 63.5 million pounds sterling of which the govern-ment of Ghana paid 66 percent (42.5 million pounds). And in terms of the smelter itself, the cost was $128 million of which $32 million was equity cap-ital (but guaranteed by a U.S. government risk guarantee) and $96 million debt financing (Rahaman & Lawrence, 2001b). Thus in return for making a risk-free investment of $32 million, Valco was guaranteed electricity at a fixed price of 2.625 mills/kwh for 50 years, where a mill refers to one-tenth of a U.S. cent. Rahaman et al. (in print) quote one of the directors of Valco as saying: "where else... could we get a 120,000 ton aluminum smelter, costing $150,000,000, of which 85% was supported by debts and 90% of that covered by the American Government."

As one of the initial lenders and as a continuing lender to the VRA, the World Bank was able to dictate minimum financial return criteria.

These types of debt covenants are intended to ensure that debtors such as the VRA have sufficient financial resources to repay the loan; furthermore in the event of a breach of such debt covenants, lenders usually have the right to demand immediate repayment of the loans. In the case of VRA, one of these covenants required that the return on investment generated by VRA assets must exceed 8 percent per year and that the asset valuation base must be reevaluated by external valuators every five years (Rahaman et al., in print).

From a governmentality vantage point, the entire financial arrangement, but especially the agreement between the World Bank and the VRA, is fascinating. The original agreement resulted in the government of Ghana providing almost 70 percent of the funding while the aluminum smelter was guaranteed approximately 60 percent of the electricity output at a fixed rate for 50 years. Furthermore, both the cost and risk to Valco were minimal in that the majority of the cost was financed with debt and the equity portion was 90 percent guaranteed by the U.S. government. Thus the entire financing structure of the project served to provide the aluminum transnationals with a cheap source of electricity at minimal risk. Similar to the Canadian and Chiapas examples, we observe how such financial incentives allow for the expropriation of wealth from indigenous territories.

If the original agreement encouraged transnational involvement along with the related environmental effects for local communities, the debt covenants ensured that the entire country would bear the costs associated with the project. In terms of local effects, the hydroelectric project flooded 8300 square kilometers, displacing "almost 80,000 people whose homes and farmlands were inundated by the reservoir" (Anane, 2001). This displacement has caused resettlement problems, and the decimation of subsistence and market based activities (cf. International River Network, 2001). On a national level, the debt covenant requirement that an 8 percent return be earned on the market value of assets (*revalued* every five years) has resulted in electricity prices that are unaffordable for large portions of the Ghanaian population. Since the transnational Valco has a fixed-price contract for 50 years for approximately 60 percent of the output, the remaining users must bear the brunt of any rate increases designed to generate an 8 percent return on assets. This has resulted in prices for other customers being *five times the rate* paid by Valco (Rahaman & Lawrence, 2001b).

The mini-case of Ghana illustrates how techniques of financial governance can be utilized by first-world governments and affiliated institutions to "govern" distant territories. In this case, the specifics of the initial loan agreement along with the debt covenants ensure that the aluminum transnationals receive the benefits of cheap electricity while the Ghanaian population bears the economic, social, health, and environmental costs. While Ghana may have technically gained its independence from Britain, these types of financial mechanisms ensure the continuation of colonial relations of exploitation.

Discussion

This chapter started from the premise that techniques of accounting and finance are banal where banal is taken to mean unoriginal, partisan, and thoughtlessly utilized and reproduced. More specifically, I have proposed that techniques of accounting/finance have been used in various colonial settings to translate macro objectives into practice. Through the combination of such softwares along with techniques of force, imperial powers have been able to dominate territories both near and far.

The empirical examples offered in the chapter have demonstrated the continuity of such techniques across temporal and spatial dimensions. The mini-case of Canada illustrated how such techniques were utilized as early as the mid-1800s and how they continue to be used today. Likewise the Chiapas and Ghana examples highlight the parallels between the use of these techniques in Canada and in other settings. In terms of temporal changes, the three mini-cases hint that incentives and changed accountability mechanisms directed at influencing the activities of transnationals which, in turn, impact on indigenous peoples and territories have become more prevalent since the early 1900s. Davis and Zannis (1973) along with Churchill (1994) refer to this as "new-style" colonialism whereby resource extraction rather than the use of cheap labor becomes increasingly important. Thus, these empirical examples indicate that accounting techniques of governance are unoriginal in the sense that they have been used almost continuously for over 150 years.

The mini-cases also highlight the partisan nature of such techniques. Techniques of financial governance have invariably been used to "govern" indigenous peoples and territory. Furthermore, when governments have attempted to use these techniques against the elites, the elites have possessed sufficient symbolic and economic capital to circumvent the regulations. However, in the case of indigenous populations, the consequences have often been genocidal. For example, the Canadian case illustrated how these techniques were used in the attempt to contain indigenous peoples on reservations and to erase indigenous language and culture through residential schooling. Likewise in Chiapas, the reforms functioned as an enclosure movement, wiping out subsistence activities and coercing indigenous peoples into the market economy. And finally in the Ghana example, we saw how the construction of the dam flooded 4 percent of Ghana's land base, decimating subsistence activities and effectively forcing the relocation of 80,000 people. In these ways, techniques of financial governance have been partisan, and have supported and reproduced colonial relations of domination.

The final claim that such techniques have been unthinkingly applied is less obvious from the empirical examples. While previous research has suggested that such techniques have often functioned as a "ready-made" solution to problems of governance and that mimetic and normative influences have encouraged the spread of such techniques (Funnel, 1998; Neu, 1999), it is difficult to discern intentionality ex-post and from a distance. Certainly the Canadian and Chiapas examples illustrate the manner in which such techniques have been used over long periods of time. Likewise an examination of World Bank activities in a variety of different settings suggests that the use of such financial governance mechanisms is not unique to the Ghana example (World Bank, 2001). Thus it seems appropriate to conclude that the use of such techniques is often unthinking both in terms of application and expected outcome. Indeed, the contrary conclusion, that techniques of financial governance might have been *consciously* applied with the expected outcome of genocide for the targeted peoples, is too chilling to contemplate.

Note

1. An aluminum smelter to be built by Kaiser and Reynolds, two giant American aluminum companies.

References

Anane, M. 2001. Courting mega disaster: Bui dam may cause havoc. [www.global500.org/feature_4.htm]

Assy, B. 1998. Eichmann, the banality of evil, and thinking in Arendt's thought. Contemporary Philosophy. [www.bu.edu/wcp/Papers/cont/ContAssy/htm]

Bartlett, R. 1978. The Indian Act of Canada. *Buffalo Law Review, 26*, 581–615.

Bell, M., Butlin, R., & Heffernan, M. 1995. *Geography and imperialism: 1820–1940.* Manchester: Manchester University Press.

Burchell, G., Gordon, C., & Miller, P. 1991. *The Foucault effect.* Chicago: University of Chicago Press.

Burchell, S., Clubb, C., Hopwood, A., Hughes, J., & Nahapiet, J. 1980. The roles of accounting in organizations and society. *Accounting, Organizations and Society, 5* (1), 5–27.

Churchill, W. 1994. *Indians are us? Culture and genocide in Native North America.* Toronto: Between the Lines.

Davis, R., & Zannis, M. 1973. *The genocide machine in Canada*. Montreal: Black Rose.

Department of Indian Affairs. 1900. *Annual Report*. Ottawa: Government of Canada.

Ejército Zapatista de Liberación Nacional 1994. First Declaration of the Lacandon Jungle, Vol. 2001: EZLN. [www.ezln.org/documentos/index.html]

Fanon, F. 1963. *The wretched of the earth*. New York: Grove Press.

Foucault, M. 1991. Governmentality. In G. Burchell, C. Gordon, & P. Miller (Eds.), *The Foucault Effect* (pp. 87–104). Chicago: University of Chicago Press.

Funnel, W. 1998. Accounting in the service of the Holocaust. *Critical Perspectives on Accounting, 9* (4), 435–464.

Galeano, E. H. 1997. *Open veins of Latin America: Five centuries of the pillage of a continent*. (25th anniversary ed.). New York: Monthly Review Press.

Grant, A. 1996. *No end of grief: Indian residential schools in Canada*. Winnipeg: Pemmican.

Harvey, N. 1998. *The Chiapas rebellion: The struggle for land and democracy*. Durham, NC: Duke University Press.

Headrick, D. 1981. *The tools of empire*. Oxford: Oxford University Press.

International River Network 2001. The environmental impacts of large dams, Vol. 2001. [www.irn.org/bascis/impacts.html]

Kieso, D., Weygandt, J., Irvine, B., Silvestre, H., & Young, N. 1991. *Intermediate accounting* (rev. 3rd Canadian ed.). Toronto: Wiley & Sons.

Knapp, A. 1998. Thoughtlessness and the banality of evil, Vol. 2001. [www.wpi.edu/~jaknapp/banality.htm]

Menchú, R., & Wright, A. 1998. *Crossing borders*. London & New York: Verso.

Miller, J. R. 1996. *Shingwauk's vision: A history of native residential schools*. Toronto: University of Toronto Press.

Miller, P., & Napier, C. 1993. Genealogies of calculation. *Accounting, Organizations and Society: 18* (7/8), 631–647.

Miller, P., & Rose, N. 1990. Governing economic life. *Economy and Society, 19*, 1–31.

Milloy, J. 1983. The Early Indian Acts: Developmental strategy and constitutional change. In L. Getty, & A. Lussier (Eds.), *As long as the Sun shines and water flows: A reader in Canadian native studies* (pp. 56–63). Vancouver: University of British Columbia Press.

Milloy, J. S. 1999. *A national crime: The Canadian government and the residential school system, 1879 to 1986*. Winnipeg: University of Manitoba Press.

Neu, D. 1999. Discovering indigenous peoples: Accounting and the machinery of empire. *Accounting Historians Journal, 26* (1), 53–82.

Neu, D. 2000a. "Presents" for the Indians: Land, colonialism and accounting in Canada. *Accounting, Organizations and Society, 25* (2), 163–184.

Neu, D. 2000b. Accounting and accountability relations. *Accounting, Auditing and Accountability Journal, 13* (3), 268–288.

Neu, D. 2001. *Birth of the nation*. Edmonton: University of Alberta.

Neu, D., & Heincke, M. (in print). The limits of governance: The case of Chiapas and Oka. *Critical Perspectives on Accounting*.

Nuu-chah-nulth Tribal Council. 1996. *Indian residential schools.* Port Alberni: Nuu-chah-nulth Tribal Council.

Paul, D. 1992. *We were not the savages.* Halifax: Nimbus.

Preston, A., Chua, W., & Neu, D. 1997. The diagnosis-related group prospective payment system and the problem of government rationing health care to the elderly. *Accounting Organizations and Society, 22* (2), 147–164.

RAIC. 1845. *Report on the Affairs of the Indians in Canada* (Sections I and II). London: House of Commons.

Ruiz, S. 1993. *A los indígenas del continente, Chiapas: La rebelión de los pobres.* Nafarroa: Hirugarren Prensa.

Russell, P. 1995. *The Chiapas Rebellion.* Austin: Mexico Resource Center.

Said, E. 1979. *Orientalism.* New York: Vintage Books.

Said, E. 1993. *Culture and imperialism.* London: Vintage Books.

SC. 1860. *Statutes of Canada.* Ottawa: Government of Canada.

Rahaman, A., & Lawrence, S. 2001a. A negotiated order perspective on accounting and financial control. *Accounting, Auditing and Accountability Journal, 14* (2), 147–165.

Rahaman, A., & Lawrence, S. 2001b. Public sector accounting and financial management in a developing country organizational context: A three dimensional view. *Accounting Forum, 25* (2), 189–210.

Rahaman, A., Lawrence, S., & Roper, J. (in print). Social and environmental reporting at the VRA: Institutionalized legitimacy or legitimation crisis? *Critical Perspectives on Accounting.*

Shkilnyk, A. M. 1985. *A poison stronger than love: The destruction of an Ojibwa community.* New Haven: Yale University Press.

Solomons, D. 1991. Accounting and social change: A neutralist view. *Accounting, Organizations and Society, 16* (3), 287–298.

Stephenson, J. 1995. *The 1994 Zapatista Rebellion in Southern Mexico: An analysis and assessment.* London: Strategies and Combat Institute.

Tinker, T. 1980. Towards a political economy of accounting. *Accounting, Organizations and Society, 9* (2), 147–160.

Tobias, L. 1983. Protection, civilization, assimilation. In L. Getty, & A. Lussier (Eds.), *As long as the Sun shines and water flows: A reader in Canadian native studies* (pp. 39–55). Vancouver: University of British Columbia Press.

Villafuentes, D., Meza, S., Franco, G., Garcia, M., Rivera, C., Lisbona, M., & Morales, J. 1999. *La Tierra en Chiapas, viejos problemas nuevos.* Chiapas: Universidad de Ciencias y Artes del Estado de Chiapas.

World Bank. 2001. *Educational change in Latin America and the Caribbean.* Washington, DC: World Bank.

Young-Bruehl, E. 1982. *Hannah Arendt, for love of the world.* New Haven: Yale University Press.

CHAPTER 9

Asserting Possibilities of Resistance in the Cross-Cultural Teaching Machine: Re-Viewing Videos of Others

Gavin Jack and Anna Lorbiecki

A s academics involved in "teaching" international management to under- and post-graduate students on degree courses run in British universities we have become increasingly dismayed by the types of videos offered by the cross-cultural training industry. Although these videos are intended to simulate experiences of what "cultural differences" to "look out for" when embarking on international careers, there is the very real danger that if used as intended, naïve management teachers could well perpetuate distorted myths and representations of the cross-cultural Other(s), despite honorable intentions to the contrary.

In order to alert more management teachers, and international students, to these discursive morphings of the Other, the cross-training cultural training industry is conceptualized here as a "kind" of teaching machine (Spivak, 1993) that privileges a reductionist view of the complexity of national culture and its constitutive politics of difference. Drawing upon the postcolonial works of Homi Bhabha, Edward Said, and Gayatri Spivak, and the post-structuralism of Michel Foucault, we provide an analytical exposition of the epistemological messages, images and coded symbolism contained within cross-cultural training videos as illustrative of our wider concerns. We argue that these messages and symbols normalize the continuing reproduction of neocolonial structures and practices as part of the contemporary global imperialism of Western management techniques and ways of knowing.

Whilst we are aware that some viewers swallow these messages whole, and see them as a kind of "truth," others watch them with resistant disdain and disbelief. As a provocative acknowledgment and encouragement of this welcome resistance, we conclude by suggesting that the cross-cultural teaching machine re-view these videos with a more "critical" pedagogical eye. To this end, we propose a mode of teaching that shifts the subject of culture away from an epistemological function to an enunciative practice (Bhabha, 1994) in which the (subaltern) agency of Others allows for a relocation and re-inscription of displaced historical and cultural meanings, thus questioning imposing Self and Other binaries.

It is a commonplace that globalization has become a central theme in numerous academic and popular business discourses over the last 20 years. Signified by such terms as the "global economy" (Hirst & Thompson, 1994), the "global marketplace" (Paliwoda, 1993), or the "global village" (McCracken, 1988), the world and its people, whether in their roles as organizational managers, employees, or customers, are presented as being increasingly interconnected as a perceived result of developments in communications, technologies, capital mobility, migration, and international labor movements. Debate exists, however, on the meaning and effects of globalization (Bradley, Erickson, Stephenson, & Williams, 2000), and its relationship to concepts of place and culture (Massey & Jess, 1995). For some, notably Levitt (1983), global connectedness creates a world of converging consumer tastes and preferences, serviceable through standardized products manufactured within a framework of increasingly universal managerial philosophies and practices deploying "one best way." From that perspective, national borders and cultural differences represent a diminishing impediment to business and hence, by extension, are a subject unworthy of further analytic attention.

For others, such as Guirdham (1999), the increasing number of cross-border interactions between various groups of people within the context of a globalizing world (be they multinational companies, international tourists, migrants, or refugees) serves to highlight the continued and ever complex ways in which we are all *different*. Such a view underlines the need for more serious debate on divergent relationships between culture, place, and global business. From a divergent perspective, the simple conflation of nation-states with national cultures, and local communities with local cultures, has been criticized heavily for its simplistic interpretations of the intensely political relationships between place and culture (Massey, 1995), especially when globalization is re-interpreted within postcolonial theory as the latest discursive metamorphosis of Western imperialism (Wichterich, 2000: 158).

From an academic perspective, an increasing amount of literature has emerged that explores the effect of perceived cultural differences on managerial and organizational thinking and practice. These include: traditional areas of comparative and cross-cultural management studies (Hofstede, 1980, 1991), selection procedures for overseas assignments (Tung, 1981), expatriate adjustment (Black, Mendenhall, & Oddou, 1991), inter-cultural communication (Guirdham, 1999), cross-cultural teamwork (Smith & Berg, 1997), and notions of international or global managers (Bartlett & Ghoshal, 1989). Organizations have also responded by investing heavily in knowledge and skills' searches (Lorbiecki, 1997) that attempt to render their employees culturally competent and linguistically proficient. Their investment has taken many forms: consultancy audits, language training, cross-cultural training manuals and videos, increased overseas secondments and assignments, and the appointment of internal HR specialists to deal with the challenges of managing people over a larger, and more dispersed, geographical area. Collectively, they form part of an increasingly institutionalized response to the cultural exigencies of doing business within a wider international or global arena. Through the course of this chapter, we refer to this as a *cross-cultural training industry.*

We view this industry as significant because it forms a highly influential network of corporations, private consultancies, government organizations, authors, business schools, and academic publications, which when taken together, provide conditions for the exercise of power in making suggestions on how to do business with Others, deemed different from oneself. At the same time, however, this industry is not without paradoxes and tensions. For example, whilst this industry might be regarded as a valuable machinery for enhancing cross-cultural managerial performance, it could equally well be interpreted alternatively, as Jaya (2001) implies in her call for a decolonization of management knowledge, as a technology of Western/American neo-imperialism. In whose interests is this industry functioning, and in terms of cultural difference, what is the Other purported to be different from? Does the cross-cultural training industry present its conceptualizations of difference as natural, obvious, and homogeneous, or is it in any way reflexive about its role in representing the cultural Other? In short, is the cross-cultural training industry a well-meaning and honest provider of an increasingly important organizational service, or is it just another form of Western/American imperialism masquerading as a socially and economically justifiable corporate provision in a globalized economy?

In the next section we show how the cross-cultural training industry has been institutionalized within academia by providing a brief historical overview of the role and conceptualization of culture within management and organization studies.

The Institutionalization of the Cross-Cultural Training Industry

As a discipline, management and organization studies has maintained a curiously paradoxical relationship to the cultural exigencies of managing internationally. Early[1] international management research was primarily concerned with the question of *why* firms internationalize and sought recourse to international trade and economic theory for explanation. This initial focus on international economics was, as Redding (1994) notes, highly significant. It not only sidelined pertinent anthropological and sociological perspectives, but more worryingly, also framed subsequent research within the narrative confines of structural functionalist epistemology and attendant positivist methodologies. Initial comparative management studies, contained notably in the research of the Aston School, provide the most significant evidence of the influence of "normal" scientific practice (Kuhn, 1962) on organization theory (Marsden & Townley, 1996). Culture and society had little explanatory and even less of an interpretative role to play in this early stage of international management research.

As the internationalization of (principally U.S.) corporations accelerated in the 1960s and 1970s,[2] increasing emphasis was placed on the challenges presented by the practice, rather than the logic, of international business. Fuelled by increasing competition from other "developed" countries, such as Japan, practitioners and academics turned their interest, Usunier (1998) observed, to *how* corporations might best internationalize, for example, their finance, marketing and HRM functions. Toward the end of the 1970s, these "how" questions provided sustenance for strong arguments against the idea of asocial and acultural organizations, as promulgated by the Aston School (Mueller, 1994). Subsequent debates on whether organizations (as entities) were either culture-free or culture-bound provided intellectual space for factoring cultural and societal phenomena into academic and practitioner agendas.

At the start of the 1990s, prompted by the emergence of globalization discourses, interest in the particularities of cross-national business interaction revived, leading, as Tung (1995) noted, to the development of two discrete areas of inquiry into cultural differences: cross-national, and intra-national management. She articulates the distinction between these two strands of management inquiry as follows (Tung, 1995: 482):

> Managing cross-national diversity refers to managing the interface between peoples of two countries, such as that between expatriates and

host-country nationals. Managing intra-national diversity, on the other hand refers to coping with the realities of an increasingly diverse, both ethnic- and gender-wise, workforce in a given country.

Within the United States and Britain, what Tung terms "*intra-national management*" is more commonly known as "managing diversity," which Litvin (1997) observed, was quickly seized by many academics and practitioners as an important and powerful tool in harnessing the energies of all organizational members in the global battle for economic success. This interest in enhancing the internal capacity of workforces in domestic and multinational organizations, as a means of responding more effectively to a "globalized" and more intensely competitive market place, has become more urgent with the sharp rise, often with overseas partners, in joint ventures, strategic alliances, mergers, and acquisitions. When, however, this instantiation of globalization is deemed to relate more to managing those "over there," the internal preoccupation with a whole range of differences (gender, age, able-bodiedness, sexual orientation, and so on) seems to be forgotten, as attention is placed primarily on race or ethnicity, under the guise of discussing national culture. Within the literature on *cross-national management*, differences in language and cultural backgrounds are often presented as awkward stumbling blocks full of opposing beliefs that manifest themselves in cultural conflicts at interpersonal, group, and leadership levels. This approach promotes the view that closer examination of the differences between national cultures is essential, as propounded in the highly influential and frequently cited works of Hampden-Turner and Trompenaars (1993) and Hofstede (1980, 1991).[3]

Both the production and consumption of management theories on cultural differences has not left academia immune to interpellations of their own ideas. They have forced business and management schools to review their own practice and seek ways of "internationalizing" their management education provision. The fears and threats presented in not understanding cultural differences, not only institutionalizes the cross-cultural training industry within academia, but it also incorporates discourses of globalization and its constitutive politics of cultural differences within its teaching machines as discussed below.

Mediation by Teaching Machines

The teaching machines of business and management schools are highly influential catalysts in both the production and dissemination of knowledge because they can have a major influence on what current or future managers learn, and on how they think about managing, when with Other(s). In recent years they have had to respond to demands (Calori & De Woot, 1994) from individuals and companies to provide courses with a stronger international orientation. Within Britain, for instance, universities now offer a proliferation of combined or joint degrees in business/management with a foreign language, and some also offer, in partnership with an overseas university, a study year abroad. Furthermore, their odyssey for internationalization also includes specifically targeting under and postgraduate overseas markets, often aided by British Council offices found throughout the world. According to Quacquarelli (1998), overseas students (those from outside Britain and the European Union) can be as high as 90 percent on some British courses, thus making international management "big business." At the start of the twenty-first century, Britain's Department of Education and Employment estimated the total value of Higher Education overseas recruitment to British exports at £1800 million per annum (Department of Education and Employment, 1998).

However, as Spivak (1993) has been at pains to point out, when the "outside" or the margin enters an institution or teaching machine, the *kind* of teaching machine that it enters will determine its contours. So what kinds of teaching machines operate in British universities? Many British universities now have a high percentage of overseas students, but what composite statistics do not tell us is that many of them are from China or the ex-colonies of Britain's erstwhile empire, such as India, Hong Kong, Indonesia, and Malaysia. Although their participation is seen by the Council of Vice-Chancellors and Principles (Heads of British universities) to enrich the cultural and intellectual environment of a university, and to foster understanding between different cultures (Council of Vice-Chancellors and Principles, 1998), their and home students' educational experiences are embedded within the peculiarities of a British university, which in turn is part of Britain's wider social landscape.

Given that a nation's social landscape has a significant effect on the kind of teaching machine that it produces, it is impossible, in the case of Britain, to ignore the continuity of its imperial past into the present, and to act as if there is a "blank sheet" to work on, rubbed clean of historical marks. Within Britain, many of its most disadvantaged women and men have ancestral roots in the colonies of Britain's erstwhile empire, and have been made to feel "out of place" as described by Baucom (1999) in his book with that title. Britain has a sustained history of racism, marked by the *Keep Britain White* campaign of the 1950s, the Nottingham and Notting Hill riots in 1958, the Deptford Marches in 1981, and the racially motivated murder of school-boy Stephen Lawrence in 1993. Although the public furor surrounding that tragic murder resulted in a charge of "institutionalized racism" being levied at the Metropolitan police (Macpherson, 1999), the 1999 Bett report also identified inequity in pay and status for British women and ethnic minority academics. As the more recent Runnymede report (2000) on the *Future of Multi-Ethnic Britain* points out, Britain has some way to go before it becomes a socially inclusive nation. Furthermore, there is a view that while the nation's rich diversity offers Britain important opportunities in world markets, there is the danger of these being squandered by racism and social exclusion. So with this backdrop, what sort of "world-class education" is the British academy providing its home and overseas students?

On the academic front, a whole body of literature, particularly from Britain, has emerged recently advocating the need to address social and political issues through a more critical approach to management education. Although the idea of critical pedagogy, Shor and Pari (2000) remarked, is not new, and has been used for some time in various adult education settings including Higher Education, applying critical theory to management in general, and to management education in particular, is a relatively new phenomenon (Alvesson & Willmott, 1992; French & Grey, 1996; Mingers, 2000). According to Fournier and Grey (2000), critical management education, with its emphasis on a Habermasian approach to emancipation, differs from traditional management education in three important ways:

1. Its focus is on analyzing the underlying assumptions of capitalism rather than on increasing job performance.
2. It seeks to "denaturalize" capitalism by taking a critical look at the realities that make up organizational life including the premise that hard science holds the truth.
3. It pays particular attention to philosophical and methodological reflexivity.

Unfortunately, however, critical management education has been left largely untouched by postcolonial inquiry, despite its presence in other disciplines such as cultural studies, history, anthropology, literary criticism, and sociology. However, as we hope to demonstrate in the next section, important ideas from postcolonial scholars, such as Said, Spivak, Bhabha, provide Western critical management education with fresh perspectives rooted in traditions far removed from traditional Western philosophical orientations.

Case Study: Videos "Making the Difference"

Over the last ten years, a series of articles has appeared in the (U.S.) *Journal of Management Education* advocating the use of films and videos in teaching. Harrington and Griffith (1990) proposed *Aliens* for teaching power and leadership. Gallos (1993) suggested several live action films for teaching "reframing"—exploring a situation from multiple perspectives. Ross (1996) described and analyzed *The Age of Innocence*, and Comer and Cooper (1998) analyzed *Disclosure* from a gender and sexual harassment perspective. More recently, Champoux (2001) proposed adding animated films such as *Antz*, *Toy Story*, and *The Little Mermaid* on the grounds that the "visual symbolism" they contain, offer a rich teaching resource for use in management courses. Animated scenes, he explains, can be used either before or after presenting management theories and concepts, with students then offering individual or group analysis of what they have seen.

The "visual symbolism" used in films and videos are not, however, standalone, innocent pieces of knowledge, to be used lightly; especially when watched by future and practicing managers, as preparation for overseas assignments or international/cross-cultural roles, as well as by students within formal international management education. They are "thick with context" (Spivak, 1993) and carry powerful messages of the cultural Other, absorbed and filtered through other bodies of knowledge. As we hope to demonstrate in the following commentary, films and videos, like Said's (1978) critique of Western European scholars' constructed knowledge of the "Orient," are *a cultural production* and contain *sets of representations*, that cannot be left to chance interpretations.

In order to alert readers to discursive morphings of the Other, we now provide an analytical exposition of the epistemological messages, images, and coded symbolism contained in the specially produced video, *Making the Difference: Living and Working Abroad*. This video was produced by TV Choice Productions in association with the Center for International Briefing, which is based at Farnham Castle in England. The Center is highly prestigious, and specializes in running two/three week preparation courses for managers who are about to embark on overseas assignments. The video lasts about 25 minutes and is accompanied by a teaching manual that includes: advice on how to use the action pack; a two-page introduction on cultural difference, and a synopsis of the key points explored. The main areas covered are different countries' orientations toward results, relationships, time, body language, attitudes toward women, and when "yes means no." The video pack also includes a copy of the script; background information containing views of the interviewees who have worked abroad; a series of questions to ask students once they have watched the video, discussion topics, and role play exercises.

Making the Difference commences with a scene at an airport and starts with the following commentary, using a female voice-over:

> The modern world is becoming smaller and smaller. Thanks to modern communications and transport, countries are closer than ever before. It's tempting to think that people are getting closer, too, but are they? In fact, there are many differences. Some large, some small.... Each culture has its own beliefs and ways of doing things—not better, not worse—just different. [Pans to children drawing at a table.] When you go abroad—to live and to work—you take your luggage with you. [Children's drawing of luggage.] But there's something else that you're taking, that you may not realize—your "cultural baggage": attitudes taken for granted, preconceived ideas about how the world works. You'll have to change and adapt to survive. (Children's drawing of airliner and parachute in trouble.) If you don't understand this simple fact, if you go out unprepared, you're heading for trouble.

The screen is interrupted by the caption, MAKING THE DIFFERENCE, the commentary then continues with:

> When you're new to a culture it is easy to make mistakes. They may be small, a wrong word or gesture, but in business they can lose deals, they can break careers. (Making the Difference script, undated: 14)

The video then moves to Chas, a trainer in a multinational company who went to work in Brunei, who talks about the "*never forgiven*" mistakes made by his predecessor. That interview is followed by five others, interspersed with commentaries on key points, shot at various locations and settings. Anne, who worked as a teacher in Colombia, advises the viewer "*not to get too depressed*" over their different time keeping. Claire is used to illustrate very subtle differences in body language, as she found out when she went to live in Greece (raising an eyebrow to signify "no"). Catherine "*discovers the cost*" of Sri-Lanka's "politeness culture": they are "*very polite people and they don't like to say 'no'*" (they kept saying "yes" when she asked, "Is the shopping center in this direction?" and she got lost). Colin, warns against thinking of the Germans as similar to "us," just because of belonging to the single European market—"*that's one of the biggest mistakes that people can make.*" The video then moves to two women's experiences of working in the Middle East; Maureen is cautious and says:

> So many times you've gone and had that innocent cup of coffee, and the next thing you find yourself fighting off very unwanted advances, and the guy does not understand why you're fighting him off. You've made eye contact with him, you've smiled at him, you've sat in a public place with him. All of these things suggest that you are behaving in a way that the women he knows would not behave and therefore you're not to be respected. A lot of women hate this when they are travelling, they absolutely hate to come to terms with this. They hate to confront it and they hate to admit it, but unless you do you are really placing yourself in danger often. (Making the Difference script, undated: 21)

Suzy, however, counterbalances the preceding view by describing her very different experiences of being in the Middle East where "*women are treated with such respect*" and "*she was treated like a queen.*" Just before the video ends, a commentator suggests:

> So the ideal is to be comfortable with difference, to tolerate ambiguity, to put up with what someone called the continual state of beleaguered self-esteem. (Making the Difference script, undated: 23)

The extracts from the script of *Making the Difference* outlined above, together with its ironic title, serve as an illustrative example of a manufactured cultural fiction of the Other, similar to Western fictions of the Orient. Several practices and sets of representations might be identified which illustrate this. First, the video buys into and replicates popular discourses on globalization and culture, representing the former as a phenomenon, which is all pervasive and a "*matter for all,*" rather than an idea constructed and emanating from the economic powers of the "developed" world. Evidence for this Westernized construction and thus "ownership" of globalization lies in the way in which its implications and exigencies are couched in the discourse of capitalism. Not dealing with the cultural challenges of globalization will "*lose deals,*" cause "*trouble,*" or "*break careers.*" In other words it poses as a threat to the maintenance and perpetuation of the rationality of Western capitalism. Second, the video holds the power to shape viewers' concepts of others' social and cultural identities. It does this, in the first instance, by conflating nation states with national and unitary cultures, for example, "*Sri Lanka's politeness culture,*" "*the Germans,*" "*Colombian time-keeping,*" thus rendering invisible the multifaceted nature and numerous cultural differences, which might be found *within* each of these societies. It might be suggested that this is a technique of control: a practice of drawing tight boundaries around and subsequently homogenizing a set of culturally diverse people such that they might be "known." Culture thus becomes a container with a socially *factitious* nature. Third, the images of the children are important. They suggest a determinist process of "learning" or "acquiring" culture, in which children are passive recipients of an already established body of knowledge with no agency for mediating these materials. Plus, they are politically and historically "neutral"—the innocence of the children renders innocent the knowledge of the cultural Other—that is to say agency and knowledge from which stories of colonization, historical repression, and violence have been expurgated. Indeed the adage in the video that each culture has its own ways of doing things—*"not better, not worse, just different"*—provides justification for ignoring the historical and political legacies of cultural colonization. Fourth and most importantly, the Other(s) have no voice in this video: they are not permitted to speak or represent themselves. The silencing, death, and preservation of the Other's cultural structures into "glass jars" and its subsequent epistemological "post-mortem" by Western eyes is reminiscent of Marsden and Townley's (1996) account of "scientification."

These four observations in sum indicate that the teaching processes involved in using videos, and their ironic attempts to bring the material of the cultural Other to "life," are just as problematic as the content of videos. As we explain in our analysis of Ellison's (1997) views on the use of videos in cross-cultural teaching, the teacher is involved in *acts of mediation*. In his paper, Ellison, a consultant at the Center for International Briefings, not only explains how he uses the video *Culture Gap* (counterpart and practical carbon-copy of the *Making the Difference* video) in his job, but also how he thinks it *ought* to be used. At the beginning of his chapter, Ellison (1997: 106–107) explains why using this video is helpful:

> [The Video] provides a degree of compromise. It allows the introduction of thoughts and ideas from another culture whilst retaining control over content and quality, within the parameters of the video, over time. Although this video [The Cultural Gap] is intended for the shipping industry (it is targeted at ships' crews and has a distinct maritime flavour), it provides general lessons to be learnt, and it "does not take long for the 'real' audience to start relating to the 'virtual' audience. It is neither too academic nor too boring."

The context for the video is important here. At the start of the cultural briefing offered by the consultant, participants are introduced to the concept of culture and asked, following a brief outline of their work, to reflect upon their own culture with specific recourse, to the studies of Hall, Trompenaars, and Hofstede. Having had this introductory session, the video is then shown. In terms of content, Ellison highlights the topics covered in the video: culture filters, culture management skills, and understanding cultural values. Using a basic *Sender–Message–Receiver* (S–M–R) model for interpersonal communication (a model, we might add, which is not without its problems), Ellison (1997: 108) uses the notion of culture filters, which equates to a type of "noise" in the terminology of the S–M–R model, as a concept which:

> . . . explains how people communicate and how what they say and what they understand will be affected by their cultural background and cultural understanding of the situation. Some people may use these filters without knowing it.

These "culture filters" are things that must be managed if communicative messages are to be encoded in a culturally sensitive way in order to ensure that the meaning of the message might be subsequently decoded and understood correctly. These two culture management skills read (Ellison, 1997: 109):

1. check, check, and check again that you interpret correctly the message sent to you by someone in another culture; and
2. make sure in your own communication to make use of your culture filters so that you really say what you mean.

The final part of the video deals with "understanding cultural values." The participants are presented with a list of "values" such as generosity, honesty, reliability, respect, openness, and fairness. They are asked to discuss the relative importance of these values and to consider which of the values means most to them. Differences in response are highlighted during discussion and act as the basis for an analysis of cultural differences.

Although Ellison does allow the Other to speak in his training sessions, ultimately he forces participants to box themselves and their identities, and Others' and their identities, into the cross-cultural theories and models he follows (i.e., within Hall's, Hofstede's, and Trompenaars' concepts and the S–M–R communication model). Culture, cultural values, and cultural identity are taught to be things that people possess, rather like a television or a microwave oven, or baggage as in *Making the Difference*. They are *taught* to be external to the individual, with cultural differences seen to determine and influence the way in which people communicate and understand one another. Culture has acquired boundaries and homogenizing values and only becomes "useful" when resident in the discursive schemata of managerialism. The Other has once again been silenced: it has been frozen into discrete and essentialist categories of difference and processed mechanically through a series of theories and models. This is the effect of Ellison's teaching machine. It is his active mediation that provides the technocratic contours of this particular form of cross-cultural teaching.

As seen in our commentary on both *Making the Difference* and the significance of mediation on the part of the teacher, perceived cultural differences are encoded, visually and textually, within a manufactured cultural fiction of the Other that draws upon Western-centric management theories as points of departure. This privileging of Western voices and their silencing of the rest is, we suggest, part of a wider managerialist perpetuation of contemporary neocolonialism. Whilst processes of neocolonialism are highly complex, as they go beyond questions of representation and include important material and affective dimensions, here we have attempted to demonstrate how the cross-cultural teaching machine creates categories and inscribes practices that relegate non-Western forms of knowing and subjectivity to the margin. In our concluding section, we suggest how resistance to this continuing neocolonialist inscription might be fostered in the cross-cultural teaching machine so that what is being professed on "'culture" becomes more of an enunciative practice (Bhabha, 1994), rather than an epistemological function, as commonly practiced. We do this by considering early conceptualizations of power and resistance within Labor Process Theory (LPT) and changes brought about by post-structuralist thinking. Drawing upon the work of Homi Bhabha, as well as Michel Foucault, we then suggest ways in which resistant spaces can be opened up within the cross-cultural teaching machine itself.

Resisting the Irresistible?

Within management and organization studies, questions of resistance and power have been of notable concern to LPT within its dominant Marxist tradition. As Jermier, Knights, and Nord (1994) explain, labor process theorists initially viewed resistance as genuine only if it emanated from one source: revolutionary class consciousness. From this Marxist point of view, workers begin to engage in class-based resistance when they become aware, through the collective consciousness of labor solidarity, of their own exploitation and alienation, generated by the extraction of surplus value under conditions of capitalist production. Recent application, within LPT, of postmodern and post-structuralist analysis has, however, rendered this Marxist interpretation of resistance, suspect. Instead of viewing resistance in terms of a grand narrative, of a class-based, dualistic struggle between (primarily blue-collar) workers and owners, LPT now points toward processes of subjectivity, including notions of the self, as more productive sites for understanding the contiguous, rather than dialectical, nature of power and resistance.

Understanding resistance, and power, through contiguous analysis allows more space to be devoted to the proximity of ideas and impressions in place and time, as a principle of association, or interconnectedness. For example, LPT's previous preoccupation with resistance as a class-based power struggle over the ownership of the means of production, is, under a contiguous principle of association, rendered much more complex. Instead of focusing on resistance as a means by which powerless workers might somehow accomplish some form of utopian destiny of a fixed universal nature (a problematic essentialist claim in itself), Foucauldian analysis urges us to step back and reconsider the, often hidden, preconceptions that lie behind the discursive terminology employed. As Foucault clearly articulates in his debate with Noam Chomsky (Rabinow, 1984), there is no external universal or essential position of certainty from which one might be "free" of power in some imagined, ideal society.

Foucault's exposure of the grand narratives of resistance and power, as a work of fiction or imagination has been taken up by Said (1978) in his book *Orientalism*. The publication of that book was a landmark not only in the author's discipline of literary criticism, but also in many of its intellectual neighbors such as cultural studies, sociology and social policy, politics and international relations, and European, Oriental, and African studies. As Gandhi (1998) explains, the success of Said's work lay in his systematic and complex unravelling of the way in which principally Western European scholars (writers, poets, linguists, philosophers, historians, *inter alia*) constructed knowledge of the "Orient" (everything that was not Europe) in their work. In particular, Said explored the sets of representations (categories, classifications, images) used by these scholars in producing their accounts of the Oriental Other, a path that we have similarly followed in our analysis of sets of representations in the video *Making the Difference*.

Said's central notion of Western accounts of the Orient as a fictional, cultural production rather than a faithful reflection of existing "reality" from plural perspectives, resonates with Bhabha's (1994) call to consider existing accounts of "culture" as a historic and literary project, too. Reconceptualizing the cross-cultural teaching machine in this way, not only allows for its artifacts (videos, management theories on cultural differences) to be seen as "literary texts." Consideration can also be given to the contiguous relationships between their authors' intentions, scriptwriting, and sources of origin, and how representations of the Other are finally produced. Cross-cultural videos are, after all, scripted pieces of fictionalized work in which representing the Other is, Spivak (1999) explains, not unproblematic. For her, "representation" is loaded with two meanings: (a) representation as "speaking for," a form of political proxy; and (b) "representation" as in art, or in a picture.

The pictures and images contained within fictionalized accounts of the Orient by Western scholars have been resisted and challenged by postcolonial unveilings of their homogenizing, colonizing impulses, and their concomitant denial of the legitimacy of non-Western epistemes and associated forms of subjectivity. Excluding localized knowledges of the Self is problematic for students, and teachers, both within, and outside, Britain, Europe, or the United States. Presenting partial knowledge (in both senses of the word) is, Trowler (2001) argues, extremely limiting as it "captures" and fixes the way in which teachers, students, and others see the world that they live in. Moreover, it also limits options available for thought and its articulation, especially in relation to the increasingly neo-colonial rhetoric of management knowledge. As Jaya (2001) points out, much of the knowledge currently transmitted through university teaching machines seems to follow increasingly a Western/American lens. In her call for, "no more colonization," Jaya asks us teachers, instructors, and professors what we really "know" and "profess"? She also asks whether teachers in management and organization studies are mindlessly repeating mainstream courses and instructional guidelines, without due consideration of their epistemological deficiencies, inconsistencies, and partialities?

In order to rise to Jaya's challenge to decolonize management knowledge by embracing multiple-world views, knowledges, and philosophies, we suggest that the cross-cultural teaching machine re-view the videos that it produces with a more "critical" pedagogical eye. Instead of using them as intended, we provocatively propose that they be viewed as literary texts, or works of fiction, for subsequent deconstruction and literary criticism (as alluded to above with reference to Bhabha, 1994), as commonly expected of students studying literature. While advocating this literary excursion as a form of "home-work," attention would be placed on culture as an enunciative practice (rather than as an epistemological function) in which different subjective readings and interpretations of the video text are expected, and then shared, thus creating the conditions for resisting the irresistible temptation to fix and know the Other, through a Western imperial lens. As Bhabha (1994: 177–178) writes:

> If culture as epistemology focuses on function and intention, then culture as enunciation focuses on signification and institutionalization; the epistemological tends towards a reflection of its empirical referent or object, the enunciative attempts repeatedly to reinscribe and relocate the political claim to cultural priority and hierarchy...in the social institution of the signifying activity.... The enunciative is a more dialogic process that attempts to track displacements and realignments that are the effects of cultural antagonisms and articulations.

Culture as enunciative practice might be seen as subversive and resistant since it aims to transgress the rationale and form of the hegemonic moment of colonial orderings of alterity by inscribing cultural incommensurability into the heart of such orderings thereby transforming polarities of Self and Other.

Post-Script

Being mindful of some of the partiality of our own arguments, we now offer a reflexive acknowledgment of this chapter's limitations. First of all, we have focused on the cultural production and sets of representations primarily of one cross-cultural training video. That video is certainly not a representative sample of the entirety of cultural texts used by the industry, and neither is it intended to be so. We do, however, believe that it is indicative of a very conventional cultural production deployed in the teaching of management students "about" cultural differences. Second, we have restricted our focus to the ways in which perceived cultural differences are encoded into the video itself, both visually and textually, and the ways in which one teacher has talked about the manner in which he uses such videos. We have not then considered how the video might be appropriated (culturally, materially, and affectively) by its viewers, though our own teaching experience tells us that responses vary enormously between one student and another. Finally, and relatedly, our euphemized exposition of imagined attempts at teaching cross-cultural management might be seen as overly "harsh" or overly "subjective," but as in all literary work, it is impossible to escape some element of fiction.

Notes

1. By early we refer to the international management research of the 1960s. Wright and Ricks (1994) explain that research into international business was very much in its infancy during this period.
2. In consonance with the emergence of the United States as a global economic power.
3. See McSweeney (2002) for a probing critique of Hofstede's work.

References

Alvesson, M., & Willmott, H. (Eds.). 1992. *Critical management studies*. London: Sage.

Baucom, I. 1999. *Out of place: Englishness, empire, and the locations of identity*. New Jersey: Princeton University Press.

Bhabha, H. K. 1994. *The location of culture*. New York: Routledge.

Bartlett, C., & Ghoshal, S. 1989. *Managing across borders: The transnational solution*. Boston: HBS Press.

Black, J. S., Mendenhall, M., & Oddou, G. 1991. Toward a comprehensive model of international adjustment: An integration of multiple theoretical perspectives. *Academy of Management Review, 16* (2), 291–317.

Bradley, H., Erickson, Stephenson, C., & Williams, S. 2000. *Myths at work*. Cambridge: Polity Press.

Calori, R., & De Woot, P. 1994. *A European management model*. London: Prentice Hall.

Champoux, J. E. 2001. Animated films as a teaching resource. *Journal of Management Education, 25* (1), 79–100.

Comer, D. R., & Cooper, E. A. 1998. Gender relations and sexual harassment in the workplace: Michael Crichton's *Disclosure* as a teaching tool. *Journal of Management Education, 22*, 227–241.

Council of Vice-Chancellors and Principals of the Universities of the United Kingdom. 1998. *International students in UK higher education*. Briefing Note.

Department of Education and Employment. 1998. The value of education and training exports to the UK economy. *Research Report No. 83*.

Ellison, D. 1997. The culture gap: A cross-cultural training video. In D. Killick & M. Parry (Eds.), *Proceedings of the Cross-Cultural Capability Conference* (pp. 106–111). Leeds, UK: Leeds Metropolitan University.

Foucault, M. 1980. *The history of sexuality: An introduction* (Vol. 1). New York: Vintage Books.

Fournier, V., & Grey, C. 2000. At the critical moment: Conditions and prospects for critical management studies. *Human Relations, 53* (1), 7–32.

French R., & Grey, C. (Eds.). 1996. *Rethinking management education*. London: Sage.

Gallos, J. V. 1993. Teaching about reframing with films and videos. *Journal of Management Education, 17*, 127–132.

Gandhi, L. 1998. *Postcolonial theory: A critical introduction.* Edinburgh: Edinburgh University Press.

Guirdham, M. 1999. *Communicating across cultures.* Basingstoke: Macmillan.

Hampden-Turner, C., & Trompenaars, F. 1993. *The seven cultures of capitalism.* London: Piatkus.

Harrington, K. V., & Griffin, R. W. 1990. Ripley, Burke, German and Friends: Using the film *Aliens* to teach leadership and power. *The Organization Behaviour Teaching Review, 14*, 79–86.

Hirst, P., & Thompson, G. 1994. Globalization, foreign direct investment and international economic governance. *Organization, 1*(2), 277–303.

Hofstede, G. 1980. *Culture's consequences.* London: Sage.

Hofstede, G. 1991. *Cultures and organizations: Software of the mind.* London: McGraw-Hill.

Jaya, P. S. 2001. Do we really "know" and "profess"? Decolonizing management knowledge. *Organization, 8* (2), 227–233.

Jermier, J. M., Knights, D., & Nord, W. R. (Eds.). 1994. *Power and resistance in organizations.* London: Routledge.

Knights, D., & Vurdubakis, T. 1994. Foucault, power, resistance and all that. In J. M Jermier, D. Knights, & W. R. Nord (Eds.), *Power and resistance in organizations* (pp. 167–198). London: Routledge.

Kuhn, T. S. 1962. *The structure of scientific revolutions.* Chicago: University of Chicago Press.

Levitt, T. 1983. The globalization of markets. *Harvard Business Review*, May–June, 92–102.

Litvin, D. R. 1997. The discourse of diversity: From biology to management. *Organization, 4* (2), 187–210.

Lorbiecki, A. 1997. The internationalization of management learning: Towards a radical perspective. In J. Burgoyne & M. Reynolds (Eds.), *Management learning: Integrating perspectives in theory and practice* (pp. 265–281). London: Routledge.

Macpherson, W. 1999. *The Stephen Lawrence Inquiry: Report of an inquiry by Sir William Macpherson of Cluny.* London: Her Majesty's Stationery Office.

Marsden, R., & Townley, B. 1996. The Owl of Minerva: Reflections on theory in practice. In S. R. Clegg, C. Hardy, & W. R. Nord (Eds.), *Handbook of organization studies* (pp. 659–675). London: Sage.

Massey, D. 1995. The conceptualization of place. In D. Massey & P. Jess (Eds.), *A place in the world?* (pp. 45–86). Milton Keynes: Open University Press.

Massey, D. & Jess, P. (Eds.). 1995. *A place in the world?* Milton Keynes: Open University Press.

McCracken, G. 1988. *Culture and consumption.* Bloomington: Indiana University Press.

McSweeney, B. 2002. Hofstede's model of national cultural difference and their consequences: A triumph of faith—a failure of analysis. *Human Relations, 55* (1), 89–118.

Mingers, J. 2000. What is it to be critical? Teaching a critical approach to management undergraduates. *Management Learning, 31* (2), 219–237.

Mueller, F. 1994. Societal effect, organizational effect and globalization. *Organization Studies, 15* (3), 407–428.

Paliwoda, S. 1993. *International Marketing* (2nd ed.). Oxford: Butterworth-Heinemann.

Quacquarelli, N. 1998. No let-up in demand for MBAs. *World Executive Digest,* March.

Rabinow, P. (Ed.). 1984. *The Foucault reader: An introduction to Foucault's thought.* London: Penguin Books.

Redding, S. G. 1994. Comparative management theory: Jungle, zoo or fossil bed? *Organization Studies, 15* (3), 323–360.

Ross, J. 1996. Scorcese's *The Age of Innocence*: An escalation interpretation. *Journal of Management Education, 20,* 276–285.

Said, E. W. 1978. *Orientalism.* London: Penguin Books.

Scott, J. C. 1990. *Domination and the arts of resistance: Hidden transcripts.* New Haven: Yale University Press.

Shor, I., & Pari, C. 2000. *Education is politics: Critical teaching across differences, post secondary.* Portsmouth, NH: Boynton Cook.

Smith, K., & Berg, D. 1997. Cross-cultural groups at work. *European Management Journal, 15* (1), 8–15.

Spivak, G. C. 1993. *Outside in the teaching machine.* New York: Routledge.

Spivak, G. C. 1999. *A critique of postcolonial reason: Toward a history of the vanishing present.* Massachusetts and London: Harvard University Press.

Trowler, P. 2001. Captured by the discourse? The socially constitutive power of new higher education discourse in the UK. *Organization, 8* (2), 183–201.

Tung, R. 1981. Selection and training of personnel for overseas assignments. *Columbia Journal of World Business, 19,* 482–494.

Tung, R. 1995. Strategic human resource management challenge: managing diversity. *The International Journal of Human Resource Management, 6* (3), 482–494.

Usunier, J-C. 1998. *International and cross-cultural management research.* London: Sage.

Wichterich, C. 2000. *The globalized woman: Reports from a future of inequality.* (P. Camiller, Trans.). London: Zed Books.

Wright, R. W., & Ricks, D. A. 1994. Trends in international business research. *Journal of International Business Studies, 25* (4), 687–701.

CHAPTER 10

From the Colonial Enterprise to Enterprise Systems: Parallels between Colonization and Globalization

Abhijit Gopal, Robert Willis, and Yasmin Gopal

> What I object to is the craze for machinery, not machinery as such.
>
> Mahatma Gandhi

L et us consider the first part of this thought in the context of information and communication technologies (ICTs). That there is a craze is hardly worth disputing. But why the craze? Who has it? How is it manifested? What are its consequences? These are seemingly innocuous questions, but in exploring them we expose a worldwide system of power, wealth, deprivation, progress, and stagnation that bears an uncanny resemblance to the colonial world to which Gandhi objected. That he saw the craze for technology as implicated in colonial "unfreedom" is telling; as he says, "Today, machinery merely helps a few to ride on the backs of millions. The impetus behind it all is not the philanthropy to save labor, but greed. It is against this constitution of things that I am fighting with all my might" (1997: 307). That he separates the technology from the craze for it is indicative of his nuanced understanding of how the manner of its creation and deployment is inherently political. His statement points also to the diffuse and widespread nature of the technological project as we know it, implying that it is an obsession that is hardly easy to overcome. Yet, he offers too, with the second part of his thought, the hope that ends other than those that have been hitherto pursued can be imagined.

This chapter takes on the task of exploring the dazzling lure of ICT in the post-development world (the craze), the disturbing similarity of its role in this context to the machinations of colonial rule (the effects and outcomes of the craze), and its relationship to the promise of post-colonial[1] liberation (the hope for other ends). The story we wish to tell is rooted in a contradiction: ICT is often held up by the (largely) Western center as the key to prosperity for peripheral economies (Madon, 2000; Natarajan & Agbese, 1989); however, the well-being of these economies in the longer term is, in fact, seriously compromised by these same technologies as they are deployed today. This latter contention remains, of course, to be established, and it is to this task that we will apply ourselves in this paper.

It is interesting to note first, however, that colonialism was rooted in a similar contradiction. Initially lauded for its potential as a means of bettering the lot of people supposedly unable to fend for themselves, it was later seen as actually degrading, and disempowering, and as a crime against humanity. As the hold of colonialism on geopolitical reality began to loosen in the middle of the twentieth century, another contradictory ideology, that of "development," took its place. On the one hand, it upheld as inviolable the notions of freedom, equality, and the right to prosperity. On the other hand, it celebrated the inexorable logic of the market that pushed the formerly colonized countries into greater levels of deprivation and dependence (Rahnema & Bawtree, 1997; Sachs, 1992a).

Today, the patronizing presence of the development era has given way to the ideology of globalization. What we hope to show is that the contradiction continues to hold sway in this new reality, which is oiled by information and its rapid communication. It is by exploring the machinations of these technologies that we will be able to see how this system of domination is disturbingly similar to the one that prevailed during the colonial era.

Development or Neocolonialism?

The large scale de-colonization of the mid-twentieth century brought with it the hope of discontinuity, a break with the oppressive past and the promise of future prosperity. Indeed, it was in the language of such hope that then U.S. President Harry Truman presented his agenda for development in 1949: "We must embark on a bold new program for making the benefits of our scientific advances and industrial progress available for the *improvement and growth* of underdeveloped areas...The old imperialism—exploitation for foreign profit—has no place in our plans...Greater production is the key to *prosperity and peace*" (cited in Ullrich, 1992: 275, italics added).

The notion of development had its origins in the colonialism-tainted past (Esteva, 1992; Mohan, 1997). Ullrich (1992: 276) asks pointedly, "Did the new orientation, in which the 'other' cultures of the world were declared to be 'developing countries' and given assistance to foster their forces of production, really introduce the end of colonialism? Or is our present era to be regarded as a new, less immediately recognizable, and therefore more effective, stage in Western imperialism?" By substituting "development" for "poverty," the west went from "exploiter" to "helper," from description to prescription, writing in its own heroic role.

The conditions for this seemingly subtle shift were, of course, perfect. The value system of the market that had been implanted in colonial times made the shift to "development" both plausible and desirable. This was aided by the fact that the only alternative system to Western capitalist thought, socialism, had built into it the same enthrallment with the "development of the forces of production" (Ullrich, 1992: 279). Reconstituted now by the development goal as "underdeveloped" countries (Esteva, 1992), the formerly colonial regions quickly adopted "the religion of progress" (Ullrich, 1992: 276).

A critical component of the machinery that exalted the development doctrine was the education system that had endured since colonial times as a key constituent of colonial policy. As Symonds (1966: 17) notes, for Lord Macaulay, "the main object of British educational policy was 'to form a class of interpreters between us and the natives we govern', a class of persons Indian in blood and color but English in tastes, in opinions, in morals and in intellect." In the development era, the functionaries of capital were being similarly schooled, and toward "the end of the 1960s...the United States' model of high-level business education was becoming the dominant organizational form for both training elite and aspiring elite managers and generating intellectual innovations about business and management in many countries" (Whitley, 1984: 335). In the Third World, these narrowly educated elites were now not only interpreters for their own countries of the dictates issuing from the metropoles, but they were also snapped up by the powerful keepers of the development torch, the Bretton Woods institutions. Not surprisingly, perhaps, the "World Bank, for example, is often described as comprised of citizens of 100 countries who attended six universities" (Kobrin, 1998: 366).

As Esteva (1992) shows, development began as a decidedly economic program, utilizing broad quantitative indicators that eventually failed to correlate with "satisfactory progress" (p. 13). From here it proceeded through guises such as *unified development* (social and economic), *human-centered development*, *integrated development*, the promising but misguided notion of *endogenous development*, and, more recently, *redevelopment*, implicit in which is the admission of the failure of earlier conceptions of development along with a willingness to tear down the results obtained earlier and start over. Redevelopment now appears to have donned the mask of *sustainable development*, which, in practice, seems to involve sustaining the project of development rather than any higher aim.

Through all its twists and turns, development has been a much-criticized project, replete with examples of "failure" in terms of its stated objective of "helping" (Gronemeyer, 1992). In spite of this, it has had wide-ranging effects. It has resulted in displacement and lopsided growth, plunging millions of people into greater misery and showering a few with enormous wealth (Sachs, 1992b); it has mobilized a disturbing process of homogenization, characterized by "a tremendous loss of diversity" (p. 4); it has precipitated an "ecological predicament" (p. 2) that, if left unheeded, threatens the viability of future generations. It has, moreover, marginalized those whom it constructs as noncontributors to the economic project of progress (Berthoud, 1992; Castells, 1998); it has sought to firmly establish the logic of the market as the only one of value to humankind, and it has created and consolidated a destructive power differential, conceived initially in terms of the developed/underdeveloped dichotomy and sustained through a fallacious program of aid and dependence.

How the System Sustains Itself

Colonization had brought with it deindustrialization (Pacey, 1991), marked by the disappearance of indigenous industry and the appearance, in its place, of the colonizer's technologies and values. With deindustrialization came the stifling of what Pacey (1991) has called technological dialogue—the idea, pervasive throughout history, of autonomous technological development within communities that were in "dialogue" with other, often far-flung, communities. With decolonization came some hope of the revival of technological dialogue but the odds were stacked against it in the face of the development discourse. Today, we claim that the development era has run its course, but are we any closer to technological dialogue? The answer must be an unqualified "no," because the same system that snuffed it out in the first place and later kept it from resurfacing sustains itself today. We now call it globalization, a word that signifies not only a *new* twist to an old theme but an eminently *cleverer* twist. Quickly retreating from common parlance are the smug references to underdevelopment and pathological essences. Language (to the dismay of many) is politically correct. Human rights and charity toward the unfortunate are high on the agenda. There appears to be a (not always dissimulated) sincerity in efforts to make a better world for all. Yet, beneath this rhetoric, the old system perseveres. Goonatilake (1995: 226–227) notes that these globalizing tendencies "are much more pervasive than the hegemonizing tendencies of empires of yore, the present cultural globalization being a stronger superimposition on the regional cultural hegemonies wrought by these past empires." It may be useful to consider why this may be so by exploring the nature of this system and its elements.

Central to this system is the "monoculture" (Shiva, 1993; Ullrich, 1992) of capitalism and the "metaphysic" of the market (McMurtry, 1998), at once an ideology, a system of values, and an authoritative presence thoroughly inscribed into popular consciousness since colonial times. This is not to suggest that capitalism or the market ideal have not changed since their early days; on the contrary, this way of thinking has suffered through several crises, has evolved and redefined itself in numerous ways (Harvey, 1989), and has established itself as synonymous with other unquestioned institutions of our day such as democracy and freedom (McMurtry, 1998). Since its earliest incarnation as the "invisible hand" to its past and current status as theology (McMurtry, 1998), its presence is so pervasive that it is unseen and, therefore, unquestioned.

Decentralized as the entire system appears, its core is small, powerful, and tightly knit. It consists of the United States–Europe–Japan nexus (Castells, 1998), flagrantly united in communities of the rich such as the Group of Seven/Eight and the Organization for Economic Co-operation and Development (OECD). These countries (at least, their elites) define the game and set the rules. Such a power differential, though, needs careful preservation even if its seeds have been planted through the institutions of colonialism and development: most people, after all, have lost more than they have gained from this system. Having given up the overtly coercive means of preserving such power that was embodied in colonialism, the functionaries of the core and their allies nurture their advantage through several means at different levels.

The most openly coercive power in the nurturing of this system is wielded by transnational companies (TNCs) based in the rich countries, which arrogantly treat the globe as their playground. "Given their ability to confer or withdraw investment from national economies in free movement across borders, regulatory standards, tax regimes, natural resource sites, and labor forces, they have no accountability to nation-states and their electorates" (McMurtry, 1998: 140). The state, weakened in its influence, plays an altered role: "Government purpose lies in a role which is generally supporting, supplemental and secondary to the needs of the firm" (Spich, 1995: 7). Slightly less arrogant, and transparently in the service of the TNCs, are the Bretton Woods institutions and the World Trade Organization. Together, they hammer out of the peripheral countries any resistance to the market model, specify the kinds of projects that may be undertaken, and broker trade agreements "as necessary preparation...for the competitiveness challenge which all country economies will inevitably face" (Spich, 1995: 21).

Yet, even such conspicuous coercion does not appear to be read as such by most people, so ingrained is the value of the market and the well-established power differential. At the receiving end of this relationship of dominance are willing allies who "want to participate in instant prosperity" (Ullrich, 1992: 284). In keeping with the market doctrine that "to be rational is to consistently seek to gain as much for oneself as possible" (McMurtry, 1998: 128), elites in peripheral countries exercise self-interest to the detriment of the societies in which they live (Berthoud, 1992).

There are structural aspects, too, to the system's sustaining machinery. In place, through the auspices of colonial rule and the development project, are entrenched technological[2] and administrative infrastructures. The social and cultural conditioning that arises from these appears impossible to reverse. And being constructed at an urgent pace is a system of interconnections through ICTs that opens up the minutest details of a country's goings-on to the scrutiny of the international market and keeps in clear and constant view the threat of capital flight. This is supplemented by the media, which extends the gaze of international markets and beams into millions of homes images of the Western (and primarily American) ways of life (Schiller, 1991). Undergirding the entire system of power and its preservation and continuance, then, is a constant flow of information, supported increasingly (in many senses of the word) by ICTs. It is to an examination of these technologies that we will turn next.

Information and Communication Technologies

If globalization is the guise now adopted by the interests of Western capital, information and its technologies are its blood and bones.[3] Its constituent character is revealed in the numbers (not all of which, unfortunately, are in accord, revealing the somewhat arbitrary nature of supposedly hard information); the *rate of growth* in telling statistics such as the number of personal computers, the number of Internet hosts, and the number of Internet users in peripheral countries has typically been higher than in well-off countries. In India, for example, the proportion of personal computers to population rose by over 100 percent between 1996 and 1999, while the corresponding increases in Canada and the United States were only around 50 percent (World Bank, 2001) during a period widely celebrated as being witness to a veritable explosion in ICT use in rich countries (OECD, 2000). The proportion of Internet hosts to population during this period increased by approximately 600 percent in India, 500 percent in the United States, and 100 percent in Canada (World Bank, 2001). The number of Internet users in peripheral countries is also quickly catching up with the numbers in the rich countries; India, for instance, had approximately 4.5 million users in 2000 while France had 9 million (CIA, 2001). Similar increases are apparent in other categories such as telephones and television sets (CIA, 2001; World Bank, 2001).

Of interest too is the increasingly global nature of ICT manufacture and trade. For example, 70 percent of India's rapidly growing software output is for export; 61 percent of this software makes its way to the U.S. (Watson, 2001). The traffic in hardware is also increasing rapidly: for example, U.S. computer hardware exports to India rose to $2.26 billion in 2000, an increase of nearly 66 percent over the previous year.

ICTs represent, to use an apt English metaphor, the new white knight. Consistent with the liberatory rhetoric of globalization, the emancipatory and self-actualizing potential of knowledge/information is persistently emphasized. Its technologies are "promoted [to peripheral nations] as a means of lessening social gaps in education and literacy and as a means of leapfrogging into the modern age" (Schiller, 1981: 18). No wonder, then, that many peripheral countries today use their mastery and promotion of ICTs as a means of signifying to the international community the extent of their "progress."[4]

We will try to show in the next section that, far from being emancipatory, as the elites of both core and peripheral societies would have us believe, ICTs might actually represent the most potentially effective means of continuing the project of dominance inaugurated during colonial times (Schiller, 1981). Before we proceed in that direction, however, a brief examination of the components and characteristics of ICTs might be useful.

While a case might be made for developing a much more elaborate and comprehensive classification of the various kinds of ICTs available, we believe a simple breakdown will suffice for our purposes: information and communications technologies. The former include primarily applications and databases. *Applications* are both widely used (e.g., SAP R/3, Microsoft Office, Netscape Navigator) and created in peripheral countries. *Databases* related to the affairs of both private and public sectors are burgeoning, much as they are in the Western world. Among communication technologies, *telecommunications* networks connect these peripheral countries both internally and externally to global markets.

These technologies, like all others, are not neutral in their influences on society and culture (Winner, 1985; Feenberg, 1991). Technologies are built to achieve certain ends, and these ends follow from the ethos of the time. The hindsight of a succeeding epoch will often betray the values inherent in a technology (Standage, 1998), such as the design principle during the industrial revolution that allowed for means of access to moving parts of machines for purposes of repair to be so small that only children could use them, as child labor was acceptable at the time (Winner, 1985). But this subsequently objectionable "value" could hardly have been visible as such to most people at the time. In our own time, we are guided by the ethic of the market, and much of what it legitimizes might be objectionable in hindsight. Whether this will be so is hard to predict. What we do understand is that the designs we create are not value-free. With this in mind, let us consider some characteristics inherent in ICTs.

One characteristic of ICTs (and of other technologies) is that they need *standardization*. It seems to be well recognized that they can be "effective" only when they can "talk to each other." Stemming from the nineteenth-century American industrial design imperative of "interchangeable parts" (Pacey, 1991, 1992), the idea of standardization fits comfortably within the rhetoric of globalization. Another characteristic is that they are, in many ways, *invisible*, possessed of a Heideggerian "ready-to-hand" quality. As DeMaio (1978) observes, "So much of this information flow takes place beneath the surface of our conscious activities that we literally take it for granted" (cited in Schiller, 1981: 20). The technologies that effect the flow are invisible, so the flow becomes invisible. One apt descriptor of such technologies is "trojan machines" (Ullrich, 1992: 285). A related characteristic is the powerful *conditioning* effect of ICTs (Hamelink, 1986). As Ullrich (1992: 285, italics added) has pointed out:

> The alleged tools of progress are not tools at all, but technical systems that worm their way into every aspect of life and tolerate no alternatives... With them... there typically comes an infrastructural network of technical, social and psychological conditions, without which the machines and products do not work... [Technology] brings with it its corresponding requirements and they can only function with their associated infrastructure and the *psycho-social* preparation of people.

Pacey (1991) sees the effectiveness and influence of technology as stemming from the principles of organization embodied in it rather than from its technical characteristics. Hence, ICTs need to be viewed as artifacts that both facilitate and, are the effects of, specific kinds of social and psychological *conditioning*. In turn, such psycho-social conditioning may become an important component of the wider repertoire of practices and processes which further social, cultural, and political control.

These three characteristics (standardization, invisibility, and conditioning), as we hope to show in the following section, also characterized the technological apparatus of colonialism. They were, as they are today, unremarkable imperatives of the Western market ethos (Adas, 1989), as well as vectors of control. To question the market ethos (and this is especially true in the case of ICTs) was and is to question the goal of progress (Berthoud, 1992; McMurtry, 1998). Today, ICTs are an integral component of the globalization project, in terms of their ability to "shrink" the world (King, 1989) and in terms of their remarkable malleability in the regime of flexible accumulation (Harvey, 1989). Their development and deployment are not in the hands only of self-interested TNCs but, as Schiller (1981) points out, they have, in "a revealing example of late capitalist development," benefited from "huge governmental research funds" (p. 30). The complicity that characterizes the relationship between capitalism and technology permits the legitimization of an important message of globalization: the market might be "tough" but invest in ICTs and you will achieve an equal footing with the rich countries and make the market work for your prosperity. We now turn to an attempt to reveal the contradictory nature of this message.

Colonialism and the New Technologies

We wish to adopt here a more emphatic standpoint than the one that merely complains that ICTs are the latest tools of an imperialism that has never died, howsoever true that contention might be. We take the position, rather, that ICTs and their attendant "infrastructural network[s] of technical, social and psychological conditions" (Ullrich, 1992: 285) have parallels in colonialist rule, a way of being that has ostensibly been rejected today. We intend to arrive eventually at a question: if we reject colonialism and its attendant machinery, can we really afford to uncritically celebrate globalization and its attendant technology? Before we proceed to examine the links between ICTs and colonial rule, it is useful to consider the parallels between structural and relational conditions in the two eras.

An important tool of the European colonizers was the colonial city (e.g., Bombay and Calcutta in India). King (1989) calls these the very first sites for the confrontation between European and non-European peoples, though, in essence they were meant for the colonizers, not the colonized. Initially port cities, they later included regional capitals and other outlying settlements. Their function was administrative, commercial, and consumptive, "concerned with extracting, organizing, and dispatching the economic surplus"—from the copper mines, sugar, coffee, or tobacco plantations where the natives worked—"to the imperial metropole" (King, 1989: 2). On one level, this arrangement corresponds to the core–periphery equation of today, in which the peripheral economies serve their extractive, resource-supplier function for the benefit of the core capitalist powers. On another level, it brings to mind the setting up of enclave economies—the Silicon Valleys of the East—within the periphery (Castells, 1996), and the exploitation of cheap labor to fuel the growth of TNCs and the metropolitan economies.

Similar, too, are the alliances that were forged, first with the landed gentry and later with the educated elite by the colonizers (e.g., the British in India) for the maintenance of the empire, and the ties between the so-called "third world capitalists and classical petty bourgeois classes" (Petras, 1978) and the TNCs. Just as the chosen ones among the natives were groomed to act as intermediaries between the "sahibs" and the multitudes, so are today's elites in the satellite states being trained to speak the language and serve as conduits to the masses.[5] In the nineteenth century, the alliances made by the British in India "were intended to delineate acceptable attitudes, so as to outlaw more 'extreme' positions and not to reach agreement on sharing power with westernized Indians" (Robb, 1992: 6). Administration was centralized and the policy makers resided at the Colonial Office "back home." In the current situation, we see a tendency toward centralization of key management functions in TNCs as the flow of information within the organization grows and new technologies are introduced (Poster, 2001). As Davenport (2001: 20) notes, present day ICTs "allow managers to keep much closer tabs on far-flung operations than they would be able to do otherwise."

It is in these new technologies that we catch other glimpses of the old colonial ways and it is these that we will now explore. We examine these technologies (applications, databases, and telecommunications) within the context of the three characteristics of ICTs we described in the previous section—standardization, invisibility, and the conditioning effect—and attempt to demonstrate that colonial situations were geared toward achieving the effects of these very characteristics. We begin with the technologies of information: applications and databases. First, in the creation of applications we see thriving software development industries in peripheral countries. Notable here is the adherence to Western specifications that enforce *standardization*. Barber points out that the worldwide software industry is controlled by a handful of corporations and "the men who dominate this extraordinary new world of technologized culture are mostly American" (1998: 82). And though a few in the peripheral economies are staking out their share in this technological boom, their "take-home" pay is limited at best. Moreover, the drive to produce software "has incurred a large opportunity cost as the finest local minds now produce software to boost the performance of American and European companies rather than using their talents to address domestic developmental needs" (Heeks, 1998: 2). In such important changes in social preferences, we may discern signs of the kind of *conditioning* discussed earlier.

We see somewhat parallel developments during colonialism. To take one example, Victorian technologies, on which indigenous talent labored, were the steamship, the telegraph, and the railway (MacLeod & Kumar, 1995). Each of these was served to provide greater physical control over the empire, and reaped sizeable benefits for the British. For instance, in India, according to MacLeod Kumar, "what 'development' took place . . . occurred within a framework which the metropolis dictated, and from which the recipient did not always seem to benefit" (1995: 20). Simultaneously, these technologies also participated in the process of bringing about large scale social change— as Marx (1972) clearly foresaw, albeit in an idiom steeped in Eurocentrism and orientalism—and concomitant changes in people's subjectivities, thus effecting the kind of psycho-social *conditioning* mentioned previously.

Second, as regards the actual content of information technologies, we see today the large-scale use of and dependence (as technology becomes *invisible*) on information systems in the offices of TNCs in the peripheral countries.[6] The quintessential information system, we might venture to surmise, is the enterprise system (Davenport, 2001), "the programs that manage a company's vital operations, from order-taking to manufacturing to accounting" (Edmondson, Baker, & Cortese, 1997: 41); a key exemplar is the R/3 system from SAP (a German company now operating worldwide), a set of "tightly interwoven programs . . . that come together as a powerful network that can speed decision-making, slash costs, and give managers control over global empires" (Edmondson et al., 1997: 41–42). The meteoric rise in the popularity of this software was based on the company's keen understanding of the globalizing trend: "SAP designed products to link every part of a company's operations . . . [and] made sure their software could handle different currencies, languages, and regulations—a big draw for multinationals" (Edmondson et al., 1997: 43). As a means of control, the system appears to help in two ways: to collect information about every aspect of peripheral operations and to ensure that the procedures carried out around the globe are *standardized*. The categories used to store information in the databases arise from the Western mind and bear little sensitivity of the cultural circumstances from which the data derives and the procedures reflect modes of operation that are widely deployed in the West. As one might expect, this aspect of databases has its own consequences as regards the mental/psychological *conditioning* of database users.

When we look back to colonial times, we see similar preoccupations. The British maintained an extensive database of papers, letters, and memoranda at the India Office in London (Farrington, 1980; Kaminsky, 1986). Cognizant of the need for detailed information, the colonial office in London had "prepared printed forms and a circular to governors instructing them to have the forms filled out by all the individual office holders in the colonies" (Young, 1961: 34) thus *standardizing* the system of reporting and control. "Official returns and reports became routine [hence, *invisible*]...and the major disciplinary spur and check for government employees at all levels," and later this "enumeration and documentation were extended to society at large, encouraging and coercing it as well" (Robb, 1992: 293). Darnton's (2001) description of the systematic development of a database of every book printed in British India highlights the exercise of colonial control via the mundane activity of the accumulation of information.

Where procedures were concerned, the colonial rulers employed a very large number of indigenous people to run the colonial machinery. Tight *control* over what these employees did, unsurprisingly, was critical. Elaborate procedures were put in place that specified the *standardized* way in which colonial employees were to complete their tasks. "Information flowed in and business was disposed of according to established routines within each office," such routinization helping to render information flows relatively *invisible* and unremarkable (Robb, 1992: 34). Other office procedures contributed toward standardization and control. For instance, every

> ...file or report was logged at each stage...Each separate function was allocated to a particular official, and tasks left *written trails which could be traced* by the supervisors...*Standardized* reports and returns recorded the conduct of business at lower levels and matters of routine, in marked contrast with the exchanges of extensive minutes and papers which contributed to decision-making at the top. (Robb, 1992: 34–35, italics added)

An interesting but somewhat hidden (*invisible*) aspect of colonial power lay in language. Robb (1992: 42) notes that, in the British Empire, "corruption and inefficiency were combated by the extension of the use of English." English in the British Empire served as a means of distinguishing between those who were "the cream of society" (Gopal, 1963: 240) and entrusted with administrative responsibilities, such as in the civil services, and those among whom "the use of vernacular languages was seen as a disability" (Robb, 1992: 42). The elites in the civil services were schooled in colonial language and its ways, often at the colonial metropoles, and were well versed in getting by in colonial society (within limits, of course). On the other hand, language proved to be a barrier for the others. For instance, during the Great Rebellion of 1857, the rebels found themselves unable to use the telegraph to their advantage because "not many . . . knew English and no telegraphic code was in vogue for any Indian language" (Ghose, 1995: 166). As Ashcroft, Griffiths, and Tiffin (1995: 283) note: "The control over language by the imperial center—whether achieved by displacing native languages, by installing itself as a 'standard' against other variants which are constituted as impurities, or by planting the language of empire in a new place—remains the most potent instrument of cultural control."

Today, language is a crucial element in the spread of ICTs. Although software such as SAP uses several languages, these are all metropolitan in nature, leading to a *standardization* of its own kind. In India or in Malaysia, English is used to run the software. Only Westernized elites, therefore, have access to such systems and the beneficial positions they imply. The Internet, too, reveals the hegemonic influence of English (Poster, 2001), as does computing vocabulary in general. Based as these are on the ASCII character set, the use of non-English text is rendered difficult (Gupta, 1997), serving thereby as powerful influences on world culture. Such processes are not only *invisible*, they also facilitate a specific psychological *conditioning* of people involved with them.

Beyond information technologies, and in concert with them, lie the technologies of communications. Perhaps the most glamorous sector in the world of ICTs, their catalysis of the globalization endeavor is pivotal to the project. They manifest themselves in many ways, such as the Internet, global positioning systems (GPS), and wide and local area networks of several kinds, creating thereby a world that is not only highly "connected" but in which the *metaphor* of the network has come to be a societal model (Castells, 1996). By its pervasiveness, the network metaphor has an important *conditioning* effect on how people think about issues of interest and imagine new possibilities. And their digital character links them seamlessly (*and invisibly*) to information technologies, enabling a system of interchange and surveillance about which the colonial rulers could only have dreamt. Through these technologies, surveillance in peripheral countries is effected in at least two important ways. First, it enables the relatively *invisible* accumulation of vast amounts of seemingly innocuous data. Moreover, as Barber (1998: 92) points out, "the current anti-regulatory fever has assured that the new data banks being compiled from interaction and surveillance are subject to neither government scrutiny nor to limitation and control." Through the development of "data warehouses," countries are constituted after the fact (following comparisons to data from other countries) as poor, lazy, corrupt, Western-like, advanced, or successful. Second, real-time monitoring of activities is made possible. Evidence of "non-normality" on any of several predefined variables is systematically accumulated and provokes unhappy consequences in forms such as capital flight, international disapproval, or, in the case of employees of TNCs, a threat to employment.

The colonial rulers, too, entertained visions of a connected world (Standage, 1998). They were very aware of the immense potential of timely information: "Rapid communication with the Headquarters of the Supreme Government for public and political purposes from all the presidencies, but most specially from the Presidency of Bengal, where political events are most likely to occur, is manifestly the first consideration for the Government of India" (Ghose, 1995: 157). The setting up of telegraph routes across the country was politically motivated and, the Court of Directors in London—which was, not surprisingly, averse to the idea of such systems falling in the hands of nongovernmental agencies—made sure that its operation would be supervised exclusively by the government (Ghose, 1995). The telegraph played a crucial role in the quelling of the Great Rebellion of 1857, making possible the summoning of reinforcements from distant corners of the empire as well as the timely delegation of authority to the officers on site. Railways and steamships were products of the same vision, used to consolidate British rule (McLeod & Kumar, 1995; Pacey, 1991). Each of these resulted in networked arrangements that had as their objective greater control over empire and the harvesting of economic benefits. But they all pale, in terms of their potential for control, in comparison with the networks of today. What is possible today, through digital networks and digital information technologies, is a revival of the colonial vision of the control of remote markets and resources *without actually having to be there*.

We return now to the question we raised at the beginning of this section, hoping that what we have described lends it meaning and urgency. If we reject colonialism and its attendant machinery, can we really afford to uncritically celebrate globalization and its attendant technology? In view of the parallels between colonial rule and our use of ICTs, do we not need to reexamine what we have set in motion?

The Way Beyond

Anthony Smith (1980: 176) has suggested that, "The threat to independence in the late twentieth century from the new electronics could be greater than was colonialism itself" (quoted in Schiller, 1981: 115). This, indeed, is what we see in the frenetic spread of ICTs and the insidious return of colonial-style control, except that ICTs command a level of discipline that colonizers only struggled to achieve. Colonial control was also palpable and clear to see, enforced as it was by the police and the armed forces (Jayaweera, 1986). What makes the problem worse today is that the control is hegemonic, a struggle not between police and civilians but "between knowledge and mis-representation" (McMurtry, 1998: 395). The challenge, in the first place, is to be able to "see" that a problem exists (McMurtry, 1998; Sachs, 1992b).

To be able to see, however, is surely not easy. So entrenched is the value system of the market (McMurtry, 1998) and so strong is the conviction that ICTs represent progress (Berthoud, 1992) that even the willingness to look is hard to find. Even among those prepared to listen, the invisible nature of ICTs, and therefore its effects, threatens the credibility of the message. And then there are the self-interested on both sides of the power equation who are predisposed, perhaps, to look the other way even in the face of the most compelling evidence. Nevertheless, we hope we have, through our essay, pointed the reader in directions that facilitate the "seeing."

What is it, though, which is visible through the smoke and mirrors? We see, hopefully, that something is missing: technological dialogue. In a world dominated by ICTs arising from the west, it is missing in two important senses. First, this most important set of technologies emanates in its most basic design from the metropoles of the world (Poster, 2001). In spite of the hopes and celebrations of the countries that have found their feet in this sector, they still excel only at a game defined beyond their borders. They succeed only in furthering the project that began with colonialism and turning, in concert with those who provide them with approbation, a blind eye to the plight of the millions of their compatriots on the wrong end of the widening gap between the rich and poor. Second, as the most effective tool to date of metropolitan control, ICTs surreptitiously promote the transformation of the globe into the markets and raw materials that Western capital has hungered for since colonial times. With the further advance of this way of thinking, the possibility of technological dialogue in all other sectors recedes even farther.

We also see, despite protestations to the contrary from the apologists of globalization, a despairingly polarized world, rent by the destructive forces of colonialism and development, and in danger of blundering into the new millennium with possibilities of even more destructive divisions, courtesy of the globalization project (Rifkin, 1995). The only players in the game are those who have something of money-value to exchange (McMurtry, 1998); the rest are consigned to the stands (as paying spectators, of course).[7] Levels of poverty and deprivation are rising to such levels that the well-meaning denizens of metropolitan societies can pick and choose the objects of their pity (and, of course, their charity).

And we see, moreover, a ravaged natural world. In the absence of dialogue among the worldwide beneficiaries of the earth's resources, the metropolitan centers of capitalism have taken at will from these resources and have precipitated an unprecedented crisis. The earth's resources and carefully nurtured indigenous knowledge about them have been "converted from commons to commodities" (Shiva, Jafri, Bedi, & Holla-Brar, 1997: 8). The market metaphysics (McMurtry, 1998) has promoted the culture of ownership and the attendant right to do with one's property whatever might result in monetary gain. This problem alone calls urgently for technological dialogue, the recovery and development of indigenous know-how by societies that can negotiate *on equal terms* about the meaning and the future of the natural world.

Once we have caught a glimpse of the problems, is there anything we can do? Interestingly, one set of possibilities is presented by the very technologies that erode the likelihood of technological dialogue, ICTs, and it is to these that we now turn our attention. The very malleability and unobtrusiveness that make them indispensable to the globalization project can quite conceivably be utilized for rather different purposes, such as (a) autonomous dialogue among those who perceive the problems of the capitalist monoculture, and (b) the reinvention of technologies following the recovery of indigenous knowledge and values.

With respect to the first of these possibilities, the initiation of dialogue, one pervasive ICT, the Internet, appears already to present interesting possibilities (Little, Holmes, & Grieco, 2001; Madon, 2000), although it, too, is firmly entrenched at this time within the ensemble of technologies that promote the existing hegemony. As Gunaratne (1997: 3) observes, the "Internet, like the codex and typeface, may one day be turned into a counter-hegemonic influence." The prospect, of course, might appear somewhat dim, as any such discourse is already being overwhelmed by the frenzy of commercial activity that has inundated the Internet since the early 1990s, before which time it did appear to present more liberating possibilities. Nevertheless, the Internet already connects concerned individuals across every continent and we can only hope that these connections lead to the real possibility of dialogue and change. Once voices unite, it becomes harder not to hear them.

The second possibility involves the notion of reinvention. Another observation from Gunaratne (1997: 3) is helpful here: "The rush to adopt the innovations of 'the West' [makes us] dependent to the point of addiction on a mode of institutional practice which may not be particularly healthy for us. Which is not to say that any innovation or technological advancement... need be rejected out of hand because it is still in the hands of the privileged. So were paper and the Latin script once upon a time." We might return here to Gandhi's observation about technology quoted at the beginning of this paper. The "craze" for technology reflects the obsessive nature of the Western capitalist impulse at the turn of the millennium, the slippery, no-holds-barred approach that presents itself as the deliverer of prosperity and shapes its technologies in its own image. The technology itself, however, is today capable of being metamorphosed into vastly different entities to reflect other systems of thought and value, unlike the industrial technologies of yesteryear such as the railways and industrial machinery.

What, then, will reinvented ICTs look like? Although McMurtry (1998) provides some interesting examples of how ICTs might be used in novel ways to counter the damaging effects of the market ideology in the West, it is, by definition, impossible to predict and inappropriate to specify how autonomous enclaves in a polycentric world might wed the elemental principles of ICTs, as we know them, to indigenous ways of knowing and being. We might venture to suggest, however, that for their effective reinvention in the quest to reestablish technological dialogue, ICTs will need to be reconstituted as belonging to the "civil commons." McMurtry (1998: 399) uses "the concept of the 'civil commons' to distinguish it from the traditional 'commons'—the shared natural lands upon which an agricultural village economy depends." For McMurtry, the civil commons includes "both the traditional commons and all other universally accessible goods of life that protect or enable the lives of society's members" (1998: 399). ICTs in the civil commons will mean their almost uniform accessibility among members of the peripheral society, with the result that ICTs would cease to be symbols of elite privilege.

This notion of access to ICTs as a privilege of the elite is true in most parts of the world (Little et al., 2001), and most decidedly in the peripheral countries. Still, we might argue that in the West, through the auspices of the state and the (not disinterested) largesse of corporations, there is a definable, if faltering, trend toward the universal accessibility of ICTs. To whatever extent this may be true, and Rifkin (1995) would probably argue that it is not, "it must not be forgotten that industrialization arose in and through European culture and is therefore not essentially alien to it" (Ullrich, 1992: 285). Whether Western non-elites have access to ICTs is moot; they are steeped in that culture. In peripheral countries, especially those ravaged by colonialism, more or less the opposite is true. ICTs are distinctively an elite privilege, the domain of those attuned to the ways of the West, and who are primarily concerned with bolstering their own positions of advantage. Attuned as these elites are to the Western systems of knowledge embodied in ICTs, the need for reinventing these technologies for the larger indigenous context—which would call for a privileging of indigenous knowledge systems—is rarely felt in elite circles. That the recovery of indigenous knowledge systems for and through the inventive use of ICTs might actually sever Western bonds and might rekindle a technological dialogue among equals is hardly spared a thought by such privileged few. For that matter, the very existence of indigenous knowledge systems remains poorly acknowledged, giving little opportunity to the proud and ancient traditions (such as Indian science, mathematics, and arts) to mould the new technologies into novel creations.

ICTs in the civil commons would mean their accessibility by a variety of enclaves. The energies expended in the burgeoning "offshore" software development contexts, such as in Bangalore, India (Castells, 1996; Madon & Sahay, 2001), could be diverted from Western-specified developments to considerably more creative projects aimed at privileging local knowledge systems (Little et al., 2001; Madon, 2000) and, by means of such technological dialogue, both recovering indigenous knowledge systems and taking them in new and fruitful directions. By re-establishing and reinforcing the notion of technological dialogue through ICTs, a similar recovery of long overdue autonomy might be effected in other sectors.

To be sure, the barriers to such programs of reinvention look daunting: barriers raised by those who profit from the current system, structural barriers in the form of internal and external infrastructures, and the barriers posed by the Western-oriented education system. But with the initial help of the state—which is increasingly being stripped of its influence by the cult of the market—and that of the nongovernmental organizations (NGOs), the recovery of autonomy at a global level might be set in motion by paying attention to the potential of ICTs as constituting, what Gunaratne (1997) has called, a "counter-hegemonic influence."

In closing, we would like to make it clear that it has not been our intention in this chapter to try to establish a grand narrative to explain the woes of the world. Rather, we have tried to pick up strands to tell a coherent story from a point of view that differs significantly from that of the proponents of the current capitalist world system. The purpose of our paper has been to try to show at least one important contradiction in the grand narrative of the market: the contradiction between the glitter of ICTs and their destructive consequences. We hope, through our essay, to have given at least a few readers the motivation to pick up the rocks strewn along their paths to see what lies underneath.

Notes

1. We treat the concept of the postcolonial in an epochal rather than an epistemological sense as we are concerned in this paper with the continuities amongst what are often presented as three distinct epochs.
2. It is important to note that the technological and industrial infrastructure, often the pride of a peripheral country, is based largely on foreign technology. As Natarajan and Agbese (1989: 26) point out, "technical progress in many countries has taken place, not due to original innovations, but due to the transfer and diffusion of technology developed elsewhere." These technologies become, therefore, the ideal carriers of (usually) Western values.
3. Any allusion to violence that the reader might pick up in the use of this terminology is intended; ICTs have all of the violent potential of science and technology eloquently revealed in Ashis Nandy's, *Science, Hegemony, and Violence* (1990).
4. Countries such as Singapore, South Korea, Taiwan, and India spring immediately to mind.
5. We do not intend to imply that citizens of peripheral countries, whether in the present day or in colonial times, were devoid of agency; rather, it was specifically the agency exercised in the forging of alliances amongst elites in both core and periphery that perpetuated a system of (coercive or hegemonic) domination of non-privileged populations during both colonial and more recent times. The non-privileged also exercised their agency in opposing colonialism; one aim of our paper is to suggest that they need once again to exercise that agency.
6. Their use, of course, is spreading rapidly to other administrative contexts as well.
7. Castells (1998) captures the plight of this periphery admirably in his treatment of what has come to be called the Fourth World.

References

Adas, M. 1989. *Machines as the measure of man: Science, technology, and ideologies of Western dominance.* Ithaca, New York: Cornell University Press.

Ashcroft, B., Griffiths, G., & Tiffin, H. 1995. Language: Introduction. In B. Ashcroft, G. Griffiths, & H. Tiffin (Eds.), *The post-colonial studies reader.* London: Routledge.

Barber, B. R. 1998. The new communications technology: Endless frontier or the end of democracy? In R. G. Noll & M. E. Price (Eds.), *A communications cornucopia* (pp. 72–98). Washington, DC: Brookings Institution Press.

Berthoud, G. 1992. Market. In W. Sachs (Ed.), *The development dictionary: A guide to knowledge as power* (pp. 70–87). London: Zed Books.

Castells, M. 1996. *The rise of the network society.* Malden, MA: Blackwell Publishers.

Castells, M. 1998. *End of millennium.* Malden: Massachusetts: Blackwell Publishers.

CIA. 2001. *The world factbook.* Washington, DC: Central Intelligence Agency.

Darnton, R. 2001. Un-British activities. *New York Review of Books,* April 12.

Davenport, T. H. 2001. *Mission critical: Realizing the promise of enterprise systems.* Boston: Harvard Business School Press.

DeMaio, H. B. 1978. Transnational information flow: A perspective. In *Data regulation: European and Third World realities,* Uxbridge, UK: Online.

Edmondson, G., Baker, S., & Cortese, A. 1997. Silicon Valley on the Rhine. *BusinessWeek,* (European ed.), November 3, 1997.

Esteva, G. 1992. Development. In W. Sachs (Ed.), *The development dictionary: A guide to knowledge as power* (pp. 6–25). London: Zed Books.

Farrington, A. 1980. *British policy in Asia: India Office Memoranda* (Vol. 2). London: Mansell.

Feenberg, A. 1991. *Critical theory of technology.* New York: Oxford University Press.

Gandhi, M. K. 1997. The quest for simplicity: "My idea of Swaraj." In M. Rahnema & V. Bawtree (Eds.), *The post-development reader* (pp. 306–307). London: Zed Books.

Ghose, S. 1995. Commercial needs and military necessities: The telegraph in India. In R. MacLeod & D. Kumar (Eds.), *Technology and the Raj* (pp. 153–176). New Delhi: Sage.

Goonatilake, S. 1995. The self wandering between cultural localization and globalization. In J. Nederveen & B. Parekh (Eds.), *The decolonization of imagination* (pp. 225–239). London: Zed Books.

Gopal, R. 1963. *British rule in India: An assessment.* London: Asia Publishing House.

Gronemeyer, M. 1992. Helping. In W. Sachs (Ed.), *The development dictionary: A guide to knowledge as power* (pp. 53–69). London: Zed Books.

Gunaratne, A. R. 1997. The virtual spaces of postcoloniality: Rushdie, Ondaatje, Naipaul, Bakhtin, and others. *Proceedings of the First Online Conference on Postcolonial Theory.* [www.as.nus.sg/staff/conf/poco/paper5.html]

Gupta, A. F. 1997. The internet and the English language. *Proceedings of the First Online Conference on Postcolonial Theory.* [www.as.nus.sg/staff/conf/poco/paper6.html]

Hamelink, C. J. 1986. Is information technology neutral? In J. Becker, G. Hedebro & L. Paldan (Eds.), *Communication and domination* (pp. 16–24). Norwood, New Jersey: Ablex.

Harvey, D. 1989. *The condition of postmodernity*. Oxford: Blackwell.

Heeks, R. 1998. Building software industries in Africa. [www.sas.upenn.edu/African_Studies/Acad_Research/softw_heeks.html]

Jayaweera, N. 1986. The Third World and the political economy of the communication revolution. In J. Becker, G. Hedebro, & L. Paldan (Eds.), *Communication and domination* (pp. 30–44). Norwood, New Jersey: Ablex Publishing Corporation.

Kaminsky, A. P. 1986. *The India Office, 1880–1910*. New York: Greenwood Press.

King, A. 1989. The new colonialism: Global restructuring and the city. *Intersight* [www.ap.buffalo.edu/~intrsght/archives/intersight1/king/king.html].

Kobrin, S. 1998. Back to the future: Neomedievalism and the postmodern digital world economy. *Journal of International Affairs, 51* (2), 361–386.

Little, S., Holmes, L., & Grieco, M. 2001. Calling up culture: Information spaces and information flows as the virtual dynamics of inclusion and exclusion. *Information Technology & People, 14* (4), 353–367.

MacLeod, R., & Kumar, D. 1995. Introduction: Western technology and British rule. In R. MacLeod & D. Kumar (Eds.), *Technology and the Raj* (pp. 11–22). New Delhi: Sage.

Madon, S. 2000. The internet and socio-economic development: Exploring the interaction. *Information Technology & People, 13* (2), 85–101.

Madon, S., & Sahay, S. 2001. Cities in the developing world: Linking global and local networks. *Information Technology & People, 14* (3), 273–286.

Marx, K. 1972. On imperialism in India. In R. C. Tucker (Ed.), *The Marx-Engels reader* (pp. 577–588). New York: W. W. Norton.

McMurtry, J. 1998. *Unequal freedoms: The global market as an ethical system*. Toronto: Garamond Press.

Mohan, G. 1997. Developing differences: Post-structuralism and political economy in contemporary development studies. *Review of African Political Economy, 24*, 311–328.

Nandy, A. (Ed.). 1990. *Science, hegemony, and violence: A requiem for modernity*. Delhi: Oxford India Press.

Natarajan, R., & Agbese, P. O. 1989. New technology, the south and technology transfer. *International Journal of Contemporary Sociology, 26* (1–2), 25–37.

OECD. 2000. *Measuring the ICT sector*. Organization for Economic Cooperation and Development.

Pacey, A. 1991. *Technology in world civilization: A thousand year history*. Cambridge, MA: The MIT Press.

Pacey, A. 1992. *The maze of ingenuity: Ideas and idealism in the development of technology* (2nd ed.). Cambridge, MA: The MIT Press.

Petras, J. 1978. *Critical perspectives on imperialism and social class in the Third World*. New York: Monthly Review Press.

Poster, M. 2001. *What's the matter with the internet?* Minneapolis: University of Minnesota Press.

Rahnema, M. & Bawtree, V. (Eds.). 1997. *The post-development reader*. London: Zed Books.

Rifkin, J. 1995. *The end of work: The decline of the global labor force and the dawn of the post-market era*. New York: Tarcher/Putnam.

Robb, P. G. 1992. *The evolution of British policy towards Indian politics: 1880–1920*. New Delhi: Manohar Publishers and Distributors.

Sachs, W. (Ed.). 1992a. *The development dictionary: A guide to knowledge as power*. London: Zed Books.

Sachs, W. 1992b. Introduction. In W. Sachs (Ed.), *The development dictionary: A guide to knowledge as power*. London: Zed Books.

Schiller, H. I. 1981. *Who knows: Information in the age of the Fortune 500*. Norwood, New Jersey: Ablex Publishing Corporation.

Schiller, H. I. 1991. Not yet the post-imperialist era. *Critical Studies in Mass Communication, 8* (1), 13–28.

Shiva, V. 1993. *Monocultures of the mind: Biodiversity, biotechnology, and the Third World*. Penang, Malaysia: Third World Press.

Shiva, V., Jafri, A. H., Bedi, G., & Holla-Brar, R. 1997. *The enclosure and recovery of the commons*. New Delhi: Research Foundation for Science, Technology, and Ecology.

Smith, A. 1980. *The geopolitics of information*. New York: Oxford University Press.

Spich, R. S. 1995. Globalization folklore: Problems of myth and ideology in the discourse on globalization. *Journal of Organizational Change Management, 8*(4), 6–29.

Standage, T. 1998. *The Victorian internet: The remarkable story of the telegraph and the nineteenth century's on-line pioneers*. New York, NY: Berkley Books.

Symonds, R. 1966. *The British and their successors: A study in the development of government services in the new states*. London: Faber and Faber.

Ullrich, O. 1992. Technology. In W. Sachs (ed.), *The development dictionary: A guide to knowledge as power* (pp. 275–287). London: Zed Books.

Watson, J. 2001. *Export IT India: An overview of India's information technology market*. Washington, DC: International Trade Administration, U.S. Department of Commerce.

Whitley, R. 1984. The fragmented state of management studies: Reasons and consequences. *Journal of Management Studies, 21* (3), 331–348.

Winner, L. 1985. *The whale and the reactor: A search for limits in the age of high technology*. Chicago: University of Chicago Press.

World Bank. 2001. *World development indicators*. Washington, DC: World Bank.

Young, D. M. 1961. *The colonial office in the early nineteenth century*. London: Longmans.

CHAPTER 11

The Practice of Stakeholder Colonialism: National Interest and Colonial Discourses in the Management of Indigenous Stakeholders[1]

Subhabrata Bobby Banerjee

> When the missionaries first came to Africa, they had the Bible and we had the land. They said, 'Let us pray.' We closed our eyes. When we opened them, the tables had been turned: we had the Bible and they had the land.
>
> Desmond Tutu

After decades of struggle, the land rights of Aboriginal people of Australia were finally recognized by the Native Title Act of 1993. Recognition of Native Title overturned the long-standing view that Australia was *terra nullius*—land belonging to no one—and finally recognized the rights of Aboriginal people over their illegally occupied land. While this was hailed as a major milestone in the process of reconciliation between indigenous and non-indigenous Australians, the implementation of the Native Title Act was fraught with problems and uncertainties. As several Aboriginal communities discovered, granting of Native Title did not always mean control of the land and its resources, especially when the clarion call of "national interest" was sounded. Tourism, the creation of national parks and mining interests were all enclosed under the rubric of national interest and in almost every case, Aboriginal interests were put last. This chapter examines one such case: the debate over the construction of the Jabiluka uranium mine in the Northern Territory, which was recently approved by the Australian government despite protests by the Mirrar community, the traditional owners of the land, and by various national and international environmental groups including UNESCO.

I begin the chapter with a critical discussion of the narratives of colonialism and postcolonialism. I discuss the historical conditions underlying the relations between mining interests and indigenous communities in Australia and examine the role that governments have played and continue to play. I then provide a history of the Jabiluka mine and examine the colonial and anticolonial discourses that inform this project. I discuss the role of other stakeholders in this process and argue that current organization theories on managing stakeholders are complicit with colonialist attitudes and values. I conclude by discussing some emancipatory possibilities of postcolonialism and provide some directions for future research.

Colonial and Postcolonial Dominations

Postcolonial theory, despite gaining currency in Western academic thought in recent years, is mired in much theoretical and political confusion (Shohat, 1992). The prefix "post-" seems to imply that the era of colonial domination has ended with the emergence of newly independent nations in Asia, Africa, and South America. However, several scholars have questioned this assumption and in problematizing the postcolonial condition, have criticized the universalist definition of culture that informs it (Mani, 1989; Radhakrishnan, 1994), doubted its political agency (Shohat, 1992), critiqued its singularity and ahistoricity (McClintock, 1992), and warned of its ability to reproduce a politics of domination (Pugliese, 1995).

The postcolonialism school of thought attempts to problematize issues arising from colonial relations (Shohat, 1992). It is, to quote Edward Said, a "retrospective reflection on colonialism, the better to understand the difficulties of the present in newly independent states" (Said, 1986: 45). However, using the term "post" in postcolonialism tends to isolate the problems caused by colonialism and place them in some past era with the assumption that colonialism as a historical reality has somehow ended (Mani, 1989; Said, 1986).

Despite its focus on non-Western spacetimes, postcolonialism is rooted in Anglo-American academy and is "a discursive practice in the specific context of the western academy" (Pugliese, 1995: 345). This aspect of postcolonialism becomes more problematic when theorizing the position of indigenous peoples in contemporary postcolonial theory, a position that often remains unspoken and invisible. As Perera and Pugliese (1998) have pointed out, postcolonial theories have very little relevance (and could in fact prove quite problematic) in accounting for ongoing struggles of indigenous people in Australia, Canada, and the United States. In these societies, where much programmatic celebrations of "multiculturalism" occur regularly, there is often a conflation of indigenous rights with other "minority" issues with little acknowledgment that the agendas of these groups are quite different and often incompatible (Banerjee & Linstead, 2001).

When discussing postcolonial perspectives of the Jabiluka uranium mine, it might be more appropriate not to focus on the term postcolonialism as it is generally understood but rather to ask, who is defining postcolonialism and for what purpose and then examine the consequences of such a position. The position I take in this paper in describing relations between indigenous communities with governments and business corporations is located in what Perera and Pugliese (1998) describe as "the fraught space riven by an ongoing colonial desire to exploit the land, its resources and peoples, and the anticolonial opposition to colonizing institutions and practices" (p. 72). Perhaps, "recolonization," a term employed by Aboriginal activist Jacqui Katona, is more appropriate.

Katona (1998) describes the discourses on Aboriginality that unfolded in the Western academe as being typical of the "academic mindset of skull measuring." Muecke (1992) describes three kinds of discourses on Aboriginality by European authors: the *anthropological,* the *romantic,* and the *racist.* All three discourses arose from perceptions of difference and relationships of dominance and all three share some commonalities. The anthropological discourse surrounding the "discovery" of the native is aptly described by Radhakrishnan (1994) as the "I think, therefore you are" syndrome. Objective knowledge of the Aborigine was produced by the canons of anthropology using a functionalist-empirical approach that excluded any possibility of dialogue (Muecke, 1992). In fact, as Said (1986) points out the basis of European ethnography *depended* on the incapacity of the native to negotiate or disrupt scientific discourse about them. Thus, knowledge of the Aborigine was constructed based on descriptions of totemic rites, rituals, kinship patterns, and other formulations that are characteristic of the tribe of European anthropologists.

Terms like "Aboriginal tragedy" and stories that mourn the "passing" of a "barbaric and primitive," yet "noble" race are characteristic of the romantic discourse. Muecke (1992) discusses one such book, *The Passing of the Aborigines* by Daisy Bates, a "Victorian adventurer" who spent twenty years "looking after" Aboriginal people, as an example of the romantic discourse. Since "civilization" had arrived in the continent, the "primitive" ways of life would be overcome: the fact that Aborigines would "disappear" was accepted as a logical outcome. Bates's aim in writing her book was "to make their passing easier and to keep the dreaded half-caste menace from our great continent. They should be left as free as possible, to pass from existence as happily as may be" (Bates, 1966, cited in Muecke, 1992). These stories did not just play out in the imagination of the colonizers but had real impacts on government policy as exemplified by the "Aboriginal Policy." In an official memorandum in 1933, J. A. Carrodus, the Secretary of the Department of the Interior, wrote "The policy of the government is to encourage the marriage of half-castes with whites or half-castes, the object being to breed out the color as far as possible" (Manne, 1999: 17).

For instance, a report by the Human Rights and Equal Opportunities Commission entitled *Bringing Them Home* (1997) describes some harrowing stories of the "stolen generation," Aboriginal children forcibly removed from their families. The logic of this policy was that the children (especially the "half-castes") should not be brought up in the "primitive" way but were to be sent to missions and schools to be "civilized." The "full-blooded" Aborigine, "racially incurable," would "pass away" in time (in effect, be "bred out") and the only remaining "problem" was to "raise the status" of the "half-castes" so they could be absorbed into the white population (Reynolds, 1989). The romantic discourse was rich in such racist metaphors. The third discourse constructed and represented Aboriginality in terms of their essential racial difference (Muecke, 1992). Thus, all Aboriginal practices, including present day social issues such as alcohol and drug abuse, are explained in genetic terms.

Some writers describe another discourse, which they see as being potentially liberating. Aboriginality as political identity, survival, resistance, and independence are themes underlying this discourse (Hollinsworth, 1992; Keefe, 1988; Sheridan, 1988). These writers argue that focusing only on cultural continuities or Aboriginal descent in constructing Aboriginality is "reductionist and essentialist" whereas the Aboriginality-as-resistance model is a more dynamic concept that is "progressive, forward-looking rather than retrospective" (Hollinsworth, 1992: 149). However, representation of Aboriginality has become a contentious issue in recent years. The fact that constructions of Aboriginality have been shaped by colonial and racist discourses should come as no surprise: what is interesting and problematic is the fact that representations of Aboriginality in "postcolonial" Australia continue to be dominated by non-Aboriginal people.

Several Aboriginal activists and academics have launched blistering attacks on non-Aboriginal representations (constructed mainly by white academics) of Aboriginal identity (Anderson, 1995; Dodson, 1994; Watego, 1989) with the quite reasonable argument that it is none of their business to define who or what Aborigines are. As Anderson (1995) argues, the creation of a particular form of knowledge about Aboriginality is linked with the power of organizing and regulating Aboriginal life and even the rhetoric of "self-determination" is often informed by colonial practices.

For example, in a recent land claim made by the Yorta Yorta people, the Federal Court of Australia ruled in December 1998 that "the tide of history had swept away any claims of the Yorta Yorta people to their traditional land" (Rintoul, 1998). In his statement of dismissal, Justice Howard Olney ruled that the claimants "had ceased to occupy their traditional land in accordance with their traditional laws and customs" and that "native title rights and interests once lost are not capable of revival" (Rintoul, 1998: 11). The judgment highlights modes of institutional forgetting in the representation of Aboriginal rights: the reason that the Yorta Yorta people "had ceased to occupy their traditional land" was because they were removed from their land by white settlers and placed in missions and the fact that their "traditions" (in this case, mainly language) were not passed on was because in the missions, speaking "native" languages was a punishable offence.

The violence of this judgment is best summed up in the words of Des Morgan, one of Yorta Yorta's principal claimants: "Do you have to be naked and dancing for them to recognize you as Aboriginal? My ancestors' spirits still walk that land, the same as my spirit will walk the land when I die and my children's spirit will follow me. How can they deny our existence? I don't need a white judge to tell me who I am. I am Yorta Yorta" (Rintoul, 1998: 11). The authority of institutional memory (in this case, of the legal system and the media) in presenting the "real" present as a representation of past realities arises from a narrative of power that is embedded in the discourse of the production of history (Banerjee & Osuri, 2000). The use of Aboriginal memory by Aboriginal peoples to produce some expression of collective identity in the present is crucial to their politics of identity: rejecting this process as being "theoretically limited" because memory contains fictitious essences, precludes transforming modes of domination into distinctively Aboriginal forms of resistance. As Lattas (1993) points out, arguments by white theorists to relinquish using "essential" forms of Aboriginality to articulate Aboriginal identity simply serves to police images of Aboriginal authenticity and is another form of cultural hegemony rather than the cultural pluralism that is so celebrated by much of contemporary social theory. So while I acknowledge the contradictions and paradoxes of using the term Aboriginal in accordance with colonial governmental processes of naming, I affirm that I am using this term in order to avow its coloniality, to mark the coloniality of its representations in Australian corporate and governmental discourse. In the next section I discuss the history of relationships between Aboriginal communities and the mining industry, which will provide the background for the Jabiluka case.

Whose Land is it Anyway?

The history of large-scale mining in Africa, the Asia-Pacific, North and South America is a long and bloody one resulting in the devastation of many indigenous communities, several of whom are engaged in struggles with governments and business corporations to this day. The global mining industry is (and has been so for more than 50 years) controlled by a handful of transnational corporations with the inevitable mergers and acquisitions that characterize global corporate hegemony. The initial postcolonial scenario has changed: whereas the large mining corporations of the 1950s and 1960s were forced to cede controlling interests to the governments of newly independent countries, more recent trends of deregulation, privatization, and relaxation of foreign ownership restrictions have led to a global restructuring of the mining industry, an industry that is increasingly resembling what it looked like during colonial times (Moody, 1996).

Mining is a key industry in Australia and has been so for nearly 150 years. Over 60 percent of Australia's commodity exports come from mining, accounting for over $36 billion of Australia's export earnings (Kauffman, 1998). The industry has a deplorable record in dealing with Aboriginal communities: from physical coercion and killings in early colonial days to institutional, political and economic coercion in more recent times (Roberts, 1981). Legal requirements and increased Aboriginal political activism have compelled most of the leading mining companies to rethink their strategy of dealing with Aboriginal communities. As we shall see later, this so-called "stakeholder approach" where mining companies position Aboriginal communities as their "preferred development partner" is also quite problematic in that it sets up neocolonial relations that manage and control Aboriginal life (Banerjee, 2001a; Howitt, 1998).

Governments and corporations defended any environmental or sociocultural impacts of mining activities by focusing on economic benefits that contribute to national development and national security (McEachern, 1995). The devastation that mining has wrought on indigenous communities throughout the world cannot be measured, in economic terms or otherwise. Apart from the damaging socio-cultural consequences caused by mining, traditional means of sustenance and support were irreversibly affected leading to the destruction of hunting land, depletion and contamination of freshwater resources, siltation and pollution of rivers, lakes and oceans, and widespread deforestation (Roberts, 1981; Walck & Strong, 2001).

Royalty payments that result from mining do not solve the fundamental problems faced by Aboriginal communities in Australia who are impacted by mining (Katona, 1998). Health, education, life expectancy, essential services and housing for Aboriginal people continue to be the worst in the country, well below national averages. Mineral wealth extracted from Aboriginal lands in the Northern Territory provided more than $10 billion in gross revenue since 1978: however most Aboriginal communities in the area live in dire poverty with little scope to access resources for education and training or gain political power (Kauffman, 1998). Even assuming that employment in the mining companies is necessarily a good thing (I for one, do not make that assumption), Aboriginal employment in the companies that mine their land is minimal and is restricted to casual, unskilled, minimum-wage jobs (Gundjehmi Aboriginal Corporation, 1997; Kauffman, 1998; Roberts, 1981).

A closer look at the alleged economic benefits of mining for Aboriginal communities reveals a somewhat less rosy picture of reality. Royalty payments are not the solution: several studies by government and nongovernment agencies have shown that royalty payments do not provide the benefits they were designed to, and the socio-economic condition of Aboriginal communities continues to stagnate (Kauffman, 1998). Very little of the millions of dollars in royalty payments over the years is seen by the traditional owners impacted by mining: most of the money goes to maintain government infrastructure and pay for land council expenses. A portion of the money is also used to provide basic services other citizens expect the government to provide. The per capita amount of money received from royalty payments is very modest, ranging from $450 to $700 per person per year. These payments do nothing to address the fundamental problems of poor health, lack of local infrastructure, absence of tertiary education, and chronic unemployment (Yencken & Porter, 2001). The rural indigenous median family income is $5256 which is 61 percent of the non-indigenous rural family median income after accounting for differences in family size. Unemployment among indigenous people is about 40 percent compared to Australia's total unemployment rate of 8 percent. Although Aboriginal people comprise 25 percent of the population in the Northern Territory (a region where more than half of all mining in Australia is carried out), they comprise only 7 percent of the workforce, mainly in minimum-wage casual jobs (Kauffman, 1998).

The impact of mining on Aboriginal communities in Australia is quite clear: whatever benefits that arise tend to be appropriated by corporations, and state and federal governments, while Aboriginal communities who face the greatest economic, social, and cultural impacts hardly receive any share of the rewards. Let us now examine how discourses of development under colonial relations framed the Jabiluka uranium mine in northern Australia.

The Case of the Environmentally Friendly and Culturally Sensitive Uranium Mine[2]

The Jabiluka uranium mine is probably one of the most controversial issues of the 1990s in Australia. It is a complex issue involving traditional Aboriginal owners, the Northern Land Council, environmental groups and other NGOs, federal and territory governments, the mining company, and the powerful mining and minerals lobby. Environmental concerns and the violation of Aboriginal land rights are the central objections of groups that oppose the mine. Recent opinion polls indicate that two-thirds of Australians are opposed to the mine (Miller, 1999). Apart from the dangerous nature of uranium itself, a major environmental concern is potential contamination caused by "tailings" (fine particles left at the end of any mining process). For each ton of uranium oxide extracted, about 40,000 tons of tailings remain behind as low level radioactive waste. These tailings have up to 85 percent of the ore's original radioactivity and can remain radioactive for 300,000 to 700,000 years (Verjauw, 1997). The proposed mine at Jabiluka is an underground mine, to be built below the flood plains in an area infamous for its long and very wet season. There are concerns about the long-term safety of the dam that is supposed to contain the tailings and the absence of a coherent wastewater management policy (Christophersen & Langton, 1995). Environmentalists cite two cases in the Philippines where similar tailings dams constructed in a similar climactic region collapsed during the wet season, contaminating lakes and streams in the region and dispossessing scores of indigenous communities by rendering large tracts of land uninhabitable (Jabiluka, 1997).

A detailed discussion on the full range of environmental impacts of the project is beyond the scope of this chapter. The debate followed a predictable pattern: the government and the pro-mining lobby produced evidence by "independent scientific experts" of the environmental friendliness of uranium mining, and the anti-mining lobby produced equally "scientific" evidence of the environmental damage the project would cause. Both parties took great pains to discredit each others' "independent, credible scientists" and one government report claimed that public opposition to the mine was as a result of negative "social perceptions" about uranium that were inconsistent with "true scientific evidence" of the relative "benign" effect uranium mining would have on flora and fauna of the region (Gundjehmi Aboriginal Corporation, 1997).

The rights of local communities in this process did not, as usual, enter the debate. Two detailed reports, one by UNESCO and the other a Senate report, were critical of the entire Environmental Impact Assessment process (Report of the Senate Inquiry, 1999; UNESCO, 1998). Aboriginal communities were given little opportunity to comment on the environmental reports. The local people resented the approval process as a whole, since it was framed by questions that evaluated the conditions under which the project should proceed rather than whether it should proceed at all, which was the key question as far as the community was concerned. Perceptions of environmental risks were not given due recognition and, as is the case when there are high levels of environmental insecurity, there was widespread community distrust of big business and government institutions responsible for ensuring public health and safety (Beamish, 2001).

The territory and federal governments as well as the mining company insisted that the mine would go ahead, stating that all environmental safeguards have been met and Aboriginal interests have been accommodated, a position challenged in courts and in the public sphere by environmental activists, Aboriginal activists, scientists, academics, political leaders, students, and many other sections of the Australian public. The protests were at national and local levels: at one stage the Gundjehmi Aboriginal Corporation representing the traditional owners, along with the main organization coordinating the nationwide protest, the Jabiluka Action Group, organized a six-month long blockade of the mine site, bussing protestors from different parts of the country to stop construction of the mine. Hundreds of protestors were arrested and jailed including Yvonne Margarula, the senior traditional owner who, ironically, was charged for trespassing in her own land. The protests did succeed in delaying the project considerably. The protests also received international attention culminating in a UNESCO World Heritage Committee investigation of the project in June 1998. In their report, the Committee found that the mine posed a serious threat to the natural and cultural World Heritage values of Kakadu National Park and called for a halt to mining construction (UNESCO, 1998), a call ignored by the Australian government and the mining company. The decision whether to place Kakadu National Park on the list of World Heritage sites "in danger" was to be taken in an Extraordinary Session of the World Heritage Committee in Paris on July 1999. A Senate Inquiry into the project conducted in April 1999 reached a similar conclusion and found "serious flaws" in the Environmental Impact Statement that was prepared for the project. This report, supported by a majority of the Australian Senate, also found

> ...serious flaws in the consideration of the social and cultural impacts of the project on Aboriginal communities. Most disturbing to the Committee was a consistent pattern of rushed and premature ministerial approvals given to the construction of the mine while outstanding concerns about tailings disposal, radiological protection, project design and cultural heritage protection remain unresolved (Report of the Senate Inquiry, 1999).

The Australian government's response to both these reports was to initially ignore any unfavorable recommendations and discredit the findings of the committees. This was followed by six months of intensive lobbying by the Department of Foreign Affairs (and an expenditure of more than $1 million) that targeted key decision-makers of the twenty-one nations of the World Heritage Committee resulting in the UN resolving not to place the world-famous park on the endangered list, thus saving the Australian government a major international embarrassment (MacDonald, 1999).

Jabiluka has one of the largest deposits of uranium in Australia, most of which is located on Aboriginal land. Uranium was first discovered in the region in the early 1970s and was accompanied by the inevitable rush of mining companies lobbying Federal and State governments for mining leases. Mining did not proceed immediately as the Labor government of 1972 placed a moratorium on new uranium mines in the wake of a national debate on the benefits of uranium mining (Jabiluka, 1997). It was felt that an official inquiry was required and the Fox Commission was appointed by the Federal government to evaluate the impact of mining in the region. This is how the 1977 report of the Fox Commission described Aboriginal reaction to mining:

> It was established to the satisfaction of the Commission that the Aboriginal people concerned were opposed to mining on their land ... while royalties and other payments ... are not unimportant to

the Aboriginal people...our impression is that they would happily forego the lot in exchange for an assurance that mining would not proceed.... It is not likely that the mining venture will add appreciably to the number of Aborigines employed. (Roberts, 1981: 128)

In its conclusion, however, the Fox Commission delivered a pro-mining judgment: "In the end, we formed the conclusion that their opposition should not be allowed to prevail." The reasons given were the "overall benefits" mining would deliver to the Australian economy. This report cleared the way for uranium mining in the region and the new Liberal government, which had a more pro-uranium-mining policy than the Labor government, supervised the final negotiations over the Ranger mine, which began production in 1981. The Kakadu region, which was declared a National Park in 1979 and listed as a World Heritage site, has the dubious distinction of being the only National Park in the world with a uranium mine, adding a bizarre twist of irony in the debate over environmental conservation. Kakadu National Park is an enormously popular tourist destination receiving over 300,000 tourists a year, and the uranium mine is included as a site in some of the "eco-tours" conducted in the park. Negotiations on a second mine at Jabiluka started soon after the Ranger deal and the government and the mining company claimed that official "consent" was obtained from the then senior traditional owner, Toby Gangale in 1982. The current traditional owner is his eldest daughter, Yvonne Margarula.

According to the land rights legislation in the Northern Territories, consent had to be obtained from Aboriginal communities before any mining agreements were signed. The Northern Land Council was authorized to negotiate on behalf of the local Aboriginal communities who would be impacted by mining. "Consent" was the key issue: the current dispute over mining in Jabiluka also focuses on consent, that the traditional owners claim was obtained fraudulently. After the Fox Commission gave their approval on uranium mining in Ranger in 1979 (overriding the wishes of local Aboriginal communities), the traditional owners decided not to consent to mining. This meant that, the traditional owners were opposing not only the federal and territory governments and the mining company but also the organization created by government to represent Aboriginal interests, the Northern Land Council. The traditional owners, the Mirrar people, expected that the land council would support their opposition to mining by helping them get their land back. They were in for a rude shock. In a meeting with the traditional owners in 1978 during negotiations for the Ranger mine, the Chairman of the Northern Land Council, Galarrwuy Yunupingu, said:

> The Northern Land Council also has to know that the community which will be affected by the mining at Ranger have had a fair chance to say what they want to say to the Northern Land Council. This does not mean that the members of the Northern Land Council do what the community says. When you make the decision have in mind that we are entitled to be pushed around by any government in power. We are being pushed around today and we will be pushed around tomorrow, and we will be pushed around forever. That is a fact of life. (Jabiluka, 1997)

After the Fox Commission made its recommendation to proceed with mining, the Land Council's approach was to make the best of a bad deal: get legal land title and negotiate decent royalty payments. This was seen as a pragmatic approach with the quite reasonable assumption that if they were not part of the negotiations, the process would go on without them (a letter to that effect was written by the mining company to the Council), which would be even more harmful. The economic view prevailed because the alternative view, an Aboriginal view of land, could not be effectively articulated within the economic rationalist and corporate government rationalist structures in which the negotiations were conducted. The Land Council, supposedly representative of Aboriginal views and aspirations, has to operate and implement policies in a legislative framework that is designed to serve non-Aboriginal interests. As Katona (1998) points out, the Land Council is an extension of the Federal Government and has no actual decision-making authority, its responsibility is largely consultative.

The traditional owners were very clear that any development proposals on their land, whether it was uranium mining (to which they were firmly opposed) or tourism, would be discussed after the land claim was successful under the assumption that once they got their land back legally, they could enforce such a ban. The organization that would help them negotiate the maze of legalities in obtaining legal title over their land was the Northern Land Council. Unfortunately, the traditional owners' desire to control development in their land, an integral part of what the Land Rights Act stood for, was negated either through political negotiation, economic coercion, or through legislative amendments. At the Ranger negotiations, Ian Viner, the then Minister for Aboriginal Affairs said:

> This has being going on for a long time. Six years it's been going on. So the question now is not whether or not there is going to be mining,

but how is it going to be carried out. We think it is a fair agreement and we think it's a proper agreement for the Aboriginal people and for the whole of Australia. And we have now reached the time when we need to make a decision. In your hearts you would prefer that mining didn't come. We know that. The government had to listen not only the voice of the Aboriginal people but to the voice of all Australia. We can make that decision today. We can take the heartache away from it. We can use the uranium agreement as a foundation for your people, to look to the future, for yourself and your children and to work to the future for yourself and your children. (Jabiluka, 1997)

Toby Gangale interrupted the Minister to say, "I'm Toby Gangale. That's my country up there. Give us time to organize. We don't have to sign agreement now. We don't have to go to mining now." But, as usual, the voice of "all Australia" had spoken without listening to the voice of Aboriginal Australia. And as for "looking to the future"? For the next six years Toby Gangale and the Mirrar people watched as bulldozers carved up their land as the Ranger mine was built and waited for the benefits that never came. Katona uses the term "ecocide" to describe the effects of mining:

Having uranium mining in the Mirrar's backyard hasn't led to any great benefits. It brought along social changes, which made them more depressed, which dispossessed them even more from their own land. And it's left them with a legacy of bad health, no houses, no infrastructure, no employment. It has brought them not economic independence, but ecocide. . . . a sense of powerlessness. Alcohol consumption in this area is a symptom of powerlessness. Alcohol has become an anesthetic in some sense in this community. People anaesthetize themselves to what they see around them to their inability to be able to control their lives. That's led to other poor health outcomes, poor educational outcomes, poor employment outcomes. There's no opportunity to change their lifestyles, the lifestyle which has come about as a direct result of the history in this area. We can't expect individuals to be able to overcome those barriers. There has to be resources provided. There has to be infrastructure which reflects indigenous values and beliefs, which is able to advocate on their behalf to be able to turn this around. (Jabiluka, 1997)

The Mirrar are opposed to mining in Jabiluka because of the adverse sociocultural impacts that mining has had in the region. This was the crux of their argument presented to the UNESCO World Heritage Committee: the Mirrar could demonstrate that their living cultural tradition was directly under threat by further mining on their land, hence their opposition to the Jabiluka project (Gundjehmi Aboriginal Corporation, 1997). According to the Mirrar submission, "the destruction of cultural sites of significance by specific mining activity and a structural decline in the Mirrar living tradition resulting from imposed industrial development" represented a loss in cultural values as well as an attack on their rights (Gundjehmi Aboriginal Corporation, 1998: 7). The question of "cultural sites" is a complex one involving multilayered interconnections between country, people, language, kinship, community, spiritual, and political systems. It is impossible to reduce this rich and complex cultural landscape to lines on a map based on Western notions of geography and property. Aboriginal notions of land and country are epistemologically and ethically incongruent with Western notions. The process of "accommodating" Aboriginal interests into a Western capitalist framework is simply a continuation of colonial control involving the imposition of an alien knowledge system and subjugation of local knowledges.

The Mirrar feel that uranium mining in the region would contribute to disempowerment and negative psychological and sociological impacts that could lead to the abandonment of traditional living culture (Gundjehmi Aboriginal Corporation, 1998). They argue that increasing mining activity in the region would increase non-Aboriginal presence of cultural, economic, and political systems that can pose a threat to Mirrar living tradition. This position was vigorously challenged by the Australian government and the company, who claimed that the project would have a "negligible adverse impact" on the Aboriginal community (Energy Resources of Australia, 1999). This, despite a 1984 government report on uranium mining in the Northern Territory that stated:

> ... the current civic culture is one in which disunity, neurosis, a sense of struggle, drinking, stress, hostility, of being drowned by new laws, agencies, and agendas are major manifestations. Their defeat on initial opposition to mining, negotiations leading to Ranger and Nabarlek, the fresh negotiations on Jabiluka and Koongarra, new sources of money, the influx of vehicles together have led the Project to an unhappy verdict: that *this is a society in crisis.* (Australian Institute of Aboriginal Studies, 1984: 299, italics added)

Aboriginal leaders also point out that fifteen years after the report, the stated recommendations are yet to be implemented. Royalties from the Ranger mine have not enhanced the economic position of Aboriginal communities.

Local Aboriginal people receive only 30 percent of the royalty payments from Ranger and a major portion of the royalties are used to maintain land councils and provide basic amenities (water, sewerage, roads, electricity, education) that other Australians claim as "citizenship rights" (Gundjehmi Aboriginal Corporation, 1998). Despite $43 million of royalties from the Ranger uranium mine since 1981, the local Aboriginal community continues to live in dire poverty. As a result of the rapid establishment of the white, company-run mining township, the local Aboriginal community was further marginalized resulting in "chronic alcohol abuse, community violence, and a chronic sense of disempowerment and hopelessness" (Gundjehmi Aboriginal Corporation, 1998: 6). Employment in the mines was also limited to menial jobs: from 1980 to 1996, ERA averaged less than five local Aboriginal employees out of a total workforce of 350 in the region. The senior traditional owner, Yvonne Margarula, was employed as a laundry attendant in the hotel owned by the Gagudju Association, the same hotel of which she is a member of the Board of Directors.

There are scores of reports and studies that discuss economic, social, cultural, and environmental impacts of mining in the region: not one of these reports ever discussed with Aboriginal people the possibility of securing an independent economic future without depending on mining (Gundjehmi Aboriginal Corporation, 1997). In a historic gesture, the traditional owners even tried returning the money they had received from the Jabiluka lease hoping that this would stop the mine. But the Land Council said they had to honor the earlier "agreement," the company's position was the same, they had their "agreement." The government was satisfied that legal requirements were met under the Native Title Act, they had their "consent."

The line between "consultations" and "negotiations" became increasingly blurred as the meetings progressed, with the traditional owners still under the impression that they had a right to veto mining. One report on the social impact of uranium mining in the area mentioned that the elders in the community complained of too many meetings and inadequate presentation of the issues (Australian Institute of Aboriginal Studies, 1984). The report also noted that failure to attend meetings was interpreted by government and company negotiators as lack of interest shown by the community instead of an expression of deliberate abstention or disapproval. The final meeting, which dealt with the actual issue of "consent," lasted more than four days. Katona describes this last meeting:

> The last meeting and the consultations and negotiations that took place over 18 months, was a meeting about consent. The agreement

had been negotiated, all points had been agreed upon by the Northern Land Council and Pancontinental. And saved until the last meeting, was the issue of consent. Yvonne's father (Toby Gangale, the senior owner) was very sick at that meeting. He was run down by the process. He was so worn down that he couldn't sit at that meeting—he spent most of that meeting lying down. And finally at the end of that meeting when the question of consent was put, he got up and addressed the legal advisers and the people attending that meeting. And he said 'I'm tired now, I can't fight anymore'. That was consent. That was officially and legally all that was required to embody legal consent for a project to go ahead. (Jabiluka, 1997)

The mining company's position was predictable and mirrored the government's position: all environmental safeguards had been met, the agreement had to be honored and any adverse social and cultural impact of the mine would be "constructively addressed" by the Federal and Territory governments as well as the mining company. Thus, the key stakeholders involved in negotiating mining agreements were the traditional owners, the Northern Territory land council, federal and state government officials, and the mining company. I will examine some key stakeholder interactions within the theoretical framework of stakeholder theory and highlight the colonial and neocolonial relations of power underlying these relations. As we will see, the stakeholder framework allows particular types of questions to be posed and particular types of answers to emerge.

The Complicities of Stakeholder Theory

Stakeholder theory continues to receive a great deal of attention in recent times as is evidenced by the publication of dozens of books and more than 100 articles in journals (Donaldson & Preston, 1995). While conventional theories of the firm focus on its responsibilities toward its shareholders, a stakeholder perspective takes a broader view and implies that a company should consider the needs of all its stakeholders. Stakeholders are defined as "any group or individual who can affect or is affected by the organization's objectives" (Freeman & Reed, 1983: 91). This broad view is not without its problems: different stakeholders have differing stakes and balancing the needs of competing stakeholders is not an easy task. Moreover, stakeholder theory is derived from Western notions of (economic) rationality and fails to address needs of groups like indigenous stakeholders (Banerjee, 2001a).

The normative basis of stakeholder theory—that business "should" be socially responsible—stems from the notion that "society grants legitimacy and power to business and in the long run, those who do not use power in a manner which society considers responsible will tend to lose it" (Davis, 1973: 314). Economic systems, governments, and institutions often determine what is "legitimate" and this power to determine legitimacy cannot be easily lost. While customers, employees, shareholders, and governments may be able to "withdraw legitimacy," forcing a corporation to either change its approach or perish, the power of Aboriginal communities to do so is constrained by the self-same notion of legitimacy: society, governments, and corporations do not doubt that Aborigines are legitimate stakeholders, however, Aboriginal notions of development and land use are not really legitimate alternatives to Western notions of progress and development. Thus, while Aboriginal stakeholders are positioned as legitimate whose needs will be "constructively addressed," the stakes that are involved for Aboriginal communities affected by mining are somehow positioned as "illegitimate" or against "national interest."

Because the scope and level of application for determining boundaries of legitimacy is institutional and societal, stakeholder theory urges organizations to be "publicly responsible, for outcomes related to their primary and secondary areas of involvement with society" (Preston & Post, 1975; Wood, 1991). This principle of public responsibility is designed to make larger societal concerns more relevant by providing behavioral parameters for organizations. The public debate in the Jabiluka case has focused on the corporation's environmental responsibility as well as its responsibility to Aboriginal stakeholders. There are several motivations for corporate ecological responsiveness including legislation, social responsibility, competitiveness, and public concern (Banerjee, 2001b; Bansal & Roth, 2001). However, social responsibilities should be relevant to the "organization's interests" (Wood, 1991) and therein lies the problem: these "public" responsibilities are defined and framed by larger principles of legitimacy, principles that are inimical to Aboriginal stakeholders in the first place. Thus, the parameters that define a "social outcome" are determined by a system of rules and exclusions that do not address Aboriginal concerns. The public–private dichotomy of stakeholder representation does not legitimize Aboriginal interests; instead it serves to regulate indigenous ways of living. Who is seeking stakeholder input? For what purpose? Public interests are represented by government agencies that seek stakeholder input to obtain information designed to legitimize support for their decisions. The input from Aboriginal communities regarding mining on their land at Jabiluka was unequivocal: they did not want it. The agencies that sought this input admitted the adverse consequences that mining had on Aboriginal society. The decision to mine was motivated by the economic gains to "the nation" (at the cost of irreversible loss to Aboriginal nations) and legitimized by promoting Aboriginal participation in "development." If the domain of public responsibility was designed to serve Aboriginal interests, it has failed them miserably, and the process of stakeholder management, far from being beneficial to Aboriginal stakeholders has further marginalized them. Institutions and agencies that were developed to assess stakeholder needs are grounded in colonial practices and serve to continue the process of internal colonialism in Australia.

If the institutional and organizational levels of corporate social responsibility are inimical to Aboriginal interests, then the principle of "managerial discretion" (Carroll, 1979) is even more constrained. According to Wood (1991), "managers are moral actors. Within every domain of corporate social responsibility, they are obliged to exercise such discretion as is available to them, toward socially responsible outcomes" (p. 698). The fallacy of managers as "moral actors" is easily revealed by the Foucauldian notion of subjectification, a mode that reveals how managers become constituted as subjects who secure their meaning and reality through identifying with a particular sense of their relationship with the firm (Knights, 1992). Individual manager's role in accommodating stakeholder interests is predefined at higher levels, and practices at this level are governed and organized by organizational and institutional discourses.

The stakeholder theory of the firm represents a form of stakeholder colonialism that serves to further marginalize indigenous communities by depriving them of their rights and resources. That (perceived) integration of stakeholder needs might be an effective tool for a firm to enhance its image is probably true (Banerjee, 2001b). However, for a critical understanding of stakeholder theory, this approach is unsatisfactory. Effective practices of "managing" stakeholders, and research aimed at generating "knowledge" about stakeholders, are less systems of truth than products of power applied by corporations, governments, and business schools (Knights, 1992). As Wilmott (1995) points out, the establishment of new organization theories is very much the outcome of the historical development of capitalism and creates value only for particular people and institutions. The fact that stakeholder management practices of mining companies that are able to negotiate compensation agreements with Aboriginal communities are touted as a "best practice" approach (Howitt, 1998; Katona, 1998) is a striking example of how pervasive and dangerous these regimes of truth can be for marginalized stakeholders. A view of the full picture of the consequences of stakeholder theory and practice requires a stepping out of the frame. A more critical examination of stakeholder theory, for instance, understanding that stakeholder relations are systematized and controlled by the imperatives of capital accumulation, may produce a very different picture. The process of stakeholder integration is informed by notions of power, legitimacy, and urgency that are contingent on the particularities of nation states, industries, organizations, or other institutions (Wilmott, 1995) and serve to either negate alternative practices or assimilate them. As Katona points out:

> . . . the types of benefits the mining companies are talking about is another form of assimilation for Aboriginal people. And it's assimilation by industry, which is highly questionable. There's already pressure been applied from governments historically over the last 200 years for Aboriginal people, to accommodate a Western system of education, for Aboriginal people to accommodate a Western system of living, and Aboriginal people have resisted that and actively resisted that. And one of the fundamental parts of this campaign for the Mirrar is the fact that their relationship with the land and all the values and beliefs that underpin that, that give them the right to say no is being challenged by this development. (Jabiluka, 1997)

It makes little difference to Aboriginal communities whether corporations' stakeholder strategies are "reactive," "defensive," "accommodating," or "proactive" (Carroll, 1979) or follow any other typology: the right to say no to development on their land does not arise in any case. Roberts (1981) documented a wide range of strategies used by mining companies in Australia to negotiate mining leases on Aboriginal land. Some of these strategies include: (1) ignore Aboriginal land councils wherever possible (or threaten to do so), (2) isolate any Aboriginal group or individual who is a "traditional owner" and focus company efforts in making a deal with them, (3) discredit advisers used by Aboriginal groups and any scientific evidence produced by "outsiders" or use the law to restrict access to the land, (4) invoke national interest and economic security of Australia, and (5) offer to employ "employable" Aborigines. Nearly twenty years later, the same strategies are still being used by mining companies and governments: in the Jabiluka case, every single strategy listed above was used at one time or another.

Conclusion and Future Possibilities

I began this paper by discussing colonial relations in a postcolonial era and some of the problems associated with the deployment of the term "post-." Perhaps it may be appropriate to conclude by discussing some emancipatory possibilities of the term.

One approach is to deconstruct the "post-" by clarifying and expanding on the reminders of colonialism and experiences of colonialism that continue into the present. Said (1986) believes this should be the role of the postcolonial intellectual. Rather than isolate colonialism as a distinct historical period with little claim on the present, it is the postcolonial intellectual's role to "look for discontinuities in apparently smooth surfaces and for continuities across the dominant and oppositional" (Mani, 1989: 13). Modernity, progress, development are all hallmarks of the nationalistic project of the postcolonial era and too often serve as continuities of colonial modes of control. Studies of Aboriginal resistance are also theorized in relation to Western cultures, and the dichotomies that result from this position (development versus no development; traditional versus modern; land use versus conservation) only serve to perpetuate Western notions of progress. Relocating and reinscribing resistance from the cultures they spring from is by itself another form of resistance, probably more empowering (Escobar, 1995).

This is where, according to Katona (1998), academia has failed Aboriginal communities. Courses on cross-cultural understanding and cultural sensitivity developed by universities and schools seem to benefit non-Aboriginal communities. The focus of much academic research today is what Katona (1998) calls "academic skull measuring," where one portion of non-Aboriginal society tries to understand more about Aboriginal communities and once the communities are analyzed, subjectified, and reconstituted, the task is done and the research over, with no value to Aboriginal communities who are the subjects of the research. An example of this approach is Whiteman and Cooper's (2000) ethnographic study of a Cree beaver trapper, which while developing a so-called indigenous land ethic, ignores histories of colonialism that indigenous peoples have had to contend with. Katona (1998) calls for efforts to demystify the dominant paradigm for indigenous communities so that they can take advantage of aspects of Western society that benefits their way of life, aspects that provide for their rights and can be used to negotiate the forms of their existence.

The diversity of social movements in different parts of the world might provide such an alternative reading guide that could transform hegemonic notions of development and modernity (Dreiling & Wolf, 2001; Escobar, 1992). The study of "traditional ecological knowledge" is becoming increasingly in vogue for Western scientists and pharmaceutical corporations. It is crucial to examine this practice with a critical lens in order to understand the stakes involved: who is doing the study and for what purpose?

Understanding and using traditional ecological knowledge of indigenous peoples for the advancement of Western science and medicine through patents and intellectual property rights is simply another violation of indigenous rights. If we have to search for alternatives to development, apart from a critique of contemporary notions of development we also need to situate our theories within appropriate social movements: for example, traditional ecological knowledge should not be separated from the political, economic, and cultural struggles of indigenous peoples (Carruthers, 1996). Aboriginal struggle for land rights is more than a fight to regain their land, as Escobar (1995) points out, "it is above all a struggle over symbols and meanings, a cultural struggle" (p. 248). The Jabiluka struggle is such a struggle. It is not a postcolonial struggle, it is an anticolonial struggle. As Perera and Pugliese (1994) assert, if our critical theories, our postmodern theories, our postcolonial theories are to have any meaning, their "genuinely transformative aspirations (should) be identified by its commitment to vital local struggles, as also by its openness to reexamining its own disciplinary premises, orthodoxies and complicities" (p. 98).

Perhaps the words of Jacqui Katona and Yvonne Margarula (Jabiluka, 1997) provide a fitting conclusion to this chapter and a reminder of the tasks that lie ahead:

Jacqui Katona:

> We had a discussion about this with people. What if we don't win the court case or what if we aren't able to influence the government? And a senior man stopped the discussion...and he said look, win or lose, it doesn't matter. What is important is that we fight, that we fight for our beliefs, we fight for the things that are important to us.

Yvonne Margarula:

> I believe my own culture. Black fella way. Right way. Proper way. Bining way. Balanda should listen. And believe. How many times we gonna tell him?

Notes

1. This chapter is an edited version of a paper that appeared in *Organization & Environment* (March 2000). I dedicate this paper to the Mirrar people of the Kakadu region and to the various groups in Australia who have joined forces with the Mirrar in their struggle against uranium mining in Kakadu.
2. I have drawn heavily from two sources in presenting the Jabiluka case. One is an excellent documentary film titled *Jabiluka* (1997) produced and directed by

David Bradbury. The other is an interview of Jacqui Katona (see Katona, 1998), who is family with the traditional owners of Jabiluka and was the Chief Executive Officer at the Gundjehmi Aboriginal Corporation, which represents the traditional owners, the Mirrar people. Other sources include Kauffman (1998), Perera and Pugliese (1998), and Roberts (1981). I have also consulted many newspaper articles and television reports on the case. The Gundjehmi Aboriginal Corporation maintains an informative website (www.mirrar.net) containing a variety of material including media releases, UN reports, and historical records.

References

Anderson, I. 1995. Aboriginal nations? In S. Perera (Ed.), *Asian and Pacific inscriptions: Identities/ethnicities/nationalities* (pp. 65–82). Melbourne: Meridian.

Australian Institute of Aboriginal Studies. 1984. *Aborigines and uranium: Consolidated report to the Minister for Aboriginal Affairs on the social impact of uranium mining on the Aborigines of the Northern Territory (1979–84)*. Canberra: AGPS.

Bachelard, M. 1998. *The great land grab*. Melbourne: Hyland House.

Banerjee, S. B. 2001a. Corporate citizenship and indigenous stakeholders: Exploring a new dynamic of organization-stakeholder relationships. *Journal of Corporate Citizenship, 1* (1), 1–17.

Banerjee, S. B. 2001b. Managerial perceptions of corporate environmentalism: Interpretations from industry and strategic implications for organizations. *Journal of Management Studies, 38* (4), 489–513.

Banerjee, S. B., & Linstead. S. 2001. Globalization, multiculturalism and other fictions: Colonialism for the new millennium? *Organization 8* (1), 711–750.

Banerjee, S. B., & Osuri. G. 2000. Silences of the media: Whiting out Aboriginality in making news and making history. *Media, Culture, Society, 22* (3), 263–284.

Bansal, P., & Roth, K. 2001. Why companies go green: A model of ecological responsiveness. *Academy of Management Journal, 43* (4), 717–736.

Bates, D. 1966. *The passing of the Aborigines*, cited in Muecke (1992).

Beamish, T. D. 2001. Environmental hazard and institutional betrayal: Lay-public perceptions of risk in the San Luis Obispo County oil spill. *Organization & Environment, 14* (1), 5–33.

Bringing Them Home. 1997. Report of the National Inquiry into the separation of Aboriginal and Torres Strait Islander children from their families. Sydney: Human Rights and Equal Opportunities Commission.

Carroll, A. B. 1979. A three-dimensional conceptual model of corporate social performance. *Academy of Management Review, 4*, 497–505.

Carruthers, D. V. 1996. Indigenous ecology and the politics of linkage in Mexican social movements. *Third World Quarterly, 17* (5), 1007–1028.

Christophersen, C., and Langton, M. 1995. Allarda! *Arena Magazine, 9* (June–July), 28–32.

Davis, K. 1973. The case for and against business assumption of social responsibilities. *Academy of Management Journal, 16*, 312–322.

Dodson, M. 1994. The end in the beginning: Re(de)finding Aboriginality. *Australian Aboriginal Studies, 1*, 2–12.

Donaldson, T., & Preston, L. E. 1995. The stakeholder theory of the corporation: Concepts, evidence and implications. *Academy of Management Review, 20* (1), 65–91.

Dreiling, M., & Wolf, B. 2001. Environmental movement organizations and political strategy: Tactical conflicts over NAFTA. *Organization & Environment, 14* (1), 34–54.

Energy Resources of Australia. 1999. *The Jabiluka Project Executive Summary: EIS findings in brief.* [www.energyres.com.au/jabiluka/eis/brief.htm]

Escobar, A. 1992. Imagining a post-development era/ Critical thought, development and social movements. *Social Text, 31 & 32*, 20–56.

Escobar, A. 1995. *Encountering development: The making and unmaking of the Third World, 1945–1992.* Princeton, NJ: Princeton University Press.

Freeman, J. 1999. Stakeholder influence strategies. *Academy of Management Review, 24* (2), 191–205.

Freeman, R. E., & Reed, D. E. 1983. Stockholders and shareholders: A new perspective on corporate governance. *California Management Review, 25* (3), 93–94.

Goldsmith, E. 1997. Development as colonialism. *The Ecologist, 27* (2), 60–79.

Gundjehmi Aboriginal Corporation. 1997. *We are not talking about mining: The history of duress and the Jabiluka Project.* [www.mirrar.net]

Gundjehmi Aboriginal Corporation.1998. *Submission from the Mirrar people to the UNESCO World Heritage Committee.* [www.mirrar.net]

Hollinsworth, D. 1992. Discourses on Aboriginality and the politics of identity in urban Australia. *Oceania, 62* (2), 137–155.

Howitt, R. 1998. Recognition, respect and reconciliation: Steps towards decolonization. *Australian Aboriginal Studies, 1*, 28–34.

Jabiluka. 1997. Documentary film produced and directed by David Bradbury. Presented by the Gundjehmi Aboriginal Corporation and Frontline Film Foundation.

Katona, J. 1998. If Native Title is us, it's inside us: Jabiluka and the politics of intercultural negotiation. Interview with S. Perera & J. Pugliese, *Australian Feminist Law Journal, 10* (March), 1–34.

Kauffman, P. 1998. *Wik, mining and Aborigines.* St Leonards: Allen & Unwin.

Keefe, K. 1988. Aboriginality: Resistance and persistence. *Australian Aboriginal Studies, 1*, 67–81.

Knights, D. 1992. Changing spaces: The disruptive impact of a new epistemological location for the study of management. *Academy of Management Review, 17* (3), 514–536.

Lattas, A. 1993. Essentialism, memory and resistance: Aboriginality and the politics of authenticity. *Oceania, 63* (2), 240–267.

MacDonald, J. 1999. A million dollars and some fancy lobbying helped sway countries. *The Age*, July 14, 12.

Mani, L. 1989. Multiple meditations: Feminist scholarship in the age of multinational reception. *Inscriptions, 5*, 1–23.

Manne, R. 1999. A cruel case of absurd historical denial. *The Age*, November 15, 17.

McClintock, A. 1992. The Angel of Progress: Pitfalls of the term "post-colonialism." *Social Text, 31/32*, 84–98.

McEachem, D. 1995. Mining meaning from the rhetoric of nature: Australian mining companies and their attitudes to the environment at home and abroad. *Policy, Organization & Society* (Winter), 48–69.

Miller, C. 1999. North shareholders protest over Jabiluka. *The Age*, June 4, 7.

Moody, R. 1996. Mining the world: the global reach of Rio Tinto Zinc. *The Ecologist, 26* (2), 46–52.

Muecke, S. 1992. *Textual spaces: Aboriginality and cultural studies*. Sydney: University of New South Wales Press.

Perera, S., & Pugliese, J. 1998. Parks, mines and tidy towns: Enviro-panopticism, 'post'colonialism, and the politics of heritage in Australia. *Postcolonial studies, 1* (1), 69–100.

Preston, L. E., & Post, J. E. 1975. *Private management and public policy: The principle of public responsibility*. Englewood Cliffs, NJ: Prentice-Hall.

Pugliese, J. 1995. Parasiting "post"-colonialism: On the (im)possibility of a disappropriative practice. *Southern Review, 28* (3), 345–357.

Radhakrishnan, R. 1993. Postcoloniality and the boundaries of identity. *Callaloo, 16* (4), 750–771.

Radhakrishnan, R. 1994. Postmodernism and the rest of the world. *Organization, 1* (2), 305–340.

Report of the Senate Inquiry. 1999. *Report of the Senate Inquiry into the Jabiluka Project*. [www.mirrar.net]

Reynolds, H. 1989. *Dispossession*. St Leonards's: Allen & Unwin.

Rintoul, S. 1998. "Tide of history" sinks land claim. *The Weekend Australian*, December 19–20, 11.

Roberts, J. 1981. *Massacres to mining: The colonization of Aboriginal Australia*. Victoria: Globe Press.

Rowse, T. 1990. Are we all blow-ins? *Oceania, 61* (2), 185–191.

Said, E. 1986. Intellectuals in the post-colonial world. *Salmagundi, 70/71* (Spring/Summer), 44–64.

Sheridan, S. 1988. "Wives and mothers like ourselves, poor remnants of a dying race": Aborigines in colonial women's writing. In A. Rutherford (Ed.), *Aboriginal culture today*, Sydney.

Shohat, E. 1992. Notes on the "post-colonial." *Social Text, 31/32*, 99–113.

Starik, M., & Marcus, A. A. 2001. Special research forum on the management of organizations in the natural environment: A field emerging from multiple paths, with many challenges ahead. *Academy of Management Journal, 43* (4), 539–547.

UNESCO 1998. *Report on the mission to Kakadu National Park, Australia*. [www.biodiversity.environment.gov.au/kakadu/pdfs/infl8e.pdf]

Verjauw, R. 1997. *Draft resolution for the European Parliament on the impact of the nuclear industry on indigenous peoples.* Brussels, Belgium: Kola (International Campaigns Office).

Walck, C., & Strong, K. C. 2001. Using Aldo Leopold's land ethic to read environmental history: The case of the Keweenaw forest. *Organization & Environment,* *14* (3), 261–289.

Watego, C. 1989. Review of R. Sykes *Black Majority Editions.* Cited in Rowse (1990).

Whiteman, G., & Cooper, W. H. 2000. Ecological embeddedness. *Academy of Management Journal, 43* (6), 1265–1282.

Wilmott, H. 1995. What has been happening in organization theory and does it matter? *Personnel Review, 24* (8), 33–53.

Wood, D. 1991. Corporate social performance revisited. *Academy of Management Review, 16* (4), 691–718.

Yencken, D., & Porter, L. 2001. *A just and sustainable Australia.* Redfern, NSW: The Australian Council of Social Service.

PART IV

Conclusion

CHAPTER 12

The Postcolonial Imagination

Anshuman Prasad and Pushkala Prasad

I do not agree that the dog in the manger has the final right to the manger, even though he may have lain there for a very long time. I do not admit that right. I do not admit, for instance, that a great wrong has been done to the Red Indians of America, or the black people of Australia. I do not admit that a wrong has been done to these people by the fact that a stronger race, a higher grade race, a more worldly-wise race . . . has come in and taken their place.

> Winston Churchill to the Peel Commission of Inquiry, 1937, quoted in Tariq Ali, *The Clash of Fundamentalisms: Crusades, Jihads and Modernity*

We see now an ever more extreme separation of a small minority that controls enormous wealth from multitudes that live in poverty at the limit of powerlessness. The geographical and racial lines of oppression and exploitation . . . have . . . not declined but increased exponentially. Despite recognizing all this, we insist on asserting that . . . [the 21st century] Empire is a step forward. . . . We claim that [this] Empire is better in the same way that Marx insists that capitalism is better than the forms of society and modes of production that came before it.

> Michael Hardt and Antonio Negri, *Empire*

In postcoloniality, every metropolitan definition is dislodged . . . all metropolitan accounts are set askew.

> Gayatri Chakravorty Spivak, *Outside in the Teaching Machine*

Despite some differences, the two metropolitan accounts—one by Winston Churchill, and the other by Hardt and Negri (2000)—which inaugurate this chapter, share something in common at a deep level: what the two metropolitan accounts may be seen to share is an absolute acceptance of the genocidal consequences of "civilization" as the price that "the wretched of the earth" must willingly pay for achieving Europe's[1] idea of the Kingdom of God on Earth. It is accounts of this nature, as well as relatively more subtle expressions of Europe's will to power, that postcolonialism seeks to "dislodge," rupture, and "set askew." Accordingly, postcolonial theory's engagement with colonialism and its continuing aftermath may be seen as representing an ethico-political project aimed at developing a uniquely radical and comprehensive critique of three monumental and mutually overlapping phenomena of great relevance to us today, namely, Western colonialism and neocolonialism, European modernity, and modern capitalism. As postcolonial critics have noted, these phenomena are overdetermined, with each serving as one of the conditions of possibility, as well as the effects, of the others. These phenomena are also extremely complex as a result of, among other things, their long and variegated history, wide spectrum of constitutive practices, and far-reaching implications whether cultural, political, economic, psychological, philosophical, epistemological, ideological, ethico-moral, aesthetic, or something else.

Postcolonial theory seeks to understand (neo)colonialism and other related phenomena by means of investigating the role therein not only of Western political and economic practices, but also, for instance, of Western culture, knowledge, and epistemology. In so doing, postcolonial theory aims to develop a fine-grained understanding of: (a) the multiplicity of instruments and causes that combine to perpetuate the current international regime of exploitation and deprivation, as well as (b) of their wide-ranging effects on peoples, cultures, economies, epistemologies, and so forth. In the process of analyzing colonialism and neocolonialism, postcolonial theory does not reduce non-Western peoples to the status of passive bystanders, but sees them instead as active agents responding to, resisting, and frequently surviving under conditions of unprecedented violence and cruelty. The ethical impulse driving the postcolonial project is the desire for a more just and equitable global order not only in political and economic terms, but also in terms that are more cultural, psychological, epistemological, and so forth. The postcolonial agenda, hence, is crucially enmeshed with the goal of assigning Europe its appropriate place in the global order of cultures and civilizations, or in other words, with the goal of "provincializing Europe" (Chakrabarty, 2000; Prasad, 1997).[2]

Postcolonial theory is a uniquely effective instrument of critique for a variety of reasons. To begin with, postcolonialism, as an inheritor of the legacy of the "theoretical practices of the freedom struggles" waged in Africa, Asia, and Latin America over the last several centuries (Young, 2001: 159), is felicitously positioned, intellectually and politically speaking, to draw upon a vast storehouse of knowledge consisting of sophisticated critiques of Western colonialism, capitalism, and modernity. Other streams of critical scholarship in the West often seem to ignore this store of knowledge. Partly as a result of this intellectual legacy rooted in Third World experiences, postcolonialism also uses Marxism in creative ways. As scholars have noted, Marxism's enmeshment in a teleological view of History as Progress, and its commitment to Eurocentrism and other, similarly problematic, Enlightenment ideals have implied that Marxism "itself remains complicit with, and even extends, the system to which it is opposed" (Young, 1990: 3).[3] Moreover, European Marxism is burdened by its legacy of Stalinism and "the imperialist nature of European socialism and communism" (Ali, 2002: 111). Marxism has been criticized also for its relative neglect of race and gender issues. Marxism, hence, would clearly appear to be somewhat inadequate as a framework for offering a sufficiently radical critique of modernity, colonialism, and capitalism.

Postcolonial theory, accordingly, operates through a relatively ambivalent and tense relationship with Marxism. In keeping with this, while much of postcolonial theory refuses to accord a canonical status to Marxism, at the same time, postcolonialism is also opposed to a full-blown rejection of Marxism in its entirety. In this way, postcolonialism attempts to insulate itself from some of the major weaknesses of Marxism while simultaneously continuing to make productive use of Marxian theory and framework of analysis. Indeed, leading postcolonial scholars repeatedly emphasize the crucial, even indispensable, role of Marx in postcolonialist inquiry.[4] However, by allowing itself to creatively deviate from Marxism, postcolonial theory is able to offer a more radical critique of colonialism, capitalism, and modernity.[5]

Somewhat similarly, postcolonial theory's complex relationship with poststructuralism seems to have enabled the former to engage more fruitfully with the materialities of (neo)colonialism, capitalism, and modernity. In order to understand this complex relationship, it may be useful to begin by noting that some scholars within the postcolonial field itself have opposed the use of post-structuralist concepts and analytical devices for a number of reasons, including a concern that the Western roots of post-structuralism may operate to give an overall Eurocentric ideological outlook to postcolonial theory, and render the latter complicit with neocolonial processes.

This viewpoint, however, is challenged by scholars more sympathetic to post-structuralism, who contend that there are ample grounds for arguing that post-structuralism is "not as straightforwardly western as is often assumed" (Young, 2001: 67). Among other things, these scholars point to a range of non-Western practices, theoretical and otherwise, that anticipate and/or inform European "high" theory (cf. e.g., Bhabha, 1994; Young, 2001), with the result that post-structuralism, for instance, comes to be seen as having "a specifically postcolonial provenance" (Bhabha, 1994: 64).

Interestingly, however, this position is not necessarily extended further by all postcolonial scholars to suggest that post-structuralism as manifested in European high theory may be sufficient/adequate for serving as postcolonialism's overarching conceptual framework. On the contrary, postcolonial scholars like Spivak seem to make a distinction between Western post-structuralist writings, on the one hand and, on the other hand, the "*staging*" of post-structuralist theory outside the West with a view to "undoing…imperialism" (1993: 145, italics in the original). In so doing, Spivak (1993) seems to hint at some limitations in the former, and may be said to be suggesting that it is the latter that is likely to be of greater value to the postcolonial critic (cf. also, Spivak, 1999; Young, 2001). Be that as it may, it can easily be argued that postcolonial theory utilizes post-structuralist insights in a more politically engaged manner and, partly as a result of this, is able to offer a more effective response to the material realities of the contemporary neo-colonial conjuncture.

Notwithstanding the above, it is common for critics of postcolonialism to frequently make the mistake of conflating post-structuralism and post-colonialism. On the other hand, however, sometimes postcolonialism is equated not with post-structuralism, but rather with postmodernism.[6] Therefore, it may be useful to point out here that postcolonialism differs in important ways from postmodernism as well. For example, postcolonialist and other scholars have criticized postmodernism for, among other things, treating uniquely Western concerns as issues of universal significance, for its ethical relativism and political quietism, for its Eurocentrism and continued complicity with the protocols of Western modernity, and for its disavowal of the colonial moment (cf. e.g., Adams & Tiffin, 1990; Bhabha, 1994; Richard, 1993). Not only do these and other limitations of postmodernism sharply differentiate it from postcolonialism, such limitations also under-score the inadequacies of postmodernism as a framework for radical critique. Among the different critical perspectives, it would appear that postcolonialism and certain streams of radical feminism (e.g., Butler, 1991; hooks, 1991) have much in common as regards their overall orientation toward issues of marginality, resistance, the politics of knowledge, and so on. Indeed, postcolonial scholarship has profited by critiquing certain aspects of liberal First World feminism,[7] while simultaneously seeking to forge strong links of solidarity with feminism's more radical strands, whether theorized in the West or elsewhere.

Among various critical approaches, therefore, postcolonialism may be seen as offering a uniquely productive and versatile framework for radical critique. It is a matter of considerable surprise, therefore, that more than two decades after the publication of Edward Said's masterpiece, *Orientalism* (1978), management and organizational scholarship mostly continues to ignore the postcolonial framework. How do we account for such indifference toward postcolonial theory? While there are no simple answers to this question, the issue is well worth investigating.

Postcolonialist scholars have noted that, even during the relatively recent past, Western academic researchers seem to have been somewhat reluctant to discuss meaningfully the phenomenon of imperialism. For instance, noting the unpopularity of the term "imperialism" in Britain, Williams and Chrisman (1994) have pointed to the refusal, till fairly recent years, of sections of British academe to seriously analyze the processes of imperialism. In a related vein, Sprinker (1995) has pointed to the discomfort experienced in sections of American academe with the characterization of the United States as a modern-day empire. Conceivably, the close association of imperialism with cruelty, plunder, rape, violence, genocide, and the like turns it into something unsavory that is jarring to the liberal sensibility. It could be this perception of the unsavory quality of the object of postcolonial inquiry that may partly explain why, consciously or otherwise, management scholars have largely stayed away from postcolonial theory.

On the other hand, some management scholars might believe that colonialism has ceased to exist; that colonialism firmly belongs to humanity's past history. In which case, such scholars could possibly imagine that the insights of postcolonial theory are useful only to historians and—in view of the widespread absence of an effective historical sensibility within the discipline (cf. Prasad & Eylon, 2001)—they might assume that such insights are unlikely to be of sufficient relevance for their own more contemporary purposes.

Finally, given the proliferation of the "posts-" in the social sciences, including management and organization studies, some management researchers might mistakenly assume that postcolonialism is simply another name for (or is a very closely allied variant of) postmodernism and/or poststructuralism. In that case, for these scholars postcolonialism ceases to be a relatively distinct scholarly approach, capable of providing insights that might meaningfully differ from the insights offered by postmodernism, post-structuralism, and so forth. This group of researchers, therefore, might decide to ignore postcolonial theory because of an erroneous belief that post-colonialism may not have much to offer in terms of theoretical/scholarly "value added" over and above the theoretical contributions of postmodernism and/or post-structuralism. This book seeks to set to rest these and other reservations about the relevance of postcolonialism for organization studies, and argues that postcolonial theory can meaningfully enhance our understanding of management and organizational processes.

Nevertheless, the long-standing and continuing aloofness of management scholarship from postcolonialism does have important consequences. Here we would like to turn to Spivak's (1999) discussion of what she calls "sanctioned ignorance" (p. 2) with a view to shedding some useful light on this issue. If we may be allowed to somewhat simplify Spivak (1999), what she seems to be suggesting is that the "axiomatics of imperialism" (p. 4) operate to make Eurocentric knowledge appear as the only appropriate knowledge. However, the success of this operation involves, in part, learning to ignore the challenges potentially posed by rival/alternative knowledges. The ignoring of alternative knowledges, in turn, requires the availability, within the Eurocentric tradition, of key texts that endorse and *sanction* such ignorance. Spivak, accordingly, deconstructs some of the writings of Kant, Hegel, and Marx—"the last Three Wise Men" of Europe (1999: 111)—as texts that sanction the kind of ignorance she has been speaking of.

In part, Spivak's (1999) deconstructive reading suggests that some of the central texts of Western philosophy are dependent upon what she calls "the native informant" (p. 6)—a figure well-known to the field of ethnography (Prasad & Prasad, 2002)—for consolidating their own position. Significantly, however, even as the moment of the native informant is crucially needed by these key philosophical texts, the native informant is also simultaneously foreclosed in such texts. Spivak's deconstruction, thus, serves to "make visible the foreclosure of the subject *whose lack of access to the position of narrator* is the condition of possibility of the consolidation of... [the] position" of major texts of Western philosophy (1999: 9, italics added)—texts that support and legitimate the "sanctioned ignorance" of those who remain enmeshed in the discursive circuitry of Eurocentric knowledge. Our concern here is to investigate whether, by refusing to seriously engage with postcolonial theory, management scholars might become complicit, wittingly or unwittingly, with similar dynamics of sanctioned ignorance within our own discipline.

Consider, for instance, the following. Writing the introductory editorial essay for a special issue on "Critical Perspectives on Organizational Control" of the *Administrative Science Quarterly*—a major American journal publishing scholarly research in the area of organizational and administrative studies—John Jermier (1998: 238), the special issue coeditor, states:

> Although much modern critical theory is still concerned with the capitalist labor process, in recent years a growing number of critical theorists have turned their attention to other social processes. For instance, critical theorists have focused attention on patriarchy and the plight of women, racism and its effects on minorities, and the impacts of postcolonialism on members of nations historically subjugated by industrial nations.

Relying upon a somewhat hasty reading, the passage may conceivably be seen as suggesting that modern critical theory[8] has begun to acknowledge and take into consideration the scholarly insights being offered by postcolonial theory and criticism. Upon closer scrutiny, however, the passage is seen to be saying something altogether different. Let us go back to the passage, and carefully read it a second time. What the passage states, our second reading shows, is not that critical theory has begun to take into account the intellectual contributions of postcolonialism, but rather that critical theory has begun to focus attention upon "social processes" other than "the capitalist labor process" and, by way of providing examples of such other social processes, the passage enumerates the following: "patriarchy and the plight of women, racism and its effects on minorities, and the impacts of postcolonialism on members of nations historically subjugated by industrial nations." Hence what the Jermier passage seems to be saying is that, just as critical theory has now begun to examine "patriarchy and the plight of women" and "racism and its effects on minorities," critical theory has also started investigating "the impacts of postcolonialism" on the historically colonized nations.

At this point we are faced with something of a dilemma. Clearly, patriarchy has negative consequences for women; it is equally obvious that racism has negative consequences for minorities. Is the Jermier passage suggesting, however improbable it may seem, that postcolonialism has negative consequences for the citizens of the ex-colonies? Postcolonialism, as this book has shown, is a well-respected critical approach that "identifies with the subject position of [the colonized]" (Young, 2001: 19), and offers radical critiques of colonialism and neocolonialism. Hence, it would be virtually impossible to successfully make the case that postcolonialism may have negative consequences for the ex-colonized, along lines parallel to the harmful effects of patriarchy on women, or the pernicious effects of racism on minorities. In other words, while it is well known that patriarchy and racism are baneful social pathologies, by no stretch of imagination can it be argued that postcolonialism belongs to the same group of social pathologies. Clearly, therefore, it would be unfair of us to insist that the Jermier passage considers *postcolonial theory* to be on par with social evils akin to patriarchy and racism. What then does Jermier's previously quoted passage mean?

Our problem may be restated as follows: how can we make sense of a passage that employs "patriarchy," "racism," and "postcolonialism" in the same breath, and seems to suggest that these three are parallel social phenomena in terms of their deleterious social consequences? We submit that, in the context of the Jermier passage, the most reasonable answer to this question is: we cannot make coherent sense of such a passage *unless*, for this passage, the term "postcolonialism" is synonymous with "neocolonialism." What is being suggested here is that Jermier's passage will indeed make sense to the reader if, in the passage, we were to substitute "neocolonialism" for "postcolonialism." Once this substitution is made, what the passage would be stating, in effect, is that "critical theory has now turned its attention toward patriarchy and the plight of women, racism and its effects on minorities, and the impacts of *neocolonialism* on the ex-colonies of the West." The substitution of "neocolonialism" for "postcolonialism," thus, removes the incoherence from the Jermier passage, and renders the passage meaningful. However, what this also implies is that the Jermier passage confuses "postcolonialism" with "neocolonialism," and suggests that the passage exhibits unfamiliarity with the very basics of postcolonial theory. Needless to say, such an error on the part of a recognized, critical, management scholar writing for a leading journal of the field is a matter of concern.[9]

However, our interest here is not in exposing some unfortunate errors or conceptual confusions in Jermier's writing, but rather in examining how such writing may become complicit with the dynamics of "sanctioned ignorance" within management and organization studies. Let us begin by noting that, as a "prestigious" journal of the discipline, the *Administrative Science Quarterly* (*ASQ*) occupies an institutionally privileged place within organizational scholarship. Hence, by virtue of appearing in the *ASQ*, the Jermier (1998) essay becomes a part of that body of "approved" knowledge that is likely to be regarded as authoritative by large sections of management researchers. To the extent, therefore, that management researchers note the term "postcolonialism" appearing in the Jermier article, they might be left with a fleeting impression—on the basis of a single mention of this term—that "postcolonialism" is a social process (similar to patriarchy or racism) having negative consequences for people, and also that issues falling under the label "postcolonialism" are already and/or increasingly being investigated by critical theory.

Impressions such as these might have the effect of creating and/or reinforcing a sense within the field of management that the scholarly agendas of postcolonial theory and critical theory are characterized more by mutual similarities than by difference, and moreover that the agenda of postcolonial theory can mostly be subsumed under that of existing approaches of critical theory. This state of affairs is likely to work to keep the gaze of management scholarship directed mostly away from postcolonial theory. Moreover, this state of affairs may also create an implicit belief that, in the process of ignoring postcolonial theory, management scholars are not ignoring something of scholarly value.

Recall our earlier discussion of Spivak's (1999) notion of the native informant, a figure both needed and foreclosed by Western philosophical texts with a view to consolidating their own position. Along somewhat similar lines, one could argue that the Jermier (1998) text also seems to both need and foreclose the issue of postcolonialism with a view to consolidating its own position. Accordingly, after mentioning postcolonialism only once, this text quickly drops the matter of postcolonialism, never to raise it again. Moreover, neither is the postcolonial perspective allowed "access to the position of narrator" (Spivak, 1999: 9) in any of the other articles comprising the *ASQ* special issue edited by Jermier. While moves like these would appear to work to consolidate the position of Jermier's text, they may also be seen as rendering his text complicit with the dynamics of "sanctioned ignorance" within organization studies.[10] The persistence of such "sanctioned ignorance" implies that Eurocentrism continues to be a key element of the disciplinary framework of organization studies.[11]

Postcolonial scholars have noted that, for the most part, the primary audience of postcolonial theory seems to be the First World academic (Gandhi, 1998; Mongia, 1996). In part, this appears to be a result of postcolonialism's desire to critically address the Eurocentrism of the First World academy with a view to reforming the latter and making it more receptive to non-Western cultures and epistemologies. Undoubtedly, such a project of reforming the West (and Western epistemology) is laudable, and—as the contemporary situation with respect to knowledge-production within the field of organization studies suggests—needs to continue in the foreseeable future. However, partly as a result of postcolonialism's deep intellectual engagement with complex issues of epistemology, discourse and the like, the language of postcolonial theory is often said to be somewhat "opaque and dense" (Young,

2001: 67).[12] One possible result of the continued use of highly specialized language could be a further narrowing of postcolonial theory's potential audience.

Partly with a view to attending to these and related dynamics, leading postcolonial scholars have begun to emphasize the importance of addressing not only issues that might appear closer to the province of epistemology, discourse, philosophy of science, and literary theory, but also issues of greater obvious materiality, such as the environmental crisis, globalization, the North–South divide, the international economic/financial architecture, and so on (Spivak, 1999). This development is a part of the wider postcolonial project of speaking more directly to urgent issues and concerns of transnational significance. In view of the sophisticated array of intellectual resources at its command, postcolonial theory would seem to be one of the more suitable and effective perspectives for addressing issues of such importance.

The contributors to this book have attempted to demonstrate the usefulness—indeed the crucial significance—of postcolonial ways of thinking about, and responding to, our organizations and the world we inhabit. This book, however, represents a mere beginning. There is an entire world of organizational, institutional, sectoral, and global processes and phenomena awaiting postcolonial investigations. It is our hope that this book acts as an encouragement for many such studies. At the same time, it is our hope also that the book has succeeded in conveying something of the ethical nature of the postcolonial project, which sees the research act as an active intervention in our worlds, with a view to working toward a progressive agenda of global justice, compassion, and hope. Postcolonial theory's invocation to "provincialize Europe" is also an insurgent call for a more humane future.

Notes

1. For our use of the term "Europe" as a synonym for "the West," see Prasad's explanation in the introductory chapter.
2. This should not be read, however, as a desire on the part of postcolonial theory to exclude or marginalize the West. Rather, the postcolonial agenda is informed by a concern to prepare the stage for a genuine "democratic colloquium between the antagonistic inheritors of the colonial aftermath" (Gandhi, 1998: x).
3. Recall, in this connection, Karl Marx's (1972) well-known writings on India, which have the effect of turning Marx into an apologist of British (or Western) colonialism.
4. Spivak, for instance, insists that her "agenda remains an old-fashioned Marxist one" (1999: 357).

5. With some relatively minor changes, our critique of Marxism is equally applicable to versions of European neo-Marxism as well. After all, let us not forget that, according to the Frankfurt School radical, Theodor Adorno (1991), jazz as a music form had a *regressive* effect on listeners.

6. This may be a result, in part, of erroneously equating postmodernism with post-structuralism. See, in this connection, Spivak (1999: 312 ff.) for some perceptive remarks on the tendency, in certain quarters, of conflating postmodernism and post-structuralism.

7. The introductory chapter briefly discusses the postcolonial critique of First World feminism.

8. Although related to the Frankfurt School version, Jermier's (1998) definition of critical theory is not strictly limited to that version.

9. While it may be possible to come up with other interpretations of the Jermier passage, our interpretation—namely, that the passage confuses "postcolonialism" with "neocolonialism"—would seem most appropriate within the overall context of this passage. In case the passage is intended to convey some other meaning, it becomes the responsibility of the passage to make it fully clear that, whereas patriarchy and racism are social ills, postcolonialism is a scholarly framework for critique. Among other things, in view of the relative newness of postcolonial theory for management researchers, we would be justified in expecting this kind of clarity in exposition.

10. For a more complex elaboration of the notion of foreclosure, see Spivak (1999: 4 ff.).

11. It is not only "scholarly" errors like Jermier's that may operate to legitimate "sanctioned ignorance" and the attendant Eurocentrism. There are other ways in which "sanctioned ignorance" may receive disciplinary endorsement. Consider, for instance, *Doing Critical Management Research*, an otherwise excellent book on critical research methods by Alvesson and Deetz (2000). Problems seem to arise in this book, however, when the book decides to use the notion of colonization. What is intriguing about the book's use of this concept is that, almost invariably, colonization is treated *metaphorically* in the book. Thus, for instance, Alvesson and Deetz (2000) refer to "corporate colonization" (p. 35), or to the "colonization of the lifeworld" (pp. 174–175). In its insistence on treating colonization as a metaphor alone, the book may be seen as unwittingly colluding with a host of Western scholarly and cultural practices that work to efface and gloss over the long and brutal history of Western colonialism. This sort of treatment may convey the impression that metaphorical understandings of colonization are adequate and/or desirable for management researchers, or that the materialities of the modern colonial encounter are of scant relevance for management and organization studies. Moreover, in the process of subsuming the metaphor of colonization within critical theory, the Alvesson and Deetz book may be seen as implicitly rejecting the need for *postcolonial* theoretic analyses of colonization. As a result, even an otherwise sound book like Alvesson and Deetz (2000) gets

fatally enmeshed in Eurocentric protocols and gestures, and may be seen as serving, in effect, as an instrument that legitimates the "sanctioned ignorance" of management and organization studies.

12. Arguably, another reason for some of the denseness of the language of postcolonial theory may be found in its close connections with literary theory.

References

Adams, I., & Tiffin, H. (Eds.). 1990. *Past the last post: Theorizing postcolonialism and postmodernism.* Calgary, Canada: University of Calgary Press.

Adorno, T. 1991. *The culture industry.* London: Routledge.

Ali, T. 2002. *The clash of fundamentalisms: Crusades, jihads and modernity.* London: Verso.

Alvesson, M., & Deetz, S. 2000. *Doing critical management research.* London: Sage.

Bhabha, H. K. 1994. *The location of culture.* London: Routledge.

Butler, J. 1991. *Gender trouble: Feminism and the subversion of identity.* New York: Routledge.

Chakrabarty, D. 2000. *Provincializing Europe: Postcolonial thought and historical difference.* Princeton: Princeton University Press.

Gandhi, L. 1998. *Postcolonial theory: A critical introduction.* New York: Columbia University Press.

Hardt, M., & Negri, A. 2000. *Empire.* Cambridge, MA: Harvard University Press.

hooks, b. 1991. *Yearning: Race, gender, and cultural politics.* London: Turnaround.

Jermier, J. 1998. Introduction: Critical perspectives on organizational control. *Administrative Science Quarterly, 43,* 235–256.

Marx, K. 1972. On imperialism in India. In R. C. Tucker (Ed.), *The Marx–Engels reader* (pp. 577–588). New York: W. W. Norton.

Mongia, P. 1996. Introduction. In P. Mongia (Ed.), *Contemporary postcolonial theory: A reader* (pp. 1–18). London: Arnold.

Prasad, A. 1997. Provincializing Europe: Towards a postcolonial reconstruction. *Studies in Cultures, Organizations and Societies, 3,* 91–117.

Prasad, P., & Eylon, D. 2001. Narrating past traditions of participation and inclusion: Historical perspectives on workplace empowerment. *Journal of Applied Behavioral Science, 37,* 5–14.

Prasad, P., & Prasad, A. 2002. Casting the native subject: The ethnographic imagination and the (re)production of difference. In B. Czarniawska & H. Hopfl (Eds.), *Casting the other: The production and maintenance of inequality in organizations* (pp. 185–204). London: Routledge.

Richard, N. 1993. Postmodernism and periphery. In T. Docherty (Ed.), *Postmodernism: A reader* (pp. 463–470). New York: Columbia University Press.

Spivak, G. C. 1993. *Outside in the teaching machine.* New York: Routledge.

Spivak, G. C. 1999. *A critique of postcolonial reason: Toward a history of the vanishing present.* Cambridge, MA: Harvard University Press.

Sprinker, M. 1995. Introduction. In R. de la Campa, E. A. Kaplan, & M. Sprinker (Eds.), *Late imperial culture* (pp. 1–10). London: Verso.

Williams, P., & Chrisman, L. 1994. Colonial discourse and postcolonial theory: An introduction. In P. Williams & L. Chrisman (Eds.), *Colonial discourse and postcolonial theory* (pp. 1–20). New York: Columbia University Press.

Young, R. 1990. *White mythologies: Writing history and the West*. London: Routledge.

Young, R. 2001. *Postcolonialism: An historical introduction*. Oxford, UK: Blackwell Publishers.

Index

Printed and bound by CPI Group (UK) Ltd, Croydon, CR0 4YY